RULING THE
WORLD

The Story of the
1992 Cricket World Cup

RULING THE
WORLD

The Story of the
1992 Cricket World Cup

JONATHAN NORTHALL
Foreword by Kepler Wessels

First published by Pitch Publishing, 2019

Pitch Publishing
A2 Yeoman Gate
Yeoman Way
Worthing
Sussex
BN13 3QZ
www.pitchpublishing.co.uk
info@pitchpublishing.co.uk

ISBN 978-1-78531-486-5

Typesetting and origination by Pitch Publishing
Printed and bound in India by Replika Press Pvt. Ltd.

Contents

Acknowledgements

My thanks go to the players, officials, broadcasters and personalities that were part of the tournament and gave up their valuable time to talk to me: Jonathan Agnew, Dr Ali Bacher, Peter Baxter, Mark Burmester, Charles Colvile, Malcolm Conn, Gerry Connolly, Andrew Cornaga, Phillip DeFreitas, Kevin Duers, Ross Dundas, Andrew Hudson, Barry Jansen, Vinod Kambli, Patrick Keane, Gavin Larsen, Jim Maxwell, Suresh Menon, Brian McMillan, Tom Moody, Dipak Patel, Derek Pringle, Meyrick Pringle, Jonty Rhodes, Mark Rushmere, Gladstone Small, Murphy Su'a, Ian Taylor, Don Topley, John Traicos, Neil Weinart, Kepler Wessels, Peter Williams.

I would like to thank the research and archive staff that have been kind enough to answer my queries. They include Malcolm Deans (senior library assistant at Dunedin Public Library), Petar Djokovic (navy history officer at the Sea Power Centre – Australia), Deborah Fitz Herbert and Barry Friend (Hamilton City Libraries), Mike Gooch (information services officer at New Plymouth District Council), Simon Jacks (research librarian at the City of Ballarat), Jane Simmons (research and technology services librarian at Napier City Council Libraries), Mandy Vaccaro (information and library collections officer at Albury City), Greg Wakeling (operations officer at Ballarat

Cricket Association), Jacque Zagotsis (local history officer at Berri Library).

I am indebted to Jamie Bell, director at the New Zealand Cricket Museum in Wellington, for his help and assistance in accessing the 1992 Cricket World Cup Committee records passed down by New Zealand Cricket.

My thanks also go out to Frank Duckworth, Tony Lewis and Steven Stern. I appreciate that all three have been generous with their time and the information they have provided.

I have spoken to fans who experienced the tournament either in person or via television, radio, or newspapers at the time: Delan Adikari, Paul Baker, Brian Beer, Chris Coleman, Nick Cummins, Dean du Plessis, Ian Gorton, James Gould, Kate Gross, Bill Hodges, Scott Kelman, Penny Kinsella, Scott MacLean, Nick Malarao, Andrew Menczel, Keith Miller, Angus Ogilvie, Richard Palmer, Akhil Ranade, Luke Reynolds, Jason Stewart, Richard Swan, Michael Wagener, Mitch Wallenhoffer.

Many thanks to Paul and Jane Camillin at Pitch Publishing for giving me this opportunity and believing in the project.

Finally, a massive thank you to my family, who have put up with my endless mutterings about 1992 for many months.

Apologies to anyone I have missed, but their omission is not due to their contributions being any less significant.

Foreword

by Kepler Wessels

The 1992 Cricket World Cup was a historic moment in South African sporting history. After the release of Nelson Mandela, South Africa made a whistle-stop one-day international tour of India. However, the 1992 World Cup was the first foray for the South African team into a major worldwide cricket event after 21 years of sporting isolation.

It was a privilege to lead the South African team back from the wilderness in this historic event. The South African team were a mature outfit with a lot of experience at domestic level but none in the pressure cauldron of the international arena. The team faced a daunting task, facing the best teams in the world after so many years out of the competition.

The tournament had its highs and lows from a results point of view. Beating Australia during the first match at the Sydney Cricket Ground was a golden moment. Going on to beat India in Adelaide to qualify for the semi-final was an awesome achievement. Especially in light of the fact that victory was achieved while waiting for the result of a referendum to continue with political reform in South Africa. Had the decision been to oppose reform, further participation in the competition would not have been a possibility.

The loss to England in the much-publicised semi-final in Sydney was a major setback. Had rain not intervened, no one knows what the outcome would have been. Suffice to say that under the current Duckworth–Lewis–Stern system, South Africa would have gone through to the final. In fact, the rain rule that was applicable at the time was changed after that World Cup, and Duckworth–Lewis came into being.

The tournament itself was a tremendous competition, played according to a very fair format. All the teams played each other once, and the top four teams went through to the semi-finals. All matches had significance, and only the strongest teams participated in the event.

Pakistan, led by the impressive Imran Khan, pulled off a superb victory against the odds after starting the tournament in poor fashion. England had a fantastic run to the final and played some superb cricket. The hosts, Australia, after starting the tournament as favourites due to an excellent run prior to the event, never got out of the starting blocks, which came as a surprise to everyone.

I'm very happy that Jonathan Northall is writing this book about a compelling World Cup where the matches were entertaining, close and of a high standard. I wish him every success with the book, and it is certain to be an enjoyable read.

Introduction

South Africa was told that it would not be allowed to enter the 1992 Cricket World Cup. In July 1991, the International Cricket Council (ICC) had readmitted the United Cricket Board of South Africa (UCB) back into the fold after it had been suspended in 1970 for the government policy of apartheid. However, they were told in no uncertain terms that a place in the following year's one-day cricket showpiece event would not be available. The ICC chairman, Colin Cowdrey, was very clear on this point. The World Cup Committee had other ideas.

On a Sunday morning in August 1991, the committee met at the offices of the Australian Cricket Board (ACB) in Melbourne. The meeting convened at 10am and was chaired by the ACB's Malcolm Gray. In attendance on behalf of the ACB were David Richards (chief executive) and Des Rundle. Gray's New Zealand Cricket (NZC) counterpart, Peter McDermott, was joined by board colleagues Barry Paterson and Graham Dowling.

On behalf of the ICC, secretary Lt Col John Stephenson attended the meeting. Pre-empting disagreement around South Africa's exclusion, Cowdrey had presumably sent 'The Colonel' to restore discipline. Stephenson was secretary of the MCC as well as the ICC and was renowned for his military discipline as well as his negotiating skills. The decision was thought to be an act of appeasement to avoid conflict with the West Indies and Pakistan. They had both been opposed to restoring South Africa to international cricket.

The meeting started cordially, with Gray welcoming Stephenson to his first full committee meeting in Australasia. The committee was subjected to an overview of the feasibility study for admitting South Africa into the following year's tournament. In the discussion that followed, it became evident that Cowdrey's statement of exclusion was in accordance with the sentiments of at least some of the ICC members. The minutes of that meeting mention that 'the mood of many countries at the July ICC meeting had been against South Africa's inclusion despite having supported the UCB's application for Full Membership'. Peter McDermott echoed these reservations, on behalf of NZC, but confirmed that there was still support if South Africa's government approved. Malcolm Gray was clear that the ACB was supportive of inclusion.

At this point, 'The Colonel' queried why this was even being discussed when South Africa had not made an application to enter. In the days before the meeting, the UCB's executive director, Ali Bacher, had stated that South Africa would only play in the tournament if there were 'full support'. Such a point of order, for an issue that was a political minefield, appeared to aggravate Gray. He fired back that an application was not required. Furthermore, Gray continued by questioning Cowdrey's authority to make comments at the July press conference, when South Africa was readmitted to the ICC, to exclude its team from the tournament. One can only imagine the debate that Sunday morning.

The meeting concluded with an agreement not to exclude South Africa. A programme would be required to extend the tournament for eight additional matches. The estimated cost would be A$600,000 and would have to be recouped from international television sales to make the proposition viable. The marketing potential, according to Colin Bryden in his book *Return of the Prodigal*, was the primary motivator for including South Africa in the tournament. The committee agreed to write to ICC full members for their support.

Over the next few weeks, a groundswell of backing for South Africa suggested that participation was a fait accompli. As had been the way for many years with South Africa, politics and sport were intrinsically linked. In this case, the link was being used positively. The African National Congress (ANC) president, Nelson Mandela, provided a letter of support. This was the catalyst to remove any uncertainty. The only disagreement came from the West Indies, who stated that they would not support South Africa joining the next year's Cricket World Cup.

The ICC met on 23 October 1991 at Sharjah in the United Arab Emirates. The meeting location was chosen because the Wills Trophy was taking place and delegates from India, Pakistan, Sri Lanka and the West Indies were already there. The emergency meeting took less than 20 minutes to conclude. The outcome was relayed, by telephone link, to South Africa. It was the ICC chairman himself, Colin Cowdrey, who imparted the news that a ninth team would be added to the playing schedule. South Africa was going to Australia and New Zealand for the Cricket World Cup.

Chapter One

In the Beginning

The first Cricket World Cup was held in 1975 in England and was a 60-over tournament. Back in those days, each game was given extra days just in case the English summer was not amenable to the world's best cricketers tussling over cricket supremacy. It was sponsored by Prudential, with East Africa and Sri Lanka joining the six Test-playing nations in a format consisting of two groups. England, India and New Zealand were in Group A with East Africa, while Sri Lanka faced Australia, Pakistan and the West Indies in Group B. The top two teams in each group would face each other in the semi-finals.

The opening match was unforgettable in how it unfolded. England, fielding batters such as Dennis Amiss, Keith Fletcher, Tony Greig and captain Mike Denness, posted a score of 334/4 from their 60 overs. An impressive score at over 5.5 runs per over gave India a tough ask. In response, India crawled to 132/3 from their 60 overs. Sunil Gavaskar batted through the innings for 36 runs from 174 balls – a phenomenally slow scoring rate in any format of cricket. There were conspiracy theories around why the scoring was so painstakingly slow. Both East Africa and

Sri Lanka played the part of whipping boys as the Test nations enjoyed the un-English sunshine. At the end of the round robin matches, England and New Zealand topped Group A while the West Indies and Australia topped Group B.

In the first semi-final at Headingley, England were fancied to beat Australia. The Australians had both Chappells, Doug Walters, Rod Marsh and Max Walker, plus Lillee and 'Thommo'. However, it was Gary Gilmour who took most liking to the greenish pitch and grey clouds. Moving the ball prodigiously, Gilmour removed six English batters for just 14 runs. With England slumping to 37/7, only a rearguard action from Denness and Geoff Arnold helped the hosts to 93 all out. Not enough runs, even in those conditions, meant that Australia had a gettable total. Despite the loss of six wickets, England lost to the old enemy.

The second semi-final, at The Oval, was more of a contest, but the unbeaten West Indies were not to be denied by a spirited New Zealand side. Andy Roberts softened up the resistance with a hostile spell before removing top scorer Geoff Howarth. Bernard Julian tore through the middle order, and New Zealand lost their last nine wickets for 66. Set 159 to win, Gordon Greenidge and Alvin Kallicharran added a second-wicket partnership of 125 to underpin a comfortable win by five wickets.

The final would be everything the ICC would have wanted. Lord's was full and swathed in glorious sunshine. Ian Chappell called correctly and asked Clive Lloyd to have a bat. At 50/3, Chappell's slightly curious decision looked vindicated. Lloyd, walking out to bat, had other ideas. Playing a mixture of pushes into gaps and expansive strokes, the West Indies skipper scored freely. Batting partner Rohan Kanhai could be considered to have anchored the partnership, but, in reality, he didn't score too many runs. Australian profligacy in the field and Lloyd's genius gave the West Indies 291/8 from their 60 overs.

In response, Australia recovered after the loss of Rick McCosker to reach 81/1. Ian Chappell was playing with steely determination. It was three pieces of excellent fielding from Viv Richards that led the run-outs, including both Chappells, which started to turn the tide of the match. As the pressure built, Keith Boyce picked up three wickets and Australia succumbed to another run-out. At 233/9, the game was as good as done. Lillee and Thomson were at the wicket, and thousands of West Indies fans were ready to rush the pitch to celebrate. The final pair were not done yet, though, as the summer evening wore on. After yet another run-out – this time Thomson was left stranded – the West Indies were winners by 17 runs.

The 1979 Prudential World Cup was also held in England. The number of competing countries remained the same. Apart from Canada replacing East Africa, the same Test-playing nations and Sri Lanka participated. In the weeks preceding the tournament, the two-year-long cricket schism ended as Kerry Packer and the ACB reconciled their differences. This released a wealth of players from World Series Cricket (WSC) to join up with their previous estranged nations. Only Australia decided to remain loyal to the players who had remained part of the 'establishment'.

The defending champions, the West Indies, were heavy favourites while England were once again looking strong on home soil. The Australian team, captained by a young Kim Hughes, could have been considered to be a second XI to the WSC players apart from Allan Border. New Zealand's main hope was Richard Hadlee, who was fast developing into a world-class all-rounder. Sunil Gavaskar's batting at the top of the order was vital to Indian success. They also unleashed a young all-rounder in Kapil Dev.

England versus Australia was the first match of the 1979 tournament, and went the way of the home side. Australia opened up with a fifty partnership and crept along to 111/2 before being restricted to 159/9 from their 60 overs. Mike Brearley's decision to throw the ball to 38-year-old Geoff Boycott was a masterstroke. In six overs, Boycott removed opener Hilditch and then tempted Kim Hughes into an expansive stroke to a diving Mike Hendrick. Not learning anything from the 1975 final, Australia suffered four run-outs, while the bowling of Willis and Edmonds strangled the scoring. In true English fashion, the batting response started off shakily as Boycott was trapped in front by Hogg before Randall's edge behind left the scoreboard showing 5/2. Mike Brearley's concentration and Graham Gooch's positive batting steadied the ship before David Gower and Ian Botham saw the game out with nearly 13 overs to spare.

Canada's bow was a short, sharp introduction to international cricket, as Pakistan easily won. Deciding to bat first, the Canadians made a decent start and reached 103/2 before being stifled and squeezed by Pakistan. Asif Iqbal and Sarfraz Nawaz took three wickets apiece, while Majid Khan's off spin conceded only 11 runs from his 11 overs. In response, Sadiq Mohammed anchored the innings as Zaheer Abbas and Haroon Rashid made light work of the total.

Both the West Indies' win at Edgbaston and New Zealand's at Trent Bridge were comprehensive nine-wicket victories. The West Indies had Gordon Greenidge's century and Michael Holding's hostile 4–33 to thank as India were no match. For New Zealand, Glenn Turner and Geoff Howarth's batting carried the Kiwis to 190/1 in less than 48 overs.

At Old Trafford, Canada's big mistake was winning the toss. Despite Manchester serving up grey and wet conditions, Canada captain Bryan Mauricette decided to have a bat. Canada were rolled over for 45 in 40.3 overs. Chris Old's 4–8 and Bob Willis's 4–11 did the damage, with Mike Hendrick finishing with 8-4-5-1. England knocked off the meagre total in 13.5 overs, but did lose the wickets of Brearley and Randall. The rest of the group games went to form apart from Sri Lanka's matches against the West Indies and India. Rain at The Oval would spare Sri Lanka from facing the might of the champions. However, an even better result for Sri Lanka was achieved at Old Trafford when India were thwarted by 47 runs. Not only adding credence to a bid for Test status, this was also the first win by an associate member over a full one.

The semi-finals were contested at Old Trafford and The Oval. England and New Zealand met in Manchester and served up a tight affair. Once again, Brearley and Gooch rescued England as New Zealand's bowlers exerted pressure. With Brearley gone, Ian Botham played a typically bullish innings before Derek Randall finally found some form with the bat. His 42 not out helped England to 221/8 from their 60 overs. John Wright masterminded the Kiwis' response as England chipped away at his batting partners. Once he had gone, run out by the effervescent fielding of Randall, New Zealand's ambitions were ebbing away. Turner, Hadlee, Lees and Cairns played important innings to get New Zealand to within 14 runs of victory from the last over. McKechnie and Troup, the tailenders left with the unlikely task, found Ian Botham's bowling too difficult to get away, and England advanced to the final.

The second semi-final featured the West Indies and Pakistan and would prove to be a batting contest. Having been inserted by Pakistan, the West Indian opening partnership of Haynes and Greenidge punished wayward bowling by adding 132 for the first wicket. Viv Richards and Clive Lloyd joined the onslaught, with only Majid Khan proving challenging to score off, as the West Indies posted a formidable 293/6. Removing Sadiq Mohammed early did nothing more than bring Zaheer

Abbas to the crease. With Majid Khan, the Pakistan batters found the wicket as benign as when they had bowled. In 36 overs, 166 runs were added in thrilling fashion, and the West Indies were in the unusual position of being challenged. Colin Croft's aggressive bowling line reaped rewards with three quick wickets as the game's momentum shifted. Viv Richards, bowling his part-time off spin, snapped up the middle order. A sharp caught-and-bowled chance to remove Imran Khan would signal that time was almost nigh. Andy Roberts delivered the *coup de grâce* with the last two wickets, and the West Indies were in the final again.

The final was held at Lord's, as it had been in 1975. England lost Bob Willis before the game started as his injured knee was insufficiently healed to play. Mike Brearley won the toss and inserted the West Indies, as was de rigueur for the tournament. Early movement from Chris Old and another Derek Randall fielding masterpiece left the West Indies at 36/2. Viv Richards was at the crease and, having failed in the 1975 final, the 'Master Blaster' was in no mood for repeats. At 99/4, England would have felt confident despite Richards pulling and driving with intent. Collis King joined Richards at the crease at a critical time in the match. Needing to find some overs from his team, Mike Brearley turned to Gooch, Boycott and Larkins as the fifth bowler. In their 12 overs, 86 runs were scored, and so the match was slipping away. At the end of the innings, Richards was 138 not out in a formidable total of 286/9. The England innings started slowly as Brearley and Boycott opened conservatively. The partnership was worth 129 by the time it was broken, but too many overs had been consumed. Randall and Gooch were left with an enormous task. Such was the building pressure, England slumped from 183/2 to 194 all out. Five batters failed to score as the West Indies cruised to a 92-run victory and retained their title.

By 1983, one-day cricket had grown in stature. More one-day internationals (ODIs) had been played, so the ICC decided that the Cricket World Cup should increase in size, with each group member playing each other twice. Once again, the competition was held in England, but more county grounds were used to accommodate the extra games. Sri Lanka, now in the fold as a Test-playing nation, joined the other six Test nations as a matter of right. The eighth place was granted to Zimbabwe as a reward for winning the previous year's ICC Trophy. They beat Bermuda at Grace Road, Leicester, to qualify.

The West Indians, Sri Lankans and English were affected by rebel tours to South Africa and the subsequent bans placed on players. In March 1982, 15 English players embarked on a tour of South Africa. Eleven of those had been Test players, including Geoff Boycott and captain Graham Gooch. Each player received a three-year ban from Test cricket. The Sri Lankan Cricket Board were far more severe on their players and meted out lifetime bans. The West Indies Cricket Board also took a similar line with their rebel players.

The West Indies entered the tournament as favourites to make it a hat-trick of wins. England, despite wholesale changes to playing personnel, were seen as a good bet. Australia came to England with the tried-and-tested formula of Lillee and Thomson, with young gun Geoff Lawson to spearhead their pace attack. An injured Imran Khan hampered Pakistan's campaign. He made himself available but only as a batter. Having had poor tournaments in 1975 and 1979, India were considered to be rank outsiders once again.

The tournament opened with all eight sides playing on the same day. At The Oval it was England's 322/6, led by Allan Lamb's 102, that was far too good for New Zealand as the home side won by 106 runs. At Swansea, Pakistan comfortably beat

Sri Lanka. The other two games would shock the tournament. Trent Bridge was the venue for Australia's expected processional victory over Zimbabwe. However, no one told the Zimbabweans that. Playing like they wanted to win, unlike their opponents, who had assumed victory was a fait accompli, Zimbabwe won the match by 13 runs. A captain's performance from Duncan Fletcher, with 69 not out and 4–42, was too good for Australia.

At Old Trafford, India's innings was fired up by Yashpal Sharma's sublime 89. Ably assisted by Roger Binny, Sharma pulled and drove the ball with style. India's final total was 262/8, which would be a test for the West Indian batters. As rain brought the game to a premature close, to be resumed the following morning, the West Indies were 67/2 and sat in a good position. On the resumption, the rain had dampened the ground, and India's medium-pacers gave nothing for the West Indians to work with. With the score on 76, Viv Richards nicked a ball from Binny, and wicketkeeper Kirmani gratefully took the catch. This was a blow that the West Indies would not recover from. Losing another five wickets for 54 runs, the champions were languishing at 130/8. Andy Roberts and Joel Garner made an unlikely last-wicket stand of 71, but India would not be denied only their second win in the Cricket World Cup. More importantly, the seemingly unbeatable West Indies had been beaten.

In Group A, England's route to the semi-finals was a straightforward one. The only blemish on their record was a two-wicket defeat at Edgbaston by New Zealand. David Gower's fine form, including a century against Sri Lanka, helped England to plenty of runs. An inspired Sri Lankan display halted New Zealand's push for the semi-finals at the County Ground in Derby. A five-wicket haul for Ashantha de Mel, plus stifling bowling from Rumesh Ratnayake and Somachandra de Silva, left the Kiwis woefully short of a competitive total. With that defeat, a final-game decider against Pakistan at Trent Bridge would follow. Needing to improve their run rate, Pakistan's batters scored 261/3, inspired by Zaheer Abbas's century and assisted by Imran Khan's aggressive 79 not out. The New Zealand innings was boosted by Geoff Howarth, Martin Crowe, Warren Lees and John Bracewell, but Jeremy Coney's run-out left the Kiwis short by 11 runs.

In Group B, the West Indies recovered from their opening defeat by winning the rest of their group games handsomely. Australia's tournament improved somewhat with a massive 162-run victory against India. Trevor Chappell's 110 and Ken MacLeay's swing bowling were the surprise highlights as India were thrashed. By the time the last round of matches came around, the same protagonists met to decide who would reach the semi-finals. The ground at Chelmsford was packed, and the Australians were confident that they could repeat the result of a week previous. India's total of 247 was achievable, but medium-pacers Madan Lal and Roger Binny took eight wickets between them as Australia slumped to a disappointing 129 all out.

In the first semi-final, outsiders India met England at Old Trafford. Winning the toss, Bob Willis chose to bat on a sunny day in Manchester. The pitch was suited to the medium-pacers of India, and England struggled. Roger Binny once again proved good value, while Kapil Dev cleaned up the tail to bowl out England for 213. Despite a good start from openers Graeme Fowler and Chris Tavaré, England lost wickets regularly. David Gower slashed and edged; Mike Gatting ran out Allan Lamb before leaving a gap for Amarnath to bowl him. India's run chase began comfortably before Paul Allott and Ian Botham combined to remove both openers. Yashpal Sharma, with Mohinder Amarnath and then Sandeep Patil, scored a vital 61 runs to make sure that India got home safely to ensure their place in the final.

The Oval hosted the second semi-final. Pakistan were at a disadvantage before the game began, with captain Javed Miandad ruled out with flu. Clive Lloyd called correctly and inserted Pakistan on a wicket where the West Indies could exploit the conditions. And so they did. At 139/3, Pakistan may have felt that they could post a decent total. Malcolm Marshall begged to differ, with a spell of fast bowling worthy of winning the tie. An outswinger accounted for Imran Khan before Wasim Raja was caught in front in the same over. Shahid Mahboob's short and not very sweet innings was ended a little time later, and Pakistan were struggling. As they crawled to 184/8, there could be only one winner. And so it proved to be, as Viv Richards and Larry Gomes added an unbeaten 132-run partnership to ease the West Indies into their third consecutive final.

The Lord's final played out to form until about 3.15pm. India were asked to bat, and the West Indies' fast bowling attack did its job. The only respite came via Larry Gomes and his spin bowling. India failed to get a score higher than 38 as they were bowled out for 183. As the response got underway midway through the afternoon, the West Indies once again exhibited hubris. India's medium-pacers were getting movement, and the batters were finding the fielders. Kapil Dev's running catch to dismiss Viv Richards would be a defining moment. Slumping to 76/6, the double world champions were in danger of being dethroned. Jeff Dujon's defiant innings was ended by Amarnath, who finished with 3–12 from seven overs, and the West Indies' last reasonable chance had gone. It was Amarnath who ended the innings by trapping Michael Holding in front, and the pitch invasion from joyous Indian fans began.

The 1987 tournament, with Reliance as the new sponsors, was held in India and Pakistan – the competition's first time outside England. It was now a 50-over-a-side competition, in line with standards for limited-over cricket. Once again, the seven Test-playing nations each received an automatic place while the eighth team would be the ICC Trophy winners. Once again, Zimbabwe prevailed against the Netherlands. India's defence on home soil was based around good middle-order batting and spin. The outlawing of bouncers had negated the West Indies' armoury. Also, injuries to Joel Garner and Malcolm Marshall robbed them of genuine match-winners. England's squad was missing both Gower and Botham, who decided they would prefer some time at home. Also, Richard Hadlee gave the tournament a miss. Pakistan's challenge would be spearheaded by Imran Khan's guile, albeit at a slower pace than previously, and the raw talent of Wasim Akram. The Australian team, led by Allan Border, had plenty of promise, but their effectiveness remained to be seen.

India and Australia easily qualified from Group A. They shared a victory each against each other; both easily beat New Zealand and Zimbabwe twice to take the two semi-final spots. Geoff Marsh's 110 in Madras helped Australia to a tight one-run win, before India's batters set up a 56-run victory in New Delhi to return the favour. Marsh went on to score another century in the group stages against a disappointing New Zealand side. Sunil Gavaskar's century and two half-centuries were just as key for India as they cruised into the semi-finals.

Unsurprisingly, Pakistan topped Group B with five wins from their six matches. Despite losing twice to Pakistan, England secured second place. For the very first time, the West Indies had failed to get out of the group stages. Only a final-game win, against Pakistan in Karachi, would rescue a little pride from a failure. Richie Richardson's fine century was backed up by Patrick Patterson's 3–34 to inflict the first defeat on the co-hosts.

The Gaddafi Stadium in Lahore hosted the first semi-final, where the home side would face the unfancied Australians. Australia chose to bat first, and their openers added 73 for the first wicket before Marsh's zest for a quick single would leave him stranded by Salim Malik's smart throwdown of the stumps. On-field injuries to wicketkeeper Salim Yousuf and Tauseef Ahmed weakened Pakistan's team. The loss of David Boon and Dean Jones, in quick succession, did little to stem the Australian scoring. Mike Veletta and Steve Waugh carved out more runs as Australia finished on 267/8.

The Pakistan response started badly when Ramiz Raja was run out from just the third ball of the innings. By the time Javed Miandad and Imran Khan were at the crease, the home side were 38/3, and the final looked far from being a possibility. The two experienced players consolidated the innings before Imran attempted to accelerate. With the partnership at 112, Border decided that he would turn his arm over. As is the way at times, Imran misjudged a delivery, and Dyer's gloves received the ball. The Australians, sensing an opportunity, appealed for anything and everything and duly got their man. New batter Wasim Akram attempted to take up where his captain had left off, but perished via McDermott's yorker. Miandad remained, doggedly, as his country's last reasonable hope. However, a tired slog at Bruce Reid missed the ball, and the bowler hit the wickets. Pakistan's hopes were as good as over. McDermott removed Yousuf, Jaffer and Tauseef in quick succession and Australia were in the final.

With the dream final in tatters, defending champions India had to overcome England at the Wankhede Stadium in Bombay. Winning the toss, Kapil Dev asked England to bat, but his team could not make an early breakthrough. It was the introduction of spin that did the trick. Graham Gooch planned to sweep the danger away. When Gatting came to the crease, at

79/2, he adopted the same method. With 117 added in 19 overs, England's innings was building rapidly. The losses of Gatting for 56 and Gooch for 115 were compensated for by Allan Lamb. At the end of the 50 overs, England had scored 254/6, and India's final ambition hung in the balance.

Hope lay in the hands of Sunil Gavaskar as the Indian innings began. After the opener had scored a boundary in the first over, Phillip DeFreitas acquired revenge by bowling him. 7/1 was not what the capacity crowd had wanted. Consolidation from Srikkanth and Navjot Sidhu soon turned to crisis when Neil Foster removed both batters. With the score on 121, Foster struck again. Mohammed Azharuddin and Kapil Dev added 47 runs in no time at all, milking the bowling of spinner Eddie Hemmings. The acceleration from Kapil Dev finally led to his downfall when he was looking for the midwicket boundary, off the same bowler, with Gatting taking the catch to reduce India to 168/5. With Azharuddin still at the crease, and Ravi Shastri successfully sweeping Hemmings and Emburey, the game was still on. As soon as he was given out, India struggled to put another partnership together. The England bowlers mopped up the tail, as India's innings disintegrated, to win handsomely by 35 runs.

The 1987 final was held at Eden Gardens in Calcutta. Despite India having lost in the semi-final, the stadium was packed. Gatting lost the toss and was asked to bowl by Border. The Australian innings started well as Boon and Marsh took control with some attacking strokeplay. Small and DeFreitas struggled to make their mark, but the introduction of Neil Foster slowed the run rate. The loss of Marsh, bowled by Foster, further slowed the scoring.

Incoming batter Dean Jones joined Boon, and took the score to 151 before losing his wicket. Border's worry was that only 15 overs were left and runs were required. The answer was to promote fast bowler Craig McDermott to bat at four. Lusty hitting achieved boundaries but also accounted for his wicket. Boon lost his soon after, and Australia were 168/4. At the crease, Border and Mike Veletta reasserted themselves with excellent batting and sharp running between the wickets. At the end of the innings, Veletta had scored 45 from 31 balls, and Australia had a total to defend with 253/6.

Three balls were all it took for Australia to get their first wicket as McDermott trapped Tim Robinson in front. Bill Athey joined Graham Gooch at the crease. Although scoring slowly, the batters ticked over the scoreboard without keeping up with the required run rate. Simon O'Donnell trapped Gooch, for the second lbw decision of the innings, and captain Mike Gatting came to the wicket with the score on 66. Off-spinner Tim May was introduced into the attack but, after four overs, was withdrawn as Gatting took a liking to his bowling. Scoring at a reasonable rate, Athey and Gatting took England to 135/2. Border, as he had done in the semi-final, brought himself on to bowl. Immediately, Gatting looked to sweep; he top-edged the ball, and the damage was done.

With the loss of Athey for 58, England went into panic mode, like the Indians had done in the semi-final. Allan Lamb was the last hope. Pressure mounting, looking for scoring shots, Steve Waugh squeezed a ball through Lamb's guard to bowl him. John Emburey ran himself out just two runs later, and England were 220/7. The game was surely over. Phillip DeFreitas had other ideas, with a six and two fours in successive balls. By the time the last over came around, DeFreitas had perished, and 17 runs were needed from the final over. The task was too much, and Australia were world champions with a seven-run victory. Australia would get the chance to defend the title as co-hosts, with New Zealand, of the 1992 tournament.

The 1992 Cricket World Cup is considered to be a collection of 'firsts' for world cricket. White balls, black sightscreens, floodlights and those revered coloured kits were all used in the tournament. A closer look reveals that none of these facets of the game were actually new. What 1992 did do was to bring them on to the world stage together, giving them prominence and showing that the game of cricket had moved on. Revolution had come from Kerry Packer and World Series Cricket in 1977. WSC used floodlights regularly, motivated by Packer's need to generate interest, and the necessity to use white balls was born. 28 November 1978 is considered to be the eureka moment when floodlit cricket became a facet of the game. The match between WSC Australia and WSC West Indies packed 50,000 into the SCG.

Coloured kits were another innovation from Packer's WSC. Photographs and old footage cannot do justice to the sheer 1970s kitsch of the choice of colours. The powder blue of the World XI and pale lemon of WSC Australia look particularly sober in comparison to the West Indies and their salmon pink kit. Gideon Haigh, in his excellent history of WSC, *The Cricket War*, names the individual responsible. Barbara Loois, later to become Mrs Ian Chappell, was 'foraging in curtain shops and department stores for pastel fabrics'. It is quite a leap of fashion from these offerings to the iconic kits of 1992.

Coloured clothing survived the 1979 reconvergence of cricket factions, and was adopted for the annual Australian summer one-day tri-series, again named World Series Cricket. 1992 may have been the first Cricket World Cup that had dispensed with cricket whites and red balls, but it was not the first international tournament to do so. In 1985, the World Championship of Cricket was played in Australia, to help celebrate the 150th anniversary of the founding of the state of Victoria. Games were played at the MCG and SCG, and featured the seven Test-playing nations of the time. The now-famous lighting towers at the MCG were constructed for the tournament, which caused much controversy at the time. The kits chosen were quite bland; New Zealand wore beige, which has now been adopted by New Zealand fans under the guise of the 'Beige Brigade'.

It was India who won, beating Pakistan in the final, to add to their 1983 Cricket World Cup victory. Several of the players from 1985 would play in 1992. Allan Border, Dean Jones and Craig McDermott would represent Australia in both. Kepler Wessels represented Australia in 1985 but would return in 1992 as captain of his native South Africa. Only Allan Lamb would be England's representative in both competitions. India's experience in 1992 was evident with the likes of Kapil Dev, Mohammed Azharuddin, Manoj Prabhakar, Ravi Shastri and Kris Srikkanth in their squad. New Zealand had Martin Crowe, John Wright and Ian Smith to rely on, while Pakistan boasted Imran Khan, Javed Miandad, Wasim Akram, Ramiz Raja and Salim Malik. Aravinda de Silva, Arjuna Ranatunga and Rumesh Ratnayake were the Sri Lankan stalwarts. For the West Indies, star players Richie Richardson, Roger Harper, Gus Logie and Malcolm Marshall were still around in 1992.

With the addition of South Africa, the number of games to be played increased to 39. The World Cup Committee decided that matches should be played in more regional areas as well as the traditional venues. The Gabba, the Adelaide Oval and WACA hosted three group matches each from Australia's share of 25. The SCG hosted a semi-final, so it had four games in all, while the MCG hosted the final, making a total of five matches allotted. Non-international venues were included in the schedule, with Lavington Sports Oval in Albury (New South Wales), Eastern Oval in Ballarat (Victoria), Berri Oval (South Australia), Manuka Oval in Canberra, Bellerive Oval (Tasmania) and the Ray Mitchell Oval in Mackay (Queensland) each being awarded a group match.

New Zealand's 14 matches were allotted with a similar approach. Eden Park in Auckland was chosen for the opening match, three other group games plus a semi-final. Wellington's Basin Reserve hosted three, with Trust Bank Park in Hamilton and Lancaster Park in Christchurch receiving two matches each. The North Island's McLean Park in Napier and Pukekura Park in New Plymouth each received one game, as did Carisbrook in Dunedin, the most southerly venue.

Before the cricket commenced in earnest, most of the countries played warm-up games as part of the lead-up to the tournament. Pakistan's match against Tasmania opened up two weeks of matches. Tasmania proved to be stiff opposition, boosted by the inclusion of David Boon, and won by 42 runs. India also found Sheffield Shield opposition too strong as Victoria ran out 33-run victors. Shane Warne's 2–37 helped the home side bowl out India for 171. Zimbabwe's match against a Queensland Second XI was disastrous as the Queenslanders won by a massive 129 runs. In South Africa's opening match at the WACA, Western Australia won a low-scoring contest by three wickets.

India's next two matches did little to improve their morale. Rain cut short their run chase against an Australian Country XI, and an inferior run rate awarded the victory to their opponents. Two days later, rain washed out the match at Toorak Park, Melbourne, to leave India without a win in three games. Their final game, in Adelaide, changed their fortunes as they comfortably beat a Cricket Academy XI by 88 runs. Kris Srikkanth's 132 and 2–22 easily beat the emerging talent from Australia. Ricky Ponting scored 23 in a total of 217 in response to India's 305/5.

Victories against Pakistan, in Canberra, and against Tasmania gave South Africa valuable match practice. Matches at the Adelaide Oval, the Gabba and Bradman Oval in Bowral were lost to rain. Kepler Wessels scored 72, and Brian McMillan took 5–32, to beat Pakistan by 17 runs. The victory against Tasmania was more comfortable as McMillan, this time with the bat, led South Africa to a seven-wicket win.

Sri Lanka were unbeaten in their warm-up games. In Sydney, they comfortably beat an NSWCA President's XI by eight wickets. Limiting the home side to 130, Kapila Wijegunawardene took 3–39 and Rumesh Ratnayake took 2–5 before Mahanama and de Silva led Sri Lanka to victory with 21.5 overs remaining. Pakistan offered up far more resistance at North Sydney Oval, but 7–41 from Champaka Ramanayake led to a 14-run win. Sri Lanka were bowled out for 210, but Javed Miandad's 80 was not enough to win the match. The only negative was the news of a dislocated shoulder for bowler Ratnayake. Participation in the tournament was looking doubtful. In their final game at Pukekura Park, where their first tournament match was played, Sri Lanka defeated A.B. Jordan's XI by six wickets.

Australia's warm-up games were limited to a match against New South Wales and one at Auckland to acclimatise to conditions in New Zealand before the opening match of the tournament. All 14 of the Australian squad played in the match; Mark Taylor, Steve Waugh and Mike Whitney played for New South Wales. Having scored 277/4 in their 50 overs, boosted by a David Boon century and Tom Moody's 63 not out, the state side came incredibly close to pulling off the victory. Steve Small's 101 and Steve Waugh's 61 set up the win, but Greg Matthews was agonisingly run out off the last ball to leave the match tied. The game in Auckland proved to be anything but close, as half-centuries from Marsh, Border and Steve Waugh meant that

Australia's 250/7 was too much for Auckland to chase down. Two wickets apiece for Craig McDermott and Peter Taylor helped bowl out the home side for 188 and deliver a win by 62 runs.

England took a more insular approach to their preparation. Having played their series in New Zealand, they decided to have a warm-up game among themselves, with Graham Gooch and Alec Stewart captaining two teams. County players such as Mark Ramprakash, Peter Martin, Paul Prichard, David Capel, Steve O'Shaughnessy, Phil Newport and Nick Knight were used to fill out the teams. Unsurprisingly, the game proved to be tight. Stewart's side batted first, and he soon lost his wicket, but opening partner Graeme Hick scored 95 out of 244/8. In response, Gooch and Ian Botham's 105-run opening stand gave the Gooch XI a good platform. However, they slumped from 200/3 to 241/8 and fell short by three runs.

Playing conditions for the tournament were set out in a Teams Agreement that each participating country was required to sign. The contents of the document set out the rules and regulations for participation. Not only did it stipulate requirements for each team, but also obligations that the World Cup Committee were liable for.

Sponsorship of the tournament was by Benson & Hedges and, as all of these arrangements stipulate, nothing could be done to 'damage' or 'denigrate' the sponsors. A sum of £3,550,000 was paid for naming rights, prominent signage at each venue, posters, commemorative signed bats, logo on cricket clothing, a drinks trolley at each venue, awards, programmes, photographs and other literature. Also, the sponsorship extended to the Australian team for the duration of the tournament in an exclusive capacity.

By the early 1990s, tobacco advertising was coming under tremendous scrutiny globally. The problem that faced the World Cup Committee was that legislation in New Zealand had already banned such advertising. The Smoke-free Environments Act had been passed in 1990, and such a sponsor was a flagrant breach. A dispensation was sought from the New Zealand government, and it was granted on the proviso that no endorsement of cigarettes could take place. The main stumbling block appeared to be the signed bats, rather than having a known cigarette brand emblazoned everywhere else.

Several functions had been planned, and attendance was a requirement. Before the tournament began, every team was required to attend a 'welcome dinner', which included umpires and 'guests invited by the committee'. It was during this gathering in Sydney that the photographs were taken of the teams on HMAS *Canberra*. In full coloured kit, all of the players were photographed sitting on temporary seating on the flight deck of the frigate. Part of the Royal Australian Navy's fleet, HMAS *Canberra* featured in many photographs, including a shot in front of the bridge with all of the team captains and the ship's captain, Commander R.W. Gates, RAN. A song called 'Who Will Rule the World?' was written as an advertising jingle. The catchy tune and lyrics were such a hit that a full song was requested.

The main controversy from 1992 was the rain rule. Wanting professional advice on the rule, I sought the assistance of Professor Steven Stern from Bond University in Queensland. Professor Stern is now the custodian of the calculations first devised by Duckworth and Lewis, who retired from their role in 2014. First, Stern provided a definition. 'The rain rule in force for the 1992 World Cup was called the Most Productive Overs (MPO) method. It was not that sophisticated (mostly because it wasn't really thought through completely, as the outcomes show). Basically, it works as follows: if the chasing team are given a total of X overs, their target is equal to the total of the team batting first's X most productive overs + 1.'

It was clearly weighted in favour of the team batting first. Professor Stern explained further. 'The fact that the MPO rain rule led mostly to victories for the team batting first is no surprise at all. The method is only really designed for the case that there is rain in the interval and the team batting second loses overs up front (admittedly this is probably the most common scenario). For other situations, the method is a major advantage to the team batting first (in particular, notice that the revised target depends only on the number of overs lost, not on when they are lost, so losing overs before the start of the second innings leads to the same target as losing them from the end of the innings, which is clearly not appropriate).'

The squads were to have no more than 14 nominated players, and teams were to be named a week before the tournament began. Replacing players, once squads were finalised, would require written permission. Two officials were allowed to accompany the squad, and the World Cup Committee would finance expenditure such as travel and accommodation for all 16 members of the party. Travel was detailed as being 'international economy travel' by the 'airline of the committee's choice'. Accommodation consisted of four single rooms and six double rooms for each country, breakfast included, plus meals and laundry costs in the form of a daily allowance.

The playing kit was provided and had to be worn for official occasions. No logos from other manufacturers were to be on show during the tournament. Each player was issued with two short-sleeved shirts, two long-sleeved shirts, two pairs of trousers, one sleeveless sweater, one long-sleeved sweater, one cap, one fielding hat, one batting helmet and one pair of pads. Any footwear, batting and wicketkeeping gloves were the player's responsibility.

Chapter Two

Dramatis Personae

One of the iconic photographs from the 1992 Cricket World Cup is of the teams sitting on temporary seating on HMAS *Canberra* in Sydney harbour, with the Opera House and Harbour Bridge in the background. All of the squad members plus officials and umpires were included in the photograph, taken on the stern of the ship. Any statistics quoted were correct at the start of the 1992 tournament. Let's meet the players who were selected in 1992:

Defending champions and co-hosts Australia were led by 36-year-old Allan Border. This was Border's fourth and final Cricket World Cup, and 'AB' would have been hoping to repeat the success of 1987. His performances in the tournament so far had been substandard for such a successful batter. In 17 innings, Border had only passed 50 once.

At the top of the order, it was David Boon, Geoff Marsh and Mark Taylor who were selected as openers. The experienced Boon (114 ODIs) and Marsh (110) had batted together many times, while Taylor had played 20 ODIs. The inclusion of the left-handed Taylor, a Test regular, gave them a different option to the slower-scoring Marsh. The Boon–Marsh partnership had been fruitful for Australia over the years, including a 75-run opening stand at Eden Gardens in the previous tournament's final against England. Having scored over 700 runs between them in the Benson & Hedges World Series that preceded the Cricket World Cup, this was a tried-and-tested formula that would lead the charge in 1992.

If Boon and Marsh's names were to be on the opening team sheet, Dean Jones's name would be on first. Jones scored runs for fun in the one-day game, at an average of 48.20, and produced *One Day Magic* like his prophetically titled book of the time. He was an early exponent of wearing sunglasses in the field, a common item in modern-day cricket.

Although Tom Moody did not play in the final, he was a member of the victorious squad from the previous tournament. By 1992, Moody was a regular in the Australian team. Playing in all ten games of the Benson & Hedges World Series, he scored 184 runs and took eight wickets. At 6ft 6in, Moody's tall frame lent itself to dominant batting, along with being a handy medium-paced bowler. Undoubtedly, the shoulder injury to Simon O'Donnell afforded Moody opportunities to play regularly. Another veteran from 1987, the Victorian held the record for the fastest fifty in ODI cricket (18 balls against Sri Lanka in Sharjah in 1990). A dislocated shoulder and subsequent poor form in the Sheffield Shield resulted in the selectors deciding to omit O'Donnell from the 14-man squad.

The Waugh twins, 26-year-old Steve and Mark, were included for their all-round abilities. Steve was a genuine all-rounder, while Mark's fielding contribution was considerable. Steve was a veteran of 121 matches including the 1987 final. The 1989 Ashes series had been a breakout one with the bat, but a back injury led to twin brother Mark getting opportunities in the Test arena. Mark's limited-over appearances had been more sparse, but he played five games in the preceding tri-series tournament without any standout performances.

The wicketkeeping duties were trusted to Ian Healy, who had made the position his own since his debut in 1988 in Pakistan. Healy's reputation was one of a fierce competitor who weighed in with aggressive batting in the lower order. From his 63 appearances, Healy had contributed 509 runs with 79 dismissals.

Australia selected a specialist spinner in Peter Taylor. The 35-year-old from Queensland had played just two matches in 1987, but was ever present in the team over the Australian summer. Seen as a limited-overs player, he provided useful batting (420 runs at 23.33) while taking 92 wickets at 28.18. The fast bowling unit consisted of Craig McDermott, Bruce Reid, Mike Whitney and Merv Hughes. It was Hughes who was the surprise selection, having not featured in an ODI since March 1991 in Georgetown, Guyana. Despite being an ever-present in the Tests against India, Hughes had not been considered for any one-day games. However, the selectors decided to go for his experience rather than Paul Reiffel. McDermott, who took 124 wickets from his 80 matches, was in form. His 21 wickets in the World Series made him the pick of the Australian bowlers. Whitney and left-armer Reid both bowled economically, conceding less than three runs per over, without taking too many wickets.

Defeat in Calcutta in 1987 was particularly bitter for Graham Gooch. This was the second time he had tasted defeat in a Cricket World Cup Final, having played in the one-sided 1979 final at Lord's, where Viv Richards inspired the West Indies. At 38, 1992 would be Gooch's final bow. A veteran of 99 ODIs, Gooch had amassed 3,734 runs at 41.03. Captaining the side, Gooch had seen his team beat New Zealand 3–0 before heading to the Cricket World Cup.

Gooch's opening batting partner was Ian Botham. In the twilight of his career, Botham was asked to play a 'pinch-hitting' role to kick-start the batting. Due to appearing in pantomime in Bournemouth, Botham joined the New Zealand tour late, and injuries to other players meant that he made some unplanned appearances. Like Gooch, Botham had played in the 1979 final but was absent eight years later.

The other batters selected by England were Robin Smith, Graeme Hick, Neil Fairbrother and Allan Lamb. Smith went into the tournament in good form. His 85 in the third ODI at Christchurch had set up England for a clean sweep. In contrast, Hick had struggled somewhat in New Zealand and was unable to replicate his form against the West Indies in the limited-overs format. His Test form, after an elongated waiting period for eligibility to play for England, had been less than convincing. Fairbrother had also reaped runs against the West Indies. His 113 in the Texaco Trophy was his highest score in 15 appearances. The most experienced of the quartet was Allan Lamb. Lamb had scored 3,787 runs in his 113 matches, one of which was the 1987 final. His 45 off 55 balls had got England within 34 runs of victory before he was bowled by Steve Waugh.

Despite the spectre of nepotism from England manager Micky Stewart, his son, wicketkeeper-batter Alec Stewart, was selected for his versatility. Being able to open or bat in the middle order, Stewart was looking to add to his batting average of 25.50. Thirteen runs from two innings in New Zealand did little to satisfy doubters.

England's balanced one-day unit could be seen in their selections of Phillip DeFreitas, Chris Lewis, Derek Pringle and Dermot Reeve. All four could easily be classed as all-rounders, which gave England a deep batting order. DeFreitas was another who had featured in the final four years earlier. With 63 matches under his belt, the Lancashire player had played well against the West Indies but only featured once in the New Zealand series. Chris Lewis made his debut in 1990 after impressing at Leicestershire. Australian coach Bob Simpson had projected a successful future for him. Injuries had limited Lewis to 17 ODIs, but his pace had snared 23 wickets at 27.73 apiece. Derek Pringle's opportunities had also been limited due to having to compete with Botham for a place on the team sheet. More suited to English conditions, Pringle's batting had been more fruitful than his bowling. Although he had played just four ODIs, the selection of Dermot Reeve was a sound one. At 28, Hong Kong-born Reeve was late to the international setup. His experience of playing and coaching in Perth meant that his experience would be useful. A handy batter and inventive medium-pace bowler, he contributed five wickets and a valuable 31 not out in the New Zealand series.

Gladstone Small was selected as the dedicated fast bowler. It was a surprise because he had not toured, but Graham Gooch rated his experience. Small featured in the 1987 final and was at the crease when England fell agonisingly short of Australia's total. A return of 52 wickets in 48 matches was not a brilliant one, especially with an economy rate of 4.20. Interestingly, the final two places were given to left-arm spinners Richard Illingworth and Phil Tufnell. Both were relatively inexperienced, having only a handful of Test and ODI matches behind them. Illingworth had proven to be economical, while Tufnell's laissez-faire attitude to fielding negated his wicket-taking ability.

Mohammed Azharuddin led India's challenge. A fine batter, Azharuddin had led India in 31 of his 129 games, but would need to pick his team's morale up after they had lost the Benson & Hedges World Series Cup to Australia. Having finished second to the Aussies, edging out the West Indies, they lost the first final easily before falling to a six-run defeat at the SCG.

At the top of the order, Kris Srikkanth and all-rounder Ravi Shastri had been the preferred options. Srikkanth, aged 32, had featured in 138 matches, while 29-year-old Shastri had 143 appearances under his belt. Srikkanth's unorthodox batting had generated almost 4,000 runs in ODIs, and he had captained his country on 13 occasions before being relieved of the position by Azharuddin. Batting as an opener or in the middle order, Shastri was close to 3,000 runs while amassing 126 wickets at 35.47. In the World Series Cricket game in Perth, Shastri's 5–15 in 6.5 overs helped bowl India to a crushing 107-run win against Australia. Despite this effort, the Man-of-the-Match award went to opening partner Kris Srikkanth. Damaged knee ligaments and resultant surgery, before the beginning of the Cricket World Cup, was not the ideal preparation for Shastri.

Already a superstar, the 'Little Master', Sachin Tendulkar, was India's top-order batter to fear. Only 18-years-old, he had already scored 894 runs and picked up 4–34 against the West Indies. Underlining his prowess, Tendulkar was second-highest run scorer in the World Series Cricket averages, with 401 runs at 44.55. Only David Boon had a better average in the series. Completing the batting line-up were Sanjay Manjrekar, Vinod Kambli and Pravin Amre. The Manjrekar name was already synonymous with Indian cricket. Sanjay followed in his father's footsteps by representing India. Manjrekar had played 37 times, but his form in the World Series Cup had slumped. In both the Wills Trophy, in Sharjah, and the hastily arranged series against South Africa, it was Manjrekar who topped the batting averages.

Twenty-year-old Vinod Kambli was selected to join the squad after making his ODI debut in the Wills Trophy. A total of 93 runs in three innings had given the selectors enough comfort to choose him. Also, Kambli and Tendulkar had played together as schoolboys and still held a world record stand of 664 runs. Kambli also took 6–37 in that game as Shardashram Vidyamandir School won their match by 602 runs. Pravin Amre was another young batter who was given an opportunity. As he made his debut in the series against South Africa, his first innings produced a half-century at Eden Gardens. In the following eight innings, he failed to score more than 33, but his excellent fielding secured his place.

In addition to Ravi Shastri, the all-rounders selected were the legendary Kapil Dev, who had 181 ODI appearances, and youngster Ajay Jadeja, who was yet to make his international bow. At 33, Kapil Dev was considered one of the best all-rounders ever. Along with Imran Khan and Ian Botham, his achievements with bat and ball would go down in cricketing history. Although his pace was dwindling, Kapil had still topped the Indian averages over the Australian summer while maintaining an economy rate of 3.12 runs per over. Under his tutelage, Ajay Jadeja's promise had come to the fore. In first-class cricket, Jadeja had scored 1,036 runs in domestic cricket, including 256 for Haryana in the Ranji Trophy. Four centuries and an average of 94.18 had led to Jadeja's elevation to the Indian squad.

Diminutive wicketkeeper Kiran More managed to shake off a hamstring injury to make the tournament. More had been first choice since 1985 and had amassed 53 catches and 26 stumpings. Understudy Chandrakant Pandit had deputised for More while he was injured.

In the spin bowling department, it was Venkatapathy Raju who was chosen. Both Anil Kumble and Narendra Hirwani had featured in the Wills Trophy and World Series Cricket, but the leg-spinners were omitted in favour of the left-arm spin of Raju. Manoj Prabhakar's experience and his attacking medium-pace bowling had topped the averages in Sharjah and Australia. A fiery character, Prabhakar was also so handy as a batter that he had opened the innings earlier in his career. A century against Pakistan in 1987 highlighted his abilities. Quicker bowlers Subroto Banerjee and Javagal Srinath completed the Indian squad. Banerjee had made his ODI debut in Sharjah and had been used sparingly. He was a student at Dennis Lillee's School of Pace Bowling in Madras, and his ability to swing the ball late had brought him to prominence in India. Srinath cemented his position in the team in Australia with 11 wickets.

Co-hosts New Zealand could be forgiven for thinking that their previous year's achievements in one-day cricket were long forgotten. Twelve months on, England had beaten them in both Test and one-day series. Captain Martin Crowe needed to find the right balance in his bowling unit. Crowe's batting was not in question, with his excellent strokeplay. His old knee injury that tended to flare up at times would need managing.

At the top of the order, the experienced duo of Andrew Jones and John Wright were selected. It appeared that they wouldn't both open, as Rod Latham had been used as an opener in the series versus England. Both Jones with 2,035 runs and Wright with 3,812 appeared destined to play an anchor role for their team, but not together. Joining Latham in the batting stakes were Mark Greatbatch and Ken Rutherford. Left-handed batter Greatbatch had been going through a rough patch. With just 19 runs in three innings against England, his selection was more on ability than form. He had scored back-to-back centuries in England in 1990, but had struggled since those innings at Headingley and The Oval. Ken Rutherford's inconsistency in batting had prevented him from playing more Tests and ODIs. In his 63 one-day matches, Rutherford had yet to reach a century despite scoring 1,565 runs. Also, Rutherford bowled medium-pacers and fielded magnificently.

With the surname of Cairns, all-rounder Chris was already steeped in New Zealand cricket pedigree and expectation. The 21-year-old had played only a handful of games, and had recovered from a stress fracture of the back on his Test debut versus Australia at the WACA. Batting in the lower order, Cairns could hit the ball hard. His bowling was just as aggressive. In addition, medium-pace all-rounders Chris Harris and Gavin Larsen were selected to carry on their fine form. Harris, 22-years-old, topped the batting averages against England, while Larsen did likewise in the bowling averages. Harris was another Kiwi following in his father's footsteps. Larsen was 27 when first selected in 1990 and played steadily without having any standout matches.

At 35, Ian Smith was a veteran and was playing in his third Cricket World Cup. Despite pressure from young wicketkeepers Brian Young and Adam Parore, Smith was retained. He was also the vice-captain that Martin Crowe would have called upon. Experience from a player with 89 ODI appearances would be invaluable if New Zealand had aspirations of doing well.

The spinning option went to Nairobi-born right-arm off-spinner Dipak Patel. Another veteran from 1987, Patel had featured only 24 times because of John Bracewell's selection. Patel had played several seasons of county cricket for Worcestershire before moving to Auckland. The fast bowling trio of Danny Morrison, Murphy Su'a and Willie Watson made up the bowling unit. Morrison's short but well-built frame allowed him to 'bend his back' when bowling, and 52 wickets from 41 ODIs was a fair return. Su'a had made his debut in the England series after playing several Test matches. He was the first Samoan, and Pacific Islander, to play Test cricket. His one wicket for 70 runs in two matches had been an inauspicious start to his limited-overs career. Watson had made the previous Cricket World

Cup, but 1992 gave him a better opportunity. As he held off medium-pacer Chris Pringle for a spot, Watson's work rate was the deciding factor.

In the months leading up to the Cricket World Cup, Pakistan could not have been accused of being underprepared. Participation, and victory, in the Wills Trophy was followed up with home series against the West Indies and then Sri Lanka. In the space of less than four months, 13 ODIs were played, with seven victories.

Having retired after the 1987 tournament, Imran Khan soon returned to the Pakistan team. At 36, this would be his swansong. Imran was a veteran of 167 ODI matches and a talismanic leader, and his batting and bowling guile was crucial for success. One player that he had to be without was pace bowler Waqar Younis. CT scans confirmed that Younis was suffering from stress fractures in his back and he was ruled out of the tournament before it started. The prognosis was rest for two to three months, and Younis returned to Pakistan.

Chosen to open the batting for Pakistan was the experienced Ramiz Raja and the young, talented left-handed batter Aamer Sohail. Ramiz's explosive approach could lead to his losing his wicket, and this was evidenced in his batting average of 33.16. In good form in the Wills Trophy and the home series, his runs guaranteed his place. Aamer Sohail, on the other hand, had only played five matches, but had scored 91 against India in just his second ODI.

The top order for Pakistan featured the experience of ex-captain Javed Miandad. A veteran of 185 matches, Miandad had scored over 6,000 ODI runs, including seven centuries. Having captained his country 46 times, Miandad's experience was vital for Imran Khan to rely on. However, their relationship hadn't always been harmonious; also a niggling back injury had dogged Miandad for a while. In contrast, yet potentially as useful, the 21-year-old Inzamam-ul-Haq was included in the squad. 'Inzi' had scored two centuries in his first seven ODIs. Having debuted against the West Indies, he had highlighted his potential with 406 runs at 67.66. He had scored at 82.52 per 100 balls, mostly from boundaries, as Inzamam was not too interested in quick singles.

Completing the batting line-up were the experienced pair of Salim Malik and Ijaz Ahmed, along with Zahid Fazal, who had played sporadically over the previous two years. Salim Malik's 138 appearances had not delivered as many runs as his quality demanded. Although he had scored five centuries, not one of his innings had gone higher than 102. Ijaz Ahmed was five years younger than Salim Malik, but was already pushing towards 100 ODIs. Ijaz's lack of runs was compensated for by his smart fielding. The Sri Lanka series brought relief from a barren spell for the right-handed batter. Good form in the Wills Trophy and against the West Indies made sure that Zahid Fazal made the squad. At just 18-years-old, he was in a position to play himself into contention if injury befell one of the established players.

Moin Khan was selected as the wicketkeeper for Pakistan. Moin had made the position his own after debuting, against the West Indies in 1990. His batting in his 14 games had not been outstanding, but 12 catches and two stumpings were enough to keep him in the position.

At 25-years-old, Wasim Akram was in the prime of his cricketing life. A fearsome bowler with a devastating yorker, Akram was also a useful batter. With Waqar Younis ruled out of the tournament, Akram would be the spearhead of the Pakistan bowling attack. Having played 112 ODIs, he had 149 wickets, including best bowling figures of 5–21 against Australia at the MCG in the World Championship of Cricket in

1985. He also held two ODI hat-tricks out of the seven achieved at that point.

The new ball duties would go to Aaqib Javed. Still 19-years-old, Aaqib was a pure pace bowler. He came into the tournament in excellent form. He had blown India away in the Wills Trophy with 7–37, including a hat-trick with the wickets of Shastri, Azharuddin and Tendulkar, to help secure a 72-run victory. His bowling figures were the best in an ODI, eclipsing Winston Davis's 7–51 in 1983. The selection of Wasim Haider was more 'left field'. Uncapped at any international level, Haider was a fast-medium bowler who could also bat.

The last two places in the squad went to leg-spinners Mushtaq Ahmed and Iqbal Sikander. Mushtaq had come into the limelight as a 17-year-old and given the mantle of being the new Abdul Qadir. In ODIs, Mushtaq had 44 wickets in 34 matches but was expensive at 4.79 runs per over. Iqbal Sikander was 33-years-old and far more experienced than Mushtaq. He was uncapped internationally, but had played well in Pakistan domestic cricket. For Karachi Whites and PIA, Sikander had taken 42 wickets at 21.11, which gave him his opportunity.

South Africa's selections were always going to be a mystery to most cricket fans. Having been in isolation since 1970, many South African cricketers had only played in their domestic competition. Some names were known due to having played in English domestic cricket, but the final selection came as a shock to many. The most contentious decisions were to omit captain Clive Rice and opening batter Jimmy Cook.

The captaincy was given to Kepler Wessels, who had played 24 Tests and 54 ODIs for Australia. One criticism of Wessels was that his style wasn't suited to the short form of the game. However, he had never been dismissed for a duck in his 54 ODI innings, and his average was 38.25. Peter Kirsten complemented

Wessels's experience. Initially discarded by South Africa, Kirsten was brought back into the squad. Having played professional cricket since 1973, Kirsten had played in the South African and English domestic leagues. His 86 not out in the third ODI against India highlighted his apparent quality at international level, and his ability to bowl off spin added to his strengths. Opener Andrew Hudson completed the top-order batting line-up. His batting style was not suited to the spin-friendly pitches in India, but 673 runs in the Castle Cup, back in South Africa, secured his place. Mark Rushmere came to prominence during the English rebel tour in 1989/90. He was a tall player who could open or bat at number three.

The middle order was bolstered with young batters in Hansie Cronje and Jonty Rhodes. Although just 22-years-old, Cronje was already captain of Orange Free State. He did not feature in the Indian tour, but his maturity, fielding and handy medium-paced seam bowling gave South Africa options. Rhodes was known as an aggressive batter, but his fielding reputation was enormous. Comparisons were made to the almost mythical fielding prowess of Colin Bland – creating a massive expectation for the 22-year-old Rhodes to live up to.

In the genuine all-rounder category were Adrian Kuiper and Brian McMillan. Kuiper was known for being a big hitter. During the 1989/90 rebel tour, he scored a century from 49 balls against the English XI. Kuiper played in all three ODIs in India, but his innings in the first match, as he scored 43 with reserved and then explosive hitting, highlighted his talents. Kuiper played one season in England, for Derbyshire in 1990, so would have been known to many of the opposing players. McMillan's series against India was uneventful, but his batting, bowling and fielding were generally excellent. In the previous domestic season, McMillan had averaged 45 with the bat and 26 with the ball. He also had experience of English county cricket, with Warwickshire in 1986.

Wicketkeeping duties went to Dave Richardson. Having been the South African wicketkeeper during rebel tours since 1986, Richardson was the preferred choice. Born into a family of cricketers, he was known as an excellent batter with first-class hundreds to his name.

Forty-year-old Omar Henry was South Africa's only spinner and only non-white player in the squad. Having played professional cricket since 1973, Henry had featured for Western Province, Boland, Impalas and Orange Free State in domestic cricket. Since 1989, he had featured for Scotland on many occasions and captained the team. The rest of the squad was made up of pace bowlers. Richard Snell was a right-arm fast-medium bowler who shared the new ball. He had played in all three ODIs in India, but had taken just one wicket. Another of the younger players who had an excellent time against the English XI, Snell's nagging accuracy posed problems. Before the tournament, he agreed to join Somerset for the 1992 English domestic season. Sharing the new ball with Snell was Allan Donald. His pace was renowned, and he was given the tagline of being the 'fastest white bowler' due to his time in England playing for Warwickshire. Donald had taken South Africa's first Test wicket since the lifting of the apartheid ban. He had taken three Indian wickets in his first four overs and finished with 5–21, and taken nine wickets overall in the Indian series. Tertius Bosch was another express pace bowler who had forced his way into the squad. A consistent performer in South Africa, Bosch had taken plenty of wickets for Northern Transvaal. Meyrick Pringle's place was also based on his domestic form – he had been the highest wicket-taker in the previous season. A bowler who could move the ball in the right conditions,

Pringle complemented the pace bowling make-up of the South African squad.

Aravinda de Silva captained the Sri Lankan team. After he had taken over the captaincy from Arjuna Ranatunga, de Silva's form had not been great. Sri Lanka had lost the ODI series in Pakistan 4–1, with de Silva scoring just 80 runs. Nicknamed 'Mad Max', inspired by his ultra-aggressive approach to batting earlier in his career, de Silva had played 92 one-day matches with an average of 28.71. He also bowled occasional off spin, which had brought 24 wickets since his debut in 1984.

At the top of the order, Athula Samarasekera and Roshan Mahanama were most likely to open. Samarasekera had played just 31 ODIs in his nine-year career. A tall and imposing opener, his main fault was a lack of concentration at times. With an average of 20.58, Samarasekera was underperforming, and his match-winning 76 against Pakistan in Multan demonstrated his potential. Mahanama was more experienced, with 58 ODIs. Formerly a middle-order batter, Mahanama had moved to opener. Although beset by injuries, he was known for his outstanding contributions in the field. He had won three Man-of-the-Match awards in his career, including a high score of 98 and a catch against India in 1988. Another option to open for Sri Lanka was Chandika Hathurusinghe, another aggressive batter who was also a medium-fast bowler. His four matches in the Pakistan series garnered 41 runs, but his form in Sri Lanka had improved. Hathurusinghe's Tamil Nadu won the floodlit one-day competition, the R Premadasa Challenge Trophy, with the opener scoring 88 in the final.

The most experienced player in the team was Arjuna Ranatunga. At number 24 in the list of Sri Lankan ODI players, Ranatunga had featured in 99 matches including 31 as captain. He had also scored the most runs in ODIs for Sri Lanka.

Ranatunga's frame was deceiving, as the left-handed batter was also a useful medium-paced bowler. Regularly batting at number three, Asanka Gurusinha bolstered the top order. A technically sound batter, Gurusinha had played in 61 ODIs with a high score of 88. His close-in fielding was also of note.

The selection of Sanath Jayasuriya filled the all-rounder role, with the left-hander having played 20 ODIs. His batting record (8.41 average) and bowling record (52.16) belied Jayasuriya's talent. His Test record was much better, and his ability to bat long innings suggested his place in the squad had merit. Topping the batting averages in the Pakistan tour helped cement his place.

Wicketkeeping duties fell to Hashan Tillakaratne, who had excelled in the ODI format. He held the world record of the most dismissals (five) by a wicketkeeper in an innings with Rod Marsh, Guy de Alwis and Syed Kirmani. A good batting average of 28.80 from 41 matches delivered useful runs in the lower order.

A fast bowling quartet of Rumesh Ratnayake, Champaka Ramanayake, Pramodya Wickramasinghe and Kapila Wijegunawardene shared the bowling duties for Sri Lanka. Ratnayake was Sri Lanka's most experienced bowler, having taken 72 wickets in 66 matches. Ratnayake's bowling action could be deceiving. However, injury had reduced his availability throughout his career and he went into the tournament with a shoulder injury. Ramanayake's primary weapon was his nagging accuracy. He was not the fastest of bowlers, but he kept batters honest. Wickramasinghe's 5–73 in the third Test against Pakistan forced him into the ODI series. He had just a solitary wicket in four ODI matches, but still managed to make the squad. Another medium-pacer, Wickramasinghe had enjoyed an excellent domestic season, including taking all ten wickets in a three-day game. He was the first Sri Lankan to achieve this feat. Wijegunawardene's international career had been limited to the one-day game. He had taken 25 wickets in 23 matches with his medium-pace bowling.

The Sri Lankan squad was completed with the spinners Ruwan Kalpage and Don Anurasiri. Kalpage was new to the Sri Lankan one-day team, with just two matches under his belt. He was also a decent batter who fielded well. Anurasiri was relatively experienced, but had struggled to maintain his place in the team. He was an aggressive spinner who was not afraid to throw the ball up to the batters. One spinner who could have made his way into the squad, as demonstrated by his bowling figures of 3–29 in the R Premadasa Challenge Trophy Final, was a 19-year-old Muttiah Muralitharan.

The West Indies went into the Cricket World Cup without Viv Richards. Discarding a player with 6,721 runs, averaging 47, including 11 centuries and 45 fifties, was a big call by the West Indies selectors. Richie Richardson had replaced Richards, who had relinquished the captaincy with a view to retiring after the 1992 Cricket World Cup, for the Wills Trophy. In his first game as captain, Richardson had scored an unbeaten 106 to guide the West Indies to a one-wicket victory. A veteran of 152 ODIs, Richardson had amassed 4,684 runs. Australia had not been a fruitful place for runs, and his average there was just 25.17 in 52 matches.

The heir apparent to Richards, before the selectors went with Richardson, was Desmond Haynes. A veteran of 193 ODI matches, Haynes had scored 7,194 runs, including the highest score and fastest century on debut. His recent form had not been affected by the disappointment of missing out on the captaincy. He had topped the batting averages, with four scores over 50, in the West Indies' disappointing World Series campaign in Australia.

At 22-years-old, Brian Lara was the youngest member of the West Indies squad. He had captained both the West Indian youth and under-23 teams before becoming Trinidad & Tobago's youngest-ever captain at the age of 20. His international career to date had not been extraordinary, averaging 23.75, but his talent was obvious. The batting department was boosted by the experience of Gus Logie and Keith Arthurton. Logie debuted in 1981 and averaged 33.27 in his 130 matches. His fielding was exemplary (52 catches), making him a useful addition to the squad. He missed the World Series Cup in Australia after a poor run in the Wills Trophy with two ducks and a top score of 11.

Selecting three all-rounders in Phil Simmons, Carl Hooper and Roger Harper gave the West Indies plenty of variation in their line-up. Simmons had batted as an opener for the West Indies in his 36 ODIs. With just one century and an average of 27.14, he had not been consistent enough to stay in the team. On his tour debut in 1988, Simmons required life-saving surgery when a ball from David Lawrence hit him in the head. Hooper was an excellent batter, off-spinner and fielder in one-day cricket. He had been second in the West Indies' batting averages in the World Series, also taking seven wickets. For Harper, it was a surprise recall after three years. His last ODI had been in Australia, after substandard performances with the bat and ball. His fielding was remarkable; his run-out of Graham Gooch in the MCC Bicentenary match in 1987 was a testament to that.

Picking up the massive wicketkeeping gloves of Jeff Dujon was David Williams. At 5ft 4in, Williams needed to work extra hard because of the bounce extracted by the West Indies quicks. He was competent behind the stumps, with 22 dismissals in 17 ODIs, but was let down by a woeful batting average.

The bowling attack was spearheaded by the legendary Malcolm Marshall and future great in Curtly Ambrose. Marshall had terrorised many a batter in the 1980s. At 33-years-old, he was in the twilight of his career. A veteran of 131 ODIs, Marshall had taken 155 wickets at 26.18 and conceded at just over 3.5 runs per over. His 4–18 against Australia at the MCG in the World Series Cup was a reminder that Marshall was still a force to be reckoned with. Ambrose was just as miserly as Marshall, but struck more regularly. He had taken 101 wickets at 19.25 and topped the West Indies' bowling averages in Australia.

The rest of the squad was made up of more pace bowling. Winston Benjamin, Anderson Cummins and Patrick Patterson were selected in the absence of Ian Bishop, who was in long-term recovery from a back injury. Benjamin was another who had been brought back from relative obscurity. Apart from two games in the Wills Trophy, he had last featured for the West Indies at the end of 1989. He was not as quick as some of the bowlers, but was a useful tail-end batter. Cummins could have featured in the all-rounder category as a bowler who could bat. A newcomer to the ODI team, he had made his debut in the first ODI in Pakistan in the previous November. His 5–31 at the Gabba in the World Series Cup, against India, was far and away his best performance to date. Raw pace and aggression was the modus operandi for Patrick Patterson. A haul of 74 wickets in 49 matches highlighted his wicket-taking ability. Graham Gooch admitted that he had feared Patterson in the 1986 Test at Sabina Park. However, the one-day arena may not have afforded Patterson the same field placings that he would have enjoyed in Tests.

Zimbabwe's squad were not given the same opportunity to play one-day matches, as the nation was not a full member of the ICC. Cricket World Cups were the only opportunity to play ODIs at that point. The possibility of full membership loomed large, and a respectable showing was a motivating factor. Leading

Zimbabwe into their third Cricket World Cup was David Houghton. Having played in all 12 of Zimbabwe's previous ODIs, Houghton was ideally placed to captain the emerging cricket nation. A fantastic batter who was able to judge his innings, he was also an outstanding slip fielder. Houghton had also played as a wicketkeeper earlier in his career. In 1987, he had scored 142 against New Zealand in Hyderabad, almost helping to pull off another shock victory.

Opening the batting was Andy Flower, who also kept wicket. The left-handed opener had played league cricket in England and the Netherlands, but it was his form in the ICC Trophy that cemented his place. Flower scored 311 runs, at an average of 77.75, to help Zimbabwe qualify for 1992. Also opening the batting was Kevin Arnott, who had played four games in 1987. Arnott was averaging 37.33, with his highest score being 60 against India in Ahmedabad. He was another good fielder who could keep wicket.

Zimbabwe's batting was bolstered by the experience of Iain Butchart and Andy Pycroft. Both had played in all 12 ODIs, like Houghton, but their styles were different. Butchart was a hard-hitting batter, while Pycroft played more classic shots. Both had similar batting averages, while Butchart bowled medium pace. Neither was a professional cricketer – they held jobs in an agricultural machine company (Butchart) and as a lawyer (Pycroft). Pycroft had suffered from knee injuries, which hampered his fielding and running between wickets.

Andy Waller had the reputation of being a big-hitting batter. A tobacco farmer by trade, Waller was tall and used his physique to good effect. Playing all six games in 1987, he had not put in any outstanding performances. Completing the batting line-up were Wayne James and Alistair Campbell. James, yet to make his ODI debut, was a batter who could keep wicket if required. His job in Zimbabwe was as a building materials supplier. Campbell was 19-years-old, but had already made a first-class century. His fielding was less impressive, which earned him the nickname 'Kamba', meaning 'tortoise' in Shona, one of the Bantu languages of sub-Saharan Africa. Campbell was playing club cricket in England as well as representative honours for Zimbabwe, despite his young age.

Another member of the squad who played in the first ODI in 1993 was all-rounder Ali Shah. Shah was more of a bowler who batted: his bowling average of 36.50 was better than his batting average of 11.77. Bowling medium-pace cutters and seamers, he provided variation to the Zimbabwe bowling attack. His business ventures had caused a lack of practice and playing, which meant he wasn't a regular in the Zimbabwe side. He was the first non-white player to play for his country.

Zimbabwe's bowling attack featured Eddo Brandes, Malcolm Jarvis, Kevin Duers and Mark Burmester. Brandes was a fast bowler with a big frame who used every sinew – not always accurate, but always looking to bowl fast. His later-order batting was more than just slogging. Using his physique, Brandes could hit the ball hard but also with purpose. Not as quick as Brandes, Jarvis needed to get seam movement or swing to cause trouble for the batters. At 36-years-old, Jarvis had been around the Zimbabwe team since 1979, and his fitness was waning. Duers made the squad when Grant Flower, Andy's brother, withdrew due to injury. He had played in the 1990 ICC Trophy, but had not been a consistent starter for Zimbabwe. Burmester's all-round performances brought him into the reckoning for the squad. With his medium-fast bowling and as an opening batter, Burmester did enough. Representative honours at under-25 and 'B' level had given him the opportunity to test his skills on the international stage.

The final member of the Zimbabwe squad was John Traicos. At 44-years-old, Traicos was easily the oldest player in the tournament. In 1970, he had played three Tests for South Africa against Bill Lawry's touring Australian team before the apartheid ban came into being. A naggingly accurate off-spinner, Traicos took ten wickets in his 12 ODI matches for Zimbabwe. He was also instrumental in the defeat of Australia in 1983. His bowling figures of 12-2-27-0 helped restrict the Australian batters. Despite his age, Traicos was still useful in the gully position.

A total of 11 umpires were selected. The host nations contributed two each: Peter McConnell and Steve Randell from Australia, and Brian Aldridge and Steve Woodward from New Zealand. The rest of the panel consisted of one umpire from each remaining nation: David Shepherd (England), Piloos Reporter (India), Khizer Hayat (Pakistan), Karl Liebenberg (South Africa), Dooland Buultjens (Sri Lanka), Steve Bucknor (West Indies) and Ian Robinson (Zimbabwe).

In order to coordinate the massive amount of data each match would create, the World Cup Committee approached Ross Dundas to perform the duty of Official Statistician. Dundas had found an interest in cricket statistics in the 1960s and spent many years compiling his own records. He also had an interest in computers and built a database of Test cricket information that was used by Channel Nine in Australia. It was this connection that led to a phone call about improvements in on-air statistics for the 1992 Cricket World Cup.

'A few years before the 1991/92 World Cup,' he recalls, 'I was sitting at the dining table with my young family having dinner when the telephone rang. I recall it was around 6pm and my youngest daughter raced to the phone. She returned to say "Greg" was on the phone for me. "Greg?" I thought. I didn't know anyone by that name. But soon the voice gave it away. It was Tony Greig who had tracked me down. I still remember the message he had for me to this day. "KP [Kerry Packer] wants the strike rates for batters in the next World Cup, can you give it to him?"'

'In those days, this information was almost non-existent, and I only had 50 to 60 per cent of data covering all the 500-odd games played to that time and mostly from Australia. Greig said he could help me in any way he could. We began a task of writing and communicating with associations all around the world. We contacted scorers, newspaper officers, reporters and anyone who would have had contact with the games of one-day cricket that had been played to that time. Soon material began to arrive, and so I began to collate it. I had to re-score many games to obtain the balls faced. Therefore, I was the first person in world cricket to begin such a process and can claim that I started the process of batting strike rates.'

Dundas collated the information from each game during the tournament, and entered the data into his database before uploading the information into Channel Nine's computers for their use. Information was also distributed to press and broadcasters. Also, Dundas attended many of the games to act as scorer/statistician. He recalls that many of the commentary boxes had a note in the front of the window to remind commentators where they were at the time.

Chapter Three

Lifting the Curtain

Despite the grey skies, Eden Park in Auckland was awash with colour. The opening match and mandatory ceremony to start proceedings had been awarded to New Zealand. Twenty-seven thousand fans packed into the ground to witness the Kiwis take on their arch-rivals from 'across the ditch'. Before the first ball was bowled, an hour-long opening ceremony celebrated the beginning of the tournament.

At a cost of A$300,000, and having taken six months to put together, the ceremony included a parade of great players from each nation. Australia were led out by Greg Chappell, New Zealand by Lance Cairns. The organisers had struggled to find a South African player, but approached Clive Rice. Despite the sensitivity of his being dropped from the South African squad, he agreed to participate.

As part of the ceremony, the Waterford crystal trophy was driven around Eden Park in a vintage car, and Sir Richard Hadlee was given the role of holding it on its journey. Brass bands, a New Zealand air force flyover and a Maori welcome filled the time before the national anthems and the coin toss.

Back in England, Charles Colvile was presenting the coverage on Sky Sports. This being the first night of coverage, things didn't go smoothly. 'They had the opening ceremony, so we went on air about 9pm, and it was a cold night. As we went on air, somebody finished work somewhere else within the company and they went out and started up their car, and they revved it up. Their car was parked up against the Portakabins in the car park. We were in the car park. So, the car started up, and for ten minutes you couldn't hear anything we were saying in the studio because all you could hear in the background was this "vroom-vroom" and then the exhaust fumes started to get into the Portakabin, so we were all starting to feel a bit woozy.'

In New Zealand, TVNZ were facing more severe problems, with threats of disruption to broadcasts. A decision had been made to temporarily cancel Maori language news programmes during the Cricket World Cup. A Maori sovereignty group, Tino Rangatiratanga, threatened to damage pitches and equipment in protest. The programmes were restored to the schedule.

Winning the toss, Martin Crowe decided that he would bat first. Opening the bowling was Craig McDermott, and he started nervously with two wides. His third delivery, the first legitimate one of the match, angled towards the leg side. John Wright, looking to work it away, played towards the on side as if to clip it away to fine leg, but the ball received minimal contact and the stumps were broken. Wright walked away disconsolately while McDermott and his team-mates celebrated the early breakthrough.

The new batter was 32-year-old Andrew Jones, and he settled his, and New Zealand's, nerves with a boundary. In the following over, Rod Latham followed suit with a boundary square of the wicket. The ball sailed through the air but was safe. The fast outfield carried the ball quickly for four, which delighted the partisan crowd. Bowler Bruce Reid thought he had exacted revenge as Latham edged a ball bowled across his body, but Tom Moody, usually a safe pair of hands, spilled the catch.

In his next over, Reid made amends. Jones played at and missed a ball that appeared to strike him high on his pad. Muted appeals came from the Aussies, but umpire Khizer Hayat was convinced and gave the batter out lbw. The crowd were unimpressed, making their displeasure known by booing – as was TV commentator Tony Greig, who vocalised his disagreement in his inimitable style. New Zealand were 13/2, and Australia were in control.

Next batter in was Martin Crowe. New Zealand needed a cool head and sensible batting, and no one better than the Kiwi captain could be at the wicket. Finally settling the nerves, both Crowe and Latham found scoring relatively easy. Latham punished bad balls from McDermott, through backward square leg, and Moody, through the covers, for boundaries. The Australians had started to bowl too short, and New Zealand were cashing in. Their fifty was brought up by Martin Crowe with an effortless boundary. He leaned into a Bruce Reid delivery, and the ball rocketed along the ground for four runs.

The third wicket to fall was that of Rod Latham, when he went after a wide delivery from Tom Moody. The thick edge flew wide of Ian Healy, the Australian wicketkeeper, but a tumbling effort and outstretched right glove led to the catch sticking, and the batter was gone for 26. Having dropped Latham early, Moody would have found this wicket particularly pleasing. At 53/3 in the 16th over, New Zealand needed a partnership.

The incoming batter was Ken Rutherford. His form was good, with 52 and 37 against England earlier in the month, and he carried this on against Australia. Using the late cut, and playing square of the wicket, Rutherford scored quickly.

In addition, Martin Crowe looked in imperious form. He was pulling anything short, and *Wisden* made mention of knee-high balls being despatched on the on side. The unusual shape of Eden Park led to this boundary being the shortest, and the New Zealand batters were intent on exploiting it.

In the 21st over, Crowe pulled another ball towards the boundary. A running Dean Jones dived despairingly towards the ball, but the catch went down. The momentum of the ball carried it over the boundary, to add to the frustration. The Australian bowlers chose far too short a length, and both batters were quick to pounce. Both the faster bowlers and the use of spin couldn't adjust to the pace of the Eden Park wicket. Martin Crowe dragged a short ball from Taylor to the boundary, through midwicket, with ease. Not learning from his previous over, Taylor dropped short again, and Crowe despatched the ball to reach his fifty in the 31st over.

Seven overs later, Bruce Reid dropped short once again, and Crowe pulled through midwicket for another boundary. As he looked to pitch the ball up, Reid's length invited a drive, and Crowe sent the ball gloriously through mid-off for another four. Rutherford's fifty came soon after with the hapless Mark Waugh being clubbed through midwicket. Later in the over, Crowe offered another opportunity, but Allan Border's running attempt to take the high catch went down. Border managed to avoid the square leg umpire, but the ball slipped out of his grasp as he hit the ground. As he got up slowly, looking confused, Border's demeanour seemed to capture the malaise of the Australians perfectly.

The partnership was broken in the next over when Crowe dropped the ball looking for a quick single, but Mark Waugh's alertness and accuracy left Rutherford short of his ground. The partnership had been worth 118 from 25 overs. Rutherford's 57 from 71 balls had done a job for New Zealand, but more work needed to be done. Martin Crowe's innings was key to setting a competitive total.

Looking to push on, Chris Harris scored 14 off 15 balls before Border and Moody combined for a run-out. Ian Smith played a similar innings with a run-a-ball 14 before Healy took a diving catch off the inside edge. The pair of partnerships had added 44 to the total, and New Zealand were 215/6.

The new batter was Chris Cairns, joining Crowe at the crease. In the 49th over, Australia thought they had Crowe when a McDermott delivery appeared to take the edge. Umpire Shepherd was unmoved, much to the chagrin of the desperate Australians. There was much shaking of heads from Australia, but Crowe's century was still on. To follow up, another pull shot from Crowe took him to 98, and McDermott looked forlorn.

The 50th over started with New Zealand on 234/6. Cairns was on strike, while Crowe was at the non-striker's end on 99. Steve Waugh bowled the final over, and Cairns missed his first ball. He then clubbed the next two for boundaries by playing across the line. Ball four was hoiked towards cow corner, and Cairns scampered, while Crowe limped, through for three. The crowd knew that their captain would get his opportunity for a well-deserved century.

Chopping the ball towards gully, Crowe ran away from the danger end while Cairns sprinted to make his ground. The resultant dive was not needed as the fieldsman missed and Crowe had his century. Many in the crowd were filled with excitement and rushed on to the ground to congratulate their hero. A leg-side wide and a leg-bye ended the innings for New Zealand. They finished on 248/6.

New Zealand's score was above par for the conditions, so Australia needed a solid start if they were to chase the total down. The opening partnership of David Boon and Marsh were the ideal batters for the occasion. Boon, the Tasmanian, faced the opening over from Chris Cairns. Using the unusual shape of the ground perfectly, Boon clipped a ball to the short boundary for four, before pushing the ball towards the longest part of the ground for an all-run four. The Australian response was underway.

Off-spinner Dipak Patel bowled the second over. A tactic that Martin Crowe had not used previously, the choice of a spinner to open the bowling was a novelty. However, it was a novelty that seemed to confuse the Australians. Patel, who had played junior cricket with Marsh, recounted the astonishment. 'I remember Geoff Marsh actually coming out and watching me making a run up at him, and he said: "You are kidding me, aren't you?" So, I think the surprise factor was a major part.'

It was not just the Australians who were shocked by this revelation. Michael Wagener, a New Zealand fan watching the game at home, remembers the moment well. 'As a young spinner growing up in New Zealand, I was captivated at the idea. I remember watching on television and running out to tell my father, who was in the garden, that we were opening with Patel. Dad just said, "That's madness, we're definitely going to lose, I'm going to stay in the garden."'

Without pace to work with, Boon and Marsh found scoring difficult. Cairns was unable to back up the plan and conceded 30 runs from four overs. Patel, on the other hand, bowled seven overs for 19 runs. I asked Patel how he came to open the bowling. 'It wasn't sort of pre-planned in terms of a pre-World Cup. I think it revolved around the fact that prior to the World Cup, we had the English series and I bowled very well during those games. Martin Crowe showed a lot of faith in me as a one-day bowler and, you know, it's something John Bracewell and I had done for Auckland

Cricket and local domestic cricket. We just talked about it at the opening of the World Cup and it sort of evolved from there really.'

The problem for Australia was that Geoff Marsh was struggling to score. In the first 18 overs, he had scored just 19 runs. Looking to break the shackles of the New Zealand bowlers, he drove at a ball from medium-pacer Gavin Larsen, and Rod Latham took a good catch at cover.

Changing the bowlers regularly, Martin Crowe did not allow the batters to settle. Dean Jones nervously cut a ball through the vacant slip area for a boundary. The Australians were struggling to come to terms with the lack of pace. In the 25th over, New Zealand's sharp fielding yielded another wicket when Dean Jones was run out from a Cairns pick-up and throw. Ian Smith whipped off the bails, and the Kiwis ran to congratulate the fielder. Dean Jones, looking aggrieved, stomped off the ground. TV replays showed that umpire Hayat might have been too quick to give it out. It would undoubtedly have been reviewed in modern-day cricket.

Allan Border joined Boon at the wicket, and the Tasmanian soon brought up his fifty. While Boon found gaps, the Australian captain found the situation frustrating. With Dipak Patel having been brought back on, Border was induced into sweeping the ball, but just found Chris Cairns in the deep to end his misery. Australia were 104/3 in the 28th over. Not in crisis mode yet, but the required run rate was now more than six an over. Sixteen runs later, Moody was the next to fall as Rod Latham took an excellent diving caught-and-bowled chance. Beaten by the lack of pace, Moody tried to stop his shot, but the ball looped towards the diving bowler. The Eden Park crowd were ecstatic, waving and cheering, while the tension increased for Australia.

Soon after, the fifth Australian wicket fell when Mark Waugh was trapped in front by Gavin Larsen for two, as Australia slipped to 125/5. With 7.49 an over needed, Boon required a batting partner to stay with him, and Steve Waugh duly obliged. Both batters, conscious of the situation, started to find gaps in the field. In the 42nd over, coming down the wicket to Willie Watson, Boon crunched a ball through the covers for four. He then put away a full toss as his century approached. Three overs later, Waugh hit Latham back down the ground for six as part of 11 runs taken from the over as the Australians looked to accelerate.

Gavin Larsen bowled the 46th over, and it started with Boon pushing a single to earn a well-deserved century. The second ball proved the adage of 'catches win matches'. Finding himself surprised by the bounce from Larsen, Waugh tried to fend the ball off, but it ballooned into the air. Making the ground, Larsen dived to take an excellent catch. The partnership had been broken at 74. Waugh had scored 38 runs from 34 balls. Was it enough to keep Australia in the game?

The fourth ball of the over would determine the result of the match. New batter Ian Healy clipped the ball towards midwicket, and the first run brought up Australia's 200. Turning for a second run, Boon was heading towards the danger end, and Chris Harris's pick-up, throw and direct hit left the centurion short, and New Zealand on the brink of victory.

The last three wickets fell cheaply as Australia slipped to 211 all out. The last five had fallen in 17 balls as the reigning world champions capitulated. The Eden Park crowd rushed on to the pitch again as the Kiwi players ran towards the pavilion in delight. Martin Crowe's batting and captaincy won him the Man-of-the-Match award. Crowe won A$500 and a gold medallion for his efforts. Allan Border was honest in his summation quoted in *Wisden Cricket Monthly*'s review of the game: 'Once again we got a good kick up the backside. Maybe it is the shot in the arm we needed.'

Looking back at the result, I asked Dipak Patel how much his bowling had contributed to winning the game. 'It certainly was a surprise element, and I played a lot of, I suppose, junior cricket against David Boon and Geoff Marsh while I was in England. So, I think the bowling changes were very astute from Martin Crowe, you know, I think he had a theory of between 20 and 21 changes during a 50-over game, so certainly that's another factor.'

Hours after New Zealand's victory in Auckland, England and India met in a day/night game in Perth. England omitted Allan Lamb due to a hamstring injury. In his 100th ODI, England captain Graham Gooch won the toss and elected to bat first on a sunny afternoon at the WACA. He opened the batting with Ian Botham, who he used as a pinch-hitter. A tight opening spell of bowling was released slightly in the seventh over, when Botham launched a ball over mid-off for a boundary as a signal of intent. Botham's *raison d'être* as an opener was to score heavily during the first 15 overs during the fielding restrictions. The experiment was soon over, as Kapil Dev's swing bowling enticed Botham into playing an expansive shot and the edge flew behind the stumps to Kiran More. Botham was gone for nine off 21 balls.

The new batter was Robin Smith, who felt at home in Perth, having played first-grade cricket there for several seasons. Playing drives, and his trademark cut shot, 'Judgie' found runs easier to accumulate than Botham had done. Balls short and wide were pounced upon, with Banerjee particularly finding the middle of Smith's bat. In the 23rd over, Gooch pulled up with a leg injury. Looking uncomfortable, the captain called for a runner and Botham duly appeared. At the other end, Smith pulled Shastri for a big six over midwicket to bring up England's hundred in the 24th over. The ball bounced between two sparsely manned stands, as just 12,902 fans were attending the match. Abandoning a batting helmet for a cloth cap, Smith continued to punish India's bowling. A push down the ground, off Shastri, brought up Smith's fifty and Gooch followed suit just after.

The 110-run partnership ended with Gooch looking to force the ball, and a thick outside edge was taken, gratefully, by Sachin Tendulkar. Next in to bat was Graeme Hick, but he soon departed. His first scoring shot was a delightful lofted off drive, before he edged a wide ball from Banerjee to give More his second catch of the innings. England were 137/3 with 18 overs left.

With Smith in full flight, Neil Fairbrother's role was to give his partner the strike. Crashing the ball around the boundary, Smith's powerful hitting was hurting the Indian bowling attack. Kapil Dev managed to find a ball to tuck Smith up, but the batter repaid in kind with a pull shot for four. Fairbrother, inspired by Smith's belligerence, swatted a loose ball over long-on for another boundary as India struggled against England's aggressive intentions.

The partnership, worth 60, was finally broken when Fairbrother skied a ball on the leg side and Srikkanth took the catch just inside the fielding circle. Azharuddin would have been doubly pleased to see the back of Fairbrother, having put down a difficult chance at backward point. The Indian captain redeemed himself when, just one run later, Smith cut a ball from Manoj Prabhakar and Azharuddin gratefully held on to the catch. Looking set for a century, which would have been the third one on the first day of the tournament, Smith finally departed for 91 runs off 108 balls to leave England on 198/5.

With England looking set for a competitive total, their final few overs did not reap as many runs as they should have done.

Chris Lewis picked up a boundary before Kapil Dev's slower ball deceived him and Banerjee took the catch on the fence. Derek Pringle soon followed after mistiming a ball from Srinath. Alec Stewart threatened to cut loose, slashing Srinath over gully for four, before Prabhakar squeezed a ball past one of Stewart's advances down the wicket and bowled him. Stewart grudgingly nodded his acknowledgement to the bowler before striding off the ground. England's stuttering innings threatened to collapse when Phillip DeFreitas looked to take a non-existent run, the ball already in the hands of bowler Kapil Dev, and was nowhere as the underarm throw broke the stumps. England had lost three wickets for three runs and were 224/9 in the 49th over.

With Phil Tufnell at the crease, the innings was expected to end quickly, such was his reputation. Tufnell's batting partner was Warwickshire all-rounder Dermot Reeve, who helped to massage the total to 236/9 off their 50 overs. The last seven overs had only produced 39 runs. England were undoubtedly disappointed with their efforts, while India would also be rueful. The Indian bowlers managed to bowl 13 wides, Kapil Dev responsible for six, and how costly this would be was unknown.

At the start of their innings, the Indian openers found the English bowling challenging to score from. Kris Srikkanth took to lofting Derek Pringle's medium-pacers over the infielders. As Pringle's bowling length wavered, Srikkanth put pressure on with a lofted off drive for four before cutting a wide ball for another boundary. In the 12th over, DeFreitas dropped short, and Srikkanth made him pay. Slicing the ball behind square, bisecting two fielders with unerring accuracy, Srikkanth picked up four runs.

The introduction of Dermot Reeve into the attack appeared to pay dividends as Srikkanth played no shot at a ball that swung into his pads. Umpire Dooland Buultjens looked contemplative, but walked away as Reeve and the England fielders appealed. Srikkanth clubbed two boundaries in the same over as Reeve's outswinger and the slower ball appeared more to the batter's liking. In his next over, Reeve gave Ravi Shastri width outside the off stump and the result was another four.

Having clubbed two boundaries off DeFreitas, Srikkanth mistimed a stroke, and Botham took the catch at extra cover. His 39 runs had included seven boundaries in an opening partnership of 63. The new batter was captain Mohammed Azharuddin, and his first ball proved to be his last. Bowling an outswinger on a line and length that had to be played at, Reeve induced the edge and Alec Stewart took a tumbling catch. With the captain on his way back, the Indian contingent in the crowd were stunned.

Sachin Tendulkar's contribution to the match was to pull DeFreitas, still dropping short, over wide mid-on for a boundary. Oozing class, Tendulkar looked to challenge England's bowlers. Phil Tufnell was brought on to bowl his left-arm spin and Tendulkar viciously cut him for four. The situation for England required experience, and who other than Ian Botham to make the breakthrough. Having tied Tendulkar down, Botham squared him up, and Stewart took the catch. Botham's celebration, a wiggle and finger-pointing, left a lot to be desired, but India were 126/3.

Shastri brought up his fifty, off a patient 95 balls, via Botham's shin as the bowler tried to use his footballing experience at Scunthorpe United to stop the ball. Playing the anchor role, while Srikkanth and Tendulkar looked to push on, Shastri was joined by left-handed batter Vinod Kambli. The youngster was also out-thought, like his old school friend Tendulkar, as he tried to hit Botham over mid-on, but the ball was too high on the bat and Hick juggled the ball before holding the catch.

With Pravin Amre at the wicket, Shastri decided he would change tactics and look for boundaries. Playing and missing at Botham before a leading edge down to third man, Shastri looked anything but comfortable in his new role. His downfall was a comedy of errors. As he tried to pull DeFreitas over the on side, the ball rocketed straight up into the air. The bowler, concentrating on the ball, almost ran straight into Shastri to take the catch. Having got to the ball, DeFreitas spilled the catch, and the ball ran past the batting crease. Amre, with no intention of running to the danger end, sent Shastri back. DeFreitas, having the presence of mind to chase the ball, threw down the stumps and ended Shastri's innings of 57 runs.

England were not the only team with a player of enormous experience on their side. Kapil Dev came to the wicket, at 149/5, with no intention of capitulation. As he despatched Pringle for four over cow corner, the aim was apparent. Adding 39 runs with Amre, Kapil Dev had kept India in the match. However, when he found DeFreitas at long-on, surely India's chances were slipping away. Once Amre was run out from a smart piece of fielding from Tufnell, via Reeve and Stewart, India's chances were diminishing fast. Kiran More and Manoj Prabhakar's visit to the crease were also short-lived as India's innings was arrested. More was run out after his hesitation, and an accurate throw from Smith to Reeve left him short of his ground. Prabhakar's wild swing and miss left India on 201/9 in the 47th over. With Subroto Banerjee and Javagal Srinath at the wicket, with 36 runs required, the match was all over. Surely.

Taking 24 runs off Lewis and Pringle, including a massive six over long-on from Srinath at the end of the 49th over, India needed 11 off the final over. They took two off Chris Lewis's first ball, and the second proved decisive. Banerjee could only squeeze the ball away and Srinath, looking for a quick single, found himself out of his ground. The fielder, Botham, decided to run towards the stumps to make sure of the run-out and secured the victory with Srinath stranded. Botham won the Man-of-the-Match award with his 2–27 off ten overs plus key fielding. Azharuddin was left to regret his bowlers' profligacy.

Sunday, 23 February saw World Cup minnows Sri Lanka and Zimbabwe meet at the picturesque Pukekura Park in New Plymouth on New Zealand's North Island, as the ground hosted its first one-day international. With the ground having short boundaries and being arboreal, the game was going to be unforgettable. It would prove to be even more so than first thought.

Winning the toss, Arjuna Ranatunga decided to bowl first. The openers for Zimbabwe were wicketkeeper-batter Andy Flower and Wayne James. James struck the first blows in anger with boundaries as the smallness of the ground foretold of runs. The fast-medium bowling of Pramodya Wickramasinghe brought the first wicket when James, looking to run the ball wide of the slip cordon, edged behind to Hashan Tillakaratne, the wicketkeeper taking a regulation catch as James departed for 17 off 21 balls.

Andy Flower, batting in a bright red Panama hat to match Zimbabwe's colours, took 12 overs to find the boundary. Another one soon followed as he punished Wickramasinghe's short delivery with a pull shot over midwicket. New batter Andy Pycroft struggled to get the ball away, taking 22 balls to score five before losing his wicket. Asanka Gurusinha's medium-pacers were proving too tempting, but Pycroft found Champaka Ramanayake at mid-on and Zimbabwe were 57/2 in the 14th over.

Next in was captain David Houghton and, like Pycroft, he struggled to score quickly, but he added 25 with Flower before losing his wicket. Gurusinha, with his busy bowling action, ran up to the stumps and bowled a line outside off stump. Houghton, pushing at the ball, left his bat hanging and the ball took the edge. The batter turned and walked off without waiting for the catch to be taken. Gurusinha had broken through for the second time in the innings, and Tillakaratne had his second catch.

The Zimbabweans were busily finding gaps, and Sanath Jayasuriya was brought on to bowl to try to stem the scoring. Both Kevin Arnott and Andy Flower found the boundary off Jayasuriya's left-arm spin. Sri Lanka brought on Ruwan Kalpage to bowl his right-arm off breaks, but he also received similar treatment. Andy Flower reached his fifty in the 29th over with Zimbabwe on 129/3, taking a quick single off Kapila Wijegunawardene to reach the landmark. The New Zealand television commentators resorted to referring to Wijegunawardene by his first name rather than attempting his surname every time he bowled.

Both Flower and Arnott continued to pressurise the Sri Lankan bowlers. The short boundaries also helped as Zimbabwe started to accelerate. Arnott brought up his fifty with a six as he despatched a low full toss over square leg. However, this was his last contribution, as Wickramasinghe bowled a wider ball and Arnott edged it. Tillakaratne took another good catch to break up the partnership. It had been worth 85 runs to Zimbabwe, who had moved on to 167/4 in the 37th over.

The new batter was Andy Waller, and his reputation as an aggressive hitter was soon witnessed as he smashed Wijegunawardene through the covers for four. He followed this up with an uppish drive in the same direction to emphasise his willingness to move the score along. Bringing on Ramanayake did nothing to stop Waller as he cut and pulled the ball with disdain. The ground at Pukekura Park was starting to look too small for the Zimbabwean. A third boundary in the over off the unfortunate Ramanayake served as a warning to Sri Lankan captain Arjuna Ranatunga.

When Andy Flower finally achieved his century, he joined Dennis Amiss and Desmond Haynes as the only players to accomplish that feat on their ODI debut. It was also the first century scored by a Zimbabwean in international cricket. He received a congratulatory slap on the cheek from his batting partner. It appeared that Waller was in the mood to hit anything in his path. Such was the speed of his scoring, his fifty from 32 balls set a new Cricket World Cup record. The belligerence continued as Waller smashed a six into the trees that surrounded the ground. The ball was finally found in an adjacent duck pond.

The last over of the innings fell to Wijegunawardene, with Waller on strike. He pulled a short-pitched ball for six, and was then dropped in the outfield before being clean-bowled by a no-ball. Waller's riposte was to swat a ball through mid-off for a boundary. The innings ended at 312/4, with Flower carrying his bat for 115 and Waller unbeaten on 83. The partnership had been worth 145 from 13 overs. In 57 minutes, the Zimbabweans had broken the fifth-wicket partnership record in the Cricket World Cup by passing Viv Richards and Collis King's total in the 1979 final. Zimbabwe had also reached their highest-ever Cricket World Cup score to date. If Sri Lanka were going to win this match, they too would need to break records.

The fans at Pukekura Park were delighted with the innings. Brian Beer, a local archivist and historian in New Plymouth, attended the game and offered his thoughts. 'Everyone was amazed at the score Zimbabwe hit. Andy Waller was spectacular at the end of their innings. I remember his batting in particular. After his innings, we certainly didn't think Sri Lanka would be able to get that total.'

Don Topley, who coached Zimbabwe in 1992, was pleased with his team at the halfway stage. 'Bundu Waller got 85 not out. He smashed it. Andy Flower's was a cultured innings. He certainly announced himself on the international stage. We were dead chuffed with 312, and we did think it was defendable, as long as we bowled well.'

If Zimbabwe thought they had a winning total, the Sri Lankan openers did not take long to question that. Roshan Mahanama and Athula Samarasekera came out with a positive mindset. Kevin Duers, on his debut, dropped short and Samarasekera pounced to bring up the first boundary of the innings. In the third over, he found the boundary again off the bowling of Malcolm Jarvis. It was Jarvis's fifth over that saw Mahanama beautifully time a shot through the on side for another four. When Samarasekera straight-drove Duers back down the wicket for another boundary before on-driving for a similar result, then pulling him for a third boundary, the match looked well poised.

The fifty partnership came up in the ninth over as Zimbabwe struggled to contain Sri Lanka. In particular, the tall, right-handed Samarasekera was playing aggressive but orthodox cricket shots. His fifty came up in 33 balls, just one more than Waller, with nine boundaries. In the 13th over, Mahanama punished Jarvis's overpitching with boundaries either side of the wicket. Both batters were finding gaps, and boundaries, with ease.

Looking to stem the flow of runs, Zimbabwean captain David Houghton turned to veteran spinner John Traicos. The plan, according to Traicos, was simple. 'Generally, I bowled to contain. Usually coming on after 15 overs and trying to restrict the run rate by bowling flattish off-spinners with an arm ball and change of pace and spin variations.' Traicos made an immediate impact. With the score on 128, Samarasekera finally mistimed a shot and Duers gratefully took the catch. His quickfire 75 came off 61 balls with 11 fours and a six.

As Traicos became difficult to score off, Sri Lanka's innings started to lose momentum and wickets. Mahanama was the next to go just 16 runs later when he drove Eddo Brandes straight to Kevin Arnott. Scoring 59, Mahanama had taken 89 balls to get there. At the crease were Sri Lankan captain Aravinda de Silva and Asanka Gurusinha, but both fell without making significant contributions. With the score on 155, it was Traicos's tight bowling that forced Gurusinha to look for a quick single, but his captain refused, and Flower took the bails off after Waller's quick fielding. Brandes took his second wicket in the 33rd over as de Silva tried to work him away, but the ball was lofted to Houghton. The Zimbabweans celebrated while Sri Lanka's captain departed. The score was 167/4 with less than 17 overs left. The victory was looking unlikely.

Ex-captain Arjuna Ranatunga and Sanath Jayasuriya, as the last recognised batters, were tasked with mounting the recovery. With Ranatunga in his 100th ODI game, Sri Lanka could not have asked for a better man for the situation. The recovery was started, however, by his junior partner. Jayasuriya played positively. A six over the cover boundary, then pulling Brandes for four, then another six into the trees. Although he finally lost his wicket for 32, top-edging Houghton, the nine-an-over required run rate was starting to decrease. Hashan Tillakaratne was the next batter in, but Ranatunga took up the mantle. Two consecutive boundaries off Houghton's bowling kept up the momentum. A big six on to the terraces from Tillakaratne helped to keep Sri Lanka in the game. Ranatunga's fifty was achieved by putting the ball into the car park, much to the delight of children on the boundary as they ran off to find it.

At 273, Jarvis clean-bowled Tillakaratne for 32 to break the partnership. With five overs remaining, Sri Lanka needed another 40 runs for what seemed, earlier in the day, an unlikely victory. Ranatunga's wicket would be crucial for Zimbabwe if they were to defend their mammoth total. New man at the crease Ruwan Kalpage smashed Iain Butchart back down the ground for a boundary. Runs were valuable for Sri Lanka, but boundaries were priceless. The spectators at Pukekura Park were enjoying the encounter despite being largely neutral. Ranatunga had a piece of luck in the 48th over when he was caught off the bowling of Jarvis. The bowler, unfortunately for Zimbabwe, had overstepped the crease and umpire Piloos Reporter signalled a no-ball. How crucial would that be?

The 49th over was bowled by Eddo Brandes with Sri Lanka needing 15 for victory. Ranatunga found the boundary with a subtle glance off his pads from the first ball. With the second, Ranatunga steered the ball fine of Flower, behind the stumps, and the ball raced away for a second boundary. After taking singles, leaving four for the win, Kalpage tried to win the game with one hit but was caught on the boundary.

Despite the game going to the last over, it was down to Ranatunga to secure victory with a four. A desperate dive to cut off the ball was not enough as members of the crowd, some of them carrying Sri Lankan flags, ran on to the field. The successful chase was the first one over 300 runs in one-day internationals, and the 625-run aggregate was the second highest on record. It was a morale-boosting victory for Sri Lanka, but a bitter defeat for Zimbabwe. Traicos, who only conceded three an over when most of his fellow bowlers went for more than double that, was realistic in his match summation: 'It was a match we should have won after scoring 300-plus and getting the run rate to ten an over with 11 overs to go. Unfortunately, we bowled poorly to the aggressive and confident Sri Lankan batters, who batted right down to number nine.'

At the end of the game, fans decided that they would collect souvenirs. Scott MacLean, who was 12 at the time, was one of those fans. 'It was a glorious day in New Plymouth: clear and warm, and the cicadas making a real racket. Also, people could bring in their own beers, and there were some pretty well-done people by the end of it. People were grabbing whatever Benson & Hedges Cricket World Cup '92 signage that they could. I think I walked out with three boundary markers and a couple of other things.'

While the Sri Lankans and Zimbabweans were entertaining fans at Pukekura Park, the fourth game got underway at the Melbourne Cricket Ground. The newly developed MCG, with the new Southern Stand, was capable of holding 90,000. However, only 14,161 fans decided to spend their Sunday watching Pakistan and the West Indies. The toss was conducted between Richie Richardson and Javed Miandad. Pakistan captain Imran Khan had injured his shoulder, and a late decision was made to rest it. Ex-captain Miandad took over for the match, lost the toss and was asked to bat by Richardson.

The opening partnership of experienced campaigner Ramiz Raja and young Aamer Sohail were tasked with seeing off the new ball in the hands of Malcolm Marshall and Curtly Ambrose. The West Indian quicks found the firmness of the MCG wicket to their liking. Ramiz found himself playing and missing as Ambrose extracted extra bounce with his tall frame. It was the seventh over before Pakistan finally scored a boundary. Marshall strayed on to Ramiz's pads, and the opener took the gift. The score moved on to 20/0 to relieve some of the pressure. Sohail's drive back down the wicket, in the 12th over, gave Ambrose a difficult caught-and-bowled chance. The bowler just deflected the ball, and very welcome runs came Pakistan's way.

The partnership was worth just 31 runs as the run rate was more akin to Test cricket than one-day internationals.

Sensing that the scoreboard needed to tick over more frequently, Aamer Sohail tucked into Marshall with two boundaries. Giving the left-hander some room outside off stump, Marshall saw the ball fly high and fast to the cover boundary. The West Indies quickie then strayed leg side, and Sohail clipped him sweetly along the ground for four more.

A change of bowling paid dividends. Winston Benjamin was brought into the attack, and almost immediately the Pakistan openers' running between the wickets led to an opportunity for a run-out. If not for a wayward throw from Ambrose, Sohail would have been short. Sohail's escape was short-lived as he pulled a ball straight into the air, off Benjamin, and Gus Logie took the catch easily at cover. The first wicket had fallen, with the score on 45 in the 15th over.

With new batter Inzamam-ul-Haq at the crease, Richie Richardson took the opportunity to bowl spinners Roger Harper and Carl Hooper in tandem. Pakistan were failing to hit boundaries, and the spinners bowled consecutively for 13 overs. The West Indian fielders found the ball somewhat elusive at times as Pakistan hit it into the wide expanses of the MCG outfield. With the partnership worth 52 between Ramiz and Inzamam, Harper made a breakthrough. Inzamam was beaten by pace and flight and could only clip the ball to Hooper for 27 off 39 balls. Pakistan were 97/2, and stand-in captain Javed Miandad came to the crease.

Showing no signs of a back injury he had had before the start of the tournament, Miandad set about pushing the run rate up. In the 32nd over, a genuine edge flew to the boundary past diving wicketkeeper David Williams. Batting partner Ramiz finally brought his half-century up in the 37th over off 116 balls, with a solitary boundary. With Miandad stealing singles, Pakistan's total began to creep up, but they were fast running out of remaining overs. With five to go, Miandad cut Benjamin to the rope for just the sixth boundary of the innings. In the same over, Benjamin thought he had his second wicket, but Williams missed the chance. Looking to pull, Ramiz nicked the ball; Williams wrongfooted himself, and the ball flew past him. Miandad strode down the wicket, beaming with delight, and offering Ramiz some words while Benjamin stood with his head in his hands. At 171/2, Pakistan were finally accelerating their innings.

Ambrose had overs left at the end of the innings, but Ramiz put his cautious approach behind him. Coming down the wicket, he lofted the ball over mid-off for four at the end of the 48th over. Marshall bowled the 49th, but he received similar treatment. The 200 was brought up, by Miandad, with an outrageous step across his stumps to get the ball through fine leg for four. He then brought his fifty up, off just 56 balls, with another quick single. It was then Ramiz's turn as he leaned into a ball and drove it through extra cover for a boundary. The over ended with Miandad stepping outside off stump to force another four through fine leg. Marshall had conceded 16 runs.

Ambrose bowled the final over, and Ramiz secured his sixth ODI hundred. Pakistan were largely restricted to taking singles, with Ambrose proving difficult to score off. More poor fielding and a dubious shoulder-high no-ball call meant that they reached 220/2 off their 50 overs. Ramiz and Miandad's unbeaten partnership was worth 123, but the question remained as to whether Pakistan had enough runs.

Having already been disadvantaged by Waqar Younis having to miss the tournament, Imran Khan's shoulder injury meant that Wasim Akram and Aaqib Javed would spearhead the bowling attack. Choosing to leave leg-spinner Mushtaq Ahmed out, Pakistan gave Iqbal Sikander and Wasim Haider their ODI debuts. Acting captain Javed Miandad would also have to find some overs elsewhere in the team.

Desmond Haynes opened with Brian Lara to face the pace barrage from Pakistan. Despite tight bowling, the West Indies managed to keep the scoreboard ticking over. The trouble early on came when Haynes was beaten for pace, and bounce, by an Akram delivery but managed not to get any bat on the ball. Batting partner Lara played elegant drives and pulls off Aaqib, and the boundaries started to flow.

The first change of bowling saw Wasim Haider, a fast-medium-paced bowler, almost get a wicket as Lara drove the ball just short of mid-off. As if to prove to himself that he could play the shot, he executed it again and bisected the fielders for the boundary. Haider was the bowler again, two overs later, when Lara viciously cut another boundary. The young West Indian was starting to take a liking to Haider's bowling. In the same over, he pulled another boundary to bring up the fifty for the West Indies in less than ten overs.

Ijaz Ahmed's medium-pacers gave Lara little trouble as he took two boundaries off his first over. Haynes, on the other hand, was faring slightly differently. The leg spin of Aamer Sohail should have grabbed a wicket with the first ball, but wicketkeeper Moin Khan put the sharp chance down. Pushing at the ball, Haynes could only find the edge, but Moin was equally beaten by the turn and couldn't take the chance. Pakistan could ill afford to be so wasteful. Soon, Haynes swept Sohail for four, and the hundred partnership came up in the 23rd over.

Two overs later, Pakistan could well have felt that things were well and truly against them. Iqbal Sikander could have removed both batters but ended up with neither. First, Lara played an unconvincing sweep, and the ball took the edge. However, Moin Khan was standing up to the stumps and the ball looped over him to safety. Then it was Haynes's turn to enjoy good fortune. On 49, he tried to whip the ball through the leg side and managed to hit it straight into the air. Sikander ran towards the ball to take a straightforward catch, but spilled the chance. Tony Greig, on commentary, declared, 'This will be caught by the bowler ... yes he's, oh – he's dropped it.' Haynes crossed himself and looked to the heavens while Sikander stood and contemplated the dropped catch. To add insult to injury, the batters ran a single to bring up Haynes's fifty.

Pakistan appeared powerless to stop the West Indies. After 30 overs, the score was 139/0, with Haynes and Lara punishing any bad balls that Pakistan bowled at them. The reintroduction of Wasim Akram changed very little. Lara, looking for anything on leg to middle stump, whipped another boundary as the West Indies raced towards their target.

With the partnership on 175, seven runs short of Turner and McCosker's record for an opening stand in a Cricket World Cup, Wasim Akram made a breakthrough of sorts. Lara was late to get his bat down on to a yorker, and the ball hit him flush on the toes. In considerable pain, Lara was escorted off the ground to be replaced by his captain, Richie Richardson. He was taken to hospital to have the toe X-rayed.

Taking up the mantle from his junior partner, Haynes drove and glanced the ball around as Pakistan toiled further. Richardson on-drove Aaqib as the Pakistan fast bowler overpitched. It was Aaqib who gave the West Indies victory with two petulant head-high no-balls. The margin of victory was ten wickets, and the West Indies would be second in the table. They had scored 441 runs for the loss of two wickets, with 344 of those coming after the last wicket fell. Haynes finished on

93 not out, while Lara's 88 secured him the Man-of-the-Match award. In his post-match interview, Richie Richardson said that the West Indies were 'here for business', and no one could doubt that statement. After the West Indies victory, the table was sorry reading for Australian fans. Surprisingly, they were at the bottom while Sri Lanka were in one of the semi-final positions.

	Pld	Won	Lost	Tied	N/R	Pts	Net R/R	For	Against
New Zealand	1	1	0	0	0	2	0.740	248/50.0	211/50.0
West Indies	1	1	0	0	0	2	0.319	221/46.5	220/50.0
England	1	1	0	0	0	2	0.180	236/50.0	227/50.0
Sri Lanka	1	1	0	0	0	2	0.105	313/49.2	312/50.0
South Africa	0	0	0	0	0	0	0.000		
Zimbabwe	1	0	1	0	0	0	−0.105	312/50.0	313/49.2
India	1	0	1	0	0	0	−0.180	227/50.0	236/50.0
Pakistan	1	0	1	0	0	0	−0.319	220/50.0	221/46.5
Australia	1	0	1	0	0	0	−0.740	211/50.0	248/50.0

Chapter Four

Early Exchanges

The fifth match of the Cricket World Cup featured New Zealand and Sri Lanka, who had both secured unlikely victories in their first games. It took place at Trust Bank Park in Hamilton, and both teams made changes to their line-ups. Danny Morrison, the New Zealand fast bowler, had impressed in the nets in practice and replaced Chris Cairns. With main bowler Rumesh Ratnayake struggling to shake off his shoulder injury, Sri Lanka chose the spin bowling of Don Anurasiri in place of Kapila Wijegunawardene.

Winning the toss, Martin Crowe asked Sri Lanka to bat first. The innings did not start well when, in the fourth over, Samarasekera injured his hamstring while taking a single down to third man. Completing the run, the batter dropped to the floor in considerable discomfort, and a runner was called for. Despite that, he brought up the first boundary with a flashing stroke outside off stump. With minimum foot movement, he cut viciously for four. Cognisant of his hamstring injury, Samarasekera tried to hit boundaries but soon fell to the bowling of Willie Watson. Trying to lift the ball over the infield, the injured batter could do no more than loft it to John Wright at mid-off. Sri Lanka had reached 18/1 in the sixth over.

The new batter was Asanka Gurusinha, promoted to number three, who joined Roshan Mahanama at the wicket. It was Mahanama who looked to push on. In the tenth over, he punched a drive through the field for four as Watson overpitched. His fortune nearly ran out when he cut a wide ball from the same bowler; an uppish shot almost carried to Rutherford in the gully. Martin Crowe turned to his medium-pacers to strangle the batters as they had done with Australia. The pressure told almost immediately as Gurusinha looked for a non-existent single. Mahanama sent him back, as a direct hit would have left the batter well short of his ground. Soon after, Chris Harris did make the breakthrough. Gurusinha played down the wrong line, with Harris getting some outswing, and nicked the edge. Umpire Piloos Reporter double-checked with fellow umpire David Shepherd at square leg before giving the batter out for nine.

With Mahanama set, captain Aravinda de Silva came in at four knowing that he needed to put a partnership together. The New Zealanders bowled a tight line, but Sri Lanka punished anything that gave them room to play their strokes. Mahanama took full advantage of Harris's width by driving a half-volley to the boundary. That shot brought up Sri Lanka's hundred in the 30th over. In the next, Mahanama turned Patel away for two runs to bring up his half-century off 97 balls. Although scoring was difficult, with New Zealand's medium-pacers offering very little to hit, Mahanama and de Silva were looking set to kick on with 19 overs left. The outfield was quick, so Sri Lanka needed to get the ball through New Zealand's tight fielding around the wicket.

With the score on 120, and the partnership worth 70 runs, New Zealand's excellent fielding generated another wicket. Mahanama dropped the ball for a quick single, and de Silva sprinted through to the danger end. Harris's alertness and diving underarm throw beat the Sri Lankan captain's run. The delighted New Zealand team and the majority of the 8,268 crowd celebrated the crucial wicket.

It was another situation, if not quite a crisis, for Arjuna Ranatunga to revel in. Crashing a boundary off the bowling of Rod Latham, Ranatunga planned to keep the scoreboard ticking over. In the next over, Morrison was on the receiving end of another flashing cut shot. His extra pace meant that the ball flew to the boundary without the fielders needing to move. Later in the over, Mahanama edged the ball, but it sailed wide of Ian Smith and brought up the 150 for Sri Lanka.

Looking to accelerate, Ranatunga picked out the fielder in the deep. Rutherford took the catch on the boundary, both feet in the air, to remove the dangerous batter. The partnership of 52 had been broken, leaving Sri Lanka on 172/4 in the 42nd over. From the very next ball, Mahanama drove straight back at Harris, who took the catch to leave Sri Lanka in disarray. Martin Crowe was first to congratulate his bowler as Mahanama departed for 81. Losing two key wickets, in two balls, had arrested the Sri Lankan innings. Tillakaratne survived the hat-trick delivery despite the ball hitting his pads.

With pressure building on Sri Lanka, they crumbled. Jayasuriya was soon back in the pavilion. As he tried to turn a comfortable single into two runs, New Zealand's fielding proved once again to be too good. An accurate throw and swift glovework from Ian Smith ran out the diving Jayasuriya for five runs. Tillakaratne followed a little later when he smashed Watson straight at Crowe at short cover. In the 49th over, Ramanayake became the third Sri Lankan of the innings to be run out. By the time Kalpage holed out to Larsen, off a Watson full toss, Sri Lanka had lost six wickets for 30 runs.

When their innings finally ended, at 206/9, the crowd rushed on to the field. It was a premature celebration of a New Zealand victory, but they were well placed for the run chase. The most damaging bowlers were Watson, who finished with 3–37, and Harris, who took 3–43. Larsen's miserly bowling conceded just 27 runs, and he was backed up by Patel to constrict Sri Lanka.

The New Zealand innings started positively. John Wright, usually the stoic partner, struck boundaries in the first two overs. Rod Latham drove Ramanayake back down the ground for a four in the third over, as New Zealand looked set to make the total look easy to get. Wright's third boundary came up in the fourth over. The Sri Lankan bowlers were bowling short and wide and were being punished for doing so. A ball that seamed back into Latham, cutting straight through his guard, proved to be a rarity. The next ball ended up going for four, and the score went to 34/0 in the seventh over.

Having fallen during fielding and injured his shoulder, Wright was showing no signs that it was hindering his batting. Two more boundaries in the 11th over, off Wickramasinghe, moved Wright and New Zealand towards their target. Aravinda de Silva, needing a breakthrough, or at least to slow the run rate, turned to Ruwan Kalpage to bowl his off breaks. Immediately, Wright was induced into a false stroke that ballooned into the air but dropped safely. A thickish cut also flew through the gully and raced to the boundary. Wright may have scored four, but Kalpage had won the exchange. As if to reassert authority, Wright pulled Kalpage for a more convincing four to move the score on to 59/0.

The next over, bowled by Gurusinha, fared no better as Wright took two more boundaries. His fifty, the third in the Cricket World Cup, was achieved with an on drive off Kalpage. The bowler was soon celebrating, however, when a ball turned sharply and bowled Latham for 20. The batter checked the pitch with a quizzical look before departing. The bowler extracted plenty of spin, but a lazy back-foot push was an inadequate defence. Sri Lanka had broken the partnership with the score on 77.

Wright clubbed another boundary, but lost his wicket to Kalpage. The bowler took a sharp, low catch to get his and Sri Lanka's second wicket. Scoring 57 off 76 balls, with nine boundaries, Wright had given New Zealand a healthy start for Andrew Jones and Martin Crowe to continue. However, it was not going to be a repeat of Eden Park for Crowe – he found the fielder in the deep and was gone for just five runs. New Zealand had slipped to 105/3 and were now only just ahead of the Sri Lankan innings.

With Don Anurasiri's spin having the same effect as New Zealand's slower bowlers, Jones went the aerial route to release pressure. A lofted drive over mid-on raced away to the boundary. New Zealand were not the only team struggling to cope with the situation. A quick single was turned into three when sloppy fielding gave Jones and new batter Ken Rutherford the opportunity to earn runs from the overthrow.

Rutherford's decisive play, from the start, heaped further pressure back on to Sri Lanka. A slog from outside off stump sailed over one of the longest boundaries for a six. Further aerial shots from Jones followed, as Sri Lanka's medium-pacers bowled slightly loosely. With both batters finding the fence, an unwelcome misfield gifted another boundary as the match was slipping away from Sri Lanka.

With the score on 186/3, Gurusinha was convinced he had trapped Jones in front. Despite vigorous appealing, umpire Piloos Reporter said no, gesticulating that he couldn't see to make a decision due to Gurusinha's follow-through. TV replays suggested that the ball was going down leg side. If only DRS had been around in 1992 to clear the matter up. However, Gurusinha would soon be celebrating as Jones, just one run later, carelessly picked the ball up from leg stump and hit it straight to Jayasuriya at midwicket. Jones was just one run short of his half-century; the partnership of 71 hadn't taken New Zealand home, but would surely guarantee victory. Only a seismic collapse would give Sri Lanka the win.

Rutherford's second successive tournament fifty came up in the next over, and the New Zealand crowd came on to the outfield to celebrate. The batter motioned for the fans to leave the field instead of celebrating. Fittingly, it was Rutherford who hit the winning boundary. With the scores tied, de Silva brought in his field, but a lofted shot over the leg side ran away as fans once again ran on to the field.

Although Anurasiri and Kalpage were not conceding runs, the rest of the bowlers struggled to make an impact. Rutherford's 65 off 71 balls secured the Man-of-the-Match award. Having been dropped at slip by Ranatunga early on, he punished Sri Lanka with an excellent innings. In an interview on TVNZ, Martin Crowe was asked what he thought about the next match of the tournament. South Africa's bow in the Cricket World Cup was against Australia in a day/night game at the SCG. Along with New Zealand great Bevan Congdon, both were interested to see how South Africa would fit back into world cricket. Also, they were New Zealand's next opponents in four days' time.

One worry was over whether John Wright would be fit for the game. He had been diagnosed with an acromioclavicular (AC) joint injury – a shoulder separation to non-medical people – which was likely to rule him out.

Wednesday, 26 February signalled South Africa's first game in the Cricket World Cup. Rain in Sydney did little to dampen their morale. Coach Mike Procter was ebullient about his team's chances. He was confident that his pace bowling line-up of Allan Donald, Meyrick Pringle, Richard Snell and all-rounder Brian McMillan would cause the Australian batters problems.

Kepler Wessels was in less confident mood. Not only was he leading South Africa in their first Cricket World Cup, but he was also returning to a country he had represented. 'I didn't know how the crowd was going to respond. So, the lead-up to that for me was personally intense. I also knew that Australia had come off a run of one-day matches. They had a really good run. Also, I didn't know how the players were going to cope with the pressure of that sort of cauldron in their first game of the World Cup. The bus trip was the quietest one I've ever been in. I just looked around, and I saw how everybody was pale and stressed, and I thought "Oh, how is this going to work out?" But fortunately, by the time the game approached, I decided that whatever was going to happen then I was going to try and keep the players really calm. I was going to try and be completely unemotional about the whole thing and give it my best shot and lead the players as well as I could.'

Allan Border was in a similarly pensive mindset after the unsuccessful run chase at Eden Park. His final line-up had just one change – omitting Mark Waugh in favour of playing an extra bowler, left-arm pace bowler Mike Whitney. Border won the toss and decided to bat.

The 39,768 crowd packed into the SCG were expecting an exciting match, and the first ball delivered that excitement in abundance. The new ball went to Allan Donald. The pace bowler's speed was well known since he had joined Warwickshire in the English County Championship in 1987. Geoff Marsh faced the first delivery and was tempted into chasing the ball. It thudded into wicketkeeper David Richardson's gloves, and the South

African fielders enthusiastically appealed. They felt they had got their man. Tony Greig, on commentary, agreed, but umpire Brian Aldridge was unmoved. Boos rang out around the SCG as Donald returned to his bowling mark. TV replays showed that Marsh had edged the ball, but South Africa had been denied a dream start.

In the opening spell of bowling, Donald and new-ball partner Meyrick Pringle were inconsistent. Boon scored freely, while Marsh was more reserved. Pringle's search for a full length was exploited by Boon when the ball was overpitched. Several crunching drives paid dividends as Australia scored at more than four an over. South African captain Kepler Wessels, becoming the first man to play ODI cricket for two nations, brought on Richard Snell as his strike bowlers were conceding plenty of runs. Marsh defended the second ball, but Boon wanted a single. Sent back by his batting partner, Boon was stranded as the bowler picked up and threw the ball to Hansie Cronje to take off the bails.

Jonty Rhodes was soon into the action, further evidencing the South African fielding skills with a diving stop and accurate throw. Meyrick Pringle's leg intercepted the ball, painfully, but the accuracy was not in doubt. Over the next ten overs, South Africa started to assert themselves in the game. Marsh and Dean Jones picked up the occasional boundary, but runs were more difficult to come by. Adrian Kuiper came on to bowl the 21st over of the match. With the score on 76, a leg-cutter left Marsh, and Richardson took the catch. This time there was no reprieve, and Marsh's 72-ball innings was over. Catastrophe struck the Australians with the very next ball, as Kuiper bowled an inswinger into Border and the Australian captain lost his off stump. Border played all around the ball, deflected on to the stumps off the pads, and was on his way back for a golden duck.

Following his failure in the first game, Border's Cricket World Cup was getting worse.

The game soon started to slide further away from Australia. Brian McMillan's leg-cutter was too good for Dean Jones; he could only manage a thick edge, and Richardson took his second catch of the match. Australia were 97/4 in the 28th over and heading towards trouble. Having been expensive in his first spell, Donald was brought back on to bowl. A fast, but low, ball accounted for Moody, and Australia's fifth wicket fell with the score on 108. South Africa had the world champions where they wanted them.

To make things even more difficult, new batter Ian Healy injured a hamstring going for a quick single and needed a runner. Steve Waugh could have been run out if Richardson's throw hadn't been inches wide. Healy was running to the safe end but tweaked his hamstring before the run had been completed. Dean Jones came out as the runner for Healy, who needed to build a partnership with Waugh if Australia were to post a reasonable total.

Restricted in his foot movement, Healy slogged two boundaries off Pringle in the 39th over. The first was an aerial shot over midwicket; the next came when he pulled the last ball of the over towards square leg. Twelve runs were taken off the over to move Australia on to 141/5. In the very next over, the pace of Donald cramped up Healy, who was trying to play a similar shot. He could only manage to loft the ball high towards cover, and McMillan took the easy catch. Peter Taylor was the new batter in, as South Africa were making inroads into the Australian lower order. Being the last recognised batter, Waugh had to score the majority of the runs, but this pressure brought about his downfall. McMillan enticed the drive from Waugh, could only pick out Cronje at short cover.

Such was South Africa's superiority, a catch going down from Peter Kirsten's dive or Cronje missing the stumps for an easy run-out didn't hurt them. Donald produced a ball that was far too good, and fast, for Taylor, and his leg stump cartwheeled out of the ground. It was Donald's third wicket, leaving Australia at 156/8. The ninth wicket fell five runs later when McDermott and Whitney tried to take on Rhodes at cover point. There was only going to be one winner, and Snell broke the stumps to run out McDermott for six.

Australia's innings ended at 170/9 after the 49th over. South Africa had not bowled their overs in the allotted time, but would not face a penalty. The time lost due to Healy's injury meant that it would be a 49-overs-per-side game. If Australia were to pull off an unlikely victory, they would need a performance akin to South Africa's. Donald recovered magnificently after conceding 20 runs off his first four overs. He finished with 3–34, while Snell's miserly 0–15 off nine overs had stifled the scoring rate. McMillan and Kuiper took two wickets apiece to leave a very gettable 171.

Healy's hamstring problems meant that he could not take the field, so Boon took the gloves for Australia. Opening the batting for South Africa were Kepler Wessels and Andrew Hudson. Wessels had played 54 ODIs in the 1980s for Australia before deciding to switch allegiance to his native South Africa. This was his 13th ODI at the SCG, where he averaged 31.58. The South African response began at a sedate pace. Not needing to score quickly, Kepler Wessels and Andrew Hudson batted cautiously. It was the fifth over before Hudson finally got off the mark, scoring his first runs in international cricket with a punch through mid-on for three. Both openers looked to pounce on any balls short and wide. Wessels played an aggressive pull shot in the 12th over, as Whitney dropped short.

Whitney strayed on to Wessels's legs a few overs later, and was duly despatched to the boundary as South Africa eased to 51/0. The bowler almost made the breakthrough soon after, but the chance went down. It was Wessels who edged towards slip, where Mark Waugh was fielding as a substitute, but Boon dived to take the catch. The ball went firmly into the left glove, but spilled out as Boon hit the ground. Australia, desperate for a wicket, looked rueful as the opportunity went begging.

Trying to pose different questions for the South African openers, Steve Waugh was brought into the attack and immediately beat Wessels with a slower delivery. The ball thudded into the pads, and Australia appealed expectantly. Wessels found the moment amusing, but Australia were less pleased with umpire Brian Aldridge's decision. Waugh almost made amends when Wessels flicked at a ball on his pads, but it dropped agonisingly short of Craig McDermott at backward square leg. Australia could be forgiven for thinking that this would not be their day.

With spin at his disposal, Border brought on Peter Taylor. With his first ball to Andrew Hudson, Taylor bowled into the footmarks, looking for some turn. Hudson came down the wicket, to get to the pitch of the ball, but played all around it and was bowled. The first wicket had fallen at 74 in the 20th over. Peter Kirsten was the new batter and, knowing that the game was well within South Africa's reach, waited for any bad balls to be bowled. Taylor, looking for similar turn to the one that removed Hudson, found none and Kirsten cut the ball away for a boundary. Both he and Wessels controlled the situation as Australia looked helpless. Border bowled a few overs of his left-arm spin, but it was to no avail.

After 34 overs, South Africa were ahead of Australia's score and had lost far fewer wickets. McDermott was brought back into the attack as a final throw of the dice, with Australia needing wickets fast. The only noteworthy moment was when Wessels drove through the covers for a boundary to bring up his fifty. It was his fourth successive ODI half-century, and he passed 2,000 runs.

The Australians looked frustrated as South Africa were cantering to victory. Kirsten mishit Taylor, but it dropped harmlessly away from any fielders. With McDermott bowled out, Reid came back into the attack, but Wessels didn't allow him to settle. Hitting him for several boundaries, the captain was leading from the front. The win was in sight, and South Africa were making sure this was a heavy defeat for Australia. Fittingly, it was Wessels who hit the winning run to secure the nine-wicket victory. He was also given the Man-of-the-Match award to complete a memorable day against his old team-mate, and rival captain, Allan Border.

After the match, the South African team went back out on the field to greet supporters. In the Bill O'Reilly Stand, a banner had been unfurled which read, 'South Africa World Champs 1970–1992 (Unbeaten)'. The apartheid ban had robbed world cricket of a nation, and their fans were not going to forget any time soon. While South Africa celebrated, Australia had far more to think about. Their second defeat had left them bottom of the table and they were already struggling to qualify. With six games left, they would need to win at least five. The next match, against India in Brisbane, would be critical.

Dr Ali Bacher, managing director of the UCB, attended the match with Steve Tshwete, who sat on the National Executive of the ANC. Bacher was at the game because of its high profile. 'I remember going into the Australian changing room with Steve Tshwete, and I said to Allan Border, "Listen, it's been predetermined up there, who was going to win this first game."'

At Bellerive Oval in Hobart, a crowd of 1,101 were in attendance for Pakistan and Zimbabwe's match. Imran Khan took his place in the team despite not being entirely fit. His leadership qualities had been lacking in the West Indies game. Ijaz Ahmed was the player to make way for his captain. Mushtaq Ahmed was also included, at the expense of debutant Wasim Haider. Zimbabwe went with the same team except that Ali Shah's medium pace was preferred to Kevin Duers. The pitch appeared to be uncharacteristically hard and fast-paced. Winning the toss, David Houghton's ploy was to bat second and hope that some of the life had gone out of the pitch. If not, Wasim and Aaqib would cause massive difficulties for the Zimbabwean batters.

Eddo Brandes, the quickest of the Zimbabwean bowlers, took the first over. The Zimbabwe Cricket Union report mentions a ball from the first over, saying that Brandes bowled a 'bouncer at Aamer Sohail, which bounced so high that the batter did not even need to duck, and it cleared the keeper to go for a one-bounce four on one of the longest straight boundaries in cricket'. With the ball coming on to the bat, Sohail was quick to pull anything short. Malcolm Jarvis was particularly guilty and conceded boundaries through square leg. In the eighth over, the extra bounce helped Jarvis as Ramiz Raja edged behind for Flower to take the catch. The opening partnership had been worth 29, and Inzamam-ul-Haq joined Sohail at the wicket. Inzamam scored uncharacteristically slowly, and he also fell cheaply. Having made 14 off 42 balls, he picked out Brandes when trying to clip Butchart away on the leg side. Pakistan were reduced to 63/2 and Zimbabwe were very much in the game.

Javed Miandad was the next man in, and he started aggressively if not a little uneasily. He soon found his form and, along with Sohail, began to score at a run a ball. Ali Shah proved to be difficult to score off while John Traicos struggled to contain. Miandad placed the ball expertly, applying sweeps and powerful hits, to score his runs. It was the 31st over when Pakistan brought up their hundred, for the loss of two wickets, but Zimbabwe needed a breakthrough. Otherwise, they would have a difficult total to chase.

Already finding themselves under pressure from the Pakistan batting, Zimbabwe did not help their cause. Sohail offered several chances, including a caught-and-bowled off Brandes when on 85, but each one went begging. His century came up from a boundary, sweeping Traicos, from 166 balls. Not to be outdone, Miandad brought out a reverse sweep to achieve his half-century. Pakistan were 185/2 in the 42nd over and were on target for a big score.

Further punishment was dealt out to the Zimbabwean bowlers. The loss of Sohail, for an impressive 114, did little to quell the runs. With Miandad at the crease, the runs flowed while Salim Malik rotated the strike. Butchart finally trapped Miandad lbw in the final over, but the damage had been done. Pakistan finished with 254/4 and Zimbabwe needed 5.10 runs an over. Sohail and Miandad's partnership of 145 came off just 151 balls and had taken the game away from Zimbabwe. Very few people, including the Zimbabweans, were expecting anything other than a Pakistan victory.

Arnott and Flower came out to bat for Pakistan and immediately found Wasim and Aaqib's pace and bounce problematic. With Flower on four, Aaqib grazed the stumps, but the bails remained in place. However, this good fortune would not last much longer. Flower tried to cut Wasim, but the extra bounce meant that he could only nick the ball, and Inzamam took the catch at first slip. Just four balls later, Pycroft played on, Wasim had his second wicket, and Zimbabwe were 14/2. It was also Wasim's 150th ODI wicket, making him just the fifth player to reach that landmark.

Pakistan's bowling superiority was making a mockery of any potential for Zimbabwe to offer a viable chase. In the first 12 overs, not one attacking shot came in front of the wicket. The third wicket fell in the 20th over, and Zimbabwe had only mustered 33 runs. Kevin Arnott was the man out, and his seven runs had come off 63 balls. Iqbal Sikander was the bowler, and Wasim Akram took an easy catch.

With the game realistically out of reach, Ali Shah and Zimbabwe captain David Houghton took advantage of Pakistan's use of spin. Boundaries were still hard to come by, but Zimbabwe put together a meaningful partnership. They managed 25 runs off the next five overs, before another 11 runs were scored to move the total on 69/3 from 30 overs.

With the partnership worth 70, it was Aamer Sohail who added to his already special day with two wickets. The first to fall was Ali Shah. Looking to sweep the left-arm spinner, Shah played on for a useful 33 off 58 balls. The crucial wicket of David Houghton fell just five runs later. Looking to score through the covers, he picked out Ramiz at extra cover for 44. The score was 108/5, and Pakistan were well on the way to a resounding victory.

With only pride to play for, Iain Butchart and Andy Waller played some expansive shots. Waller smashed a massive six over square leg off the bowling of Iqbal Sikander. Wasim Akram was hit back over his head for a boundary, but he soon exacted revenge. The partnership had reached 79 off just 54 balls when Aaqib Javed removed Butchart for 33. With only three more runs on the board, Akram clean-bowled Waller for 44 off 36 balls.

Brandes and Traicos managed to get Zimbabwe over 200 runs, but the margin of victory was 53. Only 13 boundaries were scored in the Zimbabwe innings, and the six maidens spoke volumes for the bowling supremacy. Wasim Akram had been the pick of the bowlers with 3–21. Aamer Sohail's 114 and 2–26 gave him a deserved Man-of-the-Match award. Imran Khan had not been required to bat or bowl, but was still showing signs of shoulder pain while fielding. Reports of squabbling between the Pakistan players in the field was just as big a concern.

The second match of the day was a day/night game at the MCG. England and the West Indies faced off on a moist pitch, and the toss was an important one to win. It was Graham Gooch who asked the West Indies to bat in their second successive match in Melbourne. Both teams were unchanged from their first matches. The first over, faced by Desmond Haynes, was a maiden. Brian Lara, who was playing with a bruised foot from the Pakistan game, faced Chris Lewis. As Lewis extracted extra bounce from the pitch, Lara's forward defensive shot was inadequate, and the ball crashed into his groin. Lara crumpled to the floor in discomfort, much to the amusement of the crowd, fielders and TV commentators. When he finally resumed batting, Lara nicked the next ball, and Alec Stewart took the catch. The West Indies had already lost more wickets in this game than in the previous one.

Tight bowling from England kept Haynes and Richardson subdued. It was the sixth over before the first boundary was scored when Haynes cut Lewis for four in typical West Indian fashion. Haynes then played a pull shot for three before Richie Richardson ended the over with another aggressive cut shot for four. In his next over, Lewis made amends when Richardson fended the ball towards the slips, where Ian Botham took the regulation catch. The line of the ball meant that Richardson had to play at it, but it was the extra bounce that deceived the West Indies captain. The score was 22/2, and England's bowlers were in control. Derek Pringle bowled three maidens in his first seven overs, despite the fielding restrictions.

Haynes released some of the pressure with a pull shot off Pringle, and the ball crashed into the concrete base of the boundary fence. Behind were rows of empty seats, as just 18,521 spectators populated the large-capacity stadium. The introduction of Ian Botham into the bowling attack roused the interest of the English fans who had turned up at the MCG. It took just two balls for the all-rounder to get into the action, as Hooper tried to slog him but hit the ball straight up into the air. Dermot Reeve was under the steepling catch, and he hung on to it despite making it look more difficult than it was. The third wicket had fallen with just 36 on the board, and the West Indies needed someone to take control.

Keith Arthurton was the next batter in, but it was Desmond Haynes who was key to building the innings. Haynes received a life when he edged Phil DeFreitas, but Stewart could only parry the ball towards Ian Botham at slip. The ball cannoned off the veteran's shin and went to ground. It was a painful moment for Botham as he hobbled to retrieve the ball.

In his next over, DeFreitas was bowling to Haynes again and dropped short of a length. Haynes rocked on to the back foot and hooked the ball for another boundary to take the score on to 55/3. Trying to repeat the previous shot, Haynes smashed the ball straight to Neil Fairbrother at backward square leg. With such a safe pair of hands, Fairbrother took the catch comfortably, and the West Indian opener was gone for 38.

Keith Arthurton and Gus Logie set about trying to put a partnership together to get the West Indies out of trouble. Both batted sensibly but put away the occasional bad ball that England bowled. Arthurton played an aggressive cut shot for four, while Logie struck a massive six, off Botham, into the empty Southern Stand. Botham's mood worsened when he put down a sharp caught-and-bowled chance off the same batter.

Botham was involved again with an lbw shout that led to Logie getting himself run out. A ball from Botham hit his pads, and the England fielders appealed. Logie was intent on getting out of the way of the umpire's view and looked for a run. Unbeknownst to him, Fairbrother moved quickly to the ball, and his accurate underarm throw did the rest. The partnership had been worth 36, but the West Indies were 91/5 in the 31st over.

With England in total control, it was the 35th over before the West Indies finally reached 100, but they would lose quick wickets to further their problems. Roger Harper's flick off his pads led to his demise, before Arthurton's change of mind left Malcolm Marshall stranded. Marshall responded to the call, but found his batting partner unwilling to move after getting more than halfway down the wicket. Marshall walked off forlornly as the West Indies had slipped to 114/7.

The rest of the innings carried on in the same fashion as the West Indies found it impossible to put a significant partnership together. David Williams was next to fall when he was caught by Pringle as a leading edge flew straight over DeFreitas's head to mid-on. Arthurton was the last recognised batter but his innings, in some ways charmed, ended when he gave DeFreitas his third wicket. After bringing his fifty up with a six – his second of the innings – off the bowling of Lewis, he fell when trying to force a ball through midwicket, Fairbrother taking the regulation catch. Curtly Ambrose was the last man out, slashing at a wide ball, to end the innings on 157. The England bowlers had been miserly, while the West Indies had given several wickets away needlessly. It would take a phenomenal effort from the bowlers to win the game from here. With Ambrose, Marshall and Benjamin in the team, it was possible.

England again used Botham as a pinch-hitter to partner Gooch. The first runs came off Gooch's bat, just wide of second slip, with the West Indies forced into an aggressive field to try to take wickets. Botham found scoring difficult, while the England captain began to build in confidence. Malcolm Marshall appeared to be struggling with line and length as Gooch took 12 runs off his fourth over. The score had moved on to 26/0 with England looking comfortable. With Winston Benjamin replacing Marshall in the attack, a loose ball was gloved by Gooch for four. Williams dived, in vain, to stop the ball as it ran away to the boundary. Another tumbling effort from Williams could have removed Botham in the next over, but the ball went to ground. Trying to flick Ambrose away, he could only glance the ball, but the diminutive wicketkeeper could not hang on.

Botham's time at the crease ended, with England's fifty on the board, when he edged a ball from Benjamin to the wicketkeeper. Botham had contributed just eight runs to the partnership with Gooch, and his dismissal brought Smith to the crease. He found scoring similarly difficult, and lost his wicket when trying to pull Benjamin. He mistimed the stroke as it tucked him up, and the ball looped up to Logie at square leg, who took the catch. Smith had scored eight runs from 28 balls, as had Botham. England were 71/2 in the 21st over and were still in control of the match.

New batter Graeme Hick immediately looked to get after the spinners. He played a lofted off drive, lifting Hooper over the infield for a boundary. Roger Harper's first over was greeted with three boundaries as Hick pounced on anything short and wide. Gooch also reached his fifty during the over as England's ascendancy was reiterated.

The reintroduction of Marshall and Ambrose did little to quell England's scoring. Having been worked over by the West Indies in the previous summer's Test series, Hick found it testing, but he managed to stay at the crease. The partnership was finally broken by spin as Gooch's advancement down the wicket led to him being stumped. The ball turned and bounced, which beat Gooch. It almost beat Williams behind the stumps, but he managed to recover and take the bails off.

At 126/3, England were still well placed, with 32 runs required with more than 18 overs left. Hick had already proven that he was looking to score off the spinners. He despatched Harper for six over extra cover as he looked to end the game quickly. It also brought up his half-century, off 51 balls, with the West Indian total in reach. With just one run required for victory, Hick tried to pull out of a defensive push and the ball looped towards the bowler, Roger Harper. Harper dived and claimed the catch. Hick stood his ground before both batter and bowler looked at each other inquiringly. Before the umpires could confer, Hick walked.

An edged four, wide of the slips from Fairbrother, gave England victory with more than ten overs to spare. The Man-of-the-Match award went to Chris Lewis for his 3–30. Benjamin was the pick of the West Indies bowlers, but their total was not enough. On the back of the performance, England were installed as favourites by bookmakers. The large victory helped increase their net run rate, which could be important later in the tournament.

	Pld	Won	Lost	Tied	N/R	Pts	Net R/R	For	Against
England	2	2	0	0	0	4	0.568	396/89.5	384/100.0
New Zealand	2	2	0	0	0	4	0.488	458/98.2	417/100.0
Pakistan	2	1	1	0	0	2	0.382	474/100.0	422/96.5
South Africa	1	1	0	0	0	2	0.182	171/46.5	170/49.0
Sri Lanka	2	1	1	0	0	2	−0.084	519/99.2	522/98.2
West Indies	2	1	1	0	0	2	−0.326	378/96.5	380/89.5
India	1	0	1	0	0	0	−0.180	227/50.0	236/50.0
Australia	2	0	2	0	0	0	−0.479	381/99.0	419/96.5
Zimbabwe	2	0	2	0	0	0	−0.578	513/100.0	567/99.2

Chapter Five

Raindrops and Other Drops

The central Queensland city of Mackay was chosen to host India versus Sri Lanka. Situated about 600 miles north of Brisbane, Mackay's Ray Mitchell Oval at Harrup Park was another new venue for international cricket. The ground had hosted a World Series Cricket game in December 1978 when the West Indies easily beat the WSC Cavaliers by seven wickets. West Indies greats such as Desmond Haynes, Clive Lloyd, Viv Richards, Andy Roberts and Michael Holding turned out for the game. Queensland had hosted Pakistan in 1988 for two one-day tour games at the ground, but no international matches had been played previously.

India were the first to arrive, as their journey was far more straightforward than Sri Lanka's. Having narrowly lost in Perth, they arrived two days early for the match. Many local people greeted the Indian team as they landed at Mackay airport. Only the team manager, Abbas Ali Baig, and captain Mohammed Azharuddin spoke to the press, while players chatted with the well-wishers. The Sri Lankan team flew into Mackay during the evening after travelling from Hamilton via Brisbane. The changeover in Brisbane included having to wait several hours for their flight to Mackay, resulting in them having a full day's travel due to the three-hour time difference. The Sri Lankan manager, Ranjit Fernando, was quoted in Mackay's *Daily Mercury* as saying, 'We have decided not to complain or moan about the trip. It was hard work, but we are thinking positively.'

To meet the expected demand, Mackay Cricket Association had arranged for temporary stands to be built. To add to an influx of Indian and Sri Lankan supporters, many international journalists descended on the city, including up to 50 journalists from India who were expected to cover the match. One of those journalists was Suresh Menon, and he recalled how welcome they were made to feel. 'Mackay was notable for the generosity of the organisers, who gave us a free telephone in the press box with an international call facility. Reporters, photographers, and even some players said "thank you" and made full use of this. The facility was withdrawn after some of us said it had probably ruined Mackay's economy in one afternoon!'

In the lead-up to the game, Sri Lanka were faced with the prospect of losing Rumesh Ratnayake for the rest of the tournament. The fast bowler's shoulder injury was not going to heal in time. Aravinda de Silva summed up the issue: 'His absence will affect us in a big way because he was our strike bowler.' Sri Lanka would be left to apply for a replacement and then have to fly him to the tournament.

The weather had been sunny for weeks in the lead-up to the match, but during the evening before the game, a storm came through and drenched the area. The ground staff stayed overnight to make sure that any surface water didn't seep on to the pitch and to try to get it ready for the match. The man responsible for operations on the day, and for getting the match to Mackay in the first place, was Mackay Cricket Association's president, Barry Jansen. When I met with Barry, he was on the board of Queensland Cricket and still clearly remembered the events of the day. 'But what happened is, like a normal storm it goes, and it clears up in the morning, and it's beautiful sunshine. But it stayed overcast.'

Not only did the Queensland sunshine not appear, but intermittent rain spells kept the Harrup Park surface too wet to play on. Despite the weather, many fans still came to the match in the hope of seeing some cricket. A spell of sunshine around midday led to the players taking an early lunch in case play could commence in the afternoon.

During the lunch period, entertainment was laid on for the crowd, including a local aerobics team giving a display. It was during this session that several of the Indian squad joined the ladies of Sharon's Aerobics. Much to the delight of the crowd, Kapil Dev joined in along with Subroto Banerjee and Vinod Kambli. Not only was the on-field entertainment keeping the crowd at the ground, but the refreshments available were also being consumed at a fast rate. Barry takes up the story: 'We sold out, there was something like 28 pubs in Mackay. We sold out of cold cans, we were using hot cans and washing them through with water, they drank that much beer. We were pulling cans out of the mud three months later.'

To try to dry out the pitch, Barry called in a friend of his to help. His friend owned a helicopter business, Grif-Air, and one was despatched to try to dry the wicket. As the helicopter hovered over the ground, the crowd roared in delight. Several take-offs and landings added to the entertainment while attempting to remove surface water and damp spots. By the time umpires David Shepherd and Ian Robinson inspected the pitch at 2pm, they were happy that play could commence 45 minutes later with the game reduced to 20 overs per side.

India were forced into one change, with Ravi Shastri left out due to an injury to his left knee that he had incurred in the England game. Kapil Dev was promoted to opener, with young all-rounder Ajay Jadeja making his ODI debut. Subroto Banerjee, despite his aerobic display, was left out of the team in favour of left-arm spinner Venkatapathy Raju. Sri Lanka had injury concerns of their own with Athula Samarasekera struggling with his hamstring, so Chandika Hathurusinghe was selected. In the bowling department, Kapila Wijegunawardene was preferred to Don Anurasiri.

Having won the toss, Aravinda de Silva asked India to bat. Champaka Ramanayake was given the new ball for Sri Lanka while Kapil Dev and Kris Srikkanth opened for India. It was Srikkanth who faced the new ball, and he left the first delivery alone outside off stump before edging the second ball for two runs down to third man. At that point, the rain started again, and the players left the field. Within five minutes, the umpires were left with no choice but to abandon the game, and the teams were awarded a point each. Local television station WIN Television Mackay covered the game on behalf of Channel Nine, with the game not being shown live. WIN used one camera to record what action took place. The Sri Lankans were slightly disappointed with the outcome, while India were of the opinion that the situation could have been difficult for them. India's next game would be back in Brisbane against Australia, while Sri Lanka would have to fly back across the Tasman Sea to face South Africa in Wellington.

Saturday, 29 February saw two games being played. Later in the day would see the West Indies and Zimbabwe meet at the Gabba, but first New Zealand and South Africa met at Eden

Park. South Africa had already beaten co-hosts Australia in their first game, and their tournament did not get any easier. New Zealand had beaten Australia on the same pitch, and there had been rumours before the game that it had been prepared to suit New Zealand's medium-pacers. It would also negate the effects of Allan Donald's raw pace. Martin Crowe was quick to deny the speculation, but did point out that the pitch would get slower, as it had done against Australia.

New Zealand were forced into a change when John Wright failed to recover from his shoulder injury. Mark Greatbatch came in to replace him, amid plenty of discussion as to where he would fit into the batting order. Chris Cairns was brought back into the team, with Danny Morrison making way. South Africa also made one change, with fast bowler Tertius Bosch coming into the team to replace Meyrick Pringle. Kepler Wessels won the toss and decided to bat first. His decision influenced by the preceding day's pitch discussion, he figured that batting first would yield the most runs.

Once again, Martin Crowe used Dipak Patel as an opening bowler. South Africa couldn't find runs early on, and took 13 balls to get off the mark. In his second over, Andrew Hudson looked to release some of the pressure that was already building. Trying to hit Patel over midwicket, he played all around the ball and was bowled. In 16 balls, he had scored only one run and was visibly frustrated. In the next over, Wessels also succumbed to frustration and tried to cut Watson away. Beaten by the extra bounce, the South African captain could only steer the ball to Ian Smith behind the stumps. South Africa were 10/2 in the seventh over, and New Zealand were on top. Most of the 27,450 fans were excited with how the match had started.

South Africa's new batters were the experienced Peter Kirsten and the 22-year-old Hansie Cronje. An unconvincing sweep from Cronje almost backfired as he looked to work Patel on to the leg side. Kirsten's decision to use his feet paid off with a welcome boundary as the spinner tied up the batters. In his first seven overs, Patel had conceded just 13 runs. First change bowler was Chris Harris, and he trundled up to the wicket to bowl his first delivery. The ball was wide of off stump, and Cronje hung his bat out looking to run the ball down to third man. Instead, he edged it, Smith took his second catch of the match, and South Africa had problems at 29/3.

Peter Kirsten looked to play expansive strokes when the bowling allowed, and boundaries off Harris, Larsen and Latham helped the South African cause. Latham was unusually expensive for the New Zealand medium-pacers. Richardson looked to take him on, and hit a lofted drive back over the bowler's head. Richardson nearly gave Latham an unlikely wicket, but the ball dropped just short of Mark Greatbatch. Crowe soon withdrew Latham after he had bowled only two overs for 19 runs.

Replacing Latham, Chris Cairns was introduced into the attack. Kirsten brought his fifty up, off Cairns, when lifting the ball over the infield for another boundary. Looking set, the South African opener scored two more boundaries off Patel's final over. Richardson tried to emulate his partner, but it became his undoing. In the 35th over, Cairns bowled a ball well wide of off stump. Richardson attempted to smash it through the off side. Somehow, he pulled the ball towards mid-on and Larsen took the catch. It was terrible cricket from both bowler and batter, but the breakthrough had been achieved. The partnership had been worth 79, but South Africa were still a long way from recovering from their poor start.

Jonty Rhodes had been due to bat at six on the scorecard, but all-rounder Adrian Kuiper was next in. He had been promoted to play some big shots to help Kirsten. The experiment lasted for just three runs. Kuiper, playing a hook shot, top-edged the ball behind, and Smith took the catch. The crowd went wild but hadn't noticed that umpire Reporter had signalled a no-ball. Kuiper desperately wanted to get off strike, and charged through for a single while Kirsten was reluctant. In the ensuing chaos, Cairns had the presence of mind to notice that the batting crease was devoid of batters and shouted to Smith to throw the ball. Cairns then missed the throw from Smith, but Patel was backing up and ran Kuiper out.

Two pieces of poor cricket had cost South Africa two wickets. The score was 111/5, with Rhodes coming to the wicket as the last recognised batter. The impish Rhodes was next to get out, when Crowe pulled off a spectacular diving catch. Flicking the ball off his pads, Rhodes hit the ball in the air, and New Zealand's captain dived full stretch to remove the sixth South African for just 121 runs.

Next in was all-rounder Brian McMillan. His hair was flowing as he strode to the crease having chosen to bat without a helmet or cap. Kirsten took the decision to accelerate the scoring with several boundaries. Watson had him caught, by Cairns, in the 45th over, but had overstepped the crease. Kirsten's reprieve did not last too long as the Watson/Cairns combination removed him with a legitimate delivery. Kirsten tried to clear long-on, and the ball sailed to Cairns. He was gone for 90 off 129 balls, along with South Africa's slim chance of a competitive total.

In the final few overs, McMillan and Richard Snell added another 28 runs, 15 coming off the last over, but South Africa's 190/7 looked short of a good score. Patel and Larsen both conceded less than 30 runs off their ten overs, while Watson and Cairns picked up four wickets between them. Kirsten's innings had equalled South Africa's highest ODI score since returning, but his team-mates had failed to give him support.

Only an extraordinary bowling effort would rescue the game for Wessels and his men.

After plenty of speculation before the match, Mark Greatbatch was given the opener's berth with Rod Latham. Greatbatch had not opened the batting previously and was expected to play a pinch-hitter role. It was Latham who first struck an aggressive shot when lifting McMillan over mid-on, the ball racing away for four. Greatbatch assumed his role in the third over, off the bowling of Allan Donald. As he pulled the ball for four, it was a signal of intent from the New Zealander. In the sixth over, McMillan was smashed back over his head for six as Greatbatch looked to score at a rapid pace. The introduction of Richard Snell, at the expense of McMillan, did nothing to stem the flow of runs. He too saw the ball struck cleanly over the infield for another boundary. Tertius Bosch's introduction to international cricket was to see Latham cut him viciously for four.

Greatbatch was already scoring at almost a run a ball when he accelerated. Snell was the first recipient, with a towering six over third man off the first ball of the 12th over. The second ball was driven confidently for four. South Africa were haemorrhaging runs and needed to stop the bleeding. Adrian Kuiper was Wessels's answer, but poor fielding saw him despatched to the boundary too. That four brought up Greatbatch's run-a-ball fifty, but he wasn't ready to slow down. A delicate leg glance for four was followed up with a sweetly timed shot off leg stump for six. The ball sailed high on to the roof of the North Stand. By the end of that over, the 15th, New Zealand were 103/0. In comparison, South Africa had been 29/2 at the same stage.

It was the introduction of Peter Kirsten's off spin that would finally quieten the Eden Park crowd. Greatbatch, looking to launch the ball over mid-on, missed the turning ball and was bowled. Scoring 68 from 60 balls with nine fours and three sixes, Greatbatch's innings had set New Zealand well on the way to victory. The partnership had amassed 114 runs, leaving 77 needed for victory in 32 overs. South Africa's afternoon of woe continued when Jonty Rhodes, fleet of foot in the outfield, tried to throw down the stumps as Rod Latham took a risky single. With no one backing up, the ball ran to the boundary to give New Zealand five runs. The bowler, Allan Donald, sank to his knees in dejection. Being the recipient of that benefaction, Latham soon completed his half-century from 56 balls. The new batter, Andrew Jones, added more pressure with a sumptuous cover drive to the boundary.

Richard Snell's reintroduction into the attack was greeted with another boundary from Latham. Jones almost succumbed to the bowler, but the ball bounced just short of Wessels fielding at slip. South Africa's captain thrust his right boot at the ball to stop it, but it still evaded the fielder and ran for four. With the score on 155, Latham drove at a wide ball off Snell, and this time it carried to Wessels, who took the catch. Latham's 60 came off 69 balls, with seven boundaries.

Surprisingly, wicketkeeper Ian Smith came in to bat at four instead of Martin Crowe. His first three balls all went to the boundary as a premeditated plan came to fruition, helped by Snell's inaccuracy. The first and third balls were on leg stump and were put away proficiently. The second was swatted away, with more than a touch of bottom hand, back over the bowler's head. Allan Donald was also subjected to Smith's expansive shot-making. Stepping away to make room, Smith smeared the ball over mid-off for a one-bounce four. Smith perished in the same way as he miscued the ball and Kirsten took the catch. The crowd were disappointed, but Smith's cameo was worth 19 runs off eight balls, with four boundaries. It had been nine minutes of fun for the partisan crowd, but had taken New Zealand to within 12 runs of a resounding win.

Within two overs, New Zealand reached their target for an impressive seven-wicket victory. Their net run rate would be improved massively as the total was achieved with 93 balls still to bowl. The South African bowlers' statistics looked sickly, while their coach, Mike Procter, was less than complimentary about the pitch. Mark Greatbatch took the Man-of-the-Match award as New Zealand topped the table with three wins from their three games.

Meanwhile, at the Gabba, just over 2,000 spectators saw the West Indies and Zimbabwe meet in the second game. Desmond Haynes and Curtly Ambrose were rested, with Roger Harper dropping out. Phil Simmons, Anderson Cummins and Patrick Patterson came into the side. Zimbabwe lost Wayne James to his hand injury, and Iain Butchart, so Alistair Campbell and Kevin Duers replaced them. Having played in Hobart two days previously, Zimbabwe had travelled via Sydney to Brisbane. From the temperate climes of Tasmania, they found a marked change in conditions with Queensland's humidity. Some rain had fallen too, so David Houghton felt it was a good toss to win and inserted the West Indies.

Opening the batting for the West Indies were Phil Simmons, replacing Haynes, and Brian Lara. It was the latter who started as if he wanted to make up for lost time after his second-ball duck against England. Anything on his legs was put away with impunity, while anything on off stump and wider was clattered through the covers. In particular, it was Malcolm Jarvis who was punished as he struggled to find the right line to bowl. His left-arm swing bowling was wayward, and Lara pounced.

At the other end, Phil Simmons eased his way into the innings with a more cautious approach. While his partner had already reached his fifty, off 59 balls, Simmons was scoring at less than three an over. With his score on 21 and the team's total on 78 from 15 overs, he played across his stumps at Brandes. The large fast bowler was too quick and accurate, and clean-bowled the opener.

Lara continued to play aggressively and almost lost his wicket, but the ball went wide of the diving Andy Flower behind the stumps. More boundaries followed before he finally lost his wicket for 72 off 71 balls. It was the captain, David Houghton, who took a sharp catch to remove Lara. The score had moved on to 103/2 with Richie Richardson and Carl Hooper at the crease.

A rain shower held up play for nine minutes, but no overs were lost. The West Indies batters picked up where they had left off as Zimbabwe struggled to contain them. Richie Richardson showed no sign of a fractured finger on his left hand as he flayed the bowlers. Scoring on all sides of the ground, including a six off the bowling of Ali Shah, Richardson kept the scoreboard ticking over. Jarvis had already been hit around the Gabba, but it looked like his luck had changed when Hooper offered a chance trying to clear the boundary. Eddo Brandes, fielding in the deep, put the catch down and the opportunity was gone. Both batters scored at almost a run a ball as the West Indies passed 200 and were looking to post a massive total.

With the partnership on 117, scored in just over an hour at the crease, Hooper fell to the bowling of John Traicos. Trying to hit a flattish ball from the spinner, the batter picked out Andy Pycroft on the boundary. Richardson fell just one run later when attempting to hit Jarvis for six. Brandes was the man under the ball and did not make a mistake this time. Hooper's 63 came from 67 balls, while Richardson went for 56 off 76 balls. The West Indies were now 221/4 with two new batters at the crease.

Keith Arthurton's innings helped to boost the West Indies' total, but wickets fell regularly as Zimbabwe fought back. At one end, Arthurton was looking to hit down the ground while West Indies batters fell. Gus Logie was the first, when a powerful Eddo Brandes throw from the outfield beat his run. Flower took the bails off and sent him back for five. Malcolm Marshall was next man out, adding two runs before being caught off the bowling of Brandes. When Arthurton was out for a quickfire 26, the West Indies had slumped to 255/7 from an imposing position. Williams and Benjamin, who was bowled by Brandes off the last ball of the innings, squeezed out a few more runs and the West Indies posted 264/8 from their allotted overs. Malcolm Jarvis was the bowler punished most, as demonstrated by figures of 1–71. Brandes was the pick with 3–45, but Zimbabwe's batters were left with a testing total.

Malcolm Marshall and Patrick Patterson shared the new ball, but Zimbabwe's openers, Kevin Arnott and Andy Flower, picked up singles while not getting into too much trouble. There were 21 runs on the board when Patterson did make the breakthrough. Flower was the batter, bowled for six runs, and Andy Pycroft joined Arnott at the wicket. Another 19 runs were added before Zimbabwe felt the full force of the West Indian pace attack. Pycroft struggled with a short ball from Patterson and could only deflect the ball into his cheekbone. Batting in a helmet but without a grille, Pycroft required treatment before resuming batting. The short ball had the desired effect, with the batter edging the very next ball to Williams, and Zimbabwe were 43/2.

In the next over, bowled by Anderson Cummins, Zimbabwe found themselves in far more trouble. Arnott was hit on his right hand and retired hurt immediately. Blood was dripping from the wound as he left the field. David Houghton and Andy

Waller were the new batters at the crease and in the firing line for the West Indies barrage. Waller lasted for 13 scoreless balls before Benjamin struck. When 19-year-old Alistair Campbell's 18-ball innings ended, for a solitary run, a collapse was highly probable. Zimbabwe were effectively 64/5 with Arnott unlikely to bat again.

A collapse did not occur, as Houghton and Ali Shah played uninhibited. The run rate was creeping up, but the batters played to frustrate the West Indies rather than attempt to win the game. For 87 balls, Zimbabwe held firm while scoring when the opportunity present itself. Having seen off another spell of quick bowling, the sweet relief of seeing Carl Hooper coming on to bowl was too much for Houghton. Having passed his fifty, from a pedestrian 83 balls, he took on Hooper but managed to pick out Patterson. The partnership had been worth 69 runs and taken Zimbabwe to respectability. With Houghton gone, Shah took on the senior role and constructed partnerships of 29 and 20 with Brandes and Traicos. From those 49 runs, Brandes contributed six while Traicos added eight. Shah's innings protected the bowlers and added valuable runs to Zimbabwe's cause. Malcolm Jarvis was five not out at the end, with Shah scoring 60 from 87 balls. Zimbabwe ended on 189/7 and fell to a 75-run defeat.

After the match, news came from the hospital that an X-ray showed that the joint on Arnott's right middle finger was broken. He would not be available for the next few matches at least. In his after-match interview, Houghton commented that it had been 'tough'. When asked about the game years later, John Traicos mentioned that 'the pace of the West Indies bowlers was certainly a factor. Apart from a few exceptions, our batters tended to be intimidated by the extra pace and as a result, tended to get behind the run rate.'

Richie Richardson was critical of his team's efforts despite the resounding victory. The bowlers' effort was particularly irksome, as the West Indies captain felt that they had eased back after tearing through the top order. Richardson was considering the net run rate for his team, as it could be critical later on. Lara was named Man of the Match for his sparkling innings.

On the following day, Sunday, 1 March, the Gabba hosted its second match of the weekend. Australia were attempting to win their first match of the tournament. Their opponents, India, were one point ahead by virtue of the Mackay match. Needing to win, Australia made two changes to their side. Ian Healy's hamstring ruled him out of the game, so Mark Taylor came in to open, with David Boon dropping down the order and keeping wicket. The other change was a straight swap, with Bruce Reid making way for Merv Hughes. India also made two changes, with the highly experienced pairing of Ravi Shastri and Sanjay Manjrekar replacing Vinod Kambli and Pravin Amre.

Border won the toss and decided to bat. The wicket had been used for the West Indies versus Zimbabwe game, but the dry weather and pitch encouraged the Australian captain to get runs on the board. Taylor and Marsh opened positively, looking to score, without playing any extravagant strokes. A more aggressive shot, off the bowling of Kapil Dev, gave India the breakthrough when Taylor tried to cut the ball. Instead, he edged to More behind the stumps and Australia lost their first wicket with the score on 18.

Any respite from batting by coming in at three was gone for David Boon, with the loss of Taylor in the fifth over, and the Tasmanian strode to the wicket full of confidence. Marsh hit the first boundary of the day, in the tenth over, when he drove Srinath through the covers. Scoring slowly at first, Marsh tried to push on, but played on in the next over. It was Kapil

Dev's second wicket of the day, and Marsh departed for eight off 29 balls. Australia were wobbling again, at 31/2, and needed a partnership from Boon and Dean Jones.

Both batters played their natural games, with Jones, in particular, starting aggressively. Following up after a boundary, Jones smashed Srinath for a six straight into the Sir Leslie Wilson Pavilion, where the Queensland Cricketers' Club was situated. In the 18th over, the same bowler suffered at the hands of both batters. Jones then Boon whipped the wayward Srinath through midwicket as Australia appeared to be playing the sort of cricket that their fans expected. The partisan Gabba crowd responded accordingly. With Boon in full flow, it took a good piece of bowling from Venkatapathy Raju to remove him. The partnership was worth 71 when Boon, on 43, tried to use his feet but was beaten by flight and length. Shastri took the catch, and the Tasmanian was on his way. Australia were 102/3 in the 25th over.

Steve Waugh's arrival led to the run rate slowing somewhat, but Jones still looked to put away the bad balls. A sweep for four brought up the 150 for Australia, together with Jones's fifty from 75 balls. Having scored a single boundary, Waugh came down the wicket to Srinath to make room. However, the bowler cramped up Waugh and hit his leg stump. The partnership had been worth 54 runs for Australia.

The partnership between Jones and Moody helped Australia accelerate. A change of bat brought aggressive intent from Moody as Srinath, once again, served up balls to hit. Having scored 28 at more than a run per ball, Moody's fanciful swipe across the line off Prabhakar was his downfall. After an inspired bowling change, with Prabhakar striking in the first ball of the spell, India had reduced Australia to 198/5.

Border joined Jones at the crease, but played a subservient role. With a few overs left in the innings, Jones played with far more intent. Kapil Dev, bowling the 47th over, found that to his cost. The over cost India 16 runs, with Jones taking 14 of them. The next over threatened to be as costly, when Prabhakar could only watch as Jones launched the ball for six. When he tried the same shot again, the ball flew straight up into the air and the bowler took a good catch. He then slammed the ball into the ground as the Indian fielders ran to celebrate. Jones trudged off, to the applause of the Gabba crowd, having scored 90 runs from 109 balls.

With the score on 230/6, Australia would have had designs on squeezing another 15 runs or so from the last few balls of the innings. Instead, they lost another three wickets as Border, Craig McDermott and Peter Taylor perished cheaply. Border was unlucky as Ajay Jadeja took a smart running, diving catch at mid-off, but it summed up his tournament perfectly. Australia finished on 237/9 as the Queensland sunshine, from earlier in the day, was replaced by grey storm clouds.

The Indian response started slowly, with Kris Srikkanth looking out of sorts. McDermott bowled a tight over to him before bowling him with the last ball, with six runs on the board. Srikkanth's 11-ball innings had not garnered any runs before he was put out of his misery with a ball knocking over his off stump. Indian captain Mohammed Azharuddin was at the wicket far earlier than planned. After ten overs of reasonably tight bowling from McDermott and Mike Whitney, Merv Hughes came on to bowl first change. His first ball, nothing more than a loosener outside off stump, was crashed through the off side by Azharuddin for a boundary. The next over should have seen the partnership end, when Shastri and Azharuddin got their calling massively wrong, but Australia couldn't take advantage.

At 2.49pm, rain forced the players off the field. India were 45/1 from 16.2 overs, and the Most Productive Overs (MPO) calculation would give them a revised target to chase. With 21 minutes of play lost, India were now chasing 236 in 47 overs. The loss of three overs and a single run from the target increased the difficulty of the run chase.

On the resumption, Shastri's attempt to increase his scoring rate failed. Looking to make room to hit Tom Moody over the off side, he managed to hit the ball skywards, and Steve Waugh took the catch. New batter Sachin Tendulkar pulled Moody for a four, but the bowler gained his revenge soon afterwards. As Tendulkar tried to slash the ball over cover, Waugh was in the right place once again, and Tendulkar went for 19. India were 86/3 in the 26th over, and the required run rate was close to seven per over.

With India needing runs, and quickly, Kapil Dev was pushed up the order to help Azharuddin. Both batters hit anything of a full length back down the ground. Kapil Dev went the aerial route twice as Moody overpitched. Azharuddin did the same to McDermott, as India's expansive game plan was executed. With Kapil Dev in pinch-hitting mode, Steve Waugh pitched a ball up and trapped the all-rounder in front of his wicket. Departing from straight hitting, Kapil Dev tried to pull the ball to the leg side and perished as a consequence. A run-a-ball 21 had taken India to 128, but they now needed almost eight an over.

Sanjay Manjrekar, making his first appearance in the competition, gave his team a vital boost with an energetic innings. Shots such as a lofted on drive, off the bowling of Whitney, kept his team in the match. Azharuddin, ever the clinical batter, punished any width. Although a run rate of almost ten an over was required off the last seven, India looked as though they still believed.

With two overs left, Border was looking for Merv Hughes to keep the scoring down. Manjrekar had other ideas, and played several aggressive shots. Peter Taylor's juggling stop held a lofted drive down to two runs before a deliberate move to the off side opened up the leg-side boundary, where the ball ran away. Manjrekar's aggression gave Border plenty of problems with field placement.

With India on 194, still needing 42 from less than four overs, Border swung the game back in the Australians' favour. Manjrekar clipped the ball towards midwicket, and the Indian batters took on the run. Border's quick response and his clean pick-up and throw, accurately hitting the stumps, left his counterpart short of the crease. A piece of brilliance had ended Azharuddin's innings. The partnership had yielded 66, while the Indian captain's 93 from 103 balls had kept his team in the game.

Ajay Jadeja's contribution to his team's cause was minimal as Hughes knocked him over, in the next over, for one; India were now 199/6. Aware that he was his team's final hope, Manjrekar deposited a Hughes slower ball into the stands over long-on. When Hughes bowled a low full toss on leg stump, Manjrekar cashed in again with a four. Hughes had conceded 14 runs and India now needed 26 off the last three overs. The Indian contingent at the Gabba were getting more raucous, while the Australian fans were starting to feel uneasy.

Border's miscalculation of his bowlers, due to the revised total, meant that Moody would bowl two of the last three overs while McDermott would only have one. Kiran More looked to score off every ball. A slip when turning for two left Manjrekar, on 47 off 41 balls, on strike. Manjrekar ran the ball down to third man with an intent to take two runs. The fielder was McDermott, and his powerful throw, combined with good glovework from Boon, meant that Manjrekar was on his way. Surely India were finished at 216/7.

McDermott bowled the 46th over, and Javagal Srinath needed to get More on strike. He stepped away and slashed two runs, almost too well hit. The over was a tight one, and India were left with a target of 13 runs from the last six balls with three wickets in hand. Kiran More was on strike as Moody came in to bowl the first ball. It was a low full toss on leg stump. More struck the ball firmly towards the boundary. Dean Jones's valiant dive failed to stop it. The target was now nine runs off five balls. Moody's next ball was arguably worse, and the low full toss was despatched, with an identical shot, for another four. The target was now five runs off four balls, and India were now favourites.

With a sense of bathos, More stepped across the line of the third ball, looking to paddle it away. Missing the ball by quite a distance, the ball hit the stumps and Moody had a wicket. Manoj Prabhakar took a single off the fourth ball to leave India needing four to win off two balls. Prabhakar's dalliance with being run out on the previous ball came to fruition on the fifth delivery. Srinath carved the ball straight to a fielder, but Prabhakar was halfway up the wicket. Border underarmed the ball to Moody, and the run-out was complete.

The excitement of the situation was too much for some fans, and they ran on to the field, thinking the match was over. The Australians broke off from their celebration to signal to the fans that there was one ball left. Once the outfield had cleared, the equation was simple. Srinath needed to find the boundary to win the game. Moody ran in to bowl and Srinath, expecting the ball outside off stump, swung and made contact. The ball sailed high towards the boundary, Bill Lawry erroneously called 'SIX!' on TV commentary, and Steve Waugh tracked the ball as he tried to make ground to take the catch. The ball had gone high and Waugh, doing well to get under it, then misjudged the catch, and the ball hit his wrist before going to ground. The Indian batters had run two and were coming back for a third to tie the game. Waugh composed himself, collected the ball and threw it towards the wicketkeeper's end. Raju's run was in vain, and Australia were victors by the margin of one run.

Finally, the world champions were up and running, with one win from three matches. It had been a close-run thing, but Australia had won the game. Dean Jones received the Man-of-the-Match award, but Mohammed Azharuddin could feel doubly aggrieved after his excellent innings.

Professor Stern has calculated Duckworth–Lewis–Stern (DLS) and Duckworth–Lewis (DL) totals for comparative purposes. Although both calculations are based on more recent scoring patterns, they are useful for demonstrating the inappropriateness of the MPO totals. The DL tables used were based around 2001, which is closer to cricket in 1992 than using DLS. It's also worth considering that different totals may have encouraged different behaviour in play from both sides. For this match, the DL score was 206, and the DLS score was 208. In both cases, India would have won.

At the top of the table, New Zealand were unbeaten in their three games, and England were in a similar position from one less game. Australia were now just a point off the semi-final placings, while India's point from the washout in Mackay was their only return from three games.

	Pld	Won	Lost	Tied	N/R	Pts	Net R/R	For	Against
New Zealand	3	3	0	0	0	6	0.839	649/132.5	607/150.0
England	2	2	0	0	0	4	0.568	396/89.5	384/100.0
West Indies	3	2	1	0	0	4	0.303	642/146.5	569/139.5
Sri Lanka	3	1	1	0	1	3	−0.084	519/99.2	522/98.2
Pakistan	2	1	1	0	0	2	0.382	474/100.0	422/96.5
Australia	3	1	2	0	0	2	−0.321	616/146.0	653/143.5
South Africa	2	1	1	0	0	2	−0.595	361/96.5	361/83.3
India	3	0	2	0	1	1	−0.103	461/97.0	471/97.0
Zimbabwe	3	0	3	0	0	0	−0.885	702/150.0	831/149.2

Chapter Six

Rain, Damn Rain and Statistics

While the rain clouds were gathering over Brisbane, they had already deposited much precipitation over Adelaide. England and Pakistan were due to play the 13th match of the Cricket World Cup at the Adelaide Oval. In similar circumstances to Mackay, a sustained period of dry weather had been broken by rain in Australia's driest state capital. The result was a wicket that had been covered for 40 hours. As it had sweated while the rain fell, a bowling paradise awaited the winner of the coin toss. Geoff Boycott's pitch report, for television, highlighted the patchy surface.

Imran Khan decided to rest his shoulder once again, so Ijaz Ahmed took his place. The other change made by Pakistan was to play Wasim Haider instead of Iqbal Sikander. Allan Lamb's declaration of fitness was premature, and an aggravation of his hamstring injury meant that he would miss out once again for England. Chris Lewis was suffering from a side strain, so he played as a batter only. Graham Gooch decided that he needed a seamer, rather than spin, so Phil Tufnell made way for Gladstone Small.

Under the humid conditions, Gooch won the toss and made the obvious decision to bowl. In the first over, Derek Pringle had a very good shout for lbw, but umpire Peter McConnell decided it was not out. If nothing else, it proved that there was plenty of seam movement off the pitch. The extra pace of Phillip DeFreitas soon made the breakthrough. Ramiz Raja played at a wide ball, seaming wider, and crunched it straight to Dermot Reeve fielding at point.

Things got decidedly worse for Pakistan with the very next ball. Inzamam-ul-Haq pushed tentatively at a ball seaming away and edged to Ian Botham at first slip. Botham spilled the chance, but a tumbling catch from Alec Stewart left Pakistan on 5/2. The crowd were excited, as DeFreitas had the opportunity for a hat-trick. Javed Miandad, Pakistan's stand-in captain, was the batter but wasn't required to defend the hat-trick ball, as DeFreitas's over-eagerness led to him sliding the ball down the leg side for a wide. Redemption was almost immediate, but was thwarted by Miandad's experience. Unlike Inzamam with his firm push, Miandad knew that soft hands were needed, so when DeFreitas took the edge, the ball fell short of the slips. Having played for Glamorgan and Sussex, Miandad would have experienced similar conditions where the ball would swing prodigiously.

In the ninth over, Pakistan were 9/2 and Pringle was proving to be difficult to bat against. A confident shout for caught behind was refused, again by umpire McConnell, before Miandad got one away for a welcome three runs. Batting partner Aamer Sohail looked to get after DeFreitas somewhat, but strong shots were defended well by the English fielders.

Having scored just three runs from 21 balls, Javed Miandad's frustration got the better of him, and he played on. Pringle's tight line and movement off the pitch tucked him up, and he could only get a bottom edge on to the stumps. Pakistan had 14 runs on the board for the loss of three wickets. Pringle took the wicket with the last ball of his sixth over. The first ball of his seventh saw Aamer Sohail try to hit him straight back down the pitch. Pringle stuck out his right hand, more of an automatic reaction than anything else as his follow-through took him away from the wicket, and the ball stuck for a brilliant caught-and-bowled. Pringle had his third wicket of the match and was on a hat-trick. Ijaz Ahmed defended the hat-trick ball, but Pakistan were in all kinds of trouble at 20/4 from 13 overs.

Salim Malik led the resistance with two boundaries off the next over as DeFreitas tired somewhat. They were the first of the match for Pakistan. Gladstone Small replaced Pringle and was soon amongst the wickets. Ijaz slashed at a ball and Stewart's athletic catch, in front of slip, reduced Pakistan to 32/5. After it had taken six balls for Small to break through, Ian Botham took only five as Wasim Akram tried to cut a ball that swung back into him, and played on. At 35/6, Pakistan were in dire trouble as England's bowlers were exploiting the favourable conditions. Scoring was proving to be difficult but, worryingly for Pakistan, wickets were falling regularly.

Salim Malik scored his, and Pakistan's, third boundary of the innings. However, he too perished when he pushed at a ball off Botham, and the edge just carried to Reeve at slip. Pakistan were now 42/7, and the statisticians quickly grabbed at their record books for low scores. Canada had been dismissed for 45, by England, in the 1979 Cricket World Cup, so Pakistan wouldn't want to break that record. Their lowest ever ODI score had been against England at Old Trafford in 1978, when they were bowled out for 85. Incidentally, both Botham and Miandad played in that game.

Wasim Haider joined Moin Khan at the wicket as the storm clouds increased over the Adelaide Oval. Pakistan managed to creep past 45, but more tight bowling, particularly from Botham, saw Moin cut Small to Hick in the gully, and Pakistan were on the brink at 47/8 in the 26th over. Over the next eight overs, the Pakistan tailenders pieced together the most significant partnership of the innings. Wasim Haider and Mushtaq Ahmed squeezed out 15 runs before Dermot Reeve tempted Haider into a rash shot and Stewart took another excellent catch. Haider's 13 runs came off 46 balls to move Pakistan to 62/9.

Mushtaq scored just the fifth boundary of the day off Small, with Pakistan needing to accumulate as many runs as they could. Gooch brought back Pringle, who soon removed Mushtaq, and Pakistan were all out for 74. Pringle finished with fabulous bowling figures of 8.2-5-8-3. Botham's miserly 10-4-12-2 and Reeve's 5-3-2-1 highlighted the difficulty of batting on the wicket.

Wasim Akram and Aaqib Javed opened the bowling for Pakistan. Aaqib struggled to control the ball with his extra pace, and conceded some wides. When he got the ball in the right spot, he was challenging to play. In the fourth over, a ball flew off the seam and cut straight across Gooch. The England captain nodded to acknowledge the ball. A rain shower took the players off for six minutes before play got underway again. Despite finding it slippery underfoot, Wasim removed Gooch for three. Bounce and seam movement tucked Gooch up, and Wasim appealed for caught behind. Umpire McConnell agreed while Gooch looked aggrieved, and England were 14/1.

Three more runs were added before lunch was taken because of the rain returning. This time, it was a longer delay and almost four hours was lost. Play finally recommenced at 5.12pm, with England set a target of 64 runs from 16 overs. Such was the unfairness of the rain rule, England's fine bowling display was working against them. A total that was easily achievable had become very much more difficult. If England did not face 15 overs, each team would get one point.

Seven more runs were scored from two overs, in damp conditions, before an elongated discussion between the umpires led to the players leaving the field again. The mood of the two teams was in stark contrast. Robin Smith and Ian Botham looked despondent, while Pakistan's players seemed content to take a point from the match. In Peter Miller and Dave Tickner's excellent critique of England's performances in one-day cricket, *28 Days' Data*, they sum up the situation that England faced if rain had not ended play. 'England were 24/1 after eight overs and, ridiculously, actually in danger of defeat. They still needed almost 40 from the remaining eight overs when further rain brought an ultimate end to the farce.'

Duckworth and Lewis have commented on how DL could have changed the game in Adelaide. 'Interestingly, the revised target for 16 overs would have been 36, just over two runs per over and more equitable than four per over. Had England seen rain coming then, with such a small target, they could easily have hit out to reach 36 to win in the eight overs they did have whereas 64 in eight overs was a taller task.'

A grey Monday morning in Wellington, at Basin Reserve, saw South Africa and Sri Lanka meet for the first time. A predictable northerly wind was blowing as about 4,500 fans were in attendance, with South Africa looking to bounce back after their disappointing defeat in Auckland. Sri Lanka's travels had taken them back from central Queensland to the North Island of New Zealand. The journey via Brisbane had taken 14 hours.

South Africa made several changes to their line-up, with spinner Omar Henry and batter Mark Rushmere coming in for

Tertius Bosch and Andrew Hudson. Sri Lanka, with only 12 fit players to choose from, brought spinner Don Anurasiri back into the team in place of Kapila Wijegunawardene. Both sides were reckoning on a slower-paced pitch, which had proved to be troublesome for South Africa at Eden Park.

The toss was conducted between Aravinda de Silva and Kepler Wessels and de Silva called correctly. Inserting South Africa, he was hoping for some early movement as well as his preference to chase. Wessels admitted that he too would have bowled first. Rushmere was expected to open the batting with him, but South Africa decided to promote Adrian Kuiper into a pinch-hitting role. Perhaps after they had seen Mark Greatbatch take them apart in their last game, vice-captain Kuiper was asked to perform a similar task for South Africa. If fireworks were the plan, South Africa started as if they weren't. Both openers played reservedly, and their running between the wickets wasn't exemplary. A mix-up in the fourth over almost led to a run-out as captain and vice-captain struggled with their calling.

Kuiper finally found the boundary for the first time in the sixth over with a textbook off drive. This was followed with a pick-up over midwicket for another boundary. Pramodya Wickramasinghe overpitched again, and Kuiper took full advantage. In Wickramasinghe's next over, Kuiper crashed another ball over the infield for his third boundary. It was clear that the bowler's extra pace suited Kuiper.

By the 14th over, South Africa were on 27, with both batters struggling to score. Kuiper decided it was time to accelerate against the spin of Anurasiri. Playing a shot, born of frustration and without foot movement, led to the fall of his wicket. Trying to hit over the midwicket area, he missed the ball and was bowled. Kuiper's 18 had come from 44 balls, and the pinch-hitting experiment had ended.

The introduction of Peter Kirsten initially led to an increase in the scoring rate. The pick of Kirsten's shots was a straight six back over Anurasiri's head. With de Silva rotating his bowlers and Sri Lanka fielding brilliantly, boundaries were at a premium. Wessels was still to find the boundary as the fifty partnership came up. Kirsten looked to use his feet, and that paid more dividends than Wessels's conservative approach.

With the score on 114, South Africa were rocked by the loss of two quick wickets. Kirsten's aggressive intent got the better of him when he holed out to Chandika Hathurusinghe for 47. Ruwan Kalpage's spin tempted Kirsten to use his feet, but he didn't clear the long-off fielder. Without adding to the total, Kepler Wessels also perished. As he tried to score down the wicket off the very medium pace of Arjuna Ranatunga, the ball flew invitingly for the bowler to take the catch. Wessels's innings, described as 'tedious' on the television commentary, was over for 40 from 94 balls.

South Africa found themselves with two new batters at the crease. Jonty Rhodes was in his third ODI, while Mark Rushmere was on debut. Both attempted to build a partnership, but a screamer of a catch from Sanath Jayasuriya ended Rushmere's innings for four runs. Ranatunga's inviting medium pace once again led to a South African wicket falling. Rushmere crashed the ball through the covers, but Jayasuriya's diving catch, described as the catch of the tournament so far by Henry Blofeld, left South Africa on 128/4 in the 39th over. Reflecting on his debut, Rushmere was regretful of batting down the order: 'I remember that the wicket was on the slow, and low, side and in retrospect, I probably should have opened the batting in that game which would have suited the team and me better.'

Hansie Cronje was the next man in, and he too found scoring difficult. Rhodes, on the other hand, was having more success. It was helped when Anurasiri couldn't hold a difficult chance. The technique employed by Rhodes was to play across his stumps and pull the ball square on the leg side. In a partnership of 21, Cronje added just three before Tillakaratne's smart stumping, off the bowling of Anurasiri.

Rhodes's rearguard action ended when Jayasuriya, diving to his left, pulled off his second stunning catch of the game.. Rhodes had scored 27 off 21 balls and looked as though he could pull the innings around for South Africa.

The score was 153/6 in the 43rd over, with all-rounders Brian McMillan and Richard Snell at the wicket. Snell found the boundary twice, a thick edge and a nice drive, before falling to Anurasiri. Trying to make room to play the ball square, Snell was late on the shot, and the stumps were broken. Seven wickets down became eight in the next over, when McMillan's hesitation for a run left David Richardson running to the danger end. Roshan Mahanama had one stump to aim at and, in keeping with Sri Lanka's spectacular fielding, hit to send the batter back for a diamond duck. South Africa had slipped to 165/8 with less than six overs left.

The final overs saw a lusty blow from Omar Henry go for four, the last one of the innings, but runs were still difficult to achieve for South Africa. Henry tried to repeat his successful shot in the 49th over, but Kalpage took the catch. Allan Donald was run out off the last ball of the innings as South Africa ended up 195 all out.

Champaka Ramanayake's 1–19 from nine overs made him the pick of the bowlers. Anurasiri finished with 3–41, while Ranatunga's six overs conceded 26 but picked up the wickets of Wessels and Rushmere. South Africa lost their last nine wickets for 81 runs from 85 balls as Sri Lanka stifled their batting. Already on three points from three games, Sri Lanka had the opportunity to win two games in a Cricket World Cup for the first time.

It was fair to say that Allan Donald's first two overs were eventful. The sun came out, and the new white ball was carrying through to David Richardson behind the stumps. The ball also went for six wides and an over-the-shoulder no-ball, which flew off the bat and over Kepler Wessels's outstretched hand for four. In amongst those cheap runs for Sri Lanka were two fast and nasty balls that took wickets. Hathurusinghe was first to go when he fended a rising ball to Wessels at slip. New batter Asanka Gurusinha's lack of footwork left him plumb in front of the stumps as the Sri Lankans slipped to 12/2.

McMillan shared the new ball with Donald. Mahanama and de Silva appeared to enjoy the sweet relief of not facing 'White Lightning' and scored several boundaries. McMillan's line erred slightly and he was made to pay. Sri Lanka were looking comfortable and intent on chasing South Africa's score, but Donald upset that, and de Silva's off stump, with an inswinging yorker. South Africa were back in the match as Sri Lanka's captain trudged off for seven, leaving Sri Lanka at 35/3 in the tenth over.

Mahanama and Tillakaratne set about consolidating the innings, safe in the knowledge that Donald's spell was over. The spin of Henry was more palatable while Snell, albeit fast-medium, wasn't express speed. Tillakaratne still felt Snell's pace when a ball seamed off the pitch into a delicate area of the left-hander's midriff. Having batted for 19 overs, and added 67 runs to the total, Tillakaratne's slog sweep of Henry found Rushmere on the boundary. It was an unnecessary risk, as Sri Lanka were ahead of South Africa and building the innings nicely. Arjuna Ranatunga came to the crease, bringing a wealth of experience to the situation, with Sri Lanka at 87/4 in the 29th over.

While Mahanama nudged and caressed the ball, Ranatunga played his aggressive game. Relishing the extra pace of Donald when he was brought back on to bowl, he launched into his strokes. The partnership developed as South Africa struggled to extract the same movement off the pitch that they had been subjected to. By the 42nd over, Sri Lanka reached 150 and momentum was swinging back their way.

Having been at the crease for three hours, Mahanama played a tired-looking shot off McMillan and could only edge it to Richardson, and he was out for 68 from 121 balls. Mahanama's innings of delicate shots had finally seen him perish to one. Still needing 42 from seven overs, Sri Lanka weren't home yet. With them needing a run a ball to win, Wessels didn't have too many overs left from his main bowlers. Peter Kirsten and Adrian Kuiper shared the fifth bowler duty, which proved to be the least economical of the match. Kirsten did, however, get his captain a wicket when Jayasuriya played a curious sweep shot and overbalanced. Richardson did the rest, and Sri Lanka were 168/6 in the 45th over.

If Sri Lanka were to win, it would need Ranatunga to take them home. Despite struggling to hit boundaries, he took singles with Ruwan Kalpage. A boundary did come, in the 48th over off the bowling of Donald, leaving Sri Lanka needing 13 for victory. By the time Donald came to bowl the last over, seven runs were still required. They had four wickets in hand, but the game was finely balanced.

The first delivery of the over was fast, and Ranatunga missed the ball. Kalpage decided to run to the danger end, but Ranatunga stood firm. With two Sri Lankan batters at one end, it was an easy run-out. Ramanayake went to the non-striker's end, while Donald walked back to his mark. The second ball, on leg stump, was lifted beautifully by Ranatunga into the vast open spaces of midwicket and it ran away to the boundary. The equation was now three runs required off four balls.

The third ball was squeezed out to gully, who missed the stumps with his throw, and Sri Lanka needed two from three to win. The big problem, however, was that Ranatunga was now at the non-striker's end. Ramanayake was left with the task of hitting the winning runs, or at least getting a single to tie, off Donald. A fast full toss led to a dot ball, and the equation was now two runs off two balls. The fifth ball was quick and outside off stump. Ramanayake played a flashing square drive, and the ball ran away to the vacant boundary, with all the fielders trying to save a single, and Sri Lanka had won the match by three wickets.

Ranatunga's 64 not out off 73 balls secured him the Man-of-the-Match award and Sri Lanka's second win in the tournament. Aravinda de Silva described it as 'one of our greatest victories' as Sri Lanka went joint second in the table. Kepler Wessels was left to rue the lack of runs and his bowlers conceding 13 wides, 'We lost wickets at the wrong times, I got out at the wrong time. I should have batted through.'

The politics of South Africa's entry was evident during the match, as a billboard relating to the impending referendum was present at Basin Reserve. The vote, for white South Africans, would decide whether South Africa would push on for constitutional reform. If so, apartheid would end, and the billboard was for reform: it stated 'South Africa Vote Yes on March 17'. With the vote over two weeks away, it was too early to contemplate the effects of a potential 'no' result.

The Cricket World Cup stayed in New Zealand for the next game at a grey, and then frustratingly wet, McLean Park in Napier. New Zealand and Zimbabwe selected their teams and conducted the coin toss before heavy drizzle prevented play getting off on time. Martin Crowe decided to play Danny Morrison, rather than

Willie Watson, because of the pace of the wicket. The rain soon dampened those thoughts. David Houghton, rather strangely in light of the rain rules and impending precipitation, won the toss and asked New Zealand to bat.

Like Sri Lanka, Zimbabwe had only 12 fit players, so Iain Butchart and Mark Burmester came into the team. Burmester was making his ODI debut for Zimbabwe. An earth tremor shook Napier on the night before the game, but Burmester's mind was firmly on the match, 'The first I heard of it was at breakfast the next day. Must have been all the fresh air – I slept through the whole thing.' Kevin Duers also recalls missing the tremor and finding out on the morning of the match.

By the time play did get underway, some 75 minutes after the scheduled start, the match had already been reduced to 43 overs per side. Mark Greatbatch and Rod Latham opened the batting, while Eddo Brandes took the new ball for Zimbabwe. Despite the rain, Brandes extracted some bounce out of the pitch. The first boundary came when Greatbatch appeared to glance a ball off his hip, but umpire Karl Liebenberg called byes. With rain imminent, Brandes commenced the third over and comprehensively bowled Latham. With leg stump knocked straight out of the ground, the partisan crowd were stunned. The feelings soon turned to frustration and disappointment as the umpires led the teams off the field with the rain worsening. Andrew Jones had walked out on the fall of the wicket, but had to turn right around and go back.

The delay led to the New Zealand innings being truncated once again. On the resumption, it was now a 35-over game. In the fifth over, bowled by Brandes, Greatbatch took him on. A well-timed boundary through the covers was followed up with a bottom-handed shot over the bowler's head for a one-bounce four. Twelve runs were conceded as Greatbatch continued his form from Eden Park. With the rain intensifying again, Duers squeezed the ball past Greatbatch's swing across the line. The inside edge did the rest, and New Zealand were 25/2 in the sixth over.

With the situation requiring runs to be scored quickly, both Andrew Jones and Martin Crowe played a series of controlled shots over, and through, the infield. Wet conditions made fielding difficult for Zimbabwe, and more rain made play impossible once again. In the 12th over, at 52/2, umpire Dooland Buultjens took the teams off again. Another reduction in overs meant that the contest would now be 24 overs per side, which changed the nature of the game once again. The playing conditions were not ideal, and Iain Butchart slipped over twice coming in to bowl, much to the amusement of the crowd. If he was feeling physical pain from his fall, Jones's thick edge for four added to Butchart's woes. The final ball flew down through third man for another boundary to end the over. Crowe took ten off the next over as New Zealand's acceleration continued.

Like many young New Zealanders, Jason Stewart was in awe of Martin Crowe. Stewart represented New Zealand in the 2004 Olympics in the 800 metres, but was just an admiring fan in 1992. Born in Napier, Stewart attended the game to see his heroes, but particularly Crowe, in action. 'He entered like a gladiator. The now folklore Duncan Fearnley bat, that every cricket-following kid in New Zealand wanted, under his arm and the equally legendary sweat bandana flowing out from the back of his helmet. Crowe came out, and from ball one was a man possessed. It probably took at least six balls before I started to realise that he is not just despatching balls with ease because they were bad ones, it's because he was on absolute fire, in the form of his life and simply could. Of course, it was at least a few months or maybe even years before I realised that he was doing this out of necessity given the meteorological state of play.'

Crowe and Jones's expansive play now turned to outright aggression. Zimbabwe did not help themselves in the field, partly due to the sodden outfield, but they struggled to contain the batters in full flight. Crowe hit his second six of the match, off the bowling of Shah, to the delight of the New Zealand fans. His fifty came up off 30 balls to set a new record for the fastest Cricket World Cup fifty. Andy Waller, fielding for Zimbabwe, witnessed his record of ten days disappear.

Shah, Butchart and Burmester all suffered as Crowe and Jones smashed them to all parts. With the ball flying around McLean Park, a sensational catch from Andy Waller finally broke the partnership. Jones hit Butchart back over his head, but a running catch saw him depart for 57 off 58 balls. The partnership was worth 129 in less than an hour's play. After the resumption, Crowe and Jones had scored 110 off 57 balls.

The innings was ended soon after, for 162/3 from 20.5 overs, as rain once again stopped play. Martin Crowe finished with 74 from 44 balls, having hit eight fours and two sixes. David Houghton's field placements failed to stop Crowe as he worked the ball where the fielders had moved from. It was a special innings from a special player.

The Zimbabwe bowling figures showed Duers and Brandes with respectable figures, but Butchart's 1–53 came off just four overs. Shah went for 34 off his four overs, while Burmester's 11 balls conceded 17. Duers, looking back at the game, recognised his fortune in bowling at the start: 'The game was a difficult one with the rain. Bowling and fielding became very difficult with a wet ball. I was lucky to get a few overs in early before the wet conditions made it difficult. Martin Crowe was in great form, and even a good ball was going for runs. It was just a matter of trying to contain the two of them and hope they made a mistake and got themselves out.'

One bowler who wasn't subject to the onslaught, despite being in the team, was John Traicos. He was grateful not to have to bowl in the conditions. 'David Houghton, probably correctly, felt that I would struggle to hold a wet ball although I am not sure that I would have enjoyed the experience of bowling at Martin Crowe and Andrew Jones in full flight.'

Zimbabwe's total was reduced once the rain stopped, but they faced a tall order. Their target was 154 from 18 overs, which equated to 8.56 runs per over. Andy Flower and Andy Waller, asked to perform the pinch-hitting role, opened for Zimbabwe. The first over, from Danny Morrison, was reasonably uneventful considering the required run rate was so high. Chris Cairns ran in to start the second over, and Waller heaved the first ball for four runs. A single followed before Andy Flower also took a liking to Cairns and carved him away for another boundary. Another single, from another wayward delivery, brought Waller back on strike. Cairns dropped short again and this time saw the ball sail high over the boundary for six.

With the score on 22, Morrison found some away swing and Waller was comprehensively bowled. Having made the breakthrough, Crowe wanted to keep the pressure on Zimbabwe, so he replaced Cairns with Larsen. Flower and David Houghton continued to punish anything loose, but New Zealand were tidying up the line and length. The pressure was building, and Houghton tried to use his feet to the medium pace of Larsen, but was beaten by movement off the pitch and was bowled for 11. The score was 41/2 in the eighth over, with the required run rate now above 11 per over.

Cairns was brought back into the attack, but was no more effective than in his first over. Flower punished him once again, and he had conceded 27 runs from his two overs. Larsen's last over effectively ended the contest for Zimbabwe by picking up two wickets. The first was Butchart, trying to find the boundary via the aerial route, but Cairns at long-on took the catch safely. Flower's impressive innings of 30 ended ignominiously when his slog across the line missed the ball and he was bowled. Zimbabwe were 63/4 and sinking fast. However, the incoming rain clouds suggested that the weather may still decide the game.

The dismissal of Eddo Brandes, promoted up the order for his aggressive qualities, did nothing to change the result of the game. The rain that started to fall could still earn Zimbabwe a point. Having not bowled the 15 overs required to constitute a match, Crowe and his men were anxious to keep the game moving. Between balls, the fielders ran to get into position in readiness. The left- and right-hand combination, Alistair Campbell and Andy Pycroft, added to the urgency as Crowe's anxiety to get Harris through the over became more visible. Campbell skied the fifth ball of the over and Crowe was the fielder in position to take the catch. He did so competently, but later admitted that he had considered dropping the ball so as not to lose time for the change of batters.

The last three overs of the match, effectively redundant with Zimbabwe so far behind, saw a further wicket fall before they ended their innings on 105/7. Harris's 3–15 and Larsen's 3–16 stifled the Zimbabwe batters' ability to score. The margin of victory, New Zealand's fourth of the tournament, was 48 runs. Topping the table, New Zealand needed just one more point to secure a place in the semi-finals. Martin Crowe was given the Man-of-the-Match award for his batting.

The use of more updated, revised total calculations would not have changed the result. Stern calculated that the DL total was 150, while DLS gave 156, which was higher than the MPO total that Zimbabwe chased. Whatever method was used, New Zealand would have easily won the game.

Wednesday, 4 March brought together two bitter cricketing rivals in India and Pakistan. The venue for their first clash in the Cricket World Cup was the SCG. It was a day/night game that had been threatened by days of rain in the lead-up. The weather cleared for the match as an estimated television audience of 250 million tuned in to watch. If history was anything to rely upon, Pakistan had the upper hand in ODIs. Of the 37 matches played to date, they had won 24. The recent form was even more convincing, with India having won only once in the last ten games played.

India made one personnel change, with Ravi Shastri being rested or dropped for slow scoring, depending on which source you believe, and Vinod Kambli coming back into the team. Young all-rounder Ajay Jadeja took Shastri's place at the top of the batting order. Pakistan's line-up was buoyed by the inclusion of their captain, Imran Khan, in place of Ijaz Ahmed; but they lost experienced opener Ramiz Raja to a shoulder injury. Zahid Fazal came into the team to play his first match of the Cricket World Cup.

Just over 10,000 fans were at the SCG to witness Mohammed Azharuddin win the toss and decide to bat. Fans from both sides were making plenty of noise and waving their flags, as Wasim Akram bowled the first over. A wicket could have fallen early on when Jadeja's inside edge missed the stumps, but it ran safely away for runs. Two overs later, Akram was denied another wicket as Srikkanth's edge somehow found its way to the ground rather than stay safe on Moin Khan's glove.

At the other end, Aaqib Javed was also giving Srikkanth problems. The usually aggressive opener was struggling to score. Aaqib had rapped his pads on a couple of occasions before finally teasing an edge, and this time Moin Khan held on. Srikkanth, having scored a pedestrian five runs from 41 balls, waited for the umpire's decision and David Shepherd duly sent him on his way. With 25 runs on the board, Indian captain Mohammed Azharuddin came to the wicket.

A slowish start – which had almost ended before it had started, with a suicidal single – was soon turned around by Jadeja and Azharuddin. Any width was punished with some attractive strokeplay. Pakistan captain Imran Khan decided he would have a bowl, his first of the tournament, as the partnership grew. Azharuddin hit two boundaries off Imran, in successive overs, with delightful drives. In the 19th over, India brought up the fifty with a single. The introduction of Wasim Haider did nothing to break the partnership, so Imran threw the ball to his leg-spinner, Mushtaq Ahmed. Jadeja's answer to that was to get to the pitch of the ball and hit it over the cover area for a boundary. Having seen his junior partner hit the ball in the air, Azharuddin did the same to Mushtaq. His shot was back over the bowler's head for a one-bounce four. The bowler ended the over with a victory, as the Indian captain's cut shot flicked the ball to Moin Khan. The catch was well held, as Mushtaq had spun the ball hard and Azharuddin's cut shot had flown straight at the wicketkeeper. India were 86/2 in the 25th over.

Vinod Kambli came in at four as Jadeja carried on his plan to attack Mushtaq. In Mushtaq's next over, the opener smashed the ball back down the ground. Jadeja's attacking strokeplay became his downfall when he found Zahid Fazal, at cover, off a leg-side half-volley from Haider. Jadeja stood his ground as the Pakistan players congregated to celebrate the wicket. David Shepherd, presiding over the claim, walked over to Peter McConnell for confirmation of the catch. Having received affirmation,

Shepherd raised his finger, and Jadeja walked off, fuelled by disbelief and frustration. An innings of 46 from the all-rounder left India at 101/3.

Sachin Tendulkar was batting at five, and after he had joined Kambli at the crease, the old school friends looked to push India's total on with just under 22 overs left. Tendulkar and Kambli rotated the strike, as you would expect from players who knew each other's play intimately, as Pakistan bowled their middle overs. In the 38th over, Tendulkar played two shots that oozed class. Sohail dropped short, and Tendulkar rocked back and pulled exquisitely. As he tried to adjust, a ball that was full but wide was cut away for another boundary. The maturity and shot selection were sublime even without factoring in Tendulkar's tender age of just 18 years.

The reintroduction of Mushtaq threatened to turn the game in Pakistan's direction. Kambli, using his feet to the leg-spinner, found himself slightly cramped and hit the ball straight to Inzamam-ul-Haq in the deep. Sanjay Manjrekar's tenure at the crease lasted one ball, as he edged on to the stumps to give Mushtaq two wickets in two balls. With ten overs left, India had slipped to 147/5.

It was not quite a crisis, but India were definitely in need of some positive play, and who better than Kapil Dev to come out to bat? And so it proved as the all-rounder imposed himself on the bowlers. Mushtaq was hit over the top to the cover boundary. A few overs later, an even bigger hit went for six at the same boundary. Tendulkar joined in but almost perished when Haider failed to hold on to a diving attempt. The fielder injured himself during his valiant effort and had to leave the field.

Tendulkar's fifty came up off Wasim Akram, off 57 balls, while his senior partner was scoring at over a run a ball. A poorly executed slower ball from Aaqib Javed, which manifested as a slow full toss, was despatched by Kapil Dev. But the bowler finally got his man when a better slower ball was pulled straight to Imran Khan. Pakistan's captain took the catch to leave India on 208/6 in the 48th over. During Kapil's innings of 35 runs from 26 balls, India added 60 to their total in just 49 balls.

India finished up on 216/7 after losing Kiran More to a fabulous piece of cricket from Wasim Akram. A toe-crushing yorker to More was just dug out, leaving the batter on his knees. Tendulkar decided to take the run anyway, leaving More with a sprint to make his ground. Wasim's follow-up took him almost to the ball, which he picked up; then he turned and threw down the stumps. Tendulkar was left on 54 not out from 62 balls. Pakistan were not permitted to bowl the last over, as the innings passed the 6pm cut-off time.

Under the lights of the SCG, Pakistan's innings got underway. Inzamam-ul-Haq opened, in place of Ramiz Raja, with Aamer Sohail. The first two overs generated eight runs. Having scored just two, Inzamam shuffled across his stumps to try to work a ball to the leg side. Kapil Dev exerted some swing, and the ball thundered into the pads for an easy lbw decision. The 18-year-old Zahid Fazal struggled against the movement that Kapil Dev and Manoj Prabhakar were getting. His torment was over when he pushed at another ball, unsure whether to play or leave, and edged it to Kiran More. Pakistan were reduced to 17/2 in the sixth over.

Javed Miandad's arrival at the wicket should have led to a period of consolidation. Instead, Aamer Sohail played a series of shots that could have led to his dismissal – but the ball always went wide of fielders or over the top and to safety. Both batters ran hard as India's bowlers started to look frustrated. Tendulkar was brought into the attack, but Sohail crashed the ball through the covers as his confidence began to build.

Azharuddin brought on the spin of Venkatapathy Raju to build pressure. Tendulkar also tightened the screw. Both bowlers had confident shouts for stumpings, Kiran More vociferously appealing, but no decision was given by the umpires. Tension boiled over in the 25th over when Miandad pulled away from facing Tendulkar and made several remarks to More before gesturing to David Shepherd to intervene. Finally, play resumed, and a quick single was taken. Despite Miandad comfortably making his ground, More whipped the bails off. This was the final indignation for Miandad. Grabbing his bat, he jumped up and down on the spot as if to appeal, to mock More. The crowd reacted to the incident, generally, with laughter. At the end of the over, the umpires spoke to Miandad, and Azharuddin, to end the issue. Neither the on-field officials nor the match referee would ignore the incident.

Play settled back down, and Pakistan reached 105/2 from 30 overs. India had scored the same number of runs, with the loss of one more wicket, at the same stage. At this point, Pakistan lost their third wicket. Sohail's innings of 62 ended when he picked out Kris Srikkanth at midwicket from a Tendulkar low full toss. The partnership was worth 88 but, crucially, India had the breakthrough. Salim Malik was the new batter, and Miandad was quick to offer his advice. Even when Malik found the boundary, Miandad came down the wicket to impart his views. Miandad's counsel proved futile when Malik flashed at a ball, outside off stump, from Prabhakar. The edge flew to the embattled More.

Joining Miandad at the wicket was Imran Khan. Both were immensely experienced and had played at all five Cricket World Cups, but were never ones to see eye to eye. However, their country needed them to gel, with Pakistan needing 90 to win off the last 15 overs. Three runs later, this was proven to be impossible. Imran played a defensive shot and seemed hesitant to take a single. Miandad was committed and called Imran through. Finally deciding to run, after a stop-start effort, meant that he had too much ground to cover. More's pick-up and throw to Raju was too good, and Pakistan were now 130/5 with their captain out for a five-ball duck.

Over the next four overs, India's grip on the game was tightened. Raju should have taken a caught-and-bowled chance earlier in the over as Wasim Akram's firm shot carried to the bowler. Using his feet again, Akram missed the arm ball, and More stumped the Pakistan all-rounder for four. In the next over, Javagal Srinath bowled Miandad off the bottom edge of his bat for 40. The inswinging yorker was too good for Miandad, and India were in ecstasy. The innings had taken up 113 balls, but Pakistan's chance of victory seemed to disappear with that wicket. At 141/7 with less than nine overs to go, and with Moin Khan and Wasim Haider at the wicket, the game was India's to lose.

Haider and Moin tried to keep Pakistan in the game. The latter scored off some lusty blows, but perished when hitting Kapil Dev over midwicket. Manjrekar took the catch as Pakistan self-destructed. Mushtaq was the victim of another terrible run-out from a miscommunication, before Srinath ended the innings by bowling Haider in the last over. Pakistan were all out for 173 to give India a victory by 43 runs. Having lost their last eight wickets for 68 runs, Pakistan would rue the middle-order collapse. India, on the other hand, were buoyant, claiming a win after narrow defeats against England and Australia. Sachin Tendulkar took the Man-of-the-Match award.

After the match, umpires Peter McConnell and David Shepherd reported the Miandad–More incident to the match referee, Ted Wykes. One aspect of the clash that was omitted was the verbal exchange. The players were speaking in Hindi and Urdu, so the umpires did not know what exactly was said. Wykes talked to both team managers, Abbas Ali Baig of India and Intikhab Alam of Pakistan, to sort the problem out, but no sanctions were made against either player.

The rain in Adelaide gave New Zealand clear daylight at the top of the table. India's important win pushed them up the table, while South Africa's second defeat left them in eighth place.

	Pld	Won	Lost	Tied	N/R	Pts	Net R/R	For	Against
New Zealand	4	4	0	0	0	8	1.079	802/150.5	712/168.0
England	3	2	0	0	1	5	0.568	396/89.5	384/100.0
Sri Lanka	4	2	1	0	1	5	−0.027	717/149.1	717/148.2
West Indies	3	2	1	0	0	4	0.303	642/146.5	569/139.5
India	4	1	2	0	1	3	0.226	677/146.0	644/146.0
Pakistan	4	1	2	0	1	3	−0.033	647/149.0	638/145.5
Australia	3	1	2	0	0	2	−0.321	616/146.0	653/143.5
South Africa	3	1	2	0	0	2	−0.406	556/146.5	559/133.2
Zimbabwe	4	0	4	0	0	0	−1.077	807/168.0	984/167.2

Chapter Seven

Happy and Glorious

For the 100th match in the Cricket World Cup's history, the action moved back across the Tasman Sea, with South Africa and the West Indies clashing at Lancaster Park in Christchurch on Thursday, 5 March. The West Indies Cricket Board had been opposed to South Africa's inclusion, and this was the first time that the teams had met in an officially sanctioned game. There had been two rebel tours to South Africa, in 1982/83 and 1983/84, but they hadn't previously met under ICC regulations. On the eve of the match, a Test match between the two teams was announced, for April 1992, to be played in Barbados.

It was an important game politically, but South Africa were desperate for a win. Colin Bryden, who covered the tournament for South African media, witnessed the pressure first-hand. 'Kepler [Wessels] got quite grumpy, and the team seemed pretty tense ahead of the match against the West Indies. Kepler was upset by criticism and some abusive messages from South Africa. I quoted him as making a sarcastic comment about "the South African media, those great experts who expect us to score eight runs an over against Curtly Ambrose".'

The chilly and grey weather of New Zealand's South Island would not be to either team's liking. South Africa had not adapted to the softer wickets, while the West Indies would have preferred a bouncier track. The greenish tint to the pitch led the West Indies to contemplate bowling two spinners, whereas South Africa decided to discard theirs. Despite Omar Henry being the most economical bowler against Sri Lanka, he lost his place to Meyrick Pringle.

It would be a piece of good fortune for Pringle, after having some misfortune at the team hotel, when he lost some money in a freak accident. Pringle takes up the story: 'We were called room by room by the team manager Alan Jordaan to collect our daily expenses. I held the lift door open for Allan Donald to get into the lift; [the money] slipped out of my hand and went down that tiny slit as you enter the lift. They had to get lift services to come out and try to find the cash in the envelope. I eventually received it about a week later.'

Having tried and failed with the pinch-hitter to open, South Africa resorted to Andrew Hudson's more traditional opener role, which had served well against Australia. Hansie Cronje, with just two single-figure scores so far, was the man to make way. The West Indies brought back Desmond Haynes and Curtly Ambrose, for Phil Simmons and Patrick Patterson, after resting them. Despite the amount of grass on the surface, the pitch looked as though it would carry through for the faster bowlers. Richie Richardson won the toss and had no hesitation in bowling first. South African captain Kepler Wessels, who would have bowled first had he won the toss, expected the ball to move around in the first 15 overs. The overcast conditions seemed conducive to seam bowling.

Ambrose bowled the first over, to Hudson, and could have picked up a wicket early. He was beaten by the bounce, and his inside edge narrowly missed the stumps before running away for the first runs of the day. South Africa's luck did not last for long, as Malcolm Marshall's pace extracted extra bounce; Wessels's leading edge flew straight up into the air, and Haynes took the catch. The breakthrough was made with eight runs on the board in the fourth over.

Both Marshall and Ambrose kept tight lines to stifle the scoring. Hudson and new batter Peter Kirsten had to work for scraps. In the tenth over, a sloppy piece of fielding from Winston Benjamin led to a boundary. Marshall stood at the crease, glaring in Benjamin's direction until his humour mellowed enough for him to return to his mark. In the next over, Hudson pulled Ambrose square of the wicket for another boundary to take the score to 27/1.

The change of bowling, with Benjamin and Anderson Cummins coming on, brought slight respite albeit still with fast bowling. Kirsten pulled Benjamin for four to bring up the fifty in the 17th over. Another breakthrough, Hudson cutting Cummins to Lara at point, brought Mark Rushmere to the wicket. Looking back at his innings, Rushmere commented on his trepidation: 'To be honest it was pretty nerve-wracking facing the likes of Ambrose, Marshall etc., as they were world-class fast bowlers and had been on the international stage for many, many years. I was feeling pretty good before being given out stumped off Carl Hooper – a very close call and I could have been given the benefit of the doubt.'

Before losing the third wicket, South Africa had run hard to turn singles into twos, and they were starting to increase the scoring now Hooper was bowling spin. Rushmere was out, from a good piece of glovework from David Williams, not getting his foot behind the batting crease when trying to run the ball down to third man. Mike Procter, on TV commentary, thought that the decision was a good one. Despite the disagreement of the crowd, South Africa were 73/3 in the 25th over.

Having scored 28 runs, Peter Kirsten then pulled a calf muscle. He needed a runner, and that caused much consternation. Adrian Kuiper proved he was more suited to batting down the order with some good strokes. Enjoying Hooper's leg stump line, both batters turned him down to fine leg for runs. More lackadaisical fielding from the West Indies, particularly Benjamin, leaked runs for South Africa. Benjamin was also on the end of a fantastic leg-side boundary from Kuiper to bring up South Africa's hundred. He dismissively flicked the ball over the boundary, and it sailed into the stands for six. The South African batters were gaining confidence and putting pressure on the fielding, which had already proven to be somewhat lacking.

Ambrose was brought back into the attack. He extracted some extra bounce, leaving Kirsten to fend the ball away, but the resultant single brought up his fifty. In the same over, Ambrose bowled a full toss on off stump to Kuiper, who missed it, to get himself a deserved wicket. The ball looked as though it dipped, which resulted in Kuiper yorking himself. The partnership had been broken, and South Africa were 119/4. In the same over, more poor fielding led to four overthrows, and Ambrose's good humour lessened quickly.

The return of Marshall engineered a wicket as Kirsten could only edge a sharp ball to the diving wicketkeeper, David Williams. Kirsten's painstaking innings of 56 from 91 balls was over. Marshall's potency could have removed Brian McMillan with an inside edge, but it raced away for a boundary. Marshall stood at the crease, grimacing and scratching his head. McMillan walked past him and tapped him on the back to acknowledge the ball. It was a marvellous piece of cricket in light of the historical context of the match.

Jonty Rhodes played another impish innings as he pushed the ball around the field and sprinted runs. He scored nine from the 39th over, with four twos and a single. His innings ended when he edged Cummins behind for Williams's second catch. Rhodes scored 22 from 27 balls without hitting a boundary. McMillan and Richardson added 22 runs before a miscued shot from the former flew high into the air and Lara took a good catch in front of his body. Snell didn't last too long, losing his wicket in the same manner, before Richardson and Pringle took South Africa to 200/8 from their 50 overs. Marshall's 2–26 had made him the pick of the West Indian bowlers, but the team's fielding was poor and they leaked unnecessary runs.

The West Indian response started well. Lara looked in good form with a driven four in the second over, before cutting viciously in the next over. As he tried to cut again, Rhodes took a sharp, low chance at backward point. The West Indies moved on to 19/1, and then Pringle bowled 11 balls that he would be remembered for to this day and beyond. His recollection sums up what happened next. 'It was one of those days where it all went the right way, balls put in the right place and areas, the wicket did assist a bit as well, and the overcast conditions. I think I went for eight, two fours by Lara; then all hell broke loose.'

His first victim was West Indies captain Richie Richardson. Pringle had been pitching the ball up to give it a chance to swing. Richardson tried to heave the ball through mid-on, but it beat him for pace and swing. As it thundered into his pads, right in front of the stumps, umpire Steve Randell swiftly signalled that it was out. The next victim was Carl Hooper. Playing a shot as casually as his captain had done, Hooper steered the ball towards the slips, and Kepler Wessels took a straightforward catch. South Africa were in the ascendancy, while the West Indies were in disarray. Pringle's tormenting was complete when Keith

Arthurton slashed at a wide ball and, again, the South African captain was on hand to take the catch. In the space of 11 balls, Pringle had taken four wickets to derail the West Indies' reply. At 19/4, it would be difficult to find a way back into the match.

Gus Logie was resolute in mounting a response, but, in typical West Indies fashion, was happy to throw the bat at anything wide. McMillan was guilty of straying, and Logie pounced. Also, Haynes was determined to put away any width from South Africa. However, a damaged index finger that he had come into the match with would force him to retire hurt. At 50/4, a ball from Richard Snell slammed into Haynes's hand, which was greeted by an audible scream of pain. In obvious discomfort, he left the field to be replaced by Malcolm Marshall. The West Indies were now in deeper trouble.

Logie's response to the situation was to pull Adrian Kuiper for six. It appeared that the West Indies' plan was to play their natural game, despite it not working to this point. Kuiper's reply was to bowl a similar line and length, but Logie could only help himself to four on this occasion. Wessels looked distinctly unhappy as his bowler was struggling to find the right line. Malcolm Marshall's brief resistance was ended when he smashed a wide ball from Richard Snell straight at Jonty Rhodes. Having clipped the bowler for a boundary in his previous over, Marshall's tendencies got the better of him to give Snell his first wicket of the match. One wicket soon became two when David Williams nicked behind in the same over.

With the West Indies, at 70/6, needing a miracle, it was Desmond Haynes who returned to the crease. At 13 not out, the opener resumed his innings instead of heading to the hospital for X-rays. Logie's continued aggressive streak meant that Haynes could take a back seat. Logie reached his fifty, in the 27th over, by hitting Kuiper for three consecutive boundaries. Logie's fifty came from 53 balls, as his stroke-making was not in keeping with the rest of his team's efforts.

Haynes could have been caught, off the wayward Kuiper, with the score on 100/6, but the flying attempt from David Richardson was not enough. The result was another boundary off the all-rounder. Having scored 30, a superb effort with a damaged finger, Haynes finally succumbed when he edged an attempted drive to Richardson. It was another wide ball from Kuiper, the first of a new spell, but he picked up the wicket on this occasion. The partnership had been worth 46 this time around. Haynes's earlier attempt had been worth 31, but the opener could now go to the hospital knowing he couldn't help his team any further.

In keeping with the pattern of the innings, the West Indies soon lost another wicket and any hope of victory. Logie's aggressive hitting finally failed him, and the ball lofted out to Pringle at mid-on, who took a simple catch to add to his already excellent day. It gave Kuiper his second wicket of the over. Logie's innings of 61 came from 69 balls and had prevented the West Indies from a collapse. With the score on 117/8, it was only a matter of time before South Africa would take the win.

Curtly Ambrose came in and struck two boundaries, before a mix-up with Anderson Cummins led to him being run out. Kuiper's throw was too good, with only one stump to aim at, as the tall fast bowler struggled to make his ground. Allan Donald mopped up the tail when Cummins was caught at second slip by Brian McMillan. The innings ended on 136 and South Africa's victory was by 64 runs.

Pringle's 4–11 from eight overs, with four maidens, secured the Man-of-the-Match award. He was backed up by Donald's 1–13 from 6.4 overs and Snell's 2–16 from seven overs. Kuiper's nine overs went for 51, but he did capture Haynes and Logie. The win had stopped a two-game losing streak for the South Africans as they headed back to Australia. The West Indies were heading to Auckland to take on New Zealand.

On the same day, the SCG was the venue for Australia and England's match. Games involving Australia did not need any intervention to make them tense, but comments from the Australian prime minister were used, by the British press, to fan the flames. Paul Keating had made comments about Britain 'abandoning' Australia during World War II, which were jumped upon by media outlets. More importantly, Australia needed a win to keep their semi-final aspirations on track. With them having just two points from three games, and being eighth in the table, a defeat would dent their hopes. A win for England would see them just a point behind the unbeaten New Zealanders.

Australia decided to shuffle their pack once again, and Geoff Marsh found himself surplus to requirements. Tom Moody was asked to open with Mark Taylor. Ian Healy's return to fitness gave the Australians a boost; meanwhile, Merv Hughes was left out and Bruce Reid took his place. England used the same personnel as in the Pakistan game except that spinner Phil Tufnell was preferred to Gladstone Small despite the latter having taken 2–29 in Adelaide.

Allan Border won the toss and decided, on a slow but good wicket, to post a total for England to chase. Also, England's innings would be under lights, as this was a day/night match. Almost 39,000 fans packed into the SCG to see the old enemies clash once again. The last time the two teams had met in the Cricket World Cup was the 1987 final. Having safely negotiated the first two overs, Australia's fragile batting was put under pressure. Derek Pringle's swing bowling, aided by the humid conditions, enticed Moody to push at a ball. Nicking the edge of the bat, the ball bounced agonisingly in front of Dermot Reeve at slip. Later in the over, Mark Taylor was not so fortunate and was caught in front of the stumps for a duck. Pringle moved the ball back into the left-hander, and umpire Khizer Hayat did the rest. With just five runs on the scoreboard, it was not the start that Australia wanted.

David Boon came to the crease and looked to assert himself. Having already scored 170 runs in three innings, the Tasmanian was in fine form. He cut Chris Lewis away for a boundary in the sixth over, before repeating the stroke off Pringle. Lewis gave Moody the opportunity to cut in the tenth over as England's fast bowler strayed too far outside off stump. In the same over, Boon's run-out curse struck again. Looking for a quick single, Moody soon saw the danger that Neil Fairbrother posed. Boon, however, was advancing down the wicket when Moody sent him back. Fairbrother's throw was too fast and accurate for Boon, and his innings was over for 18. It was the third run-out in four Cricket World Cup innings for Boon, leaving Australia on 35/2.

Dean Jones walked out to the strains of 'You're not singing any more' as the English fans borrowed a chant from their football counterparts. Sensible batting, plus Alec Stewart's fumble giving away two byes, brought up the fifty as Jones and Moody looked assured. The introduction of Ian Botham's gentle medium-pacers was greeted, by Jones, with a confident hit through the air on the leg side for four runs. Moody played a similar shot some time later, with a similar result. Australia's batters were finding some form, at last, and Botham's lack of pace was inviting.

In the 23rd over, Phil Tufnell was brought on to bowl and soon found himself being milked for runs. In the next over, Moody crashed DeFreitas through the leg side for four, bringing up their fifty partnership. Jones started to use his feet to Tufnell, and the young spinner was conceding runs. By the 28th over, bowled by

DeFreitas, Moody reached his fifty with more excellent running between the wickets. With that milestone and the partnership on 71, Jones launched into a wide ball from DeFreitas. Chris Lewis, at backward point, dived magnificently to his right and held on to the catch. Jones was out for 22, and Australia were 106/3.

Steve Waugh's first contribution was to cut Tufnell away towards the boundary. Graham Gooch chased, and a well-timed boot stopped the ball, but an all-run four rendered the effort pointless. Tufnell was rewarded with his first Cricket World Cup wicket later in the over when Moody dragged the ball back on to his stumps while trying to sweep. The ball was angled towards the leg side, but the batter's glove diverted the ball on to the stumps and he was bowled. Australia were now 114/4 in the 31st over and were threatening to undo the good work done so far.

The Australian captain, Allan Border, came to the wicket under massive pressure. The innings was balanced precariously, while his personal form, with 13 runs in three innings, was abject. 'AB' needed a score for many reasons. Whether it was a statement or just a shot choice, Border used his feet and planted Tufnell back over his head for a four. Perhaps this was the innings for captain and country to reverse their fortunes.

Waugh's sweeping of Tufnell paid off as the runs continued to flow. Botham was reintroduced in the 38th over, but Border tried to play positively against his old friend and rival. That said, a Botham delivery nipped back into Border and bowled him. Reminiscent of his dismissal against South Africa, Border was deceived by the gentle medium pace and lost his wicket for 16.

In the 39th over, Healy took nine off Tufnell, including a slog sweep for six. Over number 40 will go down as another one of those times when Botham got the better of his old rivals.

Not quite Headingley 1981 proportions, but 'Beefy' wasn't quite finished with Australia. Healy's aggressive intent led to him pulling Botham to midwicket, and the safe hands of Neil Fairbrother did the rest. Two balls later, Peter Taylor was trapped in front, and umpire Steve Bucknor contemplated before signalling that it was out. Craig McDermott also lasted two balls before spooning a catch to mid-on, where DeFreitas held on. Australia had slumped to 155–8 due to Botham's spell of four wickets in seven balls without conceding a run.

Botham's four wickets were all Queenslanders: Border, Healy, Taylor and McDermott. He had played with three of them during his stint in the Sheffield Shield in 1987/88. He was part of the team that reached the final before losing to Western Australia in Perth. It was an incident on the flight to Perth that led to Botham's sacking from the Queensland team. His three-year contract was terminated, along with a A$5,000 fine from the cricket authorities, as well as an A$800 fine from the resultant court case.

It was not only the Australian cricketers who were being tormented by Botham. David Townsend, who worked for Cricketcall, a premium-rate telephone information service, remembered that *The Australian*'s journalist Malcolm Conn was perplexed too. 'In pre-Google press boxes, it was often the case that writers would call out randomly, asking if anyone had a particular stat to hand. "Does anyone know the exact date he sold his soul?" Conn asked. "Because this has to be the work of the devil, doesn't it?"'

Steve Waugh was the last recognised batter at the crease, and Australia's last hope for posting a reasonable total. With Mike Whitney and Bruce Reid left to bat, Waugh needed to survive for the last nine overs. His decision to take two runs off a Chris Lewis delivery proved to be the wrong one. He guided the ball down to third man, and DeFreitas ran in quickly and delivered a strong and accurate throw towards the stumps. Stewart's glovework was impressive, and Waugh was out for 27. Reflecting on the match, Tom Moody gave his opinion on where Australia had lost their way. 'Obviously getting a solid start and not converting it was personally disappointing, but it appeared to be a theme for us in this match with our top six. Botham's four wickets did break our back, but I felt the run-outs of Boon and Steve Waugh were more critical.'

Whitney and Reid squeezed out as many runs as they could until Reeve bowled the lanky left-hander and Australia were 171 all out. Having lost their last six wickets for 26 runs in 11 overs, Australia had not even batted out their allocation. Botham had achieved his best ODI figures to date with 4–31, while Pringle, Lewis and DeFreitas were all economical. If Australia were to win the match, their bowlers would need to bowl as well as England's had done.

Craig McDermott bowled a fiery opening spell, looking for an early breakthrough. The fastest bowler on either side, McDermott tried to extract extra bounce. Botham guided a ball over the slips in the third over, to try to release some of the pressure. In the next over, the all-rounder crashed a Bruce Reid no-ball through the covers for another boundary. Later in the same over, Botham drove the ball through the infield for another four to take England to 16/0.

Gooch finally got off the mark, with a leg-side boundary off McDermott, after facing 15 deliveries. With the England captain off and running, both openers looked to punish any width, and did so with flashing cut shots. The first bowling change brought on Mike Whitney. His first ball, short and on leg stump, was pulled sumptuously by Botham for four. It also brought up England's fifty in the tenth over.

Never one to die wondering, Botham pushed his luck on several occasions, but this time his gambles were paying off. Whitney had two lbw shouts, but inside edges and height meant that the benefit of the doubt was given to the batter. Waugh and Whitney slowed the run rate, but England's openers continued to score in singles and doubles. Australia needed wickets, otherwise the game would slip away from them.

The introduction of spin also coincided with England reaching 100 without loss. The English contingent in the crowd made themselves known, waving Union Jacks and enjoying every minute, while the Australians were resigning themselves to another defeat. Botham reached his fifty in the 24th over, triggering his decision to try to hit Whitney to all parts. However, a sharp leg-side catch by Healy ended Botham's aspirations. It was his first half-century in the Cricket World Cup, but he was out for 53 from 79 balls. Job done for Botham, and nearly done for England.

The wicket of Botham meant that Whitney ran in to bowl his first ball to Robin Smith with a yard more of pace. Smith was late on to the ball, and it cannoned into his pads. The Australians appealed with as much hope as expectation, but umpire Hayat was unmoved. Bowling over the wicket, Whitney was always going to struggle to get a decision in his favour.

Gooch continued to punish any bad balls. England were cruising to victory, as Australia continued to struggle. With nine wickets in hand, the task was a simple one. Gooch's slight impatience to get the game over with became his downfall. Having scored 58, the England captain tried to slog Steve Waugh over the on side but missed the ball, and it cannoned into his stumps. The partnership added 46 runs and England were just 19 from victory.

Smith and Hick saw England through to their total without further problems. Smith hit the winning runs, with a dismissive square cut, to deliver the eight-wicket victory with 9.1 overs left. Australia had been dealt a massive body blow, while England were almost assured of a place in the semi-finals. There could only be one name for the Man of the Match, and it was awarded to Botham. His first match at the SCG in over five years had been a revelation for the 36-year-old.

The next match took place in Hamilton, after a day's break, with Trust Bank Park subject to inclement weather. India had already been affected by rain in two of their four games, while Zimbabwe had fallen foul, last time out, in Napier. It was after lunch by the time play could get underway, and the match had been reduced to 32 overs per side. Groundsman Gavin Smith and his staff had done well to keep the wicket dry and to mop up the surface water. In the lead-up to the game, both teams had practised at Galloway Park.

The pitches were prone to uneven bounce, which led to criticism from both team managers. Don Topley and Abbas Ali Baig were quoted in the *Waikato Times* with less than complimentary views of the facilities.

With Mohammed Azharuddin winning the toss, he was in no doubt about batting first. The rain rules, and the overcast weather situation, made it the sensible decision to make. David Houghton admitted, at the toss, that he would have batted first too, and cited the confusion over the chasing target against New Zealand as the main reason. India made one change to their line-up, with Vinod Kambli replacing Ravi Shastri. Kapil Dev was promoted up the order, into the pinch-hitter role, with Kambli batting at six. Zimbabwe were unchanged from the team that had played New Zealand.

Eddo Brandes took the new ball and bowled to Kris Srikkanth. The Indian opener was under some pressure, with just 45 runs in four innings so far. His account was opened when Mark

Burmester slipped over trying to stop the ball, and it raced away for four. The fielder's new boots, along with the wet outfield, were at fault, but Brandes was in no mood for excuses. That mood was further darkened when umpire Dooland Buultjens turned down a good shout for lbw against Kapil Dev. Undeterred by the appeal, Kapil launched a massive six over mid-on in the next over.

Srikkanth showed a glimpse of his ability in the next Brandes over with a powerful drive through the covers. Later in the over, Brandes finally had something go his way when Kapil Dev missed a low full toss. As he tried to work the ball on the leg side, the ball thundered into his pads, and the Indian all-rounder was out for ten from 14 balls. Srikkanth was scoring at almost a run a ball; his timing was still off, but he managed to pull Brandes for four in the seventh over. The new batter was Indian captain Mohammed Azharuddin, and he had fewer problems with timing. In the next over, bowled by Kevin Duers, he cut a wide ball for two runs before clubbing the ball straight back down the ground for a boundary.

Mark Burmester was brought on to bowl, which he found daunting. 'It was very difficult to grip the ball, and movement of the ball was non-existent, and being a swing bowler this left very few options. My great mate Andy Flower said, "This is just like England, Burmy, and the guys hold it cross seam there." I tried it out and managed to bowl a decent line and length.'

At first Burmester's line was slightly off, resulting in Azharuddin smearing the ball through the covers for a four. No foot movement, and no interest in running, but the ball flew across the outfield. Burmester was bowling a tighter line and achieving more bounce. Azharuddin's pull shot just nicked the ball, and he was out. India were 43/2 in the ninth over, with Srikkanth being joined by Sachin Tendulkar.

It didn't take Tendulkar long to get into the game. In the next over, a boundary scored each side of the wicket off the bowling of Duers took India past fifty. At the other end, Srikkanth's hitting was slightly agricultural but no less effective. The opener's timing, or lack of it, became his downfall when a Burmester yorker beat him for pace and he lost his stumps. No more than medium pace, Burmester was rewarded with his second wicket of the match. At 69/3 with 19 overs left, the partnership between Tendulkar and Sanjay Manjrekar was key to a competitive total in overcast, damp conditions.

Just when Zimbabwe needed good fortune, it deserted them. Tendulkar was beaten by the swing of a Burmester delivery and edged it. The ball slid through the vacant slip area, beyond the grasp of Andy Flower, for four runs. In the same over, a simple piece of fielding should have limited the runs scored to one. However, the ball rolled through the Zimbabwean outfielder's grasp for another boundary. It gave India momentum, which was fatal when players such as Tendulkar were at the crease. The last ball of the over was crashed through long-on by Manjrekar as India were starting to find another gear.

The introduction of Ali Shah, and spin in the form of John Traicos, was Houghton's plan to stem the flow of runs. Manjrekar's riposte was to use his feet where possible and hit the ball into the air. Tendulkar resorted to a similar strategy to bring up his fifty with a six back down the ground. Eddo Brandes came back into the attack and Tendulkar resorted to wearing a batting helmet. It could have been a sign of respect for Brandes's pace, but his shot selection wasn't. A pull shot flew to the boundary quicker than the ball was delivered.

With five overs left, and the spin of Traicos still in the attack, Manjrekar's plan was to score with boundaries. The partnership had been worth 99 from 90 balls, but Manjrekar had been playing second fiddle to the 'Little Master'. Not quite getting hold of the ball, he played a shot that sent it sailing towards long-off, and Kevin Duers took a low, diving catch to remove the batter for a run-a-ball 34. Vinod Kambli faced just two balls before his attempted slog of Traicos led to his being bowled. India were now 170/5 and had 24 balls left.

Traicos took another wicket when Shah caught Ajay Jadeja's powerful shot. The spinner had hindered the Indian momentum by taking wickets. In the next over, Burmester took the prize wicket of Tendulkar to show India further. Tendulkar was trying to force the ball through the on side, but skewed it high towards backward point, and Campbell made no mistake. Tendulkar's fine innings was over for 81 off 77 balls, his highest score in ODIs so far.

Javagal Srinath's first ball should have led to his dismissal, but another catch went begging as Andy Flower's desperate dive was not enough. The ball ran away for four and India were getting, arguably, bonus runs. Brandes bowled the final over, and Kiran More swung his bat. Taking 12 runs, including a six, More carried India to 203/7 from their 32 overs. Zimbabwe's pick of the bowlers were Traicos with 3–35 and Burmester's 3–36, which pleased the bowler. 'I was really nervous to start but settled down and in those conditions bowled OK. Three big scalps like that are always special.'

Having scored at 6.34 runs per over, India's total was not insurmountable for Zimbabwe if they could get off to a good start. Ali Shah was promoted to open with Andy Flower, as Zimbabwe were racing against the weather as well as India's total. In order to get play underway, there was just a ten-minute lunch period. In damp conditions, with drizzle falling steadily, both teams found the situation tough. Zimbabwe had to deal with deliveries skidding on, from Kapil Dev and Prabhakar, while India had to deal with a wet ball. Both batters employed the approach of deflecting and nurdling the ball rather than aggressive shots. The first boundary of the innings came from a slash by Shah that almost cannoned into the stumps.

India's immediate priority was to bowl at least 15 overs to make sure the match wouldn't be abandoned. Interestingly, Houghton's instructions to his batters were to pace the innings. The rain rule, if employed, would take India's 'best' overs, so Zimbabwe would need to face the full innings for this tactic to work. The weather suggested otherwise.

Flower looked to put the fielders under pressure whenever possible. The wet conditions made it testing for India, and extra runs were taken. At the end of the 11th over, the umpires conferred and the batters were offered the option of leaving the field. They declined, but umpire Steve Randell told Mohammed Azharuddin that they would be leaving the field anyway. As the Zimbabwe batters were walking off, they were called back, as the weather had improved. The Hamilton groundsmen, on the outfield with the covers, needed to retreat so the game could continue.

With the need to score more quickly, Shah fell to the medium pace of Tendulkar. As he made room to hit the ball over the covers, it moved off the pitch; Shah's swing missed, and he was clean-bowled. The breakthrough had come in the 17th over with Zimbabwe on 79. It was no consolation, but the opening partnership was a Zimbabwean ODI record.

The new batter was big-hitting Andy Waller, who arrived at the wicket to face the spin of Venkatapathy Raju. Sweeping the ball to leg, Waller was given a gift of a boundary due to a misfield. Waller hit another four at the end of the 18th over, but the rain started to fall harder. Raju managed to bowl the first ball of the 19th over before the players were forced off the ground.

With the rain setting in, no further play was possible, so the rain rule would decide the match. India's most productive overs amounted to 158, so the margin of victory was 55 runs.

Applying Stern's calculations to this match gives an interesting angle. Zimbabwe's approach may well have won them the game had DLS been in play. Their DLS total would have been 100, which would have been enough. The DL total was 107, so they were three runs short, but a change of rain rule would have made this game a lot tighter than the 55-run defeat that the record books show.

It had been two weeks since Australia had featured in the opening match of the tournament. At the Adelaide Oval, they were already in a must-win scenario going into the game against Sri Lanka. Another defeat would leave the world champions in the unbelievable situation of being out of their home tournament. The Sri Lankans were buoyed by the arrival of Graeme Labrooy, who had joined the team to replace the injured Rumesh Ratnayake. With two wins under their belt, confidence was good, and another upset could be within their reach. Sitting third in the table, three points ahead of Australia, a win would get them closer to an unlikely semi-final place.

Australia decided they would recall Geoff Marsh in place of Mark Taylor at the top of the order. Sri Lanka also had a change of opener, with Athula Samarasekera's hamstring being sufficiently healed. Labrooy was named as twelfth man so he could acclimatise to Australian conditions. Allan Border decided he would like Mark Waugh to bolster the batting line-up, and Bruce Reid made way for him.

Winning the toss, Border inserted Sri Lanka on a hot day in Adelaide. Steve Waugh was given the new ball, as Australia looked to innovation to kick-start their campaign. In the third over, Sri Lanka gifted the first wicket when Samarasekera and

Mahanama's miscommunication led to a run-out. Mahanama failed to respond to the call, and was left with an impossible run when Samarasekera continued trying to take a single. Jones and McDermott combined to effect the run-out as Sri Lanka lost their most effective batter of the tournament. The loss of Mahanama for seven, after he had scored three half-centuries, was disastrous.

Asanka Gurusinha was the new batter, and he got off the mark with a crunching square cut off the bowling of Steve Waugh. Having conceded 15 runs from his three overs, Waugh had not had the impact that Australia would have wanted. Border resorted to a more traditional approach by bringing Whitney into the attack. It soon paid dividends as Gurusinha was caught in front of the stumps when attempting to flick the ball to leg. Umpire Piloos Reporter had no doubts, and Sri Lanka were reduced to 28/2 in the 12th over.

Playing his natural attacking game, Samarasekera's response to the loss of the wicket was to launch Whitney over mid-on for a boundary. Although losing Mahanama was a blow for Sri Lanka, they had Samarasekera's attacking tendencies to fall back on. He added another boundary later in the over to underline his intentions. The introduction of Tom Moody into the bowling attack was greeted by a pull shot from Aravinda de Silva. Rocking back, the Sri Lankan captain hit the ball high and comfortably for four. Playing their shots, not always convincingly, Samarasekera and de Silva started to build a partnership. However, it was another change of bowling that would generate the breakthrough. Peter Taylor's spin bowling tempted Samarasekera into using his feet to get to the pitch of the ball. The ball went high, but not very far, and Healy took a running catch. The opener departed for 34, and Sri Lanka were now 72/3.

The fall of the wicket signalled the arrival of Arjuna Ranatunga. A big presence, in every sense of the phrase, for Sri Lanka, and a solid innings was required. Ranatunga drove at a ball, early on off Taylor's bowling, but it fell short of Border in the covers. It was a lucky escape for the ex-captain. It had already been clear that Border was willing to change the plan. With Sri Lanka on 99/3 after 29 overs, Australia's captain invoked his next innovation: to bowl himself. Border did have 59 ODI wickets to his name, with Ranatunga on that list of victims, but his decision demonstrated his frustration with the bowling options in his squad. His best bowling figures at Adelaide, 2–2 in 1990, were against Sri Lanka if he had any need to further justify his decision.

The bowling of spin from both ends encouraged Ranatunga to try hitting across the line. Whether it was a sweep shot or a lusty stroke, the propensity to play that way almost resulted in another wicket falling as the ball sailed out to Steve Waugh in the deep. Despite it being a regulation catch, Waugh dropped the ball, to the chagrin of his captain. It was reminiscent of Waugh's drop on the last ball of the India game.

After Border had set a field for Ranatunga on the on side, it was an off-side drive that resulted in the loss of his wicket. Taylor's flighted ball was driven straight to Dean Jones, and Sri Lanka were 123/4. The partnership had been worth 51, with Ranatunga having struggled to 23 from 52 balls. Meanwhile, de Silva was still scoring at a reasonable rate and, in the next over, brought up his first Cricket World Cup fifty from 67 balls.

In the 39th over, the match endured some controversy when Sanath Jayasuriya was unmoved despite Steve Waugh's protestations for a catch. Bowling from the Cathedral End, Waugh came in to bowl and Jayasuriya squeezed a ball out to Waugh's brother, Mark. The siblings claimed the wicket while the batter was unmoved, presumably because of a bump ball. Steve Waugh gestured to Jayasuriya to leave the field. The umpire in question, Zimbabwe's Ian Robinson, was convinced that it wasn't out, but TV replays appeared less convincing.

Border broke through in the 42nd over when Jayasuriya aimed to slog him across the line. Missing the ball completely, he was hit in front and was given out. At 151/5, Sri Lanka needed some runs quickly, and de Silva tried to oblige. He employed the reverse sweep against Border, much to the amusement of the bowler, to get the scoreboard ticking over.

McDermott came back into the attack and, almost immediately, got himself a wicket. The extra pace and bounce meant that de Silva wasn't quite in line to pull him, and Moody took an excellent running catch on the boundary. Gone for 62, de Silva was Sri Lanka's last chance to post a respectable total.

The rest of the innings was littered with run-outs as the increasingly desperate Sri Lankans imploded. Mark Waugh was involved in all three run-outs as indecision led to a fall of wickets. First, as Ruwan Kalpage stayed firm, Waugh's throw to Healy beat the helpless Hashan Tillakaratne. Next to fall was Champaka Ramanayake, who was on the receiving end of a superb pick-up and throw. The last wicket to fall was that of Ruwan Kalpage, on the last ball of the innings, when he tried to take an unlikely fourth run from a misfield. Taylor and the Waugh brothers combined to achieve the run-out. Sri Lanka ended their innings on 189/9. Australia's bowlers had kept the scoring low, and victory looked straightforward.

The Australian innings began with both Geoff Marsh and Tom Moody in a cautious mood. In the first six overs, they scored seven runs. The Australian contingent in the crowd were effusive in their disapproval about the approach. Marsh received boos from some quarters as he set off at a snail's pace. Moody struck the first boundary in the seventh over, but Marsh had scored just two runs by the tenth. An edge, wide of Tillakaratne, ran away to give Marsh his first boundary of the day. He then scored three runs from an off drive, and the crowd's mood lifted.

The introduction of Don Anurasiri's spin bowling prompted Marsh to play a sweep shot that sailed over the boundary for six. The initial caution that Australia had employed was starting to pay off now that the pace of scoring was increasing. They had reached 47/0 after 13 overs, and both batters were looking comfortable. The Sri Lankan bowling attack was struggling to penetrate as Australia picked off the runs. Only Pramodya Wickramasinghe was difficult to score off. Gurusinha's medium pace was not going to knock over a team. A speculative over of spin from Ranatunga, which Australia milked 11 runs from, highlighted the desperation from de Silva.

As a result of some aggressive shots from Moody, Australia reached 101/0 in the 26th over. As they had scored just 16 runs from the first nine overs, the acceleration was clear. First Marsh then Moody reached their fifties, via singles, off the bowling of Kalpage. With the milestone reached, Moody's intent changed, and he was looking to score quickly to help his country's net run rate. Ultimately, this led to his downfall when he tried to whip Wickramasinghe over the infield but picked out Mahanama. The fielder juggled the ball, but it held firm at the second grasp. Australia had lost their first wicket, on 120, but needed just 70 runs with almost 20 overs left.

Geoff Marsh fell soon after when, trying to put away a full toss, he was caught in the deep by a good catch from Anurasiri. The ball flew high and fast towards the cover boundary, but was taken by Anurasiri, who had made up much ground to take the ball. Marsh's innings of 60 had taken Australia to 130/2. The new batters were Mark Waugh, playing to consolidate his place in the batting line-up, and David Boon, who was in fantastic form. It was Waugh who showed his attacking intent with a towering six off Kalpage. Coming down the wicket, Waugh made crisp contact, and the ball sailed over the white picket fence into the approving Australian crowd. That was followed up, in the next over, by a sweep for another six. Waugh's contact was true, and the ball flew low and fast over the boundary. With the score on 165, the result of a rapid partnership of 35, Waugh's aggressive shot-making resulted in his downfall. In an identical shot to Moody's, Mahanama took the catch at midwicket. Scoring at a run a ball, Waugh had scored 26 without a four, but with those two well-struck sixes.

Dean Jones came to the wicket with the instruction to finish the game, and he did just that. A towering six, estimated to have travelled 110 metres, was the pick of his 12 runs from six balls. Boon finished with 27 as Australia won the match by seven wickets with six overs to spare. Wickramasinghe was the pick of the Sri Lankan bowlers with 2–29 from his ten overs, but the rest couldn't back up his display. Tom Moody's innings was deemed worthy of the Man-of-the-Match award. The result meant that Australia moved up the table one place but, more importantly, were just a point behind third-placed India.

	Pld	Won	Lost	Tied	N/R	Pts	Net R/R	For	Against
New Zealand	4	4	0	0	0	8	1.079	802/150.5	712/168.0
England	4	3	0	0	1	7	0.655	569/130.4	555/150.0
India	5	2	2	0	1	5	0.532	835/165.0	748/165.1
Sri Lanka	5	2	2	0	1	5	−0.167	906/199.1	907/192.2
South Africa	4	2	2	0	0	4	0.050	756/196.5	695/183.2
West Indies	4	2	2	0	0	4	−0.098	778/196.5	769/189.5
Australia	5	2	3	0	0	4	−0.254	977/240.0	1015/234.4
Pakistan	4	1	2	0	1	3	−0.033	647/149.0	638/145.5
Zimbabwe	5	0	5	0	0	0	−1.261	911/187.1	1142/186.2

Chapter Eight

Hitting Their Straps

The date of Wednesday, 6 February 1980 probably does not conjure up memories to anyone but keen Kiwi cricket fans. On that day, in Christchurch, New Zealand beat the West Indies for the only time in 13 ODIs. Those two teams met again on Sunday, 8 March 1992 in the Cricket World Cup. History may have been on the side of the West Indies, but they went into the game at Eden Park as massive underdogs.

On the occasion in 1980, a Gordon Greenidge century was not enough as Jeremy Coney's 53 not out saw New Zealand over the line with two balls to spare. Most of the participants were long retired, but Desmond Haynes and the now-injured John Wright had played in the match. It had been almost five years since the sides had met in an ODI. The last match had been a ten-wicket thrashing, with Greenidge and Haynes smashing the ball to all parts.

Wet weather in Auckland had given way to dry but overcast conditions. Martin Crowe won the toss and had no hesitation in asking the West Indies to bat. Only one change was made to the New Zealand line-up, with Chris Cairns, who had had a poor game against Zimbabwe, being dropped in favour of the returning Willie Watson. The West Indies went into the match with the same team that had lost to South Africa in Christchurch.

Martin Crowe's tactic of opening the bowling with Dipak Patel once again posed problems for a batting side. The West Indies scored their first runs in the third over, as Patel and Danny Morrison bowled tightly. Haynes and Lara were restricted from scoring as New Zealand looked to squeeze another batting side out of the game. While Patel offered nothing, Morrison gave up boundaries in the seventh and ninth overs. Lara's uppish strokes went for four, but the West Indies were scoring at just above two runs per over. Crowe had an established, and well executed, plan, but the West Indies looked powerless to change the course of events.

A change of bowling, with Gavin Larsen brought on, almost conjured the first wicket when Lara mistimed a pull, but the ball landed agonisingly wide of a diving Morrison. Lara made no mistake with the next Larsen short ball and despatched it clinically. Crowe's grimace suggested that Larsen's length and line was not in the plan. Adjusting his length to induce a drive, Lara put that away too. The 12th over was becoming expensive for New Zealand. Another boundary to end the over left bowler and captain with a problem to fix.

During the next four overs, only six runs were scored as New Zealand retook control. Haynes was yet to score a boundary when Willie Watson bowled the 17th over. A short ball on off stump appealed to Haynes, who summarily pulled it square for six runs. Haynes then ran the ball down for two runs to bring up the fifty partnership. The introduction of Chris Harris finally brought the breakthrough, when Haynes was caught and bowled. As he tried to drive the ball, too much bottom hand made it fly straight rather than where he aimed, and Harris took a low, tumbling catch. The partnership had been worth 65, but almost 20 overs had already been bowled.

While Richardson was struggling to put bat to ball, Lara went about his business and reached his fifty in the 28th over with a quick single. His innings ended soon after, when he slashed the ball to point and Rutherford took the catch. This was the third time in the tournament that Lara had been dismissed in this way. Larsen's lack of pace was responsible as the batter tried to find the gap. The West Indies were 95/2, of which Lara had scored 52, in the 29th over.

In Patel's last over, Carl Hooper played an ill-timed stroke, and Greatbatch took a steepling catch at long mid-on. The ball had the height but not the length and sailed out towards the boundary. With less than 18 overs left, the West Indies were 100/3 and in dire need of accelerating their scoring. Bringing on Rod Latham, Crowe was hopeful of continuing to stifle the batters. The reality was a collection of short, wide balls that the West Indies relished. Keith Arthurton played two exquisite cut shots for boundaries, before Latham slid a ball down leg side, which evaded Richardson and Ian Smith behind the stumps.

Willie Watson came back on to bowl in the 39th over, and Richardson decided that this was the time to swing the bat. Unfortunately for the West Indian captain, the ball went vertically, and Smith took the catch to reduce the West Indies to 136/4. The ever-useful Chris Harris soon turned that into 142/5 with an inswinging medium-pacer that bowled Gus Logie all ends up. The batter hung his bat out down one line, but the ball swung into the stumps.

With under ten overs left, Arthurton was joined by Malcolm Marshall. The fragility of the West Indies' batting was highlighted by the veteran bowler batting as high as seven. With just two fifties in 135 ODI appearances, the expectation to score runs was an unrealistic one. In fact, Marshall had failed to get into double figures in his last seven innings. Therefore, it was no surprise when Larsen cleaned up as Marshall tried an ambitious slog towards midwicket.

At 156/6, New Zealand's bowlers may have been confident of cleaning up the tail. However, Morrison and Watson were guilty of some errant balls, and David Williams capitalised. The diminutive wicketkeeper was the recipient of several full tosses which were despatched. He also played some expansive strokes to push the score along.

In the 47th over, Williams was particularly punishing, with Watson suffering from an agricultural heave and then a textbook cover drive. The bowler was clearly affected by the treatment. In his last over, Watson opened up with a full toss that Williams put away. Later in the over, a full toss to Arthurton was swung away for four. Watson's intent to bowl a yorker length had resulted in bad balls that had led to boundaries.

By the time Arthurton was bowled by Morrison in the last over, trying to make room to cut, the West Indies had passed 200. A quickfire partnership of 45 had taken them to a respectable total. Watson had been expensive at 1–56, slightly undoing the excellent work of Patel with his 1–19 from ten overs. He had conceded 27 runs from his last two overs. Williams's 32 from 24 balls had given the West Indies some impetus that they would carry into the New Zealand innings.

New Zealand were chasing 204 to win, and their response began sedately. Ambrose's first-ball wide did not set a trend, and it was the 18th ball of the innings before runs came from a scoring stroke. It was Greatbatch who opened his account, with a slice over gully that ran away for four. This was followed up with a short-arm jab behind square off Marshall for another boundary, and that lit the flame for Greatbatch. Ambrose found himself being cut uppishly for four before an edge flew over the slips for another boundary. If Ambrose was feeling roughly treated, it was nothing compared with the next over. Greatbatch advanced down the wicket to Marshall and smashed the ball over extra cover for six. Cummins, replacing Ambrose, also watched as Greatbatch pulled a six into a boisterous and jubilant crowd. The last ball of the over went to the boundary, guided by Latham, and took New Zealand to 53/0.

The first ball of the next over also saw Greatbatch charging down the wicket. Although the connection wasn't great, the ball still sailed into the stand for another six. The bowler, Ambrose, stood rubbing his chin wryly as the partisan crowd were revelling in the display. By now, Greatbatch was in the zone and hitting the ball sweetly. Cummins witnessed the ball fizz past his head for another four.

The game was held up while local police ejected 12 rowdy spectators who had thrown items on to the outfield where a West Indian fielder was standing. On the resumption, Latham edged a Cummins delivery, and Williams held on to the catch. The incident was responsible for Latham's break in concentration, which resulted in his dismissal. The score was 67/1 in the 12th over, and Andrew Jones came to the crease.

Greatbatch's concentration was still intact, as underlined by a sumptuous on drive for another boundary. His fifty followed with an off drive for two to demonstrate his good form. It was not so much the run-a-ball scoring rate – it was more how the runs were accumulated: 4, 4, 4, 4, 6, 1, 6, 1, 6, 1, 4, 1, 1, 4, 1, 2. Greatbatch had played and missed at balls, much to the West Indian bowlers' annoyance, but had made up with some brutal and dismissive shots.

Andrew Jones was happy to play the supporting role and give Greatbatch the strike. Having scored ten from 35 balls, he nicked a Benjamin delivery and Williams took his second catch of the innings. Just three runs later, Greatbatch's entertaining innings also came to a close. It was Benjamin who struck, when Greatbatch picked out Desmond Haynes on the cover boundary. Gone for 63 off 77, his innings had put New Zealand in a strong position, but they had two new batters in Martin Crowe and Ken Rutherford.

Crowe had already demonstrated his fine form with match-winning innings against Australia and Zimbabwe. Against the West Indies, he decided that if the ball was in the slot, he was going to play his shots. He almost holed out when sweeping Hooper, but the ball found its way to the boundary. An edge off Benjamin could have gone to Williams, but it ran away for four. That was followed up with an authoritative cut for another four. Another Hooper delivery was cut through backward point as Crowe started going through the gears.

Batting partner Rutherford had been more sedate. A pulled four had been the pick of his eight runs, before Ambrose elicited the slightest away movement and the edge flew to Williams. Such was the prominence of Crowe's contribution, the partnership had been worth 35. New Zealand required a further 69 runs from more than 15 overs. Chris Harris got off the mark with three runs from Hooper. More importantly, this gave Crowe the strike. The West Indies bowlers were finding bowling to New Zealand's captain daunting. Ambrose overpitched and was driven for four. Marshall was pulled from off stump for another boundary. Another Ambrose delivery flew high in front of square to bring up his fifty from 52 balls.

When Chris Harris edged Cummins to Williams, who took his fourth catch of the match, the partnership with Crowe had been worth 41, with Harris having scored seven of those runs. New Zealand were within 30 runs of victory, and the West

Indies needed to get Crowe if they were to have any chance of winning.

In the 44th over, the West Indies were convinced that they had run out Dipak Patel. A swift pick-up and throw from Haynes hit the stumps directly, but umpire Peter McConnell was unmoved. Haynes appeared to remonstrate before moving away and appealing to the heavens for divine intervention. TV replays showed that Patel was clearly short of his ground. Two balls later, a mix-up between the New Zealanders should have resulted in another run-out, but Haynes's appeal for help from above was ignored.

Fittingly, it was Martin Crowe who hit the winning runs in the 49th over. Another fine on drive ran away for his 12th boundary of the innings and Crowe ended on 81 runs from 81 balls. The margin of victory was five wickets, giving them a second-ever ODI win against the West Indies – but the main fact was that New Zealand were heading for the semi-finals. The Man-of-the-Match award could only go to Crowe, his third of the tournament, and his batting average rose to 263 with another not-out.

On the same day, Pakistan and South Africa played their match at the Gabba in Brisbane. Although play could get underway on schedule, 9.30am local time, there were showers forecast for later in the day. Imran Khan won the toss, and South Africa were asked to bat first. In John Crace's *Wasim and Waqar*, 'it was a decision questioned by Wasim. "The weather was very unsettled, and so I asked the captain and coach if they had consulted a weather forecast. They said they had, and that it was clear. I thought it would rain, and so did most of the other players; the reception desk at the hotel had even told me it would rain."'

Pakistan were without veterans Javed Miandad, who was suffering from a stomach problem, and Ramiz Raja, who still had not recovered from his shoulder injury. Ijaz Ahmed came in for Miandad, while Iqbal Sikander was recalled at the expense of Wasim Haider. South Africa's batting line-up was weakened when Peter Kirsten withdrew due to a calf muscle problem. Hansie Cronje replaced him in the middle order, which meant that South Africa would have to rejig their line-up. Opening the batting for them were Andrew Hudson and Kepler Wessels. For Wessels, the Gabba was familiar territory, as he had played for Queensland from 1979 to 1986. Hudson was far less familiar with the ground, but in a positive mindset. 'A good Brisbane wicket with two quicks steaming in, I was happy and comfortable.'

With the new ball, Wasim Akram had struggled to maintain control early in the innings. This continued with two short and wide balls being cut for four by Hudson. In the sixth over, Hudson repeated the feat against Aaqib Javed. The first boundary of the over was scored through the gully. The second was a much more convincing back-foot drive that flew to the cover boundary. Wessels had struggled to five when Aaqib started to bowl the eighth over. An aggressive but mistimed pull shot could have gone to a fielder, but dropped safely. It appeared that Wessels had decided he needed to play some shots. It was short-lived, though, as Aaqib soon probed outside off stump and took the edge of Wessels's bat.

Having achieved the breakthrough, Imran brought on his leg-spin bowler, Iqbal Sikander. The new batter, Mark Rushmere, drove a fullish ball for four to settle his nerves in just his third ODI. Imran brought himself on, and Hudson also took advantage and drove another ball, off the back foot, for four runs. Rushmere hit another boundary off Sikander as South Africa were building their total without any problems. Further boundaries off the bowling of Ijaz Ahmed and Imran helped the partnership towards fifty runs.

Having just achieved his fifty, Hudson loosely flicked an Imran delivery straight to Ijaz at midwicket. It was not surprising that it had come from the on side, with Hudson being so strong off side, but a more positive stroke could have gone over the infield. South Africa were now 98/2 in the 26th over. The dismissal brought all-rounder Adrian Kuiper to the crease.

With scores of 2, 18 and 23, Kuiper would have wanted to get some runs on the board. He brought up South Africa's hundred, but succumbed to Imran for five runs. As he tried to loft the ball over the on side, it flew high into the air, and wicketkeeper Moin Khan ran to the edge of the fielding circle to take a diving catch.

New batter Jonty Rhodes was soon in trouble when trying to pull his first ball. Not making contact with the bat, the ball thundered into a delicate area of the batter. Crouching before taking a 'stock take of the damage' according to Greg Chappell's less-than-sympathetic commentary, Rhodes took a few moments to compose himself. At the start of the next over, Mushtaq Ahmed bowled to Rushmere, who pulled the ball straight to midwicket, where Aamer Sohail made no mistake. Rushmere's batting against leg spin had been troubled apart from an occasional dominant shot. Two wickets had fallen quickly, and South Africa were 111/4. Pakistan were containing South Africa, and boundaries were becoming scarce.

When Hansie Cronje cut Mushtaq for four at the end of the 27th over, it was the first boundary in 13 overs. The leg-spin partnership of Mushtaq and Sikander was pressurising South Africa. That pressure intensified somewhat when, two balls later, Rhodes was caught in front trying to sweep and was given out lbw. The bowler was unmoved, but umpire Steve Bucknor accepted Moin's loud appeal. At 127/5, South Africa's innings was starting to collapse.

Pakistan's morale was sapped by their inability to perform basic fielding tasks. Wasim Akram should have easily fielded Brian McMillan's cut to backward point, but the ball ran through his legs for a boundary. McMillan and Cronje went about their business, keeping the scoreboard ticking over without being spectacular. Meanwhile, Pakistan's fielding was deteriorating. It was Akram once again, backing up a throw to his end, who misjudged the ball, and it hit him in the knee. In the 45th over, Cronje swept Mushtaq out towards deep midwicket, where Inzamam-ul-Haq was fielding. The catch should have been taken, but the ball slipped through Inzamam's hands and ran for another four.

South Africa's batters were feeding off the low morale of the Pakistan fielders – dropping singles but fully expecting a misfield for two runs. Ijaz Ahmed, in the 46th over, obliged as the fifty partnership loomed. Imran Khan stood with his hands on his hips while making his team aware of his displeasure. In the same over, Cronje used his feet to strike a ball over the top for four, before yet another gift of overthrows from Pakistan. McMillan decided that he too would use his feet to make room, but was not so fortunate as Akram's inswinging yorker cleaned up his stumps. After a useful innings of 33 from 44 balls, McMillan exited with the score on 198/6.

Aaqib Javed bowled the 49th over, and Cronje appeared to be caught by Ijaz. Umpire Brian Aldridge had already called a no-ball. Ijaz angrily threw the ball to wicketkeeper Moin Khan. Moin underarmed the ball back to Aaqib, who wasn't watching. He turned around just as the ball hit him flush on the head, and he went to ground. He finally got back to his feet and finished his over, but then left the field for treatment.

The final over was relatively uneventful by comparison. Another Akram yorker cleaned up David Richardson, while more misfielding offered bonus runs. Cronje's 47 from 53 balls was a welcome injection at the end of the innings, and South Africa finished with 211/7. Apart from numerous misfields costing additional runs, Pakistan offered up 19 in extras, including nine wides. It begged the question of how costly these runs would be at the end of the match.

Allan Donald immediately started to redress the balance of wides when he bowled six of them in the first over, including a ball he dragged down the leg side that beat batter and wicketkeeper by some distance. Aamer Sohail and Zahid Fazal started the innings brightly, while the Queensland storm clouds gathered ever more menacingly. By the 11th over, both batters had found the boundary and were building a solid total. The usually aggressive Aamer Sohail had curbed his more aggressive strokeplay for steady, but chanceless, batting.

In the 14th over, a wild South African throw generated two runs, bringing up Pakistan's fifty. However, two quick wickets would snatch the momentum back towards South Africa. The first came from an ambitious swipe across the line from Aamer Sohail that saw his off stump hit. Richard Snell's line was too good if Sohail missed the ball, and this resulted in the first wicket falling. In the very next over, Fazal's forward defensive shot to McMillan drew the edge and Pakistan were 50/2.

Inzamam-ul-Haq and Imran Khan batted conservatively until the 20th over, when Imran set about Snell's bowling. The impending storm motivated Pakistan's captain to hit out. A cut shot through backward point for a boundary was followed up with a charge down the wicket. Another boundary came from a thick edge as Imran went into full attack mode.

The umpires decided the rain was sufficient to stop play, but Imran indicated that he was prepared to stay on. The ground staff, who were rushing on to the field with the covers, were sent back momentarily, before the decision to suspend play was confirmed. Sixty-one minutes of the game were lost, and the rain rule was brought into play. Fourteen overs were deducted, but only 18 runs taken from the total. Pakistan's revised target was 194, which effectively increased their required run rate from 6.42 per over to 8.28.

Imran had no choice but to pick up where he had left off, as Pakistan's task had become more difficult. When Inzamam cracked a Kuiper full toss for four, the fifty partnership came up, as well as Pakistan reaching 100/2. Inzamam's striking was crisp and accurate. South Africa's bowlers were under pressure, with the ball flying around a damp Gabba. When Richard Snell put down a chance to remove Inzamam at third man, the South Africans looked concerned.

The partnership had reached 85 when a piece of cricket, now iconic, shattered Pakistan's momentum. Brian McMillan rapped Inzamam on his pads and he tried to take a quick single. Imran screamed at his batting partner to get back and make his ground. Jonty Rhodes takes up the story, 'It was a combination of me being desperate to get the run-out, as Inzamam and Imran were batting superbly, and the ball was a little slippery due to wet outfield conditions; as this had also made it difficult for our bowlers to find their lengths. I saw that he [Inzamam] had advanced almost half the length of the pitch, but Imran had not moved out of his crease, so I backed my speed against Inzi's, which nearly backfired, as the umpire, Steve Bucknor, could easily have given the benefit of the doubt to the batter – as there were no third umpire referrals back then! The main reason I did not throw the ball was that we desperately needed that breakthrough.'

Rhodes's speed and dive took out all three of the stumps, and Inzamam was run out. His 48 from 45 balls had given Pakistan a chance. Since the resumption, 61 runs had been added in nine overs, but Pakistan were now 135/3 and had a new batter in Salim Malik, who didn't have the luxury of time to play himself in. If the Pakistan fans thought their chances were slim with this loss, later in the over it would become far worse. Imran's desperation for runs led to an attempted slog across the line, and the top edge flew to Richardson behind the stumps.

Allan Donald came back on to bowl, and Wasim Akram managed to find the boundary, but the requirement of two runs per ball was telling on the Pakistan batters. In the next over, Adrian Kuiper picked up three wickets as Pakistan's desperation to find the boundary led to wickets falling. The first was a good catch from Donald on the midwicket boundary to remove Salim Malik. Snell's catch, making up for his previous error, removed Wasim before Ijaz's three-ball innings ended when Jonty Rhodes took a back-pedalling catch at deep point.

With the game gone, Pakistan managed to get to 173/8, but the margin of victory was 20 runs. It was a harsh defeat, due to the rain, but the fact remained that they had achieved just one victory from their first five matches. Stern's DL (162) and DLS (163) totals show that Pakistan would have won the game.

In his TV interview afterwards, Imran was critical of the rain rule and how it was 'weighted heavily' on the side batting first. He also commented that they did not know it was going to rain. When Ian Chappell asked if Imran would have done something different at the toss had he known the forecast, Imran was adamant that he had known the forecast, and had been told it wasn't going to rain.

Monday, 9 March was a public holiday in Victoria, and a bumper Labour Day crowd was expected at the Eastern Oval in Ballarat for England and Sri Lanka's match. Thousands of Melbourne's Sri Lankan community made the journey to see their cricketing heroes. Over 13,000 packed into the ground as both sets of supporters made it a noisy and colourful occasion.

Delan Adikari attended the match as a Sri Lankan fan. Having moved to Australia in 1987, Adikari followed the nation of his birth as well as his new homeland. On that day, he joined the throngs of Sri Lankan fans enjoying the occasion in Ballarat. 'They [the Sri Lankan fans] enjoyed the game regardless of the result and were there to support players representing the country. There was a saying some older uncles used to say: "Win or lose, we booze." There was a reasonable Sri Lankan community in Victoria back then. What happened for this game was that Sri Lankans flocked to Ballarat in cars, vans, minibuses. I remember the atmosphere at the ground. The Sri Lankan flags, colours, music, food. And the action so close, like a local club game. It was great.'

Any Ballarat residents would undoubtedly be backing Sri Lanka, in any case, but England's refusal to stay locally created bad feeling. England were booked to stay in the Old Ballarat Village motel, but checked out within hours of their arrival, drove to the five-star Regent of Melbourne, and returned before the match. England's management stated that the beds weren't long enough for some of the players. In the five hours that England were at the motel, Ian Botham managed to reignite his argument with Australian prime minister Paul Keating. He told local newspaper *The Courier* that he would 'flatten' the PM.

England selected the same team that had been victorious at the SCG except that Richard Illingworth was brought in for Phil Tufnell. Sri Lanka gave Graeme Labrooy, the call-up replacement, his first match in place of Ruwan Kalpage. Graham Gooch won the toss and batted first on a sunny day at the small but packed Eastern Oval.

Sri Lanka could have started the game with an early wicket when Ian Botham flicked a ball to Asanka Gurusinha at square leg, but the ball went to ground. Botham's response was to crash the ball square for four. Anything in the slot was going to be hit by Botham, as was his brief as an opener. The Sri Lankan bowlers gave him too much width or veered too much down leg side, and the ball was despatched. A six over the leg-side boundary came with ease as Botham punished wayward bowling.

Gooch, on the other hand, was finding runs less easy to come by. Apart from a clip off the pads for four, off the bowling of Champaka Ramanayake, Gooch was struggling to score. It came as no surprise when Graeme Labrooy, bowling his fourth ball of the tournament, got one through the gate to bowl him. A torturous innings of eight runs was over, and the England captain trudged forlornly off the ground.

The new batter was Robin Smith, who got straight off the mark with a single before punishing more wayward bowling with a trademark cut for a boundary. Despite having got a wicket early on, Labrooy's confidence was almost as battered as the ball. Both batters benefitted from the bowler's lack of match practice. Botham smashed the ball, at head height, straight back down the wicket as Labrooy served up a half-volley. The umpire, who had to take evasive action, was the closest person to the ball as it rocketed past for four and thudded into the advertising hoardings.

The introduction of Don Anurasiri's spin inadvertently led to the fall of Smith's wicket. The partnership was worth 36 and looking set. However, slight hesitation in running a quick single off the spinner caused Smith to be short of his ground. Mahanama's accurate throw to Anurasiri, who took the bails off, was good enough for umpire Piloos Reporter to give the decision. The thousands of fans on the newly named 'Sri Lankan Hill' were waving their flags and celebrating as Graeme Hick joined Botham at the crease. England were 80/2 in the 19th over.

Botham's onslaught continued with a six, off Anurasiri, that landed in the trees at the back of the Eastern Oval. Hick eased his way into his innings, including a well-timed pull for a boundary off the bowling of Gurusinha, while Botham continued looking to score quickly. This aggressive intent finally got the better of the all-rounder, and he lost his wicket. Trying to make room to cut Anurasiri, Botham failed to make contact with the ball, and it carried on along its line into the stumps. Botham's frustration was evident, but he was out for 47 and England were 105/3.

Although the Sri Lankan bowlers had managed to slow the run rate down, Hick and Neil Fairbrother still kept the scoreboard ticking over. Fairbrother offered a chance, with his score on just three, but Tillakaratne could not hang on to the catch behind the stumps. When Fairbrother deposited a ball in the same trees as Botham, for another massive six, the dropped catch started to look crucial for Sri Lanka.

After he had added another 59 to the total, in 14 overs, Hick's expansive drive cannoned the ball back into his stumps to give Ramanayake his first wicket of the match. At 164/4 in the 39th over, England's innings was on a knife-edge. Sri Lanka had already chased down over 300 once in the tournament, and the small boundaries at Eastern Oval would suggest that a total above 250 could still be attainable despite England's bowlers. The last recognised batter for England was Alec Stewart, and he, along with Fairbrother, would need a good score to keep England's winning streak going.

Having been brutalised by Botham earlier, Labrooy received similar treatment from Stewart and Fairbrother. Stewart crashed a ball over cover for four, before Fairbrother used his feet and struck a six back over the top into the crowd. Not wanting to be left out, Stewart hit Gurusinha for six, and the ball sailed out of the ground as England's acceleration continued. Such was the ferocity of scoring, 80 runs were scored in nine overs. In just 41 minutes, England's total had suddenly become a testing one. Fairbrother finally holed out to Ramanayake on the boundary, but England were 244/5, with all-rounders left to swing the bat at the end of the innings. Fairbrother's 63 from 70 balls had given them a platform.

The loss of Fairbrother only brought about more problems for Sri Lanka, as Chris Lewis went berserk. Before that, a brace of boundaries from Stewart brought up his fifty from 32 balls – the second-fastest Cricket World Cup half-century. Gurusinha, bowling the last over of the innings, saw the first ball to Lewis disappear over his head for six. Later in the over, Stewart was caught on the boundary for 59, but there was still time for Lewis to flat-bat another six. England's final total was 280/6, with Lewis's 20 from six balls adding an extra buffer. Anurasiri's 1–27 from ten overs made him easily the pick of the Sri Lankan bowlers, with Labrooy (1–68) and Gurusinha (2–67) conceding heavily. If Sri Lanka were to win, they would need to score at 5.62 runs per over.

Channel Nine did not cover the match in Australia, but Sky needed to televise it for the UK. Charles Colvile recollected that Sky 'had to suddenly scrape together crews because back in London they said, "What do you mean, you're not doing England versus Sri Lanka? It's England playing – we've got to show it." So the producer was scouring around, and he found a ramshackle lot, half of whom had never seen a cricket match before in their life. There was a famous moment where he said, "Camera seven, give me a crowd shot please," and the bloke gave him a shot of the clouds in the sky because he didn't understand. He thought he said "cloud shot".'

Roshan Mahanama and Athula Samarasekera opened for Sri Lanka, and the latter was permitted to bat with a runner due to a knee injury. The innings was not four overs old when Graham Gooch injured himself running to retrieve the ball from the boundary. The England captain pulled up as he ran, grabbing his left leg, before leaving the field for treatment. Gladstone Small came on to the field as twelfth man, while Alec Stewart took over the captaincy.

England's spirits were soon lifted when Mahanama tried to run a Chris Lewis ball away but steered it to Botham at slip, who took the chance with ease. Sri Lanka's bright and breezy start of 33 at more than six runs per over had been broken. Samarasekera soon followed, giving Lewis his second wicket, when he hit the ball straight to Richard Illingworth at mid-on. This left Aravinda de Silva and Asanka Gurusinha at the crease, but both perished in quick succession as Lewis struck to grab four wickets in 18 balls. The wicket of de Silva was purely down to Fairbrother's athleticism at square leg. As he dived full length, the ball stuck in Fairbrother's grasp, and Sri Lanka's captain was gone for seven. Gurusinha, already on the receiving end of a fast bouncer, meekly chipped the ball back to Lewis as Sri Lanka slipped to 60/4.

In need of an innings, Sri Lanka looked once again to Arjuna Ranatunga. Hashan Tillakaratne joined him as England were on top of the game and looking for more wickets. While Ranatunga was playing more positively, Tillakaratne was more watchful in his approach. Cognisant of the state of the match, the Sri Lankan wicketkeeper was not looking to give his wicket away. Despite the caution from Tillakaratne, Ranatunga's willingness to score led to another wicket falling. Tillakaratne was unsure of a quick single off the bowling of Botham, but his partner was already bounding towards his crease. Smith and Botham combined to effect the run-out, and Sri Lanka were now 91/5 and in trouble.

As the last recognised batters, Ranatunga and Sanath Jayasuriya were the last reasonable hope for Sri Lanka. Several boundaries brought some confidence, but it was Botham who made the decisive breakthrough. Ranatunga advanced down the pitch, looking to strike the ball over the leg side. The ball took the thinnest of edges to Stewart, and Botham's appeal was finally accepted by umpire Khizer Hayat after a moment's reflection.

The introduction of left-arm spinner Richard Illingworth was too tempting for Jayasuriya, but he did not get enough on the ball, and DeFreitas took a running catch on the boundary to leave Sri Lanka languishing on 123/7. Defeat was certain – the only doubt was about the margin.

Resistance came in the form of bowlers Labrooy and Ramanayake, who, despite scoring slowly, managed to add another 33 runs to the total. Once again, it was Dermot Reeve's array of deliveries and changes of pace that finally wore down Ramanayake: he ballooned a catch to the bowler, who caught it with a tumbling effort. After Ramanayake had fallen for 12, from 38 balls, it was Labrooy who tried to slog Illingworth, but Smith took the catch as the ball sliced off the bat. At 158/9, Sri Lanka's innings was almost over and done with.

The inevitable finally came with the score on 170, as Reeve trapped Anurasiri in front of his stumps with a slower ball. The margin of victory was 106 runs, with Lewis's 4–30 helping to secure the Man-of-the-Match award. The victory all but assured England of a semi-final place with three games still to go. More troubling were the effects of Graham Gooch's injury. Further examination showed that there was a small tear in the hamstring. The prognosis was unknown, and with Allan Lamb still out with a similar injury, England were down to 12 fit players, and the two missing were massively experienced.

Tuesday, 10 March brought two critical games in the battle for the semi-final places. At Manuka Oval in Canberra, South Africa would be looking for a victory over Zimbabwe to take them to eight points. Before that game was to start, India and the West Indies met at the Basin Reserve in Wellington. India were on five points, along with Sri Lanka, while the West Indies were on four with Australia. Whoever could secure the victory in Wellington would help their cause.

At the toss, Mohammed Azharuddin called correctly and decided to bat first. India had replaced Vinod Kambli with Pravin Amre, while the West Indies had selected Phil Simmons in place of Malcolm Marshall. It was reported that Marshall was suffering from an ankle injury, but Simmons's selection gave them an extra batter.

Opening the innings for India were regular opener Kris Srikkanth and pinch-hitter Ajay Jadeja. Kapil Dev had played the role in the last, rain-affected game, but Jadeja returned to face the West Indies. Facing Ambrose in the first over, he scored the first runs when he turned the pace bowler away off his legs for a single. More runs came from a good shot on the off side in the third over, as India's innings started slowly. Both Ambrose and new-ball partner Winston Benjamin started off with a good line and length.

By the 12th over, India had moved steadily to 30/0 when Srikkanth lofted Benjamin over the top for a welcome boundary to relieve some pressure. The West Indies were backing up a tight bowling performance with good fielding. Cummins, replacing Ambrose, could have picked up a wicket in his first over, but the ball flew agonisingly wide of Carl Hooper at slip.

Despite Jadeja and Srikkanth playing some expansive shots, West Indian fielders always seemed to be in the way or running down the ball. The fifty came up in the 16th over, and when

Jadeja found the boundary in the next, the West Indies looked as though they were desperate for a breakthrough. Jadeja duly obliged with a poor shot that found Benjamin at mid-off, off the bowling of Simmons. Gone for 27 from 61 balls, Jadeja departed with the score on 56.

Azharuddin came to the wicket and was soon off the mark when Simmons drifted one of his medium-pacers down the leg side. A delicate glance from the Indian captain ran away for a boundary. Hooper's spin bowling gave Azharuddin more opportunities to show his shot ability all over the ground with some wristy placements. Simmons thought he had his second wicket when Srikkanth nibbled outside off stump. Both bowler and wicketkeeper celebrated more than appealed, but were left astonished by umpire Steve Woodward's lack of response.

Azharuddin brought up the Indian 100 in the 27th over with a lusty blow back down the ground for four. Srikkanth's innings was ended when he flicked a quicker ball from Hooper straight to Gus Logie at square leg. The ball was a low full toss; the opener flicked at it, his bottom hand came off the bat, and the ball flew straight to the fielder. India were 102/2 in the 28th over, and now Sachin Tendulkar came to the crease. Having scored 54 not out and 81 in his last two innings, Tendulkar experienced a rare failure. A marvellous leg-cutter opened him up, and the ball took the edge for Williams to catch. Ambrose could have had the wicket of Tendulkar earlier, but Williams had put the catch down; this time there was no reprieve.

India were still in a good position, albeit with less than 20 overs left, with Azharuddin and Sanjay Manjrekar at the crease. A Simmons over cost eight runs, and India must have thought they could use that as the springboard. Azharuddin's fifty, from 62 balls, was achieved in the next over. It was his 14th in ODIs, and took him past 4,500 runs in his career. With the partnership worth 51, a flat-batted shot from Azharuddin flew straight to Ambrose, who took the catch. As he tried to get Cummins away, the ball flew straight to the fielder, and India lost their fourth wicket in the 43rd over. India were on 166, and still well placed to post a decent total for the West Indies to chase.

Unfortunately for India, they did anything but, as the loss of Azharuddin sparked a monumental collapse. Kapil Dev's slog went straight up into the air, and Haynes took the catch before Manjrekar, scoring well despite not reaching the boundary, was run out for 27. Carl Hooper's swift footwork and accurate throw left Manjrekar way short of his ground.

Kiran More smashed Cummins for four before slicing the ball to Hooper to give the bowler his third wicket. India had slumped to 180/7, but worse was to follow. Amre's ambitious shot, off the bowling of Ambrose, sailed high into the air before Hooper comfortably took his second catch in minutes. Prabhakar managed to find the boundary, courtesy of a misfield from Keith Arthurton, before Cummins secured his fourth wicket with Richie Richardson's diving catch at midwicket. Prabhakar middled the ball, but the West Indies captain plucked it out of the air to leave India with one wicket remaining.

A run-out ended the innings, when Richardson unsuccessfully tried to repeat his catch from earlier, but the Indian batters' communication was left wanting and Williams ran out Raju. India were 197 all out after collapsing from 166/3. The last seven wickets had fallen for 31 runs, including four for Cummins from the last 22 balls of his spell. Ambrose's 2–24 assisted Cummins as the West Indians were left to chase a smaller total than they would have thought with seven overs to go.

During the innings break, Basin Reserve was shrouded in dark clouds, and the famous winds in Wellington appeared to be blowing in some rain. With a delay and the dreaded rain rule looming, the West Indies openers started the innings fully expecting to chase a revised total that would be more difficult than the 3.96 runs per over they started with. The first boundary came in the first over when Haynes cut Kapil Dev for a well-placed four. Lara was also in the mood with sumptuous fours off Prabhakar and Kapil Dev. In the fourth over, he pounced on a Prabhakar delivery angling down the leg side and smashed it six rows back for a six. In the same over, he drove another boundary as the West Indies chased down the total at a swift pace.

With Lara going after the bowlers, India were struggling to contain him. After one crashing four, Kapil Dev and Prabhakar had an animated conversation at the wicket. Lara's response was to clip the ball away sweetly off his legs for yet another boundary. The score had moved on to 43/0 in the sixth over, with Lara responsible for 35 of those runs from a mere 22 balls. The fifty partnership came up in the same over when Haynes whipped a ball through midwicket for another four.

With the weather becoming more inclement, Haynes went over the top of midwicket in the next over for his third boundary of the innings. His desire to match his partner's rapidity of scoring finally got the better of him later in the over when he cracked a cut shot straight at Sanjay Manjrekar, who held on to the catch. He shook his fingers from the stinging shot before receiving the adulation of the Indian fielders. The bowler, Kapil Dev, and captain, Mohammed Azharuddin, were deep in conference while this was taking place.

It did not take Phil Simmons long to get into the action. He heaved Kapil Dev from middle stump, and the ball sailed towards the old stand for six. Venkatapathy Raju fared no better, as Simmons launched him backward of square for a one-bounce four. The West Indies were racing away at more than seven runs per over and seemed unstoppable.

At the end of the 11th over, umpires Steve Randell and Steve Woodward conferred before deciding that the weather was sufficiently wet to suspend play. The Indian team were quick to exit the field, but both Simmons and Lara were, unsurprisingly, reluctant to move. Simmons stood still, using his bat to balance, while Lara remonstrated. Play was delayed by 20 minutes in total. The target was reduced by three runs to 195, of which another 104 were required – but four overs had been lost, leaving 46 in all, and only 35 remaining.

On the resumption, it was India who struck first when Lara's whirlwind innings ended. The rain delay had broken the momentum, and Lara's sloppy drive went straight to Manjrekar, who took the catch. Having been struggling for the breakthrough, India were delighted as the West Indies had lost their second wicket with only one more run on the board. At the start of the 13th over, Simmons found the boundary again as he appeared to carry on with his aggressive intent. In the same over, he tried again to hit Kapil Dev for a boundary, but the ball flew high into the air. Tendulkar took responsibility for the catch and managed to hold on, despite hitting his head on the ground as he tumbled back. He took a little while to get back to his feet, hindered by several congratulatory pats on the head from team-mates.

Having already survived a good shout for caught behind as well as Srikkanth putting down a sharp chance, Richardson fell to Srinath to leave the West Indies on 98/4. This time, Srikkanth made no mistake as the West Indies captain hit one out of the middle but straight at the fielder. Gus Logie joined Keith Arthurton at the crease and swept his first ball for a run. It also brought up the hundred for the West Indies. Another sweep was more successful as Srinath's poor fielding, as he was left flat on his back by the spin of the ball, allowed it to find the boundary. A fielding error from Tendulkar, possibly feeling the after-effects of his knock on the head, gave Logie an additional bonus run. Logie's propensity to play across the line led to his downfall when he top-edged a ball from Raju, and Kiran More took the easy looping catch.

The West Indies had slumped from 81/1 to 112/5 in the 21st over. If they could bat through the overs, 83 runs at less than four an over was comfortable due to their fast start. However, several careless shots had put them in a far more difficult position than was necessary. India had given themselves a chance to win.

Arthurton and Carl Hooper, the last recognised West Indian batters, set about their target with a more sensible approach. Arthurton was mainly dealing in pushing the ball around for runs rather than playing big shots. Hooper hit Tendulkar over the covers for four in the 28th over, but he too was playing a more watchful innings. Another boundary came off Tendulkar's next over, this time over the leg side, before he played a deft shot that ran the ball for four. Tendulkar had gone for 20 runs in his three overs, so Azharuddin would need to act.

A measure of Arthurton's patience and willingness to nurdle the ball around Basin Reserve was the fact that he faced 77 balls before hitting his first boundary. When it came, it was a beautifully timed on drive that flew past the outstretched hand of Kapil Dev. It was the same fielder who had a chance to take a catch off Hooper, but the veteran all-rounder spilled the ball. The game was pretty much lost for India at that point, but any lingering hope was soon gone.

Fittingly, it was Keith Arthurton who hit the winning run, as his patient 58 not out had helped the West Indies to victory. Carl Hooper's 34 from 58 balls contributed to the unbroken partnership of 83, to deliver a five-wicket win with 34 balls of the innings remaining. Despite his valuable innings, Arthurton did not secure the Man-of-the-Match award, as Anderson Cummins's

4–33 was deemed more worthy. Importantly, the West Indies had become the first team in the tournament to reach a rain-adjusted target. Unsurprisingly, they also would have won the match using DL or DLS. Stern calculated that the totals required would have been 189 and 190 respectively.

New Zealand and England were sitting comfortably at the top of the table. The other two semi-final places were far from settled, with only Zimbabwe out of the reckoning. Australia and Pakistan could ill afford another defeat, with South Africa and the West Indies having six points each.

	Pld	Won	Lost	Tied	N/R	Pts	Net R/R	For	Against
New Zealand	5	5	0	0	0	10	0.860	1008/199.2	915/218.0
England	5	4	0	0	1	9	1.054	849/180.4	729/200.0
South Africa	5	3	2	0	0	6	0.118	949/232.5	868/219.2
West Indies	6	3	3	0	0	6	−0.016	1176/287.1	1169/284.2
India	6	2	3	0	1	5	0.288	1029/211.0	943/205.3
Sri Lanka	6	2	3	0	1	5	−0.564	1080/249.1	1187/242.2
Australia	5	2	3	0	0	4	−0.254	977/240.0	1015/234.4
Pakistan	5	1	3	0	1	3	−0.138	820/185.0	831/181.5
Zimbabwe	5	0	5	0	0	0	−1.261	911/187.1	1142/186.2

Chapter Nine

Guilty as Charged

Manuka Oval in Canberra hosted the clash of the African teams, with South Africa and Zimbabwe meeting in Australia's capital. The teams had met, five weeks previously, at the Harare Sports Club for the first match between the two countries. Over 9,000 fans had packed the temporary stands to witness the game. South Africa prevailed by six wickets, buoyed by Donald's 3–29 and Kirsten's 64, before the teams travelled to the Cricket World Cup.

South Africa made one change to their line-up, with Peter Kirsten returning in place of Mark Rushmere. Despite the selectors wanting Kirsten to sit the game out, he insisted on playing. It was a change that Rushmere had anticipated, 'I thought I batted pretty well against Pakistan in making 35 from the number three position with Peter Kirsten injured. I knew Peter was coming back from his injury after this game so I, unfortunately, knew that I would lose my place in the team.'

Zimbabwe decided to make two changes as Wayne James, returning from injury, and Malcolm Jarvis came in for Iain Butchart and Alistair Campbell. The damp conditions in

Canberra were not to Zimbabwe's liking, while South Africa's travel schedule led them to limit practice to a light workout. Having won the toss, Wessels asked Zimbabwe to bat. It had been a successful tactic in Harare, and South Africa's captain was willing to apply the same approach at Manuka Oval.

The decision to bowl was soon proven to be a wise one when James played across the line and Meyrick Pringle trapped him in front for just five runs. The situation soon became worse for Zimbabwe when a ball from Allan Donald, despite the slowness of the pitch, smacked into Andy Flower's finger and caused the opener to retire hurt with the score on 26/1. David Houghton and Andy Pycroft's first job was to avoid losing another wicket, and they did so with some careful play. South Africa's bowlers failed to make further inroads, and the fifty came up with the partnership worth 24. Maybe feeling more confident, Pycroft attempted a drive off the bowling of McMillan, but managed to edge the ball to Wessels at slip, and Zimbabwe had lost their third wicket. Pycroft had scored 19 runs, without a boundary, and Zimbabwe were reduced to 51/2.

More solid play from Houghton and new batting partner Andy Waller moved Zimbabwe slowly forward. Waller did find the boundary for just the second time in the innings, before the unlikeliest of bowlers left Zimbabwe in disarray. In the 25th over, Waller decided that Peter Kirsten was the bowler to single out and tried to clear the midwicket boundary. Instead, Hansie Cronje took the catch and Zimbabwe were in trouble at 72/3 with almost half of the innings gone.

Having not learned from Waller's miscalculation, Houghton tried the same stroke off the same bowler and achieved the same result. Cronje took the catch to leave Zimbabwe on 80/4 in the 27th over. The batters crossed; Ali Shah pushed at Kirsten's next ball and Wessels gratefully took the catch. Kirsten had taken three wickets in nine balls, and Zimbabwe were as good as beaten already. Desperate times require desperate actions, and Andy Flower came back in to bat despite his finger injury. Brandes played his standard, but guaranteed entertaining, innings. Where Waller and Houghton had failed, the stocky fast bowler succeeded, and he planted the ball over midwicket for six. He also scored a four to single-handedly double the number of boundaries for the innings.

A partnership of 35 from Brandes and Flower ended with Hansie Cronje nicking the edge of Flower's bat to finish his brave innings of 19. The new batter was Mark Burmester, but he too succumbed to the bowling of Cronje, for one, to leave Zimbabwe on 117/7. Brandes played one too many shots with the score on 123, and nicked off to Richardson.

More big hitting from Malcolm Jarvis added a six and a four, while John Traicos batted admirably to add a further 28 runs. Jarvis drove the ball back to McMillan to end his innings of 17. Kevin Duers then contributed five runs, before Donald's pace was too much and he lost his stumps. Zimbabwe were all out for 163 from 48.3 overs. The South African bowling had been clinical at times, but somewhat wasteful. The top scorer was extras, with 13 wides, 11 leg-byes and four no-balls generously inflating Zimbabwe's paltry score. Kirsten's 3–31 and McMillan's 3–30 had done most of the damage. In their combined ten-over spell, Kirsten and Cronje had conjured up 5–48.

With Andy Flower nursing his damaged finger, Houghton took over the wicketkeeping duties. It was the first time he had kept wicket in three years. South Africa's opening partnership of Wessels and Hudson started brightly, with 27 runs scored by the eighth over. It was during this over that left-armer Malcolm Jarvis found a peach of a leg-stump yorker to send Hudson back for 13.

With the partnership broken, Peter Kirsten joined Wessels, and they set about reaching the target safely rather than being too concerned about the net run rate. Wessels was batting with a sore thumb and did offer a chance to Duers, at fine leg, but the opportunity went begging. A conservative approach saw South Africa slowly, but surely, accumulate the runs. Five maidens demonstrated the watchful nature of both batters.

By the time Zimbabwe did make the next breakthrough, South Africa were within 25 runs of their target. Wessels was deceived by a slower ball from Ali Shah and was bowled for 70. A partnership of 112 was the first one for a South African partnership in the Cricket World Cup, and superseded their efforts in Delhi by one run. The victory was achieved in the 46th over with the loss of just one more wicket. Kuiper's drive to mid-off was taken by Burmester off the bowling of Brandes. It was too little, too late to prevent a seven-wicket victory for South Africa. It was also their third consecutive win, and it promoted them to third in the table. Kirsten's bowling efforts, and 62 not out, secured the Man-of-the-Match award.

Reflecting on the victory recently, Kepler Wessels commented on Zimbabwe's competitiveness. 'We won easily, but it wasn't that we went into the game thinking that this is gonna be like a walk in the park. You approach that match like you would approach any other game in that tournament, because they did have the personnel to – if you had a slightly off day and they were good – they could beat you.'

With the tournament proving to be a success on the pitch, Australian viewers were less than complimentary about Channel Nine's coverage. The India versus West Indies and South Africa versus Zimbabwe matches were not shown live but limited to a highlights show that wasn't broadcast until 3am. The channel's director of sport was defensive of the position when quoted in the *Sydney Morning Herald*: 'We worked out which ones to cover months ago, and we can't cover every game, because apart from the cost, it's not technically possible. We have to look at the games and work out which ones will attract the public interest. As it is, we're covering 19 games in full.'

The sun was shining at the WACA in Perth as Australia played Pakistan in a must-win day/night match. The conditions were typical for the WACA, with a hard, bouncy pitch and a fast outfield. The Australians made one change to their line-up, with Bruce Reid, playing on his home ground, coming in for Peter Taylor.

The pace of the wicket was the deciding factor in playing three fast bowlers. Pakistan were lifted by the return of Ramiz Raja and Javed Miandad into the batting order, with Zahid Fazal and Iqbal Sikander making way for them. The toss was won by Imran Khan, who preferred to bat first and let Australia chase under the lights at the WACA.

Aamer Sohail and Ramiz Raja opened for Pakistan, and Australia were denied the perfect start when Reid overstepped before Sohail nicked the ball to Healy. The opening spell by Reid and Craig McDermott offered up 11 extras in the first 13 overs. Pakistan had reached 44/0 when Mike Whitney's first ball nipped back in to Ramiz Raja, and he just managed to squirt the ball wide of Tom Moody at slip.

The partnership was up to 78 when Ramiz took two steps down the pitch to try to pull Whitney through midwicket. Instead, he picked out Allan Border, who held on to effect the breakthrough. Ramiz's innings of 34 from 61 balls brought Salim Malik to the crease. It was a short-lived innings, as Moody, in his first over, bowled the Pakistan batter for a six-ball duck. With Malik playing down the wrong line, the ball hit middle and off, and the score was now 80/2 in the 21st over.

Losing two quick wickets, Pakistan had the vastly experienced Javed Miandad coming in next. Already averaging 63 for the tournament, and scoring at 65 runs per 100 balls, Miandad put away Bruce Reid's welcome half-volley outside off stump for a four. Reid was also the bowler, an over later, when Aamer Sohail reached his half-century with a lofted clip over mid-on for another boundary. It was greeted by Javed Miandad's congratulatory pat on the back, which was accompanied by a lecture for the young opener. With Reid getting scored off too freely for Border's liking, he withdrew the 6ft 8in left-arm fast bowler for the medium pace of Mark Waugh. Aamer Sohail was in no mood to slow down and took 13 off the over. The drinks break came as a welcome relief for Australia, with Pakistan primed for a large total.

Moving on to 76, Aamer Sohail decided that Moody was to go the same way as Mark Waugh. However, Moody's height extracted more bounce, and Sohail's attempted pull over midwicket flew high into the air for Healy to take an excellent running catch over his shoulder. Moody had broken through once again, with Sohail and Miandad's partnership ended on 77. Australia had needed this, as Pakistan had accelerated from 100 to 150 in just 23 minutes. The score was 157/3 with 13 overs still left in the innings.

The fall of the wicket brought Pakistan's two experienced, and sometimes pugnacious, cricketers together, with Imran Khan being the next man in. Both batters played conservatively for a while, until a discussion signalled a change of intent. Javed Miandad's step down the wicket, crashing Whitney through the covers, marked the acceleration. In the same over, Imran jumped on a ball angled down the leg side and lifted it cleanly into the stands.

Steve Waugh bowled the 45th over and, with two balls, tore into the Pakistan batting. First to go was Miandad, trying to make room to cut but edging the ball to Healy. With Miandad gone for 46, Pakistan were 193/4. A single for Inzamam-ul-Haq brought Imran on strike. His attempted slog skewed off the bat into the air, and Moody positioned himself well to take the catch at mid-on. Imran's innings of 13 was over when his team needed him at the crease.

Inzamam scored runs around the pitch, without getting any boundaries, before Ijaz Ahmed was on strike. Steve Waugh couldn't take a sharp caught-and-bowled chance off Inzamam but excellent fielding limited the runs conceded. On his second ball, Ijaz had a huge edge, but Healy's outstretched arm couldn't hold on to it. In the confusion after the dropped catch, Ijaz looked for a run and advanced down the pitch. His partner was unsure, and Healy's quick reflexes and throw left Ijaz stranded and out for a duck.

Wasim Akram's stay at the crease lasted one ball. Steve Waugh deceived the all-rounder with a slower delivery which he could only push at, and it looped to Mark Waugh. Pakistan's innings had arrested, and they had slumped to 205/7. From there, they could only manage 220 from their 50 overs. They managed to lose another two wickets, Inzamam for 16 and Moin Khan for five, as Australia pulled them back after a total of over 250 had looked feasible. The collapse of the innings was 6–27, with Steve Waugh's 3–36 being outstanding after he had bowled several wides and conceded some boundaries early on.

The Australian response was cautious. In the first five overs just 13 runs were scored, with more coming in extras than runs off the bat. Moody had scored four from 17 balls when Aaqib bowled an outswinger which nicked the edge. Salim Malik, at first slip, took the catch. Wasim Akram was struggling with no-balls despite bowling an attacking line. His frustration was exacerbated when an edge from Boon flew near the slips but ran away for a boundary. Akram continued to remonstrate as he walked back to his mark. A change of bowling angle saw the ball run across right-handers, and he was convinced that Boon had touched a ball. Umpire Karl Liebenberg was unmoved as Akram's displeasure threatened to spill over. Imran Khan was quick to try to calm his players before the situation escalated.

With the Pakistan bowlers giving Marsh and Boon a working-over, Imran felt that he could utilise three slips. This paid off when Aaqib forced Boon into a shot that squirmed out to third slip, where Mushtaq took the catch to the delight of Pakistan's players. Australia's score was 31/2 in the tenth over, and the game was delicately poised.

Having created pressure with Wasim and Aaqib, Imran needed to get ten overs from Ijaz Ahmed. With a bowling average of 77.00 and only two ODI wickets to his name, it would be a hard task. He had bowled 14 overs in the tournament so far, but his medium pace would be welcome relief for the Australians. Imran brought himself on at the other end to try to keep Australia's scoring rate down. It was the 17th over by the time Australia reached their fifty. Dean Jones's pick-up off his legs despatched Imran to the boundary, to provide a much-needed four. Marsh's patchy form continued, so the impetus was on Jones to keep the scoreboard ticking over. Using his feet to Ijaz, he whipped a ball over the covers for just the third boundary of the innings so far.

Despite several runs from overthrows, Pakistan kept Australia in check, and it was the 29th over when the hundred came up. The required run rate was creeping up towards six per over, with the leg spin of Mushtaq to face. Jones tried to hit Mushtaq for a six, but only managed to mistime the ball for Aaqib to take the catch. The partnership of 85, in 22 overs, had been broken and Australia were 116/3 in the 32nd over.

Marsh's mammoth innings ended soon after when he tried to cut Imran away; the ball wasn't wide enough, and the edge was caught behind by Moin Khan. For his 39 runs, Marsh had taken 91 balls, and his only boundary was a French cut. If Marsh was struggling, Allan Border was desperate, and his tournament got decidedly worse. With a solitary run to his name, he swept Mushtaq to backward point, and Australia had fallen to 123/5. In his five innings, Border had amassed 30 runs – an unacceptable return from any international, let alone the captain and a massively successful batter of his calibre.

The hope would have been for the Waugh twins to mount a rescue attempt, but Steve was soon out, caught down the leg side for five. The score was now 130/6, with Pakistan in the ascendancy. Waugh appeared to be incensed by something said to him and stood at the wicket. Imran Khan gestured his apologies as his team threatened, once again, to overstep the mark. Pakistan's exuberance and Australia's sensitivity due to the pressure were not mixing well.

Mark Waugh was joined at the crease by Ian Healy, who had scored 541 runs at 22.54 for Australia, almost at a run a ball. He would need to support Waugh if Australia were to turn the situation around. A beautiful shot through midwicket, off Mushtaq, signalled that with Waugh at the crease the match was far from over. The partnership had reached 26 when Healy tried to pull Aaqib. The bowler's pace cramped up Healy, and Ijaz Ahmed got into position and took the catch. At 156/7 in the 43rd over, Australia's fate looked sealed for the match and possibly the tournament. The return of Wasim Akram accounted for Craig McDermott, for a duck, with a quick inswinging delivery that trapped him in front. It was a ball that was far too good for a tailender.

There was only one course of action left for Mark Waugh, and that was to swing the bat. Facing Mushtaq, he charged him and smashed the ball through mid-on for a four. Revenge was almost immediate – the sweep shot did not have sufficient distance, and Ijaz took his third catch of the innings. It was game over at 167/9, and only a matter of time before Pakistan secured the victory.

With Mike Whitney and Bruce Reid at the crease, Pakistan were eager to close out the game. Mushtaq was convinced that he had Whitney caught behind, but Karl Liebenberg disagreed. Mushtaq and Moin Khan were adamant, but Whitney took exception to the appeals. An altercation took place, and umpire Piloos Reporter had to physically get between an irate Whitney and several of the Pakistan players. The not-out decision seemed wrong, but the situation was just the catalyst, as friction had been building all through the Australian innings.

It was finally over when Akram bowled Whitney. Australia were all out for 172, and the margin of victory for Pakistan was 48 runs. Only three Australians managed to get into double figures as Akram (2–28), Aaqib (3–21), Imran (2–32) and Mushtaq (3–41) contained the scoring admirably. Australia lost their last eight wickets for 56 runs. Border said that Australia had got their 'just deserts' with the comprehensive loss. Ian Chappell was more forthright and labelled the team as 'world-class duffers'. Aamer Sohail was named Man-of-the-Match, which came with $500. He did lose $250 of that with a fine, along with Mike Whitney and Moin Khan, for their roles in the unsavoury incident near the end of the innings.

The following day, New Zealand and India met at Carisbrook in Dunedin. New Zealand had already qualified for the semifinals, but India needed to win this game and beat South Africa in Adelaide to go through. Mohammed Azharuddin was quoted in the *Otago Daily Times* as saying, 'We cannot fail again. If we do not win against New Zealand, we might as well go home.' Martin Crowe's concern was a potential semi-final outside of

New Zealand, but Australia's defeat against Pakistan made them far less likely as opposition.

In the lead-up to the game, New Zealand coach Warren Lees intimated that both Danny Morrison, suffering from a groin strain, and Willie Watson would be rested and that Chris Cairns and Murphy Su'a, the latter having not yet played, would come in. However, only Cairns was selected for the match. The conditions in Dunedin would not be conducive to India – cold and windy, with temperatures not due to get above 10°C. India only made one change, with batter Pravin Amre dropping out for the extra bowling option of Subroto Banerjee.

Both captains were intent on batting first if they won the toss, and it was Mohammed Azharuddin who won the option. The very first ball of the match almost led to a wicket, when Kris Srikkanth missed a full toss from Chris Cairns. Despite the confident appeals, the ball was adjudged to have missed leg stump. Opening the bowling at the other end was Dipak Patel. Once again, Crowe was confident of the off-spinner's efficacy in the situation. Srikkanth planned to hit Patel out of the attack, but his first attempt went straight into the welcoming hands of Rod Latham at long-on.

Things went from bad to worse for India when Ajay Jadeja pulled a hamstring and was forced to retire hurt. The opener limped off the ground, requiring aid to walk. Coming in to bat was Sachin Tendulkar, to join captain Mohammed Azharuddin with the score, effectively, 21/2. Both batters had, significantly, been the most consistent for India, while the rest had struggled. Unsurprisingly, they set about rebuilding the innings. Azharuddin clipped a ball off his hips for four when Cairns bowled a bad ball. The Srikkanth plan had forced India to play 'proper cricket shots', and there could not be two better players in the team to execute that.

New Zealand's plan, as it was in every other game, was to eat through the overs as economically as possible, and they did so. By the time Azharuddin slotted a beautiful drive for four, India had used up almost half of their overs and were only 77/1. Seeing his captain hit a four, Tendulkar drove a ball high over the infield for another boundary in the same Watson over. He continued to accumulate runs with sensible stroke-making, without playing aggressive shots. In the *New Zealand Cricket News World Cup Special*, Azharuddin was quoted as saying the reasoning behind this was that they did not want to 'lose a second wicket cheaply'.

It was Patel's last over that triggered the decision to accelerate the innings. It was the 38th over, and India were 141/1. Azharuddin advanced down the wicket and successfully executed the shot that Srikkanth perished with. The six also brought up Azharuddin's fifty from 97 balls. Going aerial again, this time the shot was just short of the boundary and Greatbatch took a sharp tumbling chance.

Sanjay Manjrekar joined Tendulkar at the crease with India on 149/2. They were well placed for a good total, but their cause was harmed when Chris Harris picked up the valuable wicket of Tendulkar. Harris's wide ball should have been put away, but Tendulkar could only feather an edge to Ian Smith, standing up behind the stumps. The loss of Tendulkar, gone for a valuable 84, was a body blow for India. The hitting ability of Kapil Dev, coming in at six, could give India the impetus they required. A whipped four to the leg side, bisecting the two fielders on the boundary, demonstrated his ability. Crashing a four through extra cover, Kapil Dev was motoring at well over a run a ball. Crowe's response was to take Cairns out of the attack, his pace having helped India's cause, and rely on Harris to stem the flow of runs.

Harris's first ball to Manjrekar was meekly batted back for the easiest of caught-and-bowled chances. Again, he had broken through and India were 201/4. The new batter was Banerjee: this was just his fifth ODI batting innings, but he had scored 25 not out versus England in India's first match. Kapil Dev had already hit five boundaries in his 33 not out when he tried to heave Harris over deep midwicket, but Gavin Larsen took the catch. It was Harris's third wicket of the innings, and would stop its flow.

In the last over, bowled by Watson, India lost Banerjee to another catch on the boundary before ending the innings on 230/6. It was the fourth highest total for a team batting first at Carisbrook. Also, no team had ever successfully chased more than 204 at the ground, but the total should have been more. After the early loss of Srikkanth, Azharuddin and Tendulkar had built a good platform, but 34 runs from those last five overs felt insufficient. Patel's 2–29, once again, stifled the scoring, while Harris's 3–55 included vital wickets.

A group of students managed to bring a couch into Carisbrook so they could watch the match in comfort. Another couch was brought into the ground, but was burned, presumably for heat, which caused the terrace to be enveloped by the smoke. Despite the cold and windy weather, the match was stopped by a streaker. Wearing just underpants, and a blanket for a cloak, the gentleman was escorted off the field by police at the boundary edge.

As the New Zealand innings commenced, a gust of wind estimated to be 120km/h (75mph) blew down part of the sightscreen which 'caused havoc with the spectators', reported the *Otago Daily Times*. Opening for New Zealand was the combination of Latham and Greatbatch. After a sedate first over, the second from Prabhakar saw Greatbatch in full flow. Advancing down the wicket, he smashed the ball low and hard over extra cover for the first boundary. The next over saw a deftly guided ball to the boundary as the opener showed that he wasn't all about power.

Greatbatch plundered another boundary, this time a short-arm jab for six, before Latham played down the wrong line and lost his stumps. It was Prabhakar who took the wicket, and New Zealand were 36/1 in the eighth over. The incoming batter was the vastly experienced Andrew Jones, who was well suited to batting through while Greatbatch took apart the Indian bowling attack. Prabhakar was hit for four before the opener repeated the stroke, a pick-up from middle stump crisply despatched to leg for a maximum off the bowling of Kapil Dev. A short-arm jab over the covers for four ended the over as New Zealand raced towards their target.

Srinath replaced Kapil Dev, whose first six overs had gone for 44 runs, and Greatbatch brought his fifty up from 47 balls. At the other end, Jones was happy to play the understudy but put away any bad balls. In the 18th over, Banerjee was hit for boundaries on both sides of the wicket as Jones's classical drive punctured the fielders. In his next over, Banerjee disappeared back over his head for six as Greatbatch continued his big shots.

Greatbatch finally perished for 73 with another attempted six over the leg side. This time, his sweep didn't have enough height and flew straight to Banerjee. The New Zealanders in the crowd applauded his effort, while the Indian supporters waved their flags in relief. New Zealand had reached 118/2 in the 24th over when Greatbatch departed. He was replaced by Martin Crowe.

Raju's bowling had not only removed Greatbatch, but had also slowed the run rate. Jones flat-batted him back for four, more reminiscent of Greatbatch, to relieve some pressure. He repeated the stroke in the next over, for a similar result, through mid-off. Azharuddin's answer to Crowe, who was in imperious form in the tournament, was to employ a silly point, but he swept Raju for a boundary. He then pulled Kapil Dev for six as the wind started to gust across the ground. Having just swept

Raju for another boundary, Crowe was looking to finish the game quickly. However, a swift piece of improvisation ended his innings for 26 from 28 balls. Dropping the ball backward of square, he set off for a run, but More's outstretched hand grabbed the ball and he flicked it towards the stumps. With Crowe short of his ground, the ball dislodged a bail, and New Zealand lost their third wicket with the score on 172.

New Zealand switched their batting order around by employing wicketkeeper Ian Smith at five rather than Ken Rutherford. The crowd's disappointment that their local favourite Rutherford, who was born in Dunedin and played for Otago, was demoted was palpable. Smith's task was to score quickly, and he pulled Prabhakar for four, through the leg side, before succumbing to the same shot soon after. The substitute fielder, Pravin Amre, took the catch almost on the boundary rope, but Smith was gone for nine. The score was now 172/4 in the 32nd over, and New Zealand were still in prime position.

While the other batters had been playing their shots, Jones had quietly accumulated his runs. A back-foot cut off Banerjee brought up his fifty, his 23rd in ODIs, from 89 balls. In the same over, Rutherford eased a ball behind point for a boundary. The next ball was deposited into the crowd for six, from a pull shot, as Rutherford assumed the aggressor role. Raju bowled the next over and Rutherford went aerial for a boundary, which brought up the 200. Another boundary, this time sliced off the edge but still running away for four, came up as Rutherford moved on to 21. The next ball kept low, and Rutherford's attempted pull missed the ball and hit his pads. Umpire Ian Robinson gave the batsman out and the Carisbrook crowd gasped.

Chris Harris was next man in, and he added four runs while Jones pushed his team closer to the target. Prabhakar's yorker accounted for Harris, but Chris Cairns hit a four as New

Zealand reached the required total with 17 balls remaining. Jones finished up on 67 not out – his highest score in this Cricket World Cup so far. The defeat for India, by five wickets, eliminated them from the tournament. They had been frozen out in Dunedin. Mark Greatbatch received the Man-of-the-Match award for his impressive innings and two catches. The Indian team manager questioned how long this type of batting could continue, because he felt there was a lot of 'luck' involved. New Zealand's next match was at the weekend, when they would meet second-placed England.

Before England's game with the Kiwis, they had to face a day/night math at the MCG against South Africa. In the lead-up to the game, England's lack of fit players was becoming a concern. Graham Gooch's hamstring injury was going to keep him out of the game. He had responded to treatment, but it was too early to risk him. Allan Lamb's hamstring injury was still not fully healed, so he was also ruled out. Chris Lewis's side strain prevented him from bowling, but he participated as a batter. Neil Fairbrother and Ian Botham had picked up muscle strains but were passed fit to play. Gladstone Small came into the side to join the bowling attack.

South Africa's fitness concerns were over Peter Kirsten's calf injury and Brian McMillan's ankle strain, but both were passed fit to play. They picked the same 11 that had beaten Zimbabwe in Canberra. The South African coach, Mike Procter, was buoyant about his team's prospects. England's fitness concerns and South Africa's form gave him confidence. He was quoted in the *Canberra Times* as saying that 'England have had a fantastic run but we have to look at it positively and maybe they've peaked too early'.

In Gooch's absence, Alec Stewart continued as captain. Winning the toss, he decided to insert South Africa and bowl first. Kepler Wessels and Andrew Hudson opened for South

Africa, and faced Derek Pringle and Phillip DeFreitas with the new ball. The English opening bowlers produced a tidy spell without causing South Africa too many problems. By the 15th over, the fifty partnership was up, and England were still looking for their first wicket.

Gladstone Small, on as first change, soon found that bowling was not going to be too easy. He bowled two overs for 14 runs and was replaced. I asked Andrew Hudson whether it was a conceived plan to hit Small out of the attack: 'Would like to say yes, but sadly no. If someone bowls poorly you score boundaries; we did not want to target anyone particularly.'

Small was being used sparingly by England, and his waywardness could be accounted for by a lack of match practice. Small looked back on this time pragmatically. 'You're waiting for your chance to get back into the attack and, obviously, play your part but when it doesn't come, it doesn't come. So you know you've just got to suck it up and move on. So it was really disappointing that you don't have much input into the game and you only bowled two overs out of the allotted ten.'

While Wessels was playing conservatively, Hudson was more inclined to play shots. In the 26th over, bowled by Botham, Hudson reached his fifty from 81 balls with six boundaries. The score had moved on to 94/0, but the scoring was at less than four runs per over, even though they were batting comfortably. England's bowling attack was weakened further when Dermot Reeve appeared to injure his hamstring after less than three overs. Graeme Hick finished the over and was required to bowl the rest of Reeve's allocation with his off-spinners. It was a matter of walking wounded for England, with Phil Tufnell, the last squad member, coming on to the field as twelfth man.

In the 33rd over, England were convinced that they had run out Wessels. The South African captain, who had reached his fifty in 92 balls, was going for a quick single when Neil Fairbrother's pick-up and throw appeared to leave him short of his ground. The England fielders, Fairbrother in particular, looked astonished that umpire Brian Aldridge hadn't given him out. It appeared that Botham, standing in front of Aldridge at square leg, had obscured his view so he was not in a position to make the decision.

In the next over, England were once again denied despite confident appeals. Hick was bowling to Hudson, who tried to cut him. It was a shot that had already reaped dividends, but this time Alec Stewart, behind the stumps, was convinced that Hudson had nicked the ball. However, Hick struck in his next over, as Hudson offered a simple caught-and-bowled chance and the partnership was finally broken. The opening pair had put on 151 in 218 balls, with Hudson contributing 79. It was the third time that Hudson had fallen to an off-spinner in the tournament.

The new batter was Peter Kirsten, and his first scoring shot was to hit Richard Illingworth back over his head for six. DeFreitas came back on to bowl for England, and was greeted by Wessels with an uncharacteristically aggressive pull shot for four. A single brought Kirsten on strike, and he attempted to whip the bowler through midwicket. It was a clean strike, but the ball went through the air, and Robin Smith, sweeping out on the boundary, took the catch. The score had moved on 170/2, and Kirsten had perished trying to up the run rate.

Jonty Rhodes came in at four to join Wessels and scampered singles. He was denied a four by a sliding stop from Phil Tufnell on the boundary, which was enjoyed and cheered by the England fans. A partnership of 31 runs was ended in the 46th over when Wessels tried to hit Hick towards the longest boundary. Smith ran in and took the catch at waist height to finish Wessels's innings. His score of 85 from 126 balls was achieved with just four boundaries. Rhodes joined him back in the pavilion soon after, for 18. Wanting to take two runs, Rhodes sprinted the first quickly. Adrian Kuiper, just in, wasn't keen, but Rhodes was already running towards him at the same end when Illingworth threw the ball back to the bowler, Graeme Hick. Seeing that both batters were at his end, he threw the ball to Stewart and Rhodes was out. The score was now 205/4 in the 46th over.

When DeFreitas finished his spell of bowling, he too left the field, suffering from groin soreness. England were left in the position of having to request permission to use a fielder from outside the squad. Paul Prichard, the Essex batter who was in Sydney to play grade cricket, was allowed to take the field. Adrian Kuiper and Hansie Cronje squeezed out another 31 runs at the end of the innings. Even with Hick having to bowl the last over, England only conceded one boundary in the last ten overs, Kuiper beating the infield off Pringle. Finishing on 236/4, South Africa had posted a good total, but the base laid by Wessels and Hudson should have led to a larger tally. England would have been pleased to rein the position back in, despite a 151-run opening stand and losing Reeve early in his bowling stint.

England's response started at 6.45pm under the lights of the MCG. Alec Stewart, taking over Gooch's opening role as well as the captaincy, and Ian Botham started the innings. Allan Donald and Meyrick Pringle shared the new ball and kept the scoring down in the first seven overs. Donald's frustration at an edge that flew wide of the slips was evident, while Stewart looked not to be concerned by the false stroke.

In the eighth over, bowled by Meyrick Pringle, Stewart cut him square for a boundary before following it up with an on drive that also went for four. It signalled several well-placed shots that accelerated the scoring. Botham's lofted off drive, off

McMillan, was the pick. England's charge was abruptly stopped when rain stopped play for over 30 minutes. Play resumed at 8.17pm with England's total for victory reduced by 11 runs, but with nine fewer overs to achieve it in. England were 62/0 and needed another 164 from 29 overs.

With just one further run scored, McMillan took the first English wicket when he bowled Botham for 22. Trying to work the ball to the leg side, McMillan got through the gate and demolished middle stump. Two balls later, Robin Smith tried to score off McMillan with one of his trademark cut shots, but could only edge it behind to Richardson, and South Africa were delighted. England were reduced to 63/2, and the pressure was building.

Things got decidedly worse for them in the next over when Hick's attempted drive of Richard Snell took the edge and Richardson had his second catch in two overs. The pressure of the situation, plus the wicket doing more because of the rain, pushed the momentum in South Africa's direction. At 64/3 in the 15th over, Stewart was aware that another wicket lost quickly would put England in trouble. Stewart brought up his fifty, from 61 balls, with a deft shot that raced away for a boundary. The run rate required had reached seven per over. Stewart and Neil Fairbrother needed to increase their scoring rate, or the match would slip away. At the same time, Wessels needed to rest his front-line bowlers and get ten overs from a 'fifth' bowler. This gave England the slightest of opportunities.

The sight of Hansie Cronje and his medium-pacers led Stewart to go aerial over mid-on for a boundary. Fairbrother heaved Adrian Kuiper over square leg, also for a boundary, as both batters addressed their situation. In 13 overs, they added 68 runs in just under an hour's play. Stewart's downfall came when he hesitated before running a single, off Pringle, to

Jonty Rhodes's fielding. It was nearly always suicidal taking on Rhodes, and the ball was soon back into the hands of Pringle with Stewart desperately trying to make his ground. The bowler broke the stumps to leave England on 132/4. Stewart's excellent 77 had kept his team in the game.

England's batting order was now left with unfit all-rounders who could bat, and bowlers. Dermot Reeve came in at six, despite his hamstring injury, and used Graeme Hick as his runner. When Fairbrother crashed Pringle square of the wicket for four, England reached 150 but required 76 from less than 12 overs. If the target was going to be achieved, it would need Fairbrother to stay at the crease. Reeve had rotated well but a rash shot off the bowling of Snell went up in the air, and McMillan took the catch on the edge of the fielding circle. The score had moved on to 166/5 in the 33rd over, and England still required 60 more runs to win.

The next of the 'walking wounded' for England was Chris Lewis, and his impetus was vital. A crunching drive off Kuiper through the covers, beating the fielders, ran away on the damp outfield for a much-needed boundary. In the next over, he lifted McMillan over the top for another four at the square leg boundary. Trying to adjust his length, McMillan then saw the ball race away towards the fine-leg boundary for another four. At just over a run a ball, England were still in the game, and South Africa needed a wicket to arrest the momentum. Allan Donald was brought back into the attack, but Lewis clipped the ball through midwicket. That shot also took England past 200, and the partnership was taking the game away from South Africa. In the 39th over, though, Lewis tried to take a quick single against Jonty Rhodes and, again, there was only one winner. Lewis's frustration was visible, but the partnership of 50 had been vital. In 37 balls, the tide had turned very much towards an England victory. With just ten runs required and four wickets in hand, England would win the game. Surely.

The game went to the final over, and England just required two runs. Richard Snell was bowling and managed two dots from the first two balls. Fairbrother managed to get a single off the third ball to leave Derek Pringle on strike. Trying to strike the fourth ball for the winning run, Pringle hit the low full toss straight at Adrian Kuiper, fielding at midwicket. The fall of the wicket brought Phillip DeFreitas to the crease. With a run needed from one of the last two balls, the game was far closer than England should have made it.

DeFreitas and Fairbrother had a brief chat at the wicket before facing the fifth ball. DeFreitas crashed the ball square of the wicket for a single, and England had clinched their 11th win, with one no-result, in their last 12 ODIs. The clock had struck 10.45pm when the winning run was hit. Playing conditions demanded that play end at 10.15pm so the floodlights could be turned off 15 minutes later. The rain-adjusted innings somehow allowed for the game to go on until a result was achieved. Stern's calculations of 205 (DL) and 208 (DLS) would have been easily made by England.

I asked Andrew Hudson why he thought that South Africa had lost the game despite getting a good start to the match: 'We possibly batted too slowly to start with on a very good Melbourne wicket and were unable to push it in the middle/later overs to post a competitive score.' Jonty Rhodes was slightly less critical of South Africa: 'It was a different game back then, on a really big MCG oval. We had a steady, but slow start and even our clean hitters like Cronje and Kuiper were unable to clear the ropes in the last few overs. It was always our belief that, with our fielding backing our bowlers, any score over 220 we could make difficult to achieve. We also came off for a rain break, which meant that the ball came on to the bat a lot better batting second. Neil Fairbrother was a vastly experienced cricketer and did a great job in getting his team across the line.'

The victory assured England of a place in the semi-final, while South Africa would need to beat India to secure their participation. Alec Stewart was given the Man-of-the-Match award, despite Fairbrother's 75 not out from 83 balls, which had put England in a position to win the game.

	Pld	Won	Lost	Tied	N/R	Pts	Net R/R	For	Against
New Zealand	6	6	0	0	0	12	0.754	1239/246.3	1145/268.0
England	6	5	0	0	1	11	0.895	1075/221.3	954/241.0
South Africa	7	4	3	0	0	8	0.142	1338/319.0	1257/310.1
West Indies	6	3	3	0	0	6	−0.016	1176/287.1	1169/284.2
India	7	2	4	0	1	5	0.177	1259/261.0	1174/252.4
Pakistan	6	2	3	0	1	5	0.099	1040/235.0	1003/231.5
Sri Lanka	6	2	3	0	1	5	−0.564	1080/249.1	1187/242.2
Australia	6	2	4	0	0	4	−0.376	1149/290.0	1235/284.4
Zimbabwe	6	0	6	0	0	0	−1.113	1074/237.1	1306/231.3

Chapter Ten

Revenge and Redemption

The 29th match of the tournament took place in the small town of Berri, in the Riverland region of South Australia. Berri is over 200 miles north-east of Adelaide. Its main economy is horticulture, and fruit – particularly oranges – dominates the town. It is also home to 'The Big Orange', a 15-metre structure in the shape of, you guessed it, an orange – one of many 'big' objects scattered around Australia.

Berri's suitability for hosting a Cricket World Cup was proven in 1988. As part of Australia's bicentennial celebrations, the ACB hosted a Youth Cricket World Cup. The Berri Oval successfully staged four matches in that competition, and was awarded the West Indies versus Sri Lanka game in 1992 as a result.

Several players from the tournament had played in that youth version: Chris Lewis (England), Pravin Amre, Subroto Banerjee, Venkatapathy Raju (all India), Chris Cairns (New Zealand), Aaqib Javed, Inzamam-ul-Haq, Mushtaq Ahmed (all Pakistan),

Sanath Jayasuriya, Chandika Hathurusinghe (both Sri Lanka) and Brian Lara (West Indies).

The oval was more suited to Aussie Rules than cricket, so a new scoreboard was required, along with the construction of sightscreens and improving the facilities. Neil Weinart was the man responsible for preparing the pitch for the game. Working for Australia Post in his day job, Weinart was not a full-time curator ('groundsman' for readers from the northern hemisphere). 'I actually took a week off work to do it because, as country cricketers, we prepared our own wickets, so normally we did a bit on Thursday night at practice and a bit on Friday night and a bit on Saturday morning. In this situation, we had to do extra, so I took the week off from work. Les Burdett, who was the curator at Adelaide Oval at the time, came up and gave us advice on what to do and what kind of wicket they liked at that level.'

Having continuously worried in the run-up to the match, Weinart awoke to the sound of rain on the windows and roof on the morning of the game. It was just after 6am, and he rushed outside to see how badly the rain was falling. He was greeted by a predictably sunny South Australian morning and his wife with the hosepipe spraying the house. Why? Because she thought it might relieve his worries about the match. Weinart says he was not happy at the time.

The match was played under baking sunshine, with temperatures reaching almost 40°C. A crowd of 3,107 attended, fewer than the organisers had hoped, as Aravinda de Silva won the toss and asked the West Indies to bat. The West Indies were unchanged from their game in Wellington. Malcolm Marshall's injured ankle was given more time to heal. Champaka Hathurusinghe and Ruwan Kalpage were brought into the Sri Lankan team, with Sanath Jayasuriya and Graeme Labrooy losing their places after the comprehensive defeat in Ballarat.

First blood was drawn by Sri Lanka when Brian Lara was out early. After he had scored a single from his first five balls faced, Ramanayake took a caught-and-bowled chance. A rare failure from Lara in the tournament, and the West Indies were 6/1. Phil Simmons joined Desmond Haynes at the crease and was soon in the runs.

Both batters played their shots, and the West Indies were quickly recovering from the early loss of Lara. Simmons was dropped when on six, but did not appear to be concerned. Having played little part in the tournament to this point, he seemed intent on making hay in the sunshine. Several brutal strokes left Aravinda de Silva and his men short of ideas about how to break the partnership. Haynes had clubbed three fours and a six when Arjuna Ranatunga, an unlikely wicket-taker, enticed the West Indies opener and he nicked behind to Hashan Tillakaratne. Haynes's innings of 38 from 47 balls had helped the West Indies on to 72/2.

The West Indies captain, Richie Richardson, was next in, but he played a junior role as Simmons showed no signs of curbing his aggression. He gave two chances in successive balls off the bowling of Ranatunga when on 47, but neither could be taken. At the other end, Richardson scored eight off 23 balls before being run out. The captain had played second fiddle to Simmons in their partnership of 31. Keith Arthurton joined Simmons and kept the scoreboard ticking over with smart running between the wickets. As he often did in the tournament, Arthurton rotated the strike rather than crashing the ball to the boundary. Simmons filled that role with two sixes and nine fours in his 110 from 125 balls. Finally succumbing in the 40th over, he had achieved his highest ODI score yet. Critically, Simmons and Arthurton's partnership of 94 had moved the West Indies on to 197/4 with plenty of overs left.

Gus Logie faced two balls in the next over, and one of them bowled him. Don Anurasiri was the bowler, and the West Indies were five wickets down but still with 9.4 overs left to bat. At this point, they succumbed to the gentle medium-pacers of Chandika Hathurusinghe. It was his bowling that ended Simmons's innings when Pramodya Wickramasinghe took the catch. His next wicket was Carl Hooper for 12, before he followed up with David Williams for two. The key wicket of Arthurton followed when the batter edged behind for 40. The West Indies had slumped to 228/8, while Hathurusinghe had his best ODI bowling figures to date.

Winston Benjamin and Curtly Ambrose ended the West Indies innings with a flourish, managing 40 runs from the last few overs – including a four and a six – to leave Sri Lanka having to chase down 269 to win. Hathurusinghe's 4–57 was the pick, while Ramanayake bowled just seven of his allotted overs. His economy rate was 2.4, while Kalpage conceded 64 runs from his ten overs.

Athula Samarasekera led the Sri Lankan response, as he had done in previous matches. The opener was scoring at a run a ball off the bowling of Ambrose and Benjamin. At the other end, Roshan Mahanama was playing a more sedate innings. The opening partnership was worth 56, of which Samarasekera had scored 40 from 41 balls before Carl Hooper struck. Samarasekera was hit on the pads, and his innings was over. Hathurusinghe was the new man in, and assumed a more positive frame of mind while Mahanama continued his cautious approach to batting. Although neither batter found the boundary, it was Hathurusinghe who tried to keep the runs coming. A tight attempted run saw the West Indies pull off the run-out. The call was close, but the batter was on his way for 16 from 25 balls. Sri Lanka were 80/2, but their situation was soon to get much, much worse.

Mahanama's painfully slow innings ended soon after when Arthurton took a catch off the bowling of Anderson Cummins. His score of 11 had taken up 50 balls, and Sri Lanka were quickly losing touch with the match. The introduction of Carl Hooper's spin bowling slowed the run rate even further. Hooper was soon amongst the wickets when he took a caught-and-bowled chance to remove Sri Lankan captain Aravinda de Silva. Falling to 99/4 and still 169 runs from their target, Sri Lanka were dependent on Asanka Gurusinha and Arjuna Ranatunga, once again, to rescue the innings. Richie Richardson gave Keith Arthurton his first extended bowl of the tournament. Having bowled five overs so far, he was required to bowl a full complement of his left-arm spin. He too was difficult to score off as Sri Lanka's required run rate soared. Ranatunga and Gurusinha occupied the crease, but the possibility of a win ebbed away.

Richardson brought back Ambrose to break the partnership, and he did just that. Captain and bowler combined to remove Gurusinha to leave Sri Lanka on 130/5. The wicket signalled a collapse as the West Indies took 5–19 to decimate the batting line-up. Tillakaratne lasted just nine balls before Ambrose rearranged his stumps. Ranatunga, the last line of defence, succumbed to Arthurton for 24 before Ramanayake became his second victim. When Benjamin bowled Anurasiri for three, Sri Lanka were teetering on the edge of defeat at 149/9.

Resistance came in the form of Kalpage and Wickram-asinghe. Although it was futile with regard to the result, their unbroken partnership of 28 stubbornly prevented the side being bowled out. Wickramasinghe hit a six in his innings, but the West Indies bowlers had closed the game out. Hooper's 2–19 from ten overs and Ambrose's 2–24 from nine were the stand-out figures. It was Phil Simmons who picked up the Man-of-the-Match award – well deserved and quite remarkable considering the head injury he had overcome. After the victory, Richie Richardson was confident that his team would make the semi-finals. With one match left, a win against Australia would secure their place. As for Sri Lanka, they were out of contention for the semi-final places and were on their travels again to face Pakistan in Perth.

The action moved to Tasmania on Saturday, 14 March when Australia and Zimbabwe met at Bellerive Oval. Australia's World Cup campaign was hanging by a thread, and they needed other results to go their way. The only controllable element was for them to win their last two matches, against Zimbabwe and the West Indies. Allan Border highlighted that his team were playing for pride in their last two games. With Zimbabwe winless so far, Border was confident of a victory that would help them forget the demoralising defeat against Pakistan. The table showed that this was a meeting of the bottom two teams.

Zimbabwe had famously beaten Australia in the 1983 tournament. Ali Shah, Andy Pycroft, David Houghton and John Traicos had all played in that game, and I wondered how much of a motivator it was. Mark Burmester offered his recollections. 'We spoke about it, but all knew the game had changed a lot in those few years and we were always going to play above ourselves to compete. To be honest, their poor form in the competition was our motivation. We thought we had a real chance that day.'

Australia's team had just one change from the Pakistan game, with Geoff Marsh dropping out to make way for the spin option with Peter Taylor. Ian Healy was still suffering from the effects of his hamstring injury but retained his place. Zimbabwe made two changes as they searched for an unlikely victory. Malcolm Jarvis had picked up a groin injury, and Wayne James was omitted, so Kevin Arnott and Alistair Campbell came into the team.

The nine teams gather on HMAS Canberra. Docked in Sydney Harbour, the ship was used to take pictures for publicity purposes.

Gooch, Imran Khan, Azharuddin, Houghton, de Silva, Border, Crowe, Richardson and Wessels endured a grey Sydney day as part of the lead-up.

From the archives of the Navy History Section, Allan Border and Rear Admiral David Holthouse, AO, RAN sit on the bow of HMAS Canberra - reproduced by the kind permission of The Sea Power Centre - Australia

Martin Crowe in imperious form. Playing superbly at Eden Park, the New Zealand captain led his team to an upset victory against world champions, Australia.

Zimbabwe's Wayne James hits the ground whilst trying to run out Arjuna Ranatunga.

The post-match celebrations as South Africa trounced Australia. Coming back after 22 years of sporting isolation, South African fans produce a banner to mark the moment.

England's great all-rounder being celebrated at the MCG

A Mark Greatbatch pinch-hitting session against South Africa.

Two cricket icons: Sydney Cricket Ground pavilion and Pakistan captain Imran Khan.

David Boon at the crease at the Gabba. Australia and India played out a tight game.

Javed Miandad shows his disapproval of Kiran More's appeals.

The camera caught Dean Jones before the clash with England at the SCG.

Botham in irresistible mood against Australia. One more magical performance against the old enemy.

Jonty Rhodes beats Inzamam-ul-Haq and the stumps with his Superman dive.

A packed Eastern Oval enjoyed international cricket as England and Sri Lanka clashed in Ballarat.

Ramiz Raja hit the Australian attack to all parts of the WACA.

What is it about South Africans demolishing stumps? This time, it's Brian McMillan at the MCG against England.

Sri Lanka's Kapila Wijegunawardene bowling against Pakistan.

The Zimbabwe team celebrate their win in Albury.

Mike Whitney was unsuccessful this time but his 4-34 was too good for the West Indies.

Wasim Akram and Chris Harris clash as Pakistan upset New Zealand in the first semi-final.

England fans in full voice at the SCG in the second semi-final.

Brian McMillan's protestations were in vain as rain interrupted a close encounter...

...and the rain rule ruined it as a contest.

The captains of England and Pakistan face the press before meeting in the final.
Aamer Sohail points the way to the pavilion as Botham departs for a duck.

Wasim Akram cleans up Allan Lamb with an unplayable delivery.

Imran Khan with the winners' spoils.

A glorious Melbourne evening at the end of the 1992 Cricket World Cup.

This was the second match Zimbabwe had played in Hobart, with a comprehensive defeat at the hands of Pakistan in the first one. The conditions were overcast, so David Houghton, on winning the toss, decided to ask Australia to bat first and hopefully get help for his bowlers. Houghton's decision was fraught with danger if rain affected the game. The now infamous rain rule would make Zimbabwe's run chase more difficult.

Eddo Brandes bowled the first ball of the match to Tom Moody, who tried to leave the ball outside off stump. Brandes extracted plenty of bounce, and the ball cannoned off the inside edge and ran away for a boundary. It was a piece of good fortune for Moody that would be short-lived. Moody was hit on the thigh pad by a Kevin Duers delivery. The ball bounced away, and David Boon ran towards the danger end before deciding to retreat. Moody was left stranded as Houghton threw the ball to Flower to leave Australia on 8/1 in the second over.

After this early setback, Boon and Dean Jones scored at a sedate pace for the next few overs. Boon clipped a ball away for four when Brandes strayed on to the leg side, while an all-run four, off the same bowler, helped Jones to some runs; but they were scoring at less than four an over. The batters were, however, running confidently between the wickets. When Jones reached 12, he had amounted 5,000 ODI runs and was the second Australian to do so. In the ninth over, Boon almost lost his wicket when he tried to pull Brandes, but Kevin Arnott, at square leg, couldn't hold on to the catch. In subsequent overs, Boon's pull shot was more controlled, as boundaries off Duers and Burmester demonstrated. Rain showers started at the ground, but play continued.

By the 12th over Australia had reached 50/1, with the run rate starting to increase. The fifty partnership followed, from 69 balls, as Boon and Jones began to dominate. Houghton turned to the medium pace of Ali Shah, with Burmester, at the other end, finding Jones challenging to bowl to. The rain intensified and play was halted at 11am for 35 minutes. The lost time reduced the match to 46 overs per side.

When the players got back on to the field, Zimbabwe thought they had Boon when John Traicos's arm ball deceived the batter. Despite a confident appeal, umpire Brian Aldridge did not agree. In sight of his fifty, Boon finally succumbed to Shah when he was beaten by a leg-cutter and bowled on his off stump. The partnership with Jones was worth 94 from 131 balls, leaving Australia on 102/2. The fall of Boon brought the beleaguered Border to the crease. His intent was positive, and he looked to take on the bowlers. A beautiful lofted drive over the cover region demonstrated his willingness to play his shots. At the other end, Dean Jones was scoring in singles as he approached his fifty.

Just when the Australian captain looked set for his first big score of the tournament, a lapse of concentration ended his hopes. Traicos tempted him down the wicket, which resulted in him overbalancing. Border was unable to turn quickly enough to make his ground, and Flower broke the stumps despite a less than clean take. Border's score of 22 was his highest so far, but still a woefully inadequate return. The score had moved on to 134/3.

By the time Mark Waugh joined him at the crease, Jones had clipped a single to the leg side to bring up his fifty from 65 balls. Just six balls later, he too was on his way, after playing on while trying to run Burmester down to third man. Instead, he chopped an inside edge on to the leg stump to be on his way for 54. At 144/4, Australia's innings was wobbling.

Steve Waugh joined his brother at the crease, and with just his second ball edged Burmester to Flower behind the stumps. Although Flower got his right glove to the ball, the impact of his dive somehow dislodged it, and the chance was gone. From that inauspicious start, the Waugh twins started to score quickly. Flowing drives and improvisational flicks kept the scoreboard ticking over. Within six overs, the fifty partnership had been achieved. The Zimbabwean bowlers were struggling to contain as both Waughs found the gaps in the field. Eddo Brandes put down a difficult caught-and-bowled chance, with Steve Waugh on 37, as the ball rocketed towards him. It was the second chance that Steve had offered and Zimbabwe had spurned.

With three overs remaining, Australia were 232/4, with Mark Waugh on 44, from 31 balls, and Steve on 45 from 36 balls. From Duers's next over, both Waughs reached their fifties. Steve achieved his half-century first, before Mark made his milestone with a massive hit over the leg-side boundary. Another six brought the 250 up for Australia. A spectator's enthusiasm to catch the ball guaranteed a maximum as he leaned over the boundary, when a four was just as likely a result. Umpire Steve Bucknor contemplated before signalling the result of his deliberation.

The partnership was ended when an excellent slower yorker, following Steve Waugh as he tried to make room, was played on. The twins had added 113 runs in 69 balls, with Steve scoring 55 from 43. Ian Healy was next man in, but he lasted just two balls. Kevin Duers, bowling the last over, beat his slog towards the leg side and hit him in front of the stumps. From the last four balls, another seven runs were scored to take Australia to 265/6 from their 46 overs. Mark Waugh's 66 from 39 balls had given his team the impetus they needed. The last ten overs had yielded 106 runs as Zimbabwe failed to contain the innings. Only Traicos had maintained reasonable figures, 1–30, as the rest of the bowlers conceded more than five runs per over.

Zimbabwe opened with Ali Shah and Andy Flower, while usual opener Kevin Arnott batted in the middle order. Having recovered sufficiently from his broken finger against the West Indies, it was thought that batting down the order would give Arnott better protection. Facing McDermott and Reid with the new ball, the Zimbabwean openers took a cautious approach. The bounce from the pitch was not as pronounced as in the Pakistan game, but Zimbabwe still struggled. The bowlers constantly beat the batters on their outside edge, but couldn't extract a nick.

Shah and Flower scored at three an over, but never looked comfortable. The introduction of Mike Whitney into the attack produced similar results. The partnership was finally broken by a miscalculated run rather than an edge. Shah's desire to take two runs to Reid at third man was too ambitious. Out for 23 from 47 balls, with two boundaries, Shah was replaced by Alistair Campbell. The wicket precipitated a collapse, as Australia tore through the batting order. First to go was Andy Flower, caught by Border off the bowling of Steve Waugh for 20 in the 19th over. Next in to bat was Andy Pycroft, but he fell to a golden duck, with Mark Waugh taking the catch. Zimbabwe had slipped to 51/3, with Campbell and David Houghton at the wicket.

Mike Whitney was in the middle of a miserly spell of bowling, and was rewarded when he removed Campbell. Mark Waugh was on hand to take the catch, and the batter was on his way for just four runs from 20 balls. The Zimbabwean captain also found batting difficult and was bowled by McDermott for two. Border sensed an opportunity to improve the net run rate, in case that became a deciding factor, and his strike bowler duly obliged. Zimbabwe had fallen to 69/5, and it would only be a matter of time before they were defeated.

The Australian fans were revelling in a rare good performance in the tournament. Kate Gross was one of those fans at the match, with her cousin. 'Bellerive Oval was a pretty modest ground in those days, but it may as well have been Lord's or the MCG as far as I was concerned. I was in cricket heaven. For the first time, cricket became three-dimensional for me. Our seats were the wooden benches in the Stuart Spencer Stand on the western side of the ground, which is now occupied by the much more salubrious (by comparison) Ricky Ponting Stand. I could hear AB bark orders to his fielders when he wanted to move them. I even heard him reprimand Deano for signing autographs on the boundary when he was supposed to be fielding. We delighted in taking part in the crowd chants (not the rude ones ... our mums were sitting with us!) and the Mexican wave. We ate our chips and drank our soft drink and soaked up the atmosphere.'

Tom Moody was given the opportunity to bowl his medium-pace deliveries, but it temporarily released some pressure from Zimbabwe. Andy Waller crashed a couple of boundaries before Peter Taylor caught him off the bowling of Moody. His four overs had taken a wicket, but for the loss of 25 runs, so Border brought back Whitney, who had been difficult to score off. He picked up his second wicket soon after when he bowled Arnott for eight runs. The Zimbabwean had struggled with the pace of the pitch in his 15 balls faced. Zimbabwe were now 97/7, and Australia were pushing to end the match swiftly.

With Eddo Brandes at the crease, he was going to score quickly if he stayed in. Several lusty blows signalled that he was intent on hitting the ball hard. Border had closed in the field to put pressure on and take the remaining wickets. While Brandes was frustrating Australia, Tony Greig became fascinated with the bowler. It had been disclosed that the big Zimbabwean was a chicken farmer, and Greig, along with his fellow commentators, was intrigued.

Brandes's partnership with Burmester had added 20 before the latter became Reid's first victim. Traicos joined him at the wicket, adding another 15 runs before Peter Taylor struck to remove his fellow spinner. After Brandes survived a missed stumping when on 12, his and Zimbabwe's innings finally ended when McDermott took a catch off Taylor. With 23 from 28 balls, the Zimbabwean had achieved his highest ODI score yet, but his team were well beaten by 128 runs.

Australia's bowling figures were exemplary, with Whitney taking 2–15 from his ten overs while Reid took 1–17 off nine and McDermott chipped in with 1–26 from eight overs. Whitney stayed on the ground for almost an hour after the match, signing autographs. His tight spell was not enough for the Man-of-the-Match award, which went to Steve Waugh.

Looking back at the match, Mark Burmester rued a potential missed opportunity. 'The Waugh brothers tore into us after that, so it would have been nice to have one of them in the hut. Whenever we are in contact his [Andy Flower's] first comment is "Don't remind me of dropping Steve Waugh." There is no doubt the game was in the balance, and if we had got a couple more, who knows – some more history could have been made – but not to be.'

On the following day at Basin Reserve in Wellington, the top-of-the-table clash between New Zealand and England took place. The unbeaten New Zealanders faced an England side that had whitewashed them in the ODI series. New Zealand were able to select John Wright, fit after missing four games, at the expense of Rod Latham. England's selection was very much driven by fitness, or lack of it, with several players carrying injuries. Gooch's hamstring was still not healed enough for his inclusion, but Allan Lamb was finally fit enough to play. He replaced Neil Fairbrother, who had contracted a virus and was ruled out. Despite Phillip DeFreitas and Dermot Reeve not being fully fit, they retained their places. Lewis, once again, played as a batter only, with his side strain not repaired.

Over 13,000 fans packed into Basin Reserve before the gates were closed for the eagerly anticipated match. The weather was warm and typically windy, for Wellington, when Martin Crowe and Alec Stewart conducted the toss. Crowe won it and inserted England. He reasoned that he felt his team were competent chasers, while Stewart was 'more than happy' as he would have batted had he won.

England's innings started with them having to face more Crowe tactics, as Dipak Patel opened the bowling with Chris Harris. Botham struck the first boundary, in the second over, when Harris strayed down the leg side. Stewart struck his first off the next Harris over as England eased their way into the innings. Against Patel's bowling, Stewart and Botham employed different approaches. Stewart used his feet, but a wild swing almost led to a stumping, though Ian Smith could not take the ball as it turned significantly. Later in the over, Botham was caught in two minds as to whether to play off the front or back foot. He did neither, and the ball turned and struck leg stump. Botham was gone for eight, leaving England on 25/1 in the seventh over.

The new man in was Graeme Hick, and he was off the mark straight away. A well-timed cut shot in the next over, off Willie Watson, brought up his first boundary of the day. Hick took a liking to the bowling of Watson, and pulled him twice through midwicket in the 12th over as the England total grew. In the 14th over, Stewart smashed Watson for two fours as England passed fifty. At this point, Ian Smith left the field holding his head. Suffering from a migraine, Smith was unable to continue, and Mark Greatbatch took over the wicketkeeping duties. Henry

Blofeld conjured up a pun, on commentary, about 'Paddy' (Greatbatch's nickname) putting on pads.

Stewart continued to punish any bad balls. Cairns overpitched and was comprehensively driven to the boundary. Later in the over, Cairns pitched short to Hick, who cleared the fence for a six. By the 17th over, the fifty partnership came up, and New Zealand's bowlers were leaking runs apart from Patel. It was Patel who made the breakthrough, when Stewart played another aggressive shot, trying to sweep the ball to leg, but picked out Harris at midwicket. The partnership had been worth 70 in 14 overs, and the stand-in captain's 41 runs had come off 59 balls.

Robin Smith joined Hick, who soon brought up his fifty. Both batters played some delicate shots square and behind the wicket, to counteract the New Zealand game plan of using slower bowlers to keep the pace off the ball. Hick succumbed to Harris, as an attempted cut shot ended up in the gloves of Greatbatch. It was an excellent innings of 56 from Hick, from just 70 balls, and his dismissal brought Allan Lamb in to bat for the first time in the tournament.

In Harris's next over, Smith unleashed an aggressive shot high over the covers for four. With Lamb on strike, his rustiness was evident when he edged the same bowler to Greatbatch. The stand-in keeper couldn't hold on, but it was the sort of chance that Smith would have taken had he not been ill. Aware that his batting partner would need a little time, Smith played several aggressive shots, including using his feet to Watson. In the 41st over, he attempted to hit Andrew Jones over mid-on for six but picked out Patel on the boundary. With Smith gone for 38, England were 162/4 in the 41st over. The problem that England now faced was that the players left to bat were all carrying some kind of injury. It was not going to be easy.

Facing Willie Watson at the beginning of the next over, Chris Lewis received his first ball. As he played a back-foot defensive shot with far too much bottom hand, the ball spooned up off the bat, and Watson took the catch at the second attempt. Gone for a golden duck, Lewis trudged back off the ground disconsolately while the mainly New Zealand-supporting crowd were in raptures of delight. Allan Lamb was the next man to fall when he tried to release the pressure, partly built by his lack of form and partly by the bowling. He tried to hit Watson over the top, but picked out Cairns, who took the catch at long-off. Lamb was gone for 12 from 29 balls and England were 169/6 with less than six overs left.

Derek Pringle and Dermot Reeve tried their best to move England forward while Martin Crowe kept Jones on. In the 49th over, with Pringle trying to hit a boundary, he was easily caught out at deep midwicket by substitute fielder Rod Latham, as England's innings continued to falter. Later in the over, Dermot Reeve managed to find the boundary with a paddle sweep, but it was the first one since the 37th over.

Chris Harris bowled the final over, in which Phillip DeFreitas holed out to Cairns as England limped to 200/8 from their 50 overs. The score appeared to be insufficient as the innings meekly petered out. In the final 18 overs, England scored just 68 runs as New Zealand's bowlers once again restricted a batting team. Patel's 2–26 and Larsen's 0–24 had been particularly parsimonious, while Andrew Jones's part-time bowling had picked up 2–42 from nine overs.

New Zealand opened with Greatbatch and John Wright. The first over was a reasonably sedate one from Derek Pringle. Phillip DeFreitas bowled the first ball of the second over to Wright. The ball took a line on leg stump, and the batter leaned across to work the ball away. He missed it, it crashed into leg stump, and Wright was gone for a single. It was a carbon copy of his dismissal against Australia in the opening game. England had drawn first blood to leave New Zealand on 5/1.

Greatbatch's response was to smash Pringle, in the next over, over midwicket for six. Despite the loss of an early wicket, New Zealand adhered to their game plan, which had produced the success they had achieved in the tournament so far, and Greatbatch stuck to his pinch-hitting role. Jones, on the other hand, played more orthodox cricket strokes, but with no less intent. In the ninth over, Greatbatch found the boundary twice as he looked to put pressure on the England bowlers. To Botham's first ball, Greatbatch advanced down the wicket and struck the ball high in the air, but it fell safe. Jones's modus operandi proved more successful when he ran Botham through the vacant slip area for four. The shot also brought up New Zealand's fifty, while the veteran all-rounder seethed as he strode back to his bowling mark. The 12th over, bowled by DeFreitas, proved to be expensive as Jones and then Greatbatch found the boundary.

Botham's next over proved to be Greatbatch's undoing, when another aerial shot did not have enough on it and found DeFreitas on the boundary. The partnership of 59 was broken to leave New Zealand on 64/2 in the 13th over. Greatbatch's 35 from 37 balls had given them another good start, but it would need Jones and new batter Martin Crowe to put a partnership together. Jones punished any width, as DeFreitas and then Botham found out. He played on both sides of the wicket, striking the ball purposefully to the boundary. Botham looked frustrated and complained about field placings. Richard Illingworth, introduced in the 18th over, fared no better as Jones cracked a low full toss to the leg-side boundary. Even mishits dropped safe and ran away for four. England's bowlers were failing to contain New Zealand.

By the 26th over, New Zealand were over halfway to their target as England had no idea where a wicket was going to come from. Jones achieved his fifty later in the over with another classy front-foot drive. Martin Crowe took a liking to the bowling of Hick and scored several boundaries with cut shots. Given the width, New Zealand's captain took the opportunity to put the balls away. In the 32nd over, Jones scored his third boundary in two overs from Illingworth. It also brought up Jones's highest score yet in a World Cup. Another slog sweep to end the over took New Zealand to 156/2. Soon after, the hundred partnership was achieved and New Zealand were cruising to a very comfortable victory. Not only would they be maintaining their unbeaten run in the tournament – they would also be ending England's streak of 20 victories since arriving in the southern hemisphere at the end of 1991.

In the 36th over, Jones attempted a single off the bowling of Gladstone Small. Almost ambling down the wicket, Jones gave Hick the opportunity to aim and throw at the stumps. The throw was accurate, leaving Jones short of the crease. It was a sad way to end such a good innings. With 78 runs scored from 113 balls, including 52 runs from boundaries, Jones's innings had set up the inevitable victory. Ken Rutherford joined Crowe at the wicket, but it was New Zealand's captain who took up the mantle. Once he brought up his fifty, Crowe played as if he wanted to end the game as quickly as possible. Pringle was clubbed down the ground for a boundary before being lofted, from a more orthodox shot, in the same area. In the 41st over, from DeFreitas, Crowe scored the 11 runs needed for victory. The final blow was a shot through midwicket to secure a seven-wicket win.

One of the New Zealand fans in the R.A. Vance Stand was James Gould. Attending the match with his younger brother, James remembered how the New Zealand fans were celebratory.

'It was almost a party mode as we ran down the score without many problems. I remember there were Mexican waves going round the ground ... it was the first time I'd seen such a thing. The embankment got really rowdy in those days, so, given our ages, it was probably for the best we were on the other side of the ground. It was so enjoyable that when we hit the winning runs, it was almost a surprise to look up and see we'd done it so easily, with nine overs left. There was also definitely a bit of pride around the place that it was the two local Wellington players in Jones and Crowe who got the majority of the runs in the chase.'

England's defeat was compounded by Pringle injuring his back and having to leave the field before the end of the match. Injuries were mounting up for England, with one group game left before the semi-finals. In his post-match interview, Alec Stewart was quick to refute the suggestion that injuries were responsible for the defeat. It was England's lack of 'execution' that was responsible, he said, but they would look to win their last game, against Zimbabwe, before the semi-finals.

Sunday, 15 March featured matches at the Adelaide Oval and the WACA in Perth. The first, in Adelaide, was India's game against South Africa. The start was delayed by rain until 1.15pm, when Kepler Wessels won the toss and asked India to bat first. Vinod Kambli and Pravin Amre were selected in place of Subroto Banerjee and the injured Ajay Jadeja. South Africa were unchanged as they attempted to cement their place in the semi-finals.

Allan Donald took the new ball, and claimed the first wicket without India having scored a run off the bat. Facing his fifth ball, Srikkanth tried to push the ball down the leg side, but a leading edge flew above Kirsten's head. The fielder thrust his hand high into the air and took a spectacular catch to leave India

1/1 in the first over. It was the third time in the tournament that Srikkanth was out without scoring. In his eight innings, the opener reached double figures on only three occasions.

Mohammed Azharuddin was the new batter, and it was not the first time he had been in this situation. This was the third time in seven matches that India's opening partnership had been broken for single figures. Their captain would have to lead from the front again. Crashing Allan Donald through the covers for four, Azharuddin signalled he was ready for the challenge. He and Manjrekar started off cautiously, but the ninth over marked a watershed with the introduction of Richard Snell. Bowling slightly wide, Azharuddin could not quite time the ball through the covers at first, but took two runs. Snell bowled a similar line and length, and this time India's captain found the boundary with ease. A second boundary followed as Snell failed to adjust his line. In his next over, Azharuddin crashed the ball through midwicket for four as India closed in on 50.

Brian McMillan came on to bowl, despite a sore Achilles, and kept the scoring shots down to a minimum. With the pitch damp and the sky overcast, he was able to extract some movement off the pitch, which kept the Indian batters honest in their shot-making. Although Azharuddin and Manjrekar were looking to accelerate, McMillan was not going to make it easy. The introduction of Adrian Kuiper broke the partnership. Manjrekar advanced down the wicket and hit the ball high towards deep midwicket, but it dropped short of the fielder, Hansie Cronje. Having taken two runs, Manjrekar tried another aggressive shot, but Kuiper squeezed the ball through and bowled him. It was a terrible, wild slog, without footwork, and India were 79/2 in the 17th over.

The new man in was Sachin Tendulkar, who had little time to play himself in. Tendulkar had scored 269 runs in the tournament so far, with three half-centuries, but this was a different scenario. He took India past 100 with a glorious shot through midwicket, before a slog across the line sailed up into the air and Wessels took the simplest of catches. It was 14 runs from 14 balls from Tendulkar, but India were now 103/3.

If the 'Little Master' was slightly out of his comfort zone, Kapil Dev came to the wicket with the armoury for the occasion. At 33 years-old, the great all-rounder was unlikely to play in another Cricket World Cup, and he played with the freedom that the situation afforded him. At the other end, Azharuddin passed his fifty from 54 balls, knowing his team needed a significant effort in the last few overs. Both batters kept the scoreboard ticking over quickly with some smart hitting, picking up boundaries and pushing the ball into gaps. By the 28th over, the fifty partnership was reached as the scoring rate stayed around the six-runs-per-over mark. Azharuddin survived a very close run-out attempt, before Kapil Dev worked a Meyrick Pringle full toss to the midwicket boundary.

With two overs left, India were 162/3 with two overs left. Allan Donald bowled to Kapil Dev, with the Indian looking to make room. Donald tried to cramp him up, but he despatched the ball over deep fine leg for six with a short-arm pull that seemed effortless. He then squeezed a full-pitched ball through midwicket for four. Incensed, Donald came screaming in and, as he beat Kapil Dev's pull shot for pace, the ball cannoned into the top of middle stump. The entertainment was over, but Dev's 42 runs from 29 balls had helped set a competitive total. At 174/4, there were still a few balls left in the innings.

Pringle bowled the final over, as India lost two more wickets before posting a challenging 180/6. Vinod Kambli lasted three balls before being run out by Wessels, who had just spilled a difficult chance, with an accurate underarm throw. The other wicket to fall was that of Azharuddin, when he holed out to Kuiper. Out for 79 from 77 balls, the Indian captain had once again fought bravely for his team. If he could get his bowlers to execute, India might leave the tournament with a victory.

Kepler Wessels's challenge, to secure the victory and a place in the semi-finals, was to ensure his batters scored at a reasonable rate. To do that, he decided to demote himself down the order. Peter Kirsten was in a rich vein of form and was asked to open with Andrew Hudson. Kirsten had only failed once, scoring 11 against England, and was averaging 79.80 with 399 runs already.

Although they needed to score at six an over, the first two overs of the innings yielded just one run. In the third, Kirsten found the boundary with a square cut to start the run chase in earnest. More tight bowling contained South Africa and it almost generated a wicket when Hudson lofted the ball towards mid-on, but Tendulkar couldn't take the catch. With the sun now covering the Adelaide Oval, South Africa's fifty was brought up when Andrew Hudson pulled Srinath over the top of midwicket for four. Keeping pace with the Indian innings, South Africa had the game under control without having to take undue risks. Azharuddin turned to spin, introducing Venkatapathy Raju into the attack. Kirsten's response was to use his feet, and he drove the ball for four despite a desperate dive from Pravin Amre.

There was a contentious decision in the 16th over, when Tendulkar's superb stop and throw, off his own bowling, hit the wickets as Kirsten made his ground. Neither umpire, Khizer Hayat or Dooland Buultjens at square leg, thought it was out, but TV replays showed that Kirsten was short of his ground. India did not complain about the lack of a decision, although the replay showed that there was something to feel aggrieved about.

Taking his good fortune in his stride, Kirsten brought up his fifty just after the hundred partnership was achieved. His half-century was completed from only 55 balls, and with more than ten overs left and all ten wickets in hand, India needed to take wickets quickly. Azharuddin's problem was where he could get a wicket from. Raju and Srinath had been expensive, while Tendulkar was bowled out. Hudson reached his fifty a few minutes later as South Africa looked comfortable. Srinath was brought back on, having bowled just two overs for 19 runs. Hudson backed away to leg, trying to make room to cut. Srinath spotted his movement and bowled an excellent full delivery that hit the stumps. Hudson and Kirsten's partnership of 128 was broken with South Africa needing another 53 runs from 40 balls. Adrian Kuiper was sent in because of his big-hitting prowess.

With Prabhakar being brought back to bowl at the death, Azharuddin and the bowler were particular about their field placings. Kirsten's answer was to flat-bat the ball back over Prabhakar's head for four. The pressure started to tell, as Prabhakar was no-balled and a misfield gave South Africa an extra run. Continuing to scamper singles in the 26th over, Kuiper was almost caught short of his crease before an lbw shout led to his run-out. Srinath rapped Kirsten's pads and appealed before Kirsten attempted to take a single. Kuiper spotted the danger, but sacrificed himself as Srinath had an easy throw at the stumps. South Africa were 149/2 in the 26th over, and Jonty Rhodes was sent in. If South Africa were to run singles for victory, Rhodes would be their man.

With Kirsten's luck with him again, as Srinath's lbw shout looked plumb, he then smashed Kapil Dev for a boundary in the next over. His luck did finally run out when he tried to make room by stepping away to the leg side, as did Hudson, but Kapil Dev's yorker uprooted his stumps. Kirsten was gone for 84 from

86 balls, and South Africa were 24 runs short of victory. The asking rate was close to eight runs per over. It was time for the captain, Kepler Wessels, to come to the crease.

It was Jonty Rhodes who made a dash for glory. The first ball he faced went for a single. The second, bowled by Prabhakar, was crisply hit over square leg for a six. There was some debate, confusingly, as to whether the ball had gone over the ropes. The TV replay showed the ball scattering the crowd, but a short delay ensued before Khizer Hayat signalled a maximum. The third ball he faced was struck straight to Raju at point, and Rhodes was gone. South Africa were now 163/4, with three wickets having fallen for 14 runs. The over ended with Wessels being hit on the pads, but South Africa managed to run two due to another misfield.

Kapil Dev bowled the 29th over, as Wessels and Hansie Cronje pushed the ball into gaps and ran furiously. The last ball of the over was a low full toss, and Wessels drove the ball through the covers, beating the fielder, for a boundary. South Africa needed four runs off the last over to reach the semi-finals. It was to be bowled by Prabhakar, and the field was set to stop singles. Cronje launched the ball over midwicket and victory was assured by six wickets.

In his post-match interview, Mohammed Azharuddin could not hide his disappointment at the end of the four-month tour. 'I thought the least we could have done was qualify for the semi-finals. The most disappointing aspect was the younger players.' His fury was directed at Amre, who had scored 27 runs in four appearances, and Kambli, with 29 in five. Tendulkar, on the other hand, had scored 283 runs at 47.17.

South Africa were delighted to have reached the semi-finals, but their participation was still to be decided back home. The constitutional reform referendum was taking place two days later, and Geoff Dakin, president of the United Cricket Board of South Africa, said that withdrawal would be the only option should the 'no' vote prevail.

The last semi-final place would go to the West Indies, Australia or Pakistan. Somehow, Pakistan were still alive in the tournament. They needed to win both their games and rely on Australia beating the West Indies, but were still able to make the semi-finals. If they didn't, the Australia versus West Indies game would effectively be a play-off for the last semi-final place.

	Pld	Won	Lost	Tied	N/R	Pts	Net R/R	For	Against
New Zealand	7	7	0	0	0	14	0.782	1440/287.2	1345/318.0
England	7	5	1	0	1	11	0.598	1275/271.3	1155/281.5
South Africa	8	5	3	0	0	10	0.138	1519/348.1	1437/340.1
West Indies	7	4	3	0	0	8	0.257	1444/337.1	1346/334.2
Australia	7	3	4	0	0	6	0.059	1414/336.0	1372/330.4
India	8	2	5	0	1	5	0.137	1439/291.0	1355/281.5
Pakistan	6	2	3	0	1	5	0.099	1040/235.0	1003/231.5
Sri Lanka	7	2	4	0	1	5	-0.776	1257/299.1	1455/292.2
Zimbabwe	7	0	7	0	0	0	-1.385	1211/283.1	1571/277.3

Chapter Eleven

Friends Reunited

The second match of Sunday, 15 March took place on the west coast of Australia, with Pakistan and Sri Lanka meeting at the WACA. It was a must-win game for Pakistan if they were to retain any chance of reaching the semi-finals, while Australian fans were in dire need of a Sri Lankan victory. Sri Lanka's gruelling itinerary was almost at an end. However, travelling from Berri across the Nullarbor Plain to Perth meant that they wouldn't be able to get any practice in before the game. Pakistan benefitted from having three days off between games as well as not having to travel. Their line-up was unchanged from the victory against Australia. Sri Lanka made one change, with the harder, bouncier WACA wicket being more appealing for the bowling of Kapila Wijegunawardene rather than Don Anurasiri's spin bowling.

Pakistan were expected to make light work of Sri Lanka. The clinical nature of their victory against Australia made them huge favourites. However, some of the bad habits of earlier in the tournament appeared to be creeping back in. Wasim Akram's problems with controlling the new ball and sloppy fielding gave Sri Lanka some breathing space. Roshan Mahanama and

Athula Samarasekera pushed the ball around for singles, and received some good fortune when a catch was put down by Ijaz Ahmed. With the score on 28, Akram found an absolute gem of an inswinging yorker to uproot Mahanama's stumps. In came Champaka Hathurusinghe, and he found scoring difficult. Samarasekera was also cautious in his approach, which was not in keeping with the rest of his tournament.

Hathurusinghe's innings ended when Mushtaq Ahmed bowled him for five. The Sri Lankan batter had struggled through his 29 balls before his ordeal was over. The loss of his wicket, with the score on 48, brought the Sri Lankan captain, Aravinda de Silva, to the crease. The change of partnership saw Sri Lanka up their run rate. The WACA pitch was less lively than usual, and Sri Lanka took advantage.

The fifty partnership was achieved within ten overs, and Sri Lanka were looking comfortable. Samarasekera's natural attacking intent led him to use his feet to Mushtaq. Not picking the googly, the opener was beaten, and Moin Khan smartly took the bails off to break the partnership. Sri Lanka were 99/3, and Asanka Gurusinha was next in to bat. Gurusinha was in a terrible slump and had only reached double figures once, in the last match against the West Indies, with an average of six for the tournament. With his captain, he finally started to get a few runs under his belt. The modus operandi for scoring employed by de Silva was singles – 23 of them, in fact, before he hit Ijaz Ahmed to Aamer Sohail to end a partnership of 33. Scoring 43 from 56 balls, de Silva had scored relatively quickly but only found the boundary twice.

The fall of the fourth wicket, with the score on 132, brought Arjuna Ranatunga to the crease. While Gurusinha played the senior role, Ranatunga played an unusually subservient innings. He too struggled to score and was eventually out for five. He fell to Aamer Sohail, who had him caught by substitute fielder Zahid Fazal. It was Ranatunga's worst score of the tournament, and just when his team needed him. Sohail got through four overs for 14 runs as Pakistan's bowlers contained rather than threatened to blow the Sri Lankan batting apart. Sri Lanka were 158/5, and in need of a stand in the last few overs to post just a modestly challenging total.

Recognising the need to score quickly, Gurusinha took up the mantle. He tried to get after the bowling. Ijaz was despatched to the leg-side boundary with a well-timed shot. His luck ran out when he attempted to pull Imran over square leg. The ball tucked him up too much, and sailed high off the top of the bat. Salim Malik came running in, almost mistiming his run before taking a low, diving catch to leave Sri Lanka on 187/6.

Joining Tillakaratne at the wicket was Ruwan Kalpage, and he helped Sri Lanka to get past the 200 mark. His contribution of 14 was scored at almost a run a ball. Tillakaratne struck three boundaries as he finished on 25 not out from 34 balls. Sri Lanka finished on 212/6, which looked at least 20 runs short of a reasonable total. Imran Khan would not have been happy with his bowlers, though, as they conceded 32 extras. Also, they did not look like ripping through the Sri Lankan batters.

Wasim Akram was critical of the performance when quoted in John Crace's book. 'We were determined to try and play positively, but some of our snappiness was missing.' He continued, 'We were lucky in that Sri Lanka had no strategy for their innings; they never worked out what was a good score on that wicket, and they let things drift. Against their mediocre medium pace attack, we always fancied getting the runs.'

Despite the confidence from Wasim, it was the medium-pace attack which struck first. Aamer Sohail played one of his naturally aggressive strokes, but smashed it straight to

Mahanama at gully. Sohail was gone for a solitary run, from an uncharacteristically slow ten balls, and Pakistan were 7/1 in the third over. Imran Khan promoted himself up the order to number three, to lead from the front. However, he too struggled to score, and remained scoreless for a while before getting off the mark. In his first 37 balls faced, Imran scored just two runs. Ramiz Raja found things slightly easier, but was never going to score quickly with a career rate of 63.93 per 100 balls.

The partnership reached 55 before Ramiz managed to pick out Gurusinha off the bowling of Wickramasinghe. The opener's 32 had taken 56 balls, and Pakistan were now behind the run rate. Somehow, Sri Lanka were still in a game that they had no right to have any interest in. When Imran Khan's mistimed shot was caught by his Sri Lankan counterpart, Pakistan's run chase was far from easy. The fall of the third wicket brought Salim Malik to the crease to join Javed Miandad. So far in the tournament, Salim Malik had failed to score more than 17, with a miserable return of 55 runs from five innings. Much in the same way as Gurusinha had found form when he needed it, Salim Malik did too. Creative strokeplay and good running between the wickets started to turn the innings around.

With the scoring at five runs per over, the partnership moved on towards 100, helping Pakistan towards what would be a welcome victory. Miandad's fifty came up with a single, taking 95 minutes, but the Sri Lankan total was getting ever closer. A simple bat lift to acknowledge the milestone was all that he could muster, as Miandad knew there was still work to be done. Several runs later, he decided to flick Gurusinha off his pads. The shot was not well placed, and Wickramasinghe was waiting at deep square leg to take the catch. The partnership of 101, in 21 overs, had put Pakistan within 28 runs of victory.

Inzamam-ul-Haq joined Salim Malik, looking to end a game that was far closer than it should have been. A further 16 runs were added before panic set in. First, Malik threw his wicket away when chasing a wide ball from Kalpage, scooping his shot to Ramanayake. Just five runs later, Inzamam was run out by a direct hit from Mahanama. Not known for his running between the wickets, Inzamam fell foul of Ijaz Ahmed's desire for a single.

With Pakistan on 205/6, Wasim Akram came to the crease and soon found the boundary. Wickramasinghe was given the impossible task of bowling the final over with the scores tied. Ijaz's on drive, off the first ball, pierced the field for a boundary to secure a four-wicket win.

Miandad's innings of 57 secured the Man-of-the-Match award and, more importantly, kept Pakistan in with a chance of qualifying for the semi-finals. After they had played so poorly for the first few games of the tournament, it seemed inconceivable. Despite falling back into bad habits, Pakistan had won the game to give themselves a chance. Each game was effectively a knockout match, and they played as such. Their final game, in Christchurch, was against the unbeaten New Zealanders. Win that match, and they were in the last four; lose, and they would be on their way home. The game marked the end of Sri Lanka's campaign. Apart from their journey back, the arduous series of flights was over. The draw had taken Sri Lanka to the regional locations of New Plymouth, Mackay, Ballarat and Berri. Trips back and forth across the Tasman Sea added to the punishing schedule.

Wednesday, 18 March marked the final day of the round-robin games. The last three were played across three different time zones. The first, starting at 10.30am local time at Lancaster Park, Christchurch, was Pakistan's match against New Zealand.

The second was played on the Victoria–New South Wales border, in Albury, where England met winless Zimbabwe in a match whose result would not affect the semi-finals. The game would start an hour later, while Australia and the West Indies' key clash was to commence at 2.30pm in Perth, almost at the end of the match in Christchurch.

The scenario playing out across the three games was the question of whether Pakistan, Australia or the West Indies would take the last remaining semi-final place. If Pakistan lost, it would be a straight shoot-out between Australia and the West Indies. A Pakistan win would give them a chance, as well as knocking Australia out, but they would need the West Indies to lose comfortably. To add to the complexity, a New Zealand victory could lead to them playing their semi-final against Australia at the SCG. A defeat would guarantee playing at Eden Park, but their unbeaten record would be gone.

New Zealand made two changes for the game at Lancaster Park. The faster, bouncier track led to Danny Morrison replacing Chris Cairns, while John Wright made way for Rod Latham. Pakistan were unchanged from their line-up at the WACA from three days earlier. Winning the toss, Imran Khan quickly decided to bowl first. New Zealand had successfully chased five times in their seven wins, so Pakistan were more comfortable chasing. Being interviewed after the toss, Martin Crowe admitted that he would have bowled first. He was also asked whether New Zealand were playing to win, to which he quickly replied, 'You bet!'

An autumnal South Island wind blew across the ground, so Wasim Akram took the new ball wearing his sleeveless sweater. An eventless first over was followed up by Aaqib Javed. Greatbatch clipped down through fine leg for four, before going high over square leg for another boundary. The best shot was left for last, when he smashed a ball over mid-on for six. The ball was coming on to the Greatbatch bat and leaving it with interest as 14 runs were taken from the over.

Rod Latham joined his fellow opener's aggressive start with a beautiful square cut, off a Wasim Akram no-ball, in the next over. However, a loose shot against Aaqib was caught by Inzamam, and New Zealand lost their first wicket. Aaqib extracted more bounce and Latham, opening the face of the bat, could only guide it to slip. The fall of the wicket brought Andrew Jones to the crease. His innings lasted just three balls before Wasim produced an inswinging yorker to leave him trapped in front. Steve Bucknor had no hesitation in giving the decision, and New Zealand were 26/2 in the fifth over.

With the New Zealand fans feeling uncomfortable, a back-foot shot from Greatbatch raced to the boundary to ease the mood. Martin Crowe was struggling to get the ball away for runs when a Wasim Akram delivery angled towards the leg side. The New Zealand captain was slightly off balance as he clipped the ball, and Aamer Sohail took the chance at backward square leg. The mood turned to stunned silence as Crowe walked off while the jubilant Pakistan players congratulated themselves on such an excellent start. New Zealand were 39/3 in the ninth over, and under pressure for the first time in the tournament.

Ken Rutherford joined Greatbatch at the wicket. Perhaps the situation warranted more conservative play, but Greatbatch was in no mood to change. A slightly uppish delivery from Wasim Akram was uppercut over the infield, and bounced once before going over the rope. The opener was far more comfortable with the pace of Akram than Mushtaq's leg spin, but he kept the score moving. Rutherford was far more circumspect, but should have gone when Imran teased an edge, only for Moin Khan to drop the regulation catch. Pakistan gifted New Zealand several overthrows with unnecessary shying at the stumps, which aggravated their captain even further. Rutherford's preference for a quick single, though, became his undoing in the 20th over. Pushing the ball out on the off side, he miscalculated Akram's left-armed throw and was left short of his ground when Greatbatch sent him back. He had used up 35 balls for his eight runs, and New Zealand's innings was stuttering at 85/4.

Chris Harris came in, and could only manage a single off Imran before he fell to Mushtaq. As Harris charged down the wicket, Mushtaq's googly drifted away from the oncoming batter and Moin Khan quickly executed the stumping. Despite the umpire calling wide, Harris was out, and New Zealand had slumped to 88/5. This was proving to be the first stern test of Kiwi mettle, and it was proving to be fragile. Although the pitch conditions were the most unfavourable to the New Zealand style of play, Pakistan's mercurial form was peaking at the right time.

It was down to Greatbatch to stay at the crease, but his propensity to score fast saw him sweep the ball around the corner to Salim Malik, and Pakistan had six New Zealand wickets with fewer than a hundred runs on the board. Perhaps Crowe or Jones would not have chosen to play that shot in the situation, but Greatbatch perished by the same sword that he had used to slay bowlers in the tournament. Ian Smith's innings lasted four balls before he chopped an Imran Khan delivery on to his stumps. It was another poorly selected shot, and New Zealand were 96/7 with half their allotted overs remaining.

Dipak Patel squeezed the ball to backward square leg to bring up New Zealand's 100, in the 27th over, before he too played a rash shot. Looking to crash the ball through the covers, he picked out Mushtaq and was out for seven. The catch was a quality one, picking the ball up low and to his right, but Patel's execution of the shot had created the opportunity. The scoreboard showed 106/8, with most of Lancaster Park looking on in disbelief.

Danny Morrison was the new batter, joining Gavin Larsen, and would not have inspired confidence. His batting average was 5.75, with a top score of nine not out. It had been 15 months since he had batted in an ODI. Larsen's record was not much better, but he did have a first-class century to his name and had averaged 18 in the Shell Cup, New Zealand's domestic one-day competition.

A drive through the covers for four settled Larsen's nerves as well as giving New Zealand a welcome boundary. At the other end, Morrison's doggedness was matched only by his inability to score. His first 28 balls faced were scoreless, while a dubious stumping decision could have sent him on his way much earlier. The 29th delivery was pushed away for a single and was greeted with cheers from the crowd. Morrison raised his bat as if his score was much more significant.

Confidence seemed to flow from there, and Morrison played a few shots. The pick of them was a slog sweep, off Aamer Sohail, for a four down to cow corner. By the 43rd over, New Zealand had reached 142/8. Their match position was still dire, but the partisan crowd were being given something to cheer. Wasim Akram was brought back into the attack and produced a ball that silenced the crowd once more. The pace and bounce too was far too much for Morrison, and he could only edge the ball to Inzamam at slip. Morrison's 12 from 45 balls had been imperative for New Zealand, but the partnership was broken. The partnership had been worth 44 from 17 overs, but stopped Pakistan from rolling New Zealand over.

Larsen and Willie Watson squeezed 16 more runs, but Wasim's smart yorker, in response to Larsen trying to make room, ended the innings. All out for 166, New Zealand had recovered somewhat, but Pakistan's challenge was not a difficult one. Mushtaq's 1–18 had been the pick with his leg spin; New

Zealand did not hit any boundaries off his bowling. Akram's late wickets gave him 4–32, but Pakistan still conceded 42 extras, the joint top score.

Meanwhile, match 35 of the tournament took place in Albury. Despite being in New South Wales, the city is closer to Melbourne, which is over three hours' south via the Hume Highway. England and Zimbabwe met for their last group match – the first meeting between the two nations. The players flew to Albury and trained at the venue, the Lavington Sports Oval, on the day before the match. Ian Botham caused excitement with some massive hitting in the nets. Even a passing butterfly found the middle of Botham's bat before the all-rounder offered an interview, which he conducted spikily, with a local journalist.

Lavington Sports Oval was not unknown to six of the England players, who had featured in a tour game there on the 1990/91 tour to Australia. Allan Lamb had captained an England XI against New South Wales in a four-day match, which the state team won. Robin Smith, Alec Stewart, Phillip DeFreitas, Gladstone Small and Phil Tufnell also played in the six-wicket defeat.

England's fitness problems showed no signs of abating despite Gooch being able to train after missing two games. His leg was heavily strapped, but he came through the training session and was declared fit to play. Neil Fairbrother was declared fit after a stomach virus, as Derek Pringle (torn rib cartilage), Chris Lewis (side strain) and Dermot Reeve (hip) all missed out. Trying to put a positive spin on Gooch's forced return, manager Micky Stewart felt that he needed some batting time before the semi-final. Zimbabwe, with one final chance to win a game, picked a more experienced line-up, with Alistair Campbell, Mark Burmester and Kevin Duers making way for Wayne James, Iain Butchart and Malcolm Jarvis. Zimbabwe had the extra motivation, and additional information, from their coach, Don Topley – a team-mate of Gooch's with Essex in the County Championship.

Peter Baxter, who produced BBC's *Test Match Special* for over 30 years, covered the 1992 Cricket World Cup. 'We only had a staff of two to cover the tournament, which, of course, went over the distance from New Zealand to Western Australia. I had asked for a third person and been refused. I used Henry Blofeld to cover various games in a freelance capacity, and we linked with the ABC and Radio New Zealand, of course. Christopher Martin-Jenkins was available for England games, too. Otherwise, it was Aggers following England and me dashing all over the place, either to join him for difficult venues or to report or commentate from other vital games. I did produce the programme from what looked like a railway signal box in Ballarat, but I didn't go to Albury, because there were three key games that day.

'One of the things that made it very complicated was the number of different playing hours because of the different time zones, day/night games and the change of clocks during the tournament in New Zealand, New South Wales, Victoria and the UK – all, as far as I remember, on different dates. We had to produce a little publicity card about that and the fact that *TMS* changed networks halfway through!'

The facilities at Albury were very much of a temporary nature, and Jonathan Agnew remembers the broadcasting booth as he prepared to cover the match for the BBC. 'Climbing up through a little hatch, in a roof of a little box, that looked more like an upturned box of matches. Up on to the first floor of that, and having to go up on a stepladder and through a hole in the ceiling.'

The city of Albury embraced the match, with an official attendance of 5,645. Mitch Wallenhoffer, who attended the game as a seven-year-old schoolboy, remembers the day clearly. 'We were all pretty hyped up in our sports uniforms, sun-creamed up, wearing our white floppies and legionnaire hats. Being mid-March, it was still summer in Albury. Everyone in town seemed to be there, dancing in front of the news cameras in the hope we would get on TV and just the sheer excitement of being at an international cricket match in our home town. At school, we had a family of Zimbabweans who, of course, were very excited to be able to support their native team. The boys and their mother brought along and unfurled a massive Zimbabwean flag that they had displayed in the area, which attracted a lot of attention. So much so, one of the players came across and signed a few autographs for us.'

Winning the toss, England inserted Zimbabwe on a pitch that was slow and two-paced. An early gift of a misfield did not set the right tone for England, but then DeFreitas deceived Andy Flower and the ball cannoned into his stumps without him playing a shot. Flower's batting partner, Wayne James, should have followed, but Gooch's rustiness led to the slip catch being dropped. England's captain rectified his mistake when Botham enticed a Pycroft drive and held on to the catch. Zimbabwe were 19/2, with batting conditions proving to be testing.

Spin, in the form of Richard Illingworth, gave no respite as England tightened their grip on the game. James, frustrated by the lack of scoring opportunities, tried to drive him, but the bowler took a tumbling, juggling caught-and-bowled chance. James had laboured to 13 runs from 46 balls, while Kevin Arnott also struggled. Zimbabwean captain David Houghton joined Arnott, with a view to hanging around rather than playing forcing shots and losing more wickets. The approach, though slow-scoring, pushed Zimbabwe on past fifty before Botham took his second wicket with an lbw decision. Arnott was out for 11 and Zimbabwe were 52/4.

England had selected two left-arm spinners, mainly due to the lack of fit players, and it was Phil Tufnell who took two quick wickets to reduce Zimbabwe to 76/6, leaving them in plenty of trouble. First, it was big-hitting Andy Waller who tried to slog Tufnell across the line and lost his stumps. Shah followed with another naïve shot across the line, this time a sweep, and top-edged to Allan Lamb. Tufnell didn't have it all his own way, though. After the fall of the sixth wicket, Houghton went on the offensive and swatted Tufnell over the covers for a welcome boundary. Houghton's change of tactic was short-lived. Trying to pull Small, he managed only to loop the ball to Fairbrother at midwicket. He had added 29 runs from 74 balls, and the job appeared only half done with Zimbabwe languishing on 96/7.

Butchart and Brandes continued their captain's more aggressive intent, and it paid off. Scoring at a far faster rate than their colleagues, including three boundaries, another 31 runs were added before both fell with the score on 127. Botham ended Butchart's innings of 24 as Fairbrother held on to the catch. Brandes's wander down the wicket to Illingworth led to Stewart's regulation stumping. The England fans were in full voice, 'You'll Never Walk Alone' drifting across the ground, as Zimbabwe's number 11, Malcolm Jarvis, came to the wicket. Illingworth soon wrapped up the innings and Zimbabwe were all out for 134.

During the innings break, England were feeling confident. Gladstone Small recapped the position of the game at that point: 'The pitch wasn't the best. It was a bit of sticky, tacky pitch. The ball wasn't coming on, but we thought with the quality of our batting and the experience we had in our batting line-up we were very confident that we were able to get that score.' Such was the confidence from the England team, Don Topley received a few bread rolls at the dining room table, which were thrown in jest, plus several comments. Topley did not have to wait too long for the balance to be redressed. At the beginning of the England innings, things turned back towards Zimbabwe, as Topley recollects.

'The England boys are coming down the steps, Botham and Gooch. And I'm waiting; I've moved away from third man where the lads were. They got out, and I'm standing there. And Gooch and Botham come down and they sort of, they both look at me. I think I said, "Good luck, chaps", something like that, you know. I'm not going to say "Go and get a nought." So, they went out, and as I turned around, I was checking the field, and I said to third man, "Move a bit squarer for Goochie, don't go fine third man, squarer for Goochie."

'The first ball was bowled, and Brandes got him out lbw – it was a full toss which Goochie missed. He's played around it, hit him on the pads, everyone has gone up, and he's been given out. As he's walking back down to third man, where I'm standing, the gate man runs down the steps to open up the gate. So, as the gate man gets down to the bottom of the picket fence, I told him to "piss off". I said, "Don't worry, this one's mine!" So, as Goochie got closer, I opened the gate, and as he walked past I said, "Bad luck, Gray."'

Allan Lamb joined Botham at the crease, and both enjoyed the extra pace of Brandes. Lamb found the boundary, then Botham crashed a square cut for another four. Moving steadily on to 32/1, Lamb then tried to pull Brandes, but only looped the ball to James at point. The ball was still in mid-air when Lamb started to walk back to the pavilion. Robin Smith was the next man in, playing cautiously, and Botham continued to bat positively. With the score on 42, the all-rounder nicked one to Flower off the bowling of Shah and was on his way for 18.

With England's innings starting to take on water, Brandes soon caused it to flounder with two devasting deliveries. Robin Smith lost his off stump for Brandes's third wicket, for just two runs from 13 balls. For his fourth wicket, Brandes took the prize wicket of Graeme Hick. The prize was very much personal, with Hick and Brandes having been school friends at Prince Edward School in Harare. Hick suffered a six-ball duck with the ignominy of a yorker that uprooted his stumps. It would have been reminiscent for Hick of his miserable English summer against the West Indian quicks.

After 15 overs, England's innings had capitulated to 43/5, and the target of 135 was looking a long way off. Zimbabwe were finding that the wicket was just as friendly to their bowling, with England having lost four wickets for 11 runs. Neil Fairbrother and Alec Stewart were left with the job of getting to the target, to end the spirited display from a team that had nothing to lose and everything to gain. Needing to stay at the crease and accumulate runs, Stewart and Fairbrother did precisely that. Stewart reined in his more natural attacking game. Fairbrother was ideally suited to the occasion with his resolute, nurdling approach. Both batters were watchful and were happy to get the runs in singles. Stewart hit three boundaries, when the opportunities arose, as the target got closer with England looking as though they were extinguishing the Zimbabwean fire.

The partnership was worth 52 when Stewart tried to push an Ali Shah delivery towards the leg side. Instead, the ball flew off the leading edge and looped towards cover. Butchart took a good diving catch to leave England on 95/6 and still in need of another 40 runs for victory.

DeFreitas was the next man in, and he helped England past 100 before advancing down the wicket to Butchart and nicking the ball to Flower behind the stumps. Zimbabwe had firmly taken back control, with England on 101/7 and still needing 34 runs for victory.

Richard Illingworth joined Fairbrother at the crease, but it was the latter who would be England's best chance of victory. However, Fairbrother's resistance was broken seven runs later, when he fended a short ball off his hip and Flower made good distance to the leg side to take the tumbling catch. The Zimbabweans were ecstatic, as they knew the importance of the wicket. Next man in was Small, but he strode to the crease feeling positive despite the precarious position. 'I took pride in my batting. I was a lower batter, but I wasn't a complete novice. We weren't chasing a big total, and we had overs [in hand], so I was determined that if we could be given a bit of luck, maybe we could still win the game.'

Illingworth and Small contrived to eke out any runs they could, and managed to get England to the position where they needed 15 off the last two overs. Having scored four off the 49th over so far, Illingworth attempted a quick single with a view to retaining the strike for the last over. The ball squirted off his bat towards midwicket, where Arnott was fielding. Illingworth knew he was running to the danger end and it was a matter of whether the fielder could hit the stumps. His throw was accurate, and his team-mates swamped him. According to John Traicos, it was this moment where the victory felt assured. 'It was tight the whole way, but when Kevin Arnott ran out Richard Illingworth, I knew we were going to win the match.'

And so they did. Small tried to clip the first ball of the last over, a slower ball from Jarvis, in the air, but picked out Pycroft. England were bowled out for 125 and Zimbabwe were victors. A field invasion ensued, mostly schoolchildren, while the Zimbabwean players grabbed stumps as mementoes of a historic occasion. It had been nine years since Zimbabwe's last win, another Cricket World Cup giant-killing, but Houghton thought that this win was 'probably a bit better than the last one'.

Eddo Brandes picked up the Man-of-the-Match award with his 4–21. John Traicos's spell of 0–16 off his ten overs had been pivotal in the success, though. Ali Shah's 2–17 was important too, as Zimbabwe bowled extremely well on a bowlers' wicket. Gooch said his team were disappointed, but reflected on the fact that they had qualified for the semi-finals. As for Zimbabwe, they could return home on a high and would be given full member status of the ICC in July of the same year.

Back at Lancaster Park, the Pakistan innings had started with Aamer Sohail facing Danny Morrison as they chased the target of 167. The New Zealand quick charged in and bowled a bouncer. Sohail tried to hook the ball. It sailed down towards Dipak Patel at fine leg, who took the catch, and the crowd sensed a fightback. Patel came sprinting in, high-fiving as he went, while Aamer Sohail stayed in his ground waiting for a shoulder-high no-ball call.

Disappointed and frustrated, the opener finally walked off. In John Crace's book, he gave his opinion on the decision. 'It was clearly a no-ball; I even played it deliberately uppishly because I thought there was no risk. At first, I had thought about leaving it, but then I said to myself, "Why waste the opportunity to get off the mark with a free hit?" I couldn't believe the square leg umpire didn't give it.'

Inzamam came in at three and was greeted, in his next over, with a bouncer from Morrison. This time the ball flew to the boundary. Later in the over, Inzamam was caught in two minds and found himself bowled off the inside edge. Morrison had two wickets, and Pakistan were 9/2 in the third over. Moreover, Morrison was pumped up and determined to bowl fast. He also had a few words for Inzamam as he left the wicket. In the next

Morrison over, Ramiz Raja played two good strokes on the leg side for boundaries. The Pakistan opener was not intimidated, had the temperament for the occasion and would capitalise on any loose bowling. Javed Miandad was not so assured against Morrison or Dipak Patel. In the ninth over, he tried to hit Patel through the off side, but the ball was far too close to the bowler. Patel dived full-length to catch the ball, but it spilled on landing. Temporarily exasperated, Patel stayed motionless before slowly getting to his feet. Crowe went over to his bowler with words of encouragement, but both must have contemplated the opportunity lost when New Zealand had so little to play with.

Ramiz Raja played various strokes across the line to Patel to negate the spinner. Miandad pulled out a reverse sweep to bring up the Pakistan fifty as momentum started to shift back once again. Despite finding some touch against Patel, Morrison caused Miandad issues, and he completely lost a bouncer as it arrowed towards his head. The ball landed safely, before a shoulder-height no-ball was called. The introduction of Larsen and Harris did nothing to quell Ramiz Raja's innings. The opener found that less pace gave him time to get into position, and executed pulls and cuts to perfection. Whether the motivation was to engineer a breakthrough or to prepare for the semi-final, Crowe made several bowling changes. Again, Ramiz Raja capitalised, and Pakistan inched closer to victory. A slither of a chance went begging when Larsen failed to gather a throw from Harris with Ramiz Raja well short of his ground. Harris was quick to the ball, but a wayward throw left Larsen with too much to do. New Zealand's unbeaten run was coming to an end.

Crowe made yet another bowling change, and Morrison was brought back in. When he bowled too short, the ball fizzed to the boundary from another attacking stroke by Ramiz. Morrison's pace did get the breakthrough, though, when Miandad was caught in front. Too little, too late, but the partnership was ended. Adding 115 valuable runs from a precarious position had given Pakistan every chance of making the semi-finals.

Needing another 43 runs from 14 overs, Salim Malik came to the crease knowing his partner was well set. Not only was Ramiz Raja playing aggressively, but his shot selection was also superb. Any width was punished with impunity, as Morrison found out in the 38th over. Even mishits fell safe as the opener enjoyed his innings. His century was reached when he turned a ball, uppishly, on to the on side and ran two. A reluctantly appreciative crowd, interspersed with delirious Pakistan supporters, marked the landmark with applause.

More generous bowling from Latham and Rutherford was despatched as Pakistan, led by Ramiz Raja, raced towards the victory. The end came, from who else but Ramiz, with a slog through mid-on. The win had been achieved with 32 balls remaining. More importantly, Pakistan had done all they needed to do to reach the semi-finals. The victory had ended Australia's hopes before their match had started. Pakistan now required Australia to do them a favour and beat the West Indies.

Ramiz Raja's innings of 119 not out, including 16 boundaries from 155 balls, was not deemed to be a performance worthy of Man of the Match. Mushtaq won the award with his 2–18, and was described by Imran Khan as having a 'big heart', though he said it had been a gamble to select him for the match. Pakistan returned to their hotel to watch the rest of the game at the MCG.

In the lead-up to the match, Allan Border intimated that he would consider batting second to help any run chase to improve Australia's net run rate. Not knowing the result in Christchurch at the toss, Border won it and decided to bat first, which was the preferred plan for Australia. After their convincing win in Hobart, no changes were made to the Australian line-up. The

West Indies retained their team from Berri as the sides took to the field in what they both thought was a must-win match.

David Boon and Tom Moody opened for Australia on a good batting track. Ambrose and Benjamin took the new ball for the West Indies and kept it tight early on. Boon found the boundary with an on drive to release some pressure, and Australia went on from there. In the eighth over, it was the West Indies feeling pressure as an Ambrose delivery was called a no-ball and David Williams was deceived by late swing. The ball flew to the boundary, while Ambrose glared, unamused. A lack of amusement then turned to utter fury as a thick edge from Moody dropped just short of Hooper at slip before squirting through for another boundary.

The introduction of Cummins was greeted with a well-timed drive from Boon as Australia's batters started to assert themselves over the West Indian bowling. Moody drove Ambrose on the up, down the ground, for another boundary. Boon was fortuitous when Piloos Reporter ignored two convincing shouts in Cummins's next over. The first was an appeal for a catch down the leg side, but the umpire was unmoved despite a clearly audible noise as the ball passed Boon's gloves. The second was for a bat-pad catch to slip but, again, Reporter was not interested. The news had come through to the MCG that Pakistan had won, and so Australia's game would be their last in the tournament.

By the 14th over, Australia reached fifty, while Richie Richardson needed to counsel Cummins as he showed frustration. Moody and Boon launched into any short and wide balls. Boon's timing and Moody's shot-making kept the scoreboard ticking over. Boon's fifty came up in the 24th over, before he pulled Hooper over midwicket for four. The hundred partnership came up soon after, and Moody decided that he would play his shots. Having just clubbed Simmons for four, he tried to repeat the stroke but picked out Benjamin at deep midwicket. Despite misjudging the catch, Benjamin took it cleanly to send Moody on his way. Australia were 107/1, with Moody out for 42.

With Boon playing and scoring with ease, Dean Jones's frustration lead to his demise. As he tried to run Cummins down to third man, the lack of contact gave Williams an easy catch behind the stumps and Jones was gone for six. The fall of the second wicket brought the Australian captain to the crease. Border's miserable time with the bat continued when right-arm seamer Simmons trapped the left-hander in front. Umpire David Shepherd had no doubts, and TV replays appeared to agree. Border was out for six runs, to take his tournament total to 60 from seven innings. An average of 8.57 from the captain was abysmal. Australia were now 141/3 in the 35th over, and were handing back the advantage attained from a good opening partnership.

In the next ten overs, Boon and Mark Waugh scored at above four an over. Boon crashed Hooper to the boundary, while Waugh stroked the ball around for his runs. When Waugh did try to match his batting partner, Hooper and Williams combined for a smart stumping. Seeing Waugh advance down the wicket, Hooper fired the ball towards leg stump for Williams to whip the bails off and break the partnership. Having added another 44 runs, Australia were now 185/4 and in a decent position to finish the innings strongly.

Boon was closing in on his second century of the tournament. A nervy single to get to 99 not out also brought up the milestone of 4,000 ODI runs. A more comfortable single down to long leg finally brought up the century, but as soon as he had reached 100, a careless slog across the line brought about the fall of his wicket. As he tried to hit Cummins to the leg side, the ball flew up into the air and Williams made the distance to backward square leg. A disappointing end for Boon, and a blow for Australia, with just under five overs left.

Healy and Steve Waugh scampered between the wickets until Cummins, with his last ball, produced a yorker. Waugh played all around the ball and lost his stumps. At 200/6, Australia needed as many runs as they could get from the last few balls. The unlikely source of Peter Taylor found the boundary, chipping Ambrose over the infield, as 16 runs came from the last two overs. Australia finished their innings on 216/6, leaving the West Indies with a target of 217 runs to qualify for the semi-finals at the expense of Pakistan.

The West Indies' reply started very slowly, with Reid and McDermott keeping it tight. In the fifth over, Haynes finally got off the mark with a flick off his hips. Later in the over, Lara crashed a drive through the covers for another boundary as McDermott overpitched. In his next over, McDermott was on the receiving end again when Haynes played a vicious pull shot that rocketed to the boundary.

One Australian fan at the MCG who was a 12-year-old at the time was Luke Reynolds. He remembers the moment when the news came in from Albury. 'I recall the England v Zimbabwe scores being put up on the scoreboard, very early in the second innings, as the light was transitioning from day to night. It was seriously the biggest roar of the day. More so than Boon bringing up his hundred.' Reynolds commented on the general feeling that the game played out to at the MCG. 'I thought the atmosphere was a bit flatter than any ODI I'd been to at the MCG previous to that, maybe, because Australia was already out of finals contention.'

McDermott got his revenge when Haynes middled a full toss off his legs but hit the ball straight to Jones. Haynes was gone for

14, and Phil Simmons walked to the crease. His first ball faced was on off stump, and Simmons thrust his pad outside of the line before half-heartedly effecting a batting stroke. The ball crashed into the front leg; umpire Piloos Reporter agreed with the Australian appeals, and Simmons was gone for a golden duck. The West Indies had lost two wickets in two balls and were 27/2.

Their captain, Richie Richardson, was next in and played conservatively. While Lara looked to score, Richardson played within himself. By the 19th over, Richardson had faced 43 balls for ten runs. His 44th ball, from Whitney, went past the outside edge. Australia claimed a catch, while Richardson repeatedly gesticulated that his bat wasn't accountable for the noise. His protestations were in vain, and he was on his way. The West Indies were 59/3, and their semi-final hopes were starting to look distant.

Lara was in excellent touch, and Arthurton came out with intent. Both left-handers crunched the ball into the outfield, but the ball appeared to be slowing up. A thick edge, in the 21st over, found its way to the boundary. It was the first one in 14 overs as the West Indies were struggling to keep pace with the run rate. Arthurton drove Steve Waugh through the covers for four, then on-drove Whitney for another boundary, before playing one too many shots. Trying to drive Whitney, he hit straight to McDermott at mid-off. When Logie nicked behind for five to give Whitney his third wicket, the West Indies were in trouble at 99/5.

With the West Indies having lost five wickets, Lara and Carl Hooper gave them their last realistic hope for victory. Lara swept Taylor for four to reach his fifty and to bring up the West Indies' hundred. At the other end, Hooper was also finding batting difficult and became Whitney's fourth victim. He tried to run the ball wide of the slip area, but could only direct it to the safe hands of Mark Waugh.

Lara was running out of partners, and David Williams didn't stay around for long. As he tried to fend off a short ball from Reid, who had bowled economically, the ball looped up to Border for an easy catch. The result was decided when Lara, trying to get on strike, took a suicidal single. Benjamin remained motionless as Lara ran to his end. The non-striker's end was bereft of batters, and Moody had the simple job of breaking the stumps. The West Indies were 137/8, while Pakistan, in their hotel in New Zealand, were celebrating.

The last two wickets fell and, at 9.47pm, Australia secured victory by 57 runs. Apart from Lara's 70, the next highest score was 15. Australia's bowlers, particularly Reid with his miserly 1–26 and Whitney with 4–34, benefitted from the West Indies batters' panicking. David Boon was Man of the Match, while the autopsy started in the Australian media.

Malcolm Conn, who was a journalist for *The Australian* in 1992, summed up the feeling. 'It was a long tournament at the end of a long season. And the most bizarre thing about that Sheffield Shield game tacked on the end was that Australia had actually just played a one-day series. Now, the logical thing would have been to go from that triangular one-day series straight into the World Cup having played one-day cricket. To tack a Shield game in there, when everyone had already had a long season, and then come back and play the World Cup, it was just the height of lunacy.'

In his autobiography, *Hands and Heals*, Ian Healy echoed those sentiments. 'In hindsight, I think we made the mistake of trying too hard to treat the World Cup like any other tournament, as if it was an extension of the World Series rather than something special. Instead of going into camp in the lead-up to the Cup, we went back to the red ball in the Sheffield Shield and then had just two warm-up one-dayers ... twenty-four hours later, the Cup was on! It might have been more than coincidence that our best performance in the World Cup was our last, when we hammered the West Indies at the MCG.'

Tom Moody concurred that the preparation was inadequate to defend their title of world champions. 'I agree with Ian; there is no doubt we were underprepared, and the team lacked role clarity. At no stage did the team have a settled or balanced playing eleven.'

The final table showed that New Zealand were top and would face Pakistan, again, at Eden Park. In the second semi-final, England and South Africa would play at the SCG. Rain had decided several of the matches, but the no-result in Adelaide had given Pakistan the extra point they needed despite them being bowled out for 74. Australia's net run rate was superior, but their form had let them down in their defence of the Cricket World Cup.

	Pld	Won	Lost	Tied	N/R	Pts	Net R/R	For	Against
New Zealand	8	7	1	0	0	14	0.592	1606/337.2	1512/362.4
England	8	5	2	0	1	11	0.470	1400/321.3	1289/331.5
South Africa	8	5	3	0	0	10	0.138	1519/348.1	1437/340.1
Pakistan	8	4	3	0	1	9	0.166	1423/328.5	1381/331.5
Australia	8	4	4	0	0	8	0.201	1630/386.0	1531/380.4
West Indies	8	4	4	0	0	8	0.076	1603/387.1	1562/384.2
India	8	2	5	0	1	5	0.137	1439/291.0	1355/281.5
Sri Lanka	8	2	5	0	1	5	−0.686	1469/349.1	1671/341.3
Zimbabwe	8	1	7	0	0	2	−1.142	1345/333.1	1696/327.3

Chapter Twelve

The Agony and the Ecstasy

In the lead-up to the first semi-final, Imran Khan drew parallels between New Zealand's position and Pakistan's in the 1987 tournament. The Pakistan captain suggested that the pressure was on New Zealand, and not his team, after losing their last qualifying game as did Pakistan in 1987. Martin Crowe refused to be drawn into the mind games, and chose to focus on New Zealand enjoying the occasion and playing their natural game. Despite intimating that Pakistan would remain unchanged, Imran chose Iqbal Sikander to come into the side at the expense of Ijaz Ahmed. Playing two leg-spinners suggested that Pakistan were trying to counteract the slow-paced pitch at Eden Park. New Zealand decided to bring back the experience of John Wright, with Rod Latham making way.

Winning the toss, Martin Crowe elected to bat, and the opening pair of Mark Greatbatch and John Wright strode out in front of a vocal crowd. Wasim Akram and Aaqib Javed kept Greatbatch quiet until the fifth over, when an Akram delivery gave the opener enough width. He ferociously cut the ball up in the air, and it sailed into the crowd. In Akram's next over, Wright played a more technically correct cut shot which pierced the infield and ran away for four.

In the eighth over, Greatbatch charged down the wicket to Aaqib Javed, and connected with a shot that sent the ball sailing over mid-on and landed in the second tier of the stands. The New Zealand fans were excited as Greatbatch was once again tearing into the opposition's bowling attack. Aaqib's response was to bowl a slower ball which almost caught Greatbatch out. In his next over, Aaqib bowled the delivery again, spotting Greatbatch advancing, and the ball spun into the stumps. It was the Pakistan fans' turn to celebrate.

New Zealand were 35/1, with Andrew Jones joining Wright in the middle. Mushtaq came into the attack, and his first meaningful act was to draw Wright into an uncharacteristic hit down the ground. Ramiz Raja didn't have to move to take an easy catch, and New Zealand were two wickets down with just 39 runs on the board. Having faced 44 balls, Wright had consumed a lot of the strike for only 13 runs. New Zealand needed some impetus. Martin Crowe was the next batter in.

Taking control of the strike, Crowe started to score much faster, so Imran Khan decided he needed to take action and brought himself on to bowl. Straying on to the leg side, Imran could only watch as Crowe flicked him effortlessly for four. Accelerating the innings, Crowe soon passed Jones's score. A long hop from Sikander was despatched easily by Crowe as New Zealand's captain looked in ominous form. Imran kept Mushtaq bowling to try to get the breakthrough. Having found huge turn earlier in the over, Mushtaq managed to trap Jones in front to get his captain a vital wicket. Trying to work the ball away on the back foot, Jones was beaten by the spin, and umpire Steve

Bucknor had no doubts. New Zealand had reached 87/3 in the 24th over.

Ken Rutherford's first task, having just got to the crease, was to try to dig out a Wasim Akram inswinging yorker. The ball, having missed the bat, crashed into Rutherford's foot and was plumb in front of the wickets. The Pakistan team's appeals were soon stifled by the sight of David Shepherd's right arm extended to signal a no-ball. Akram put both his hands to his face, knowing that his front-foot digression had cost his team a wicket. Rutherford gladly accepted his second chance.

Crowe and Rutherford took to the Pakistan bowling. As they mixed solid cricket shots with aerial improvisation, interspersed with scampering between the wickets, the runs were starting to flow. Iqbal Sikander did not have the same repertoire or control as Mushtaq. Rutherford played an array of strokes that extra width encouraged. Crowe brought his fifty up in the 37th over with an effortless push towards mid-off. From just 51 balls, his was the wicket that Pakistan sorely needed, otherwise they would be chasing a massive total.

The milestone acted as a release for Crowe, as a slog sweep off Mushtaq flew for six. Rutherford launched Sikander back over his head for a maximum. With just over ten overs to go, New Zealand put their foot on the accelerator. Wasim Akram was not immune to the same treatment, as Crowe put him into the stands with a short-arm pull. The return of Aaqib Javed into the attack was greeted with another excellent aerial shot from Rutherford, and New Zealand were approaching 200.

Rutherford brought up his fifty with that shot, but fell in the next over. As he tried to pull Akram, the ball flew skyward, and Moin Khan ran forward to take the catch. New Zealand's fourth-wicket partnership had added 107 runs and, more importantly, given them a firm foundation for a big total. The majority of the crowd appreciated Rutherford and gave him a massive cheer as he made his way off the ground.

While the batters were crossing, Crowe felt something wrong with his leg. Despite trying to carry on, he required medical attention, and it appeared to be his hamstring that was causing him trouble. Greatbatch came on to the ground while Crowe was being attended to to act as a runner once his captain could get back to his feet. Having come in to bat with the fall of Rutherford, Chris Harris bisected outfielders to score a boundary, but then tried to hit Sikander back down the ground; he was beaten by the spin, and Moin Khan effected the stumping to leave New Zealand on 214/5 in the 46th over.

Although the seriousness of the injury was still unknown, and he was clearly inhibited by it, Crowe was still able to smear an Imran Khan delivery across the line for another six. However, the very next ball he faced would be his last. After he had pushed the ball through the covers for two runs, Smith and Greatbatch's miscommunication led to a run-out. Crowe's brilliant innings of 91 was over. Off 83 balls, with seven fours and three sixes, Crowe had led from the front yet again. The job was not done, though, with the score on 221/6 in the 47th over. More importantly, there was the question of how badly Crowe was injured.

Dipak Patel's first scoring stroke was to work Imran wide of Moin Khan, and the ball ran away for four. Ian Smith's wristily played clip off his legs, using the pace of Aaqib Javed, also went for four. He repeated the stroke later in the over for good measure. Pakistan's bowlers could not contain New Zealand, and the team were facing a massive total to chase. Even another Wasim Akram yorker, this time a legitimate delivery, could not stop the momentum. Patel was replaced by Gavin Larsen, who, with Smith, garnered 11 runs off the final over to take the total to 262/7. The required run rate for Pakistan would be 5.26 per over.

The New Zealand fans were confident of reaching the final. Some were already discussing buying tickets for Melbourne. Angus Ogilvie was a university student at the time, and recalls the party atmosphere at Eden Park. 'We had no idea what had happened to Crowe when he limped off the field. We were nonetheless ecstatic. His knock set us up for certain victory. After all, 262 was a mountain to climb in the early 1990s. By the end of the first innings, the terraces were electric. No doubt assisted by the amount of beer being consumed.

'There was no way we could lose from here. Mexican waves were all the rage back then, and they went around the ground endlessly with beer flying.'

As New Zealand took to the field for the Pakistan innings, Martin Crowe was absent. During the changeover, the decision was made that he would need to rest his leg for the final in case they were to reach it. John Wright was New Zealand's most experienced player, an ex-captain, and would be given the job of leading the side. Crowe imparted words of encouragement and a precis of the plan to Wright.

Patel opened the bowling with Morrison as Pakistan started their run chase steadily. Morrison conceded a couple of boundaries, but there was no Greatbatch-like hitting from Ramiz Raja or Aamer Sohail. In the ninth over, Sohail attempted to sweep Patel and top-edged the ball to Andrew Jones at backward square leg.

New Zealand were delighted with the breakthrough and the majority of Eden Park was in raptures. Imran promoted himself up the order to bat at number three again. He planned to bat through the innings by restricting the number of wickets lost. In the 12th over, a tired-looking Danny Morrison bowled his sixth straight over. Ramiz took full advantage by taking 14 off it, including two boundaries off the last two balls. It was the first sign that the New Zealand masterplan was not being adhered to.

Dipak Patel bowled eight straight overs, which also was one too many when Ramiz hit him for four before Imran used his feet to plant him into the stands for six. The introduction of Willie Watson restored some control for New Zealand, Imran choosing to let the ball pass without a shot, such was his resolution to stay at the crease. Ramiz was not so discriminatory about Watson's bowling. He tried to loft him, and the ball fell safely before succumbing to a mistimed hit. It spiralled into the air, and Morrison took a good catch at mid-on. Pakistan were now 84/2 in the 22nd over, with another 179 runs still required.

Gavin Larsen came on to bowl and was straight on the money, giving Pakistan nothing to hit. Imran and Javed Miandad appeared content to be restricted for a while. In the 27th over, Imran went down the wicket to Larsen and drove him back down the ground for six. Suddenly, Imran had decided that his time to accelerate had come. Chris Harris came on to bowl, but found Pakistan in no mood to let him settle. He did, however, contribute to a breakthrough when Imran holed out to Larsen on the boundary edge. A valuable 50-run partnership had ended, bringing Salim Malik in to bat. He would last only two balls, though, and the momentum shifted back to New Zealand. At 140/4, Pakistan needed another 123 runs from the last 16 overs. They needed a hero. Inzamam-ul-Haq, not wearing a batting helmet, walked to the crease.

Having squeezed a boundary off Larsen early on, Inzamam looked confident. According to Martin Crowe in *Out on a Limb*, Wright came into the dressing room during the drinks break for a bowling plan for the rest of the game. Despite Crowe providing a plan, he alleges that Wright just took a quick look at it and 'stuffed it deep into his pocket'.

Chris Harris conceded 14 runs in the 38th over, with Inzamam hitting him to all parts of the ground. The momentum had swung back Pakistan's way. Inzamam scored the next 40 runs in 21 balls to reach his half-century. Patel's last two overs conceded 22 runs, and by the start of the 44th over New Zealand's bowling attack had been rendered ineffective. Both Larsen and Patel were bowled out, Morrison had conceded 31 from six overs, and Harris was 1–59 with an over left. Only Watson had reasonable figures, with just two overs remaining. Inzamam found the boundary twice off Morrison's seventh over, and the required run rate was now down to less than seven per over.

Hope sprung for New Zealand in the following over when Miandad and Inzamam's running between the wickets fell apart. Trying to take two off Watson, Miandad almost found himself run out turning for the second. Not learning from this close shave, he called Inzamam through for a tight single, and Harris's throw beat the young batter to the crease. The game-changing innings was over, but the damage was done. In 47 minutes, Inzamam's 60 from 37 balls had brought Pakistan back into the game.

Wasim Akram came in and scored nine runs from eight balls before Watson bowled the all-rounder as he tried to charge him. Pakistan were now 238/6, with Moin Khan in as the new batter. A rare bad ball from Watson was hit to the boundary to leave Pakistan needing 19 from three overs. By the time Harris came on to bowl the penultimate over, the target had diminished to 12 runs. Several singles were traded between Moin and Miandad as the New Zealand fans' worst fears were being realised. The game ended as a competitive tie when the fifth ball, from Moin Khan's cross-bat slog, sailed way back over long-off for six. Pakistan's win came off the next ball, when Moin Khan's pull shot beat a despairing slide on the boundary and Pakistan were victors by four wickets.

Miandad ran towards his team-mates with his arms aloft as they ran on to the ground to celebrate. Anyone slightly associated with New Zealand was left stunned, none more so than the crowd. Pockets of Pakistan fans celebrated, while the rest were trying to contemplate how New Zealand had lost.

Another fan at the game, Keith Miller, summed up the feelings on the day. 'All of a sudden the New Zealand bowling attack (which throughout the tournament had mastered the low, slow wickets on offer) were given their first look at Inzamam-ul-Haq. The fans in green and white started to bang their drums a little faster – and taunting the local fans in the process – as he tore the attack to shreds. Smacking 60 off just 37 balls (unheard of in 1992), he left New Zealand hopes in tatters. Wright was unable to stem the flow, and when Moin Khan slapped a drive into the crowd over long-off, landing a few metres from where I was sitting, no less, it was all over bar the shouting. Pakistan had prevailed, snatching what appeared to be a victory from the jaws of defeat. As local fans, we were left with the sight of our home team in tears conducting a slow lap of honour. It was all over, and nobody really knew how.'

Although they had done so well, New Zealand had been pipped by an inspired Pakistan team. First Imran then Miandad had given the innings a backbone before Inzamam's whirlwind performance. Pakistan were going to the final. As for New Zealand, they would have plenty of time to contemplate what could have been.

The main question I wanted to be answered, when I spoke to New Zealand players, was to find out whether they were of the opinion that Crowe's injury had ultimately cost them a place in the final at the very least. An unfair question, in some ways, as

John Wright had captained the team in Crowe's absence. Gavin Larsen was adamant.

'I believe we would have won the World Cup. I believe we had the team to win the World Cup. I don't believe we did in the other three World Cups that I played in. I'm a firm believer that with Marty [Crowe] at the helm, and playing the way he was playing, the way that he was orchestrating matters then we had a team that could have lifted that trophy. With him off the park, that second innings at Eden Park was just soul-destroying.

'We deviated when Wrighty took over the reins, and we deviated away from our tried and proven bowling plan, and some of the field placings were quite different to how Marty had them. Now, I totally respect that all captains are different and they go about things in a different way, but what we did was we basically ripped our blueprint up, and we put it in the rubbish bin.'

Dipak Patel was of a different opinion and felt that defeat was down to Pakistan's brilliance. 'That's, I suppose, the million-dollar question. Certainly, from a technical perspective, things changed. It certainly didn't feel the same on the field, but at the end of the day, you know, when you're playing a World Cup semi-final, you can't take that into account. You've got a job to do, and the person who is making that decision is Wrighty. I don't think that Wrighty could have done anything better than what Martin Crowe would have done. The simple fact is that one particular player took the game away from us, that's how simple it was, to be honest with you.'

Seeking some perspective, I asked the opinion of Peter Williams, who fronted the TVNZ coverage in 1992. Williams has conducted countless interviews with Crowe and Wright over the years. 'That afternoon, those three-and-a-half hours in charge, might not have been his [John Wright's] finest hour, I think is the best way to put it. But then, in some respects, you can hardly blame him. I mean, he was out of practice as the captain. He had been the captain up until 1990, but I think he was relieved to have passed the job on to Martin. He was very happy just to be in the team as a player. And I think when, even though he was the senior pro, this responsibility was thrust upon him, he wouldn't have had any inkling of it.'

The manager of the New Zealand team, Ian Taylor, recalled how frustrating things had got in the dressing room as Wright's captaincy differed from the plan. 'I sat with Martin Crowe, just about, throughout the Pakistan innings and he was giving his own little commentary at times about "well, we need to do this", and "we need to do that" and whatever. And it didn't quite work out that way – but, you know, everyone is going to do these things differently, and we'll never know what difference it would have made.'

And with New Zealand's defeat at the hands of Pakistan, Murphy Su'a saw his last opportunity to play in the tournament disappear. Out of the 126 squad players, only Su'a failed to feature in any of the games. Speaking to Su'a, his disappointment at not playing was tempered. 'While I was disappointed not to get a game, I was certainly grateful, firstly being picked in the team, secondly being part of a team and environment that was positive and created self-belief, especially after the win over Australia in the first game. Martin [Crowe] was amazing throughout the tournament, but everyone did their part and came together in creating a special time for New Zealand cricket. A special mention for Warren Lees, who coached and managed many personalities during this time – he was outstanding.'

Having to attend every game must have been tough, but New Zealand's success dictated team selection. With their game plan, it was the medium-pacers who strangled the game to create pressure. The efficacy of fast bowling in New Zealand was negligible, and Su'a was lower than Danny Morrison in the pecking order. I asked whether there was an expectation to play. 'I certainly thought I would get a game at some stage, especially with the form the team had in the series against England prior to the Cricket World Cup. Indications and preparations leading into the tournament were that everyone should prepare to play each game.' That didn't happen, but Su'a was present at every game to perform twelfth-man duties when required.

In Sydney, England and South Africa prepared to clash for the right to play Pakistan. England's injury list improved slightly, with Graham Gooch feeling no after-effects with his hamstring and Dermot Reeve declaring himself fit. Derek Pringle's rib cartilage tear ruled him out, though, while Robin Smith had a pinched nerve in his back, so he also missed out. Phil Tufnell was the other player to miss out, as England preferred to play one spinner. South Africa had no such worries and fielded an unchanged side.

A short rain delay prevented the match from starting on time, but it was still going to be 50 overs per side. Looking back at the toss, Kepler Wessels recounted how his years in Australian cricket had helped to form his decision. 'We decided to bowl first. I knew one of the guys really well in Sydney, having played there often, and I asked him about the weather, and he said to me, "Look, it's probably going to rain for about 15 to 20 minutes during this match at some time, but my radar is not telling me exactly when. So you can't really let that influence what you're going to do." When we did bowl first, the ball was doing a lot.'

Allan Donald bowled the first over and found the edge of Ian Botham's bat, but the ball flew wide of second slip for a boundary. Botham's next boundary was more convincing as he drove Meyrick Pringle through the on side. England were off to a flying start, helped by some wide deliveries. In Donald's second over, though, South Africa were the beneficiaries of a generous decision. A rapid delivery appeared to catch the inside edge of Gooch's bat, and South Africa appealed for the caught behind. TV replays concurred with the England captain's displeasure by showing that the ball had missed the bat. However, the scorecard showed that South Africa had their breakthrough, with England at 20/1, and Alec Stewart came out to bat.

Botham continued to pursue his pinch-hitter brief. He was struggling against Pringle, slicing one just over the slips before chopping a ball on to the stumps. With Botham gone for 21, England were 39/2 in the eighth over. South Africa's bowlers were threatening to get on top. The new batter was Graeme Hick, and it felt as if South Africa's pace bowlers would pose similar problems for his batting technique to those he had faced in the English summer against the West Indies.

Immediately, Pringle found sufficient movement off the pitch to beat Hick's bat and hit his pads. Umpire Brian Aldridge was not convinced, despite the appeals for lbw. Wessels shook his head in disbelief. Worse was to follow when Pringle teased Hick into playing and extracted an edge. The ball flew to Wessels, who caught the ball, but umpire Aldridge had called a no-ball. Luck appeared to be on Hick's side, while South Africa were left to rue the possibility of a third wicket.

South Africa were literally, and metaphorically, under a cloud when the drizzle started. The ball became difficult to hold, and plenty of time was used up trying to dry it. England had no complaints as the pace of the outfield quickened, with the ball skidding off the surface. It also coincided with Hick and Stewart finding confidence and runs. Less pace from Snell and McMillan allowed the batters time to adjust and get into position to play their shots. Stewart found McMillan to his liking, with pulls and drives for boundaries.

With Stewart looking set for a big total, he tried to run McMillan down to third man, but Richardson took the catch at full length. Stewart's 33 as part of a partnership of 71 had helped England score at above five runs per over. Their 110/3 was an excellent platform to build upon.

South Africa found that the run rate was not the only problem they needed to address. Their over rate was pedestrian, and the incoming batter, Neil Fairbrother, was left-handed, which would exacerbate the time required to set fielding positions. They were without a spinner – Omar Henry had played just one match. South Africa needed to quicken up or face the consequences later.

Hick reached his fifty with an uncharacteristic fumble in the field. Having had such an inauspicious start to the innings, Hick reached his half-century from 55 balls. At the other end, Fairbrother was playing another typical innings, with plenty of nudges and nurdles for singles. The England fans were enjoying the occasion with a raucous Mexican wave. Wessels tried to improve the over rate, and get a wicket, by introducing medium pace in the form of Hansie Cronje and Adrian Kuiper. Both managed to get the ball to seam, but Kuiper's length was too short, and Hick, in particular, was quick to punish. By the end of the 30th over, England had moved on to 150/3 and were on target for a big total for South Africa to chase.

Donald came back into the attack, but his extra pace saw the ball rocket to the boundary quicker. Hick was now seeing the ball well and punished any width. In the 35th over, a cut shot and a cover drive demonstrated his dominance over Donald. By the end of it, he had conceded 14 runs, and South Africa needed a wicket. Pringle had been South Africa's best bowler so far and, as if to underline that fact, picked up a wicket in his first over back. Fairbrother had been beaten several times before a ball nipped back off the seam and took leg stump out of the ground. The partnership of 73, the second significant one of the innings, was broken – but England were 183/4, with South Africa significantly behind on their over rate.

With just four more runs on the board, South Africa struck again. Hick played a well-timed cut shot, off Snell, but far too close to Rhodes, who took a two-handed catch. Hick's superb innings was over for 83 off 90 balls. At this point, it was clear that South Africa would not bowl their allotted 50 overs, so Allan Lamb and Chris Lewis were tasked with trying to gauge how many overs were left.

Having had a few sighters, Lewis launched into the bowling. A well-timed boundary from a classic on drive was followed up with a wristy cut shot that flew for four. Also, Lewis was prepared to take on the South African fielders. Lamb was not quite as quick between the wickets, but pushed the ball into the gaps for runs. Trying to push the pace, Lamb nicked a ball behind, and the ever-reliable Richardson took the catch. The score had moved on to 221/6, and Dermot Reeve was next to bat.

Pringle bowled the 44th over, and found that both batters tried to hit him back down the ground. Both scampered furiously to pick off valuable runs. Reeve played an improvised pull shot on one leg for a boundary before calling Lewis through for a bye off the last ball to retain the strike. Reeve and Donald were colleagues at Warwickshire, and it appeared that Reeve was intent on facing the South African quick for what would be the final over. Wandering around his crease when Donald came in to bowl, Reeve created room and improvised shots into gaps for boundaries. The England innings closed at 252/6, with Lewis 18 not out from 17 balls, and Reeve with a whirlwind 25 from 14 balls. Donald had conceded 69 from his ten overs, including five wides and two no-balls. South Africa had failed to bowl five overs, which would attract a financial penalty, as well as leaving them to chase 253 from 45 overs.

South Africa's innings started with Ian Botham taking the new ball. England had scored heavily off pace bowling, so Botham's medium-pacers would force Wessels and Hudson to generate speed off the bat. Two wides were not the start that England wanted, but Botham extracted some movement off the pitch, which Wessels let through to the wicketkeeper.

Hudson, then Wessels, found the boundary as Lewis and Botham bowled too short. South Africa were keeping pace with the required run rate. Wessels was belying his reputation as a slow ODI scorer with well-placed shots into the gaps. In Botham's next over, Wessels's aim was lacking, and Lewis took the catch. Wessels climbed into a wide delivery but hit it straight to backward point, and South Africa were 26/1. The captain was out for 17, and Peter Kirsten was next to the crease. Kirsten had injured his hamstring during the England innings, and Wessels stayed on the field to be his runner.

Hudson preferred pace, and used Lewis's bowling by pulling two short balls for four to keep South Africa's run rate above where it needed to be. DeFreitas came on to bowl and found some movement off the pitch. Causing plenty of problems for both batters, he found a superb delivery to remove Kirsten. Beaten for pace and movement, Kirsten lost his off stump. He was out for 11, and South Africa were 61/2 in the 12th over.

Sensing the pressure building for South Africa, Gooch took a gamble and threw the ball to Richard Illingworth. Although the fielding restrictions were still in place, Gooch thought that spin was needed. At the other end, DeFreitas's leg cutters were causing problems for Hudson. The batter tried to pull the ball, but only managed to flat-bat it down the ground for a single. The required run rate was creeping up, while England were getting through the overs.

Illingworth bowled the 19th over, and Hudson was struggling to get the ball away. Misreading Illingworth's arm ball, he played a cut shot and was trapped in front. Umpire Brian Aldridge took his time before giving the decision. Hudson was gone for 46 to leave South Africa on 90/3. Speaking to Hudson, I asked about his liking of facing spin. 'I always felt more comfortable with pace bowling and the ball coming on to the bat. As an opener in South Africa, I mostly faced fast bowlers, and never had the experience of facing quality spinners for long periods of time, especially in the domestic set-up.'

Needing a boundary, Adrian Kuiper used his feet to Illingworth and hit him back down the ground into the sightscreen. The umpires conferred before signalling a four, which was greeted by a chorus of boos from the South African fans. Local conditions dictated that the sightscreen needed to be cleared, with it being placed two metres inside the boundary, for a six to be called. In some ways, the shot deserved more, but it did bring a useful boundary for South Africa. Kuiper repeated the stroke in Illingworth's next over for the same result.

Gladstone Small was brought on to bowl and immediately found that Kuiper and Hansie Cronje were more comfortable with the ball coming on to the bat quicker. Three successive fours to end the 26th over gave England notice that South Africa were far from out of the match. Kuiper was starting to live up to his big-hitting reputation. At the start of the next over, Illingworth bowled to Kuiper, who tried to sweep him. The ball hit Kuiper's leg, but the appeal was unsuccessful. Having run two byes, Kuiper set himself to face the next ball. As he tried to slog, his wild swing missed it by a considerable distance, and he was bowled middle and leg stump. A promising innings of 36 was over, and South Africa were pegged back again.

Fine drizzle started to fall as Cronje and Jonty Rhodes stroked the ball around the MCG. Rhodes got off the mark with an uppish on drive. Cronje also found the boundary, his first, as Illingworth tried to contain the run chase. By milking runs off the bowling, particularly of Botham and Small, South Africa moved swiftly past 150. Both sides played 'cat and mouse'; a dot ball would put the pressure on South Africa, a well-run two would redress the balance.

The score was 176/4 when Cronje tried to heave Small over the square-leg boundary. Good contact was made, but there was too much height on the shot and Hick positioned himself perfectly to take the catch. The England team celebrated the wicket and its importance. The fall of Cronje meant that Rhodes was the last recognised batter. Brian McMillan was up next and was a competent all-rounder, but the situation was becoming a difficult one.

Rhodes stepped up to the task. Lightning quick between the wickets, he pushed the first run hard and was happy to back himself in a race against the outfielders. In the 39th over, he swung Botham away towards the on-side boundary. DeFreitas tried to stop the ball with his foot, unsuccessfully, and a four brought South Africa to 199/6. Rhodes decided the next over was the one to go hard. Small was the bowler, and he found Rhodes charging down the wicket. Another well-run two meant that he retained the strike. Lewis was moved to backward point, and Rhodes hit a four through the newly made gap. Another fielding change from England moved Lewis again, but Rhodes repeated the shot. Lewis took the catch and Rhodes was out for 43 off 39 balls. A crucial wicket for England, as the South African had been keeping his team in the game.

Talking to Rhodes, he was honest about the shot. 'I had exactly eight international matches under my belt, so, without doubt, I got a little carried away, especially as I had just sliced a ball over point for a boundary. I hit the next ball in the same spot, sadly, to where they had just moved Chris Lewis. With both Cronje and Kuiper out, I felt it was my responsibility to try and hit the boundaries.'

The equation for McMillan and Dave Richardson was that South Africa needed 47 from 32 balls. A tight over from Lewis was followed up by Small. Both McMillan and Richardson were committed to running twos by taking on the fielders. Lewis started the 43rd over, and Richardson gave himself some room to a short ball and cut the ball for four. An agricultural shot back down the ground should have found the boundary but for Fairbrother's athletic slide and throw, limiting Richardson to two. He then scrambled a single to bring McMillan on strike. Then the rain started to fall.

Lewis bowled the next ball, which McMillan squirted away for two, as the crowd reached for umbrellas and any other item to shield themselves from the worsening rain. Gooch approached umpire Aldridge, who then walked towards his colleague, Steve Randell. They debated the situation before speaking with Gooch. Then, the decision was made to halt play with South Africa on 231/6 with 13 balls left. The time was 9.52pm.

Much deliberation took place in the middle as the umpires were joined by England manager Micky Stewart, South Africa coach Mike Procter and their manager, Alan Jordaan. The covers were taken off and, at 10.03pm, the scoreboard showed that one over had been lost and South Africa's revised total was 22 runs from seven balls. Boos rang out from the crowd at the news, and increased in volume as England came back out on to the field. The umpires, once again, spoke to the England captain as he walked on to the outfield. News filtered through via the TV broadcast that *two* overs had been deducted from the total, but the crowd were not aware at this point. An announcement was made, over the tannoy, that contradicted the news. The semi-final had turned from a gripping cricket match into a farce.

McMillan and Richardson walked back out to the crease. At 10.08pm, the scoreboard changed again to confirm that South Africa needed 22 runs off one ball. The crowd's disappointment and frustration could be heard clearly. McMillan faced the final ball, which he pushed for a single, before magnanimously shaking the hands of the embarrassed England players. Intriguingly, had DL or DLS been available for the semi-final, four runs off the last ball would have been South Africa's target.

In the final wash-up of the match, the revised total was 21 runs to win. The chaos of the occasion had caused confusion, but England were going through to the final by virtue of a 19-run victory. Ross Dundas, the official statistician, was responsible for the scoreboard at the SCG. He was the man who typed in the figures to update the board. The calculations were done and provided to him to enter. 'I remember the feeling in the room when the info came through,' said Dundas when asked about the occasion.

The crowd and press projected their anger at England. Although the South African line was to accept the defeat, it was done with mitigating factors, such as the rain which fell during the England innings having been no worse than the rain near the end of the match. Disappointingly, there was no mention of the reserve day that had been set aside for the semi-final. It seems strange that the game was not allowed to be finished on the following day. Not ideal from a fan perspective, but still much better than the scenes at the SCG when bottles and other items were thrown on to the outfield after the game had ended.

Chapter Thirteen

Cornered Tigers and Injured Lions

On the eve of the final, the World Cup Committee held the 'Benson & Hedges World Cup Banquet'. It was held in the Great Hall of the Royal Exhibition Building in Melbourne, and the guests of honour were the players from England and Pakistan. It seems absurd now that such an occasion would be held the night before the final – but the teams were required to attend. In the Teams Agreement, which each country's cricketing authority signed before the tournament, a clause specified that attendance 'in team uniform' was to be 'ensured'.

Over 2,000 guests attended the black-tie event and were served with a four-course dinner. Speeches from ICC chairman Colin Cowdrey and Richie Benaud were accompanied by musical and comedy entertainment. Undoubtedly, it was the comedy entertainment that caused one of the memorable moments of the tournament.

One of the performers was Gerry Connolly. Outside of Australia, it's unlikely that his name would have been known.

Famous for impersonations, he was asked to appear as the Queen at the banquet. At first, his act seemed to be received without any problems. Speaking to Connolly about the evening, he said that as he passed the England table when on his way to the stage, he was motioned to come and sit down with them.

Starting his act, Connolly made some satirical comments about the Duchess of York before performing an impersonation of ex-UK prime minister Margaret Thatcher. It was at this point that England captain Graham Gooch and Ian Botham got up and left the banquet. At the end of his act, Connolly left the stage and said to Richard Kenny, the producer, 'I think I've created an international incident.' Kenny responded, 'What do you mean?' and Connolly explained that Botham (and Gooch) had walked out. Kenny's response, factually incorrect with the benefit of hindsight, was, 'Oh no he didn't, he would have just been going to the loo ...'

Jonathan Agnew was covering his first Cricket World Cup for the BBC, and recalls how the events turned what should have been a relaxing evening into a journalistic nightmare. 'We, all the journos, were in a karaoke bar in Melbourne somewhere just down from the Rockman's Regency Hotel, where we were staying. And suddenly this news came through, and there were no mobile phones or anything in those days. We'd all had a few – it was a day/night final. It was coming to the end of the tour, and everything was great, you know, we'd had a few drinks. This news came through that the England team had stormed out of the dinner. My God, you've never seen journalists have to sober up so quickly and work so hard on the back of a karaoke evening. I had to try and file something from a phone box to the BBC outside the club. It was extraordinary. An extraordinary evening really.'

Connolly recollects that he was at home, just after 11pm that evening, when his telephone started ringing. News agencies such as Channel Nine and the BBC were desperate to get an interview. Over the next day, Connolly was inundated with interview requests and publicity. 'And I did interviews, and then the London papers broke. Then there was the Australian response to the London papers, blah, blah, blah. It went around in circles, and it was all a bit of a joke.'

The *Sun* newspaper in England went with 'Don't take the XXXX' as journalists quickly used the episode for their purposes. Australian PM Paul Keating couldn't resist taking another dig at Botham by suggesting that the players had been 'a bit precious' by walking out. Botham's justification was that 'I love my country and I can't put up with that sort of crap.'

England coach Micky Stewart said later that the whole team would have walked out had it not been the pre-final dinner. When I spoke to Gladstone Small, he commented on the dinner that 'we all had a laugh about that [the walkout]. And that it was crazy. We didn't want to be there.'

He also told the story of what Imran Khan had said after witnessing the walkout. Imran observed that 'only the colonials were left'. Most of the England team had been born elsewhere in the old British Empire: Derek Pringle in Kenya, Allan Lamb and Robin Smith in South Africa, Graeme Hick in Zimbabwe, Gladstone Small in Barbados, Phillip DeFreitas in Dominica, Chris Lewis in Guyana and Dermot Reeve in Hong Kong.

One of the guests, Bill Hodges, recalled the immediate impact of the incident. 'All I can tell you is that the majority of people in the room did not know that they had left. But they did know, I subsequently learned later, that Richie Benaud had to adjust his speech. If you're being honest, you could tell that he had to adjust it. It was still a very enjoyable speech, but it perhaps wasn't the speech that we all expected. Benaud subsequently admitted that he did have some references to Botham in that speech and

I'm sure people at the front of the room knew that those guys had left.'

After the rain debacle in Sydney, Pakistan had petitioned the World Cup Committee to change the rain rule for the final. Imran Khan was particularly critical and suggested that it had helped make the tournament the worst Cricket World Cup in history. England's management, though, felt that a change for the final would be unfair to the rest of the teams who had played under the controversial rules.

Before the final got underway, the 87,182 fans inside the MCG witnessed the official opening of the Great Southern Stand. The A$150 million stand had been in use since the World Series Cup, but had been built for use in the Cricket World Cup. The new stand had a capacity of 45,000, with four levels of seating and a cantilever roof over the top tier. The old stand had become unstable, with its concrete beginning to deteriorate, so a deal was struck with the Australian Football League to ensure the capital was available for the new construction. It is thought that this promise of a new stand was enough for the decision-makers to give the final to Melbourne rather than Sydney.

Pakistan made the unsurprising move of recalling Ijaz Ahmed in place of Iqbal Sikander. Otherwise, they were unchanged going into the final. England's team was not decided until just before the start of the match. Derek Pringle needed a late fitness test to prove that he had recovered enough to play. Robin Smith was in serious doubt, as his back injury was still restricting movement. Despite wearing a back brace and having a cortisone injection, he could not field in practice. He did spend time in the nets batting, where three local left-arm pace bowlers and two leg-spinners were employed to recreate the problems that would be faced against Wasim Akram and Mushtaq Ahmed.

Warming up in readiness, Gladstone Small was told that it was in vain because he was dropped for the final. 'I remember doing my stuff because I was hoping to play, and then I saw Goochie walking over to deliver the bad news, for me, that Pringle had passed the fitness test. So, I was going to miss out on the final. I remember at one stage, soon after Robin Smith heard his bad news that he wasn't going to make the team as well, he and I sat on the roller in the middle of the MCG sort of consoling each other.'

The toss, conducted by Ian Chappell, was won by Pakistan. Graham Gooch called incorrectly, and Imran Khan decided to bat first. With good batting conditions and the apparent advantage in the event of rain, Imran had no doubts over his decision. He was wearing a bright white T-shirt with a tiger printed upon it. The motto that he had asked his team to play by was 'like cornered tigers', and their recent results proved that it was working.

England's bowlers started positively, with Ramiz Raja and Aamer Sohail struggling to get the innings off to their usual positive start. Pringle overpitched in the third over, and was driven for four, but that delivery was not representative of the early stranglehold. In the next over, Lewis had Ramiz caught by Hick in the gully, but umpire Steve Bucknor somewhat controversially called a no-ball. In the resultant chaos, Ramiz started to walk off, before thinking that he could be run out and desperately grounding his bat.

England's disappointment did not last long, as Pringle extracted an edge, moving the ball away from Aamer Sohail, for Stewart to take the low catch. In his next over, Pringle trapped Ramiz in front to leave Pakistan on 24/2 in the ninth over. Both openers were gone for single-figure scores, and England's bowlers were well on top. Pakistan's most experienced players, Imran

Khan and Javed Miandad, were left with the task of recovering the innings. They were in a more serious position than in the semi-final, and Imran and Miandad would need all of their guile to dig them out of an awkward situation.

Early in his innings, Miandad struggled with the pace of Lewis. He played several shots uppishly, and an array of half-chances and encouragement was on offer. One delivery, on the leg side, completely deceived Miandad and ran away to the boundary for four leg-byes. Miandad fared no better against Pringle, who had a confident shout for lbw, but umpire Bucknor shook his head. The next ball also rapped Miandad's pads, but Bucknor was not in agreement with the appeal.

Pakistan's scoring was pedestrian. Imran had been content to see the ball go past the bat rather than play a shot. At one point, it was 31 consecutive deliveries before a run came off the bat. Botham and DeFreitas replaced Lewis and Pringle, and it was Botham's bowling that finally triggered some scoring shots. Imran worked him down the leg side for twos to a labouring Pringle. In the 18th over, Imran came down the wicket and hit Botham over the top for four. At the end of the over, Pakistan were 43/2 with a run rate of 2.39 runs per over.

With Imran playing more aggressively, he miscued DeFreitas, and the ball went into the air off the top edge. Gooch gave chase from midwicket, got to the ball but spilled the catch, and it hit the ground. It was a massive missed opportunity to remove Imran, who had scored just nine runs. A few overs later, Imran hit Illingworth down the ground with Gooch at long-on, but he could only watch the ball land in the stands. It looked as though it could be an important miss for England.

Miandad brought up the milestone of 1,000 runs in the Cricket World Cup with a thick edge for four. Another landmark was reached in the 35th over when the century partnership was achieved thanks to Imran's delicate leg glance to the boundary. Another leg glance, in the next over, brought up Miandad's fifty from 91 balls. That was quickly followed by Imran's fifty, from 88 balls, as the captain and vice-captain were steering their team into a position to accelerate later in the innings.

Miandad's back strain had flared up, resulting in him striking the ball clean rather than running. He called for a runner, and his aggressive intent increased before he fell to Illingworth for 58. Trying to reverse-sweep the spinner, Miandad hit the ball straight at Botham, who took the catch easily. Finally, England had broken the partnership, but it had amassed 139 runs. However, the wicket of the injured Miandad brought the hero of the semi-final to the crease: Inzamam-ul-Haq.

In the late-afternoon sunshine, England's bowlers started to toil. Inzamam found the middle of the bat straight away. Botham suffered as the young batter played several intelligent cricket shots. Excellent placement beat the infield, and the fast outfield did the rest. Botham did take the wicket of Imran, who tried to hit down the ground, with a straightforward catch from Illingworth. Pakistan were 197/4 in the 44th over. Imran's innings of 72 had steadied his team when needed, and underpinned a position from where Inzamam and Wasim Akram could kick on.

Scoring at more than a run a ball, Pakistan were making a concerted effort to get towards 250. Botham was hit for 12 off the 46th over as Wasim hit cleanly. In the 49th over, Wasim hit Lewis for 17 with several lusty blows as England failed to contain the momentum. The final over, bowled by Pringle, was a disappointment for Pakistan. Inzamam was bowled by a slower ball for 42, from 35 balls, before Wasim's 19-ball 33 ended when he was run out trying to take a quick single off the last ball.

Pakistan ended their innings with 249/6, which left England needing exactly five runs per over to win the Cricket World Cup.

Pringle's 3–22 was easily the best bowling for England with the other bowlers taking some punishment. Such was Pakistan's acceleration after Imran's hitting in the 18th over, from that point the run rate was 6.44 per over.

Between innings, there was entertainment for the crowd. Nine skydivers parachuted into the ground wearing the colours of each participating nation. Australian singer Glenn Shorrock sang the Cricket World Cup anthem, 'Who'll Rule the World?'

In the third over of England's response, Pakistan made the breakthrough, much to the disillusionment of the batter concerned. Wasim Akram found prodigious bounce, and Ian Botham gloved the ball to Moin Khan. The great all-rounder was not convinced, but he had to go. Botham left his final Cricket World Cup with a duck, Aamer Sohail's verbal volley and a chorus of booing from a partisan crowd. Only the England fans were sad to see Botham gone with just six runs on the board in reply. In his autobiography, Botham maintained that the ball had hit his sleeve. He also confessed to smashing his bat in frustration at the decision when getting back into the dressing room.

Things got decidedly worse for England when Alec Stewart followed an Aaqib Javed delivery and Moin had his second catch. Stewart had already survived a confident lbw shout from Wasim before nicking behind. He was on his way for six, and England were in a spot of bother at 21/2.

Graham Gooch and Graeme Hick managed to see off the initial pace danger. However, the threat of Mushtaq soon caused problems. Hick had reached 17 without looking confident against the leg-spinner. He failed to pick a Mushtaq googly, woefully playing for leg spin that wasn't there, and was trapped in front. It was the 20th over, and England were 59/3. Neil Fairbrother joined his captain at the crease. The required run rate and the pressure were mounting.

Gooch's answer to Mushtaq was to be aggressive. In Mushtaq's next over, Gooch looked to hit the ball high over extra cover. Instead, it squirted past Moin's grasp. Not deterred, Gooch played a sweep shot later in the over, which flew off the edge towards deep square leg. Aaqib Javed ran in to take a low, diving catch to leave England languishing at 69/4. The England captain's innings of 29 was over, and the possibility of a third Cricket World Cup Final defeat was looking likely for Gooch.

England's road back into the final lay with Neil Fairbrother and Allan Lamb. Both set about their task with placement rather than aggression. Picking up the occasional boundary, both batters were intent on pushing the ball into gaps to milk runs. Imran brought on Aamer Sohail to bowl, and England found scoring easier. The partnership added 72 runs, which more than doubled England's score.

Imran decided that Wasim Akram would bowl the 35th over. The instruction was just to bowl fast. Lamb, on 31 and looking in touch, played a defensive shot down the line of the ball. The ball pitched and jagged towards off stump and crashed into it. Just what Pakistan needed. The new batter was Chris Lewis, and he prepared to face his first ball. He played outside off stump, the ball swung viciously, and the hapless Lewis could only look down to see his stumps rearranged. Two wickets in two balls for Wasim Akram, and it left England with a mountain to climb.

Fairbrother was the last genuine hope for England. His fifty was brought up with a scrappy run, very much in keeping with the battling innings he was conjuring up. England had reached 165/6 with ten overs left. Dermot Reeve was an all-rounder with ability, and England could bat right the way down to Richard Illingworth at number 11. Fairbrother, though, was the prize wicket. Aaqib Javed almost bowled him, but the under-edge missed the stumps and ran away for four. It was fortuitous, but very much needed. The equation was 70 runs needed from 44 balls. Dot balls were not required, and Fairbrother tried to pull a short ball, which shot up into the air. Moin Khan sprinted from behind the stumps to catch the ball at point.

Reeve followed soon after with a miscued shot off Mushtaq. Even a potential collision could not put off Ramiz Raja as he took the catch cleanly. England's innings was almost over at 183/8. Reeve was out for 15, and Phil DeFreitas joined Derek Pringle. Pringle swept Mushtaq for four, while DeFreitas took Akram for a well-run three, but it was not enough. With three overs left, 43 runs were still required.

Imran brought himself on to bowl, and his first ball was hit towards the leg side by DeFreitas. It was an easy single, but DeFreitas, recognising singles would not suffice, decided to turn for two, knowing he was running to the danger end. Malik's throw was unsurprisingly accurate, considering Pakistan's ascendancy, and Moin Khan easily took the bails off with DeFreitas agonisingly short. At 208/9, the game was almost over. Richard Illingworth walked to the crease knowing that it was almost mission impossible.

England struggled to the final over. Illingworth clipped the first ball, off Imran, for four, but ball three was hit up in the air, and Ramiz Raja took the catch. Pakistan were world champions. England had been bowled out for 227 and lost by 22 runs. Man of the Match went to Wasim Akram for his devastating bowling spell (finishing with 3–49), earning him $3,000 and a gold medallion in the process.

Sir Colin Cowdrey presented Imran Khan with the trophy, a Waterford crystal globe, before Pakistan's captain gave his speech. 'I just want to give my commiserations to the England team. I want them to know that by winning this World Cup, personally, it means that one of my greatest obsessions in life, which is to build a cancer hospital, I'm sure that this World Cup will go a long way towards completion of this obsession. I would also like to say that I feel very proud that at the twilight of my career, finally, I've managed to win the World Cup.'

It was a curious speech. Imran failed to mention any of the squad. It was definitely 'him' and not 'us' who had prevailed. For sure, Imran's belief in himself and his players had been a big factor. But to not mention names such as Wasim Akram, Inzamam-ul-Haq, Mushtaq Ahmed, Ramiz Raja or Aamer Sohail seemed remiss.

In Pakistan, fans were delirious with the win. Guns were fired into the air to celebrate, but unfortunately at least five people were killed by stray bullets. One fan died of a heart attack while watching Imran receive the trophy. The gentleman shouted 'Pakistan Zindabad' – 'Long live Pakistan' – before collapsing and dying.

Contemplating where England had lost the final, Derek Pringle summed up the game. 'Steve Bucknor twice turning down plumb lbws against Javed Miandad; Ian Botham going for a duck in contentious circumstances (he claims he didn't hit the ball) and Wasim Akram's double strike to get rid of Allan Lamb and Chris Lewis, were all big moments. Basically, though, we allowed them to get too many runs after restricting them well for the first 35 overs of their innings.'

In July 1992, the final report on the tournament was presented to the ICC. A 15-page document, written by the World Cup Committee, reviewed the tournament from its inception to the final at the MCG. It was signed by Malcolm Gray and Peter McDermott on behalf of the committee, and concluded that the objectives of the tournament had been met.

It began by reviewing the start of the process, up to the decision on the winning bid to host the tournament, made in

January 1989. As part of the bid proposal, guaranteed financial amounts were offered. The eight ICC full member countries received £150,000 each, while Zimbabwe, an associate member, received £125,000. The other 18 associate members were given £40,000 each, while £100,000 was provided to support the ICC Trophy Series, which Zimbabwe had won to qualify. In total, £2,145,000 was provided as part of the deal to organise the fifth Cricket World Cup.

The report then went on to discuss the format of the tournament, South Africa's inclusion and the effects of that decision. It confirmed that CSI Limited, in London, sold the television rights overseas on behalf of the World Cup Committee. The deals made led to 60 countries receiving broadcasts. They included three unnamed African countries, Bangladesh, Bermuda, Canada, India, Israel, Italy, Malaysia, the Netherlands, Pakistan, Saudi Arabia, Singapore, Sri Lanka, Thailand, the UK, the USA and the West Indies (treated as a single country for these purposes).

Also, a deal was done with AsiaSat and their satellite network to reach other markets such as China, Japan and states within the former Soviet Union. Interestingly, emerging cricketing nations of the future such as Afghanistan, Hong Kong and the UAE also received broadcasts. More obscure markets such as North Korea were included too. Radio coverage was less well spread, with deals done in Pakistan, South Africa and the UK. The BBC World Service would have opened up the coverage somewhat. A total of 742 individuals received media accreditation for the tournament. Print (white), TV (blue) and radio (green) passes were issued, mainly from the ACB offices in Melbourne, which gave passes to the international media for matches played in New Zealand as well as in Australia. NZC handled only their domestic media accreditations.

The report moved on to the agreement that each competing country was required to sign. It stated the eight basic requirements of the agreement, before becoming critical of several breaches. The report stated its 'disappointment that neither Javed Miandad or Kapil Dev made themselves available to sign the limited edition official souvenir bats'. As part of the meet-up in Sydney, encapsulated by the iconic photographs on HMAS *Canberra*, each team was required to sign 250 bats.

Another requirement was to wear the officially supplied kit, such as caps, hats, helmets and pads. In particular, two players each from Australia and England had flagrantly flouted the agreement, and legislation was taking place. A.G. Thompson Pty Ltd (Kookaburra) and Gray Nicolls Pty Ltd were in a legal battle over manufacturer logos being placed over the official Kookaburra logo on batting pads. Although no players were named in the report, meeting minutes from 18 June disclosed that it was Geoff Marsh and David Boon from Australia, and Chris Lewis and Robin Smith from England. A fine of £2,000 was levied against each country's cricket board for the breach. Other fines were issued during the tournament for disciplinary reasons (Mike Whitney, Moin Khan and Aamer Sohail), and for slow over-rates. South Africa were fined £1,080 for bowling too slowly on two occasions.

Considering the playing conditions, it was surprising to see that the rain rule was not criticised. Even putting the disastrous end to the semi-final to one side, most of the rain-affected games produced less than equitable targets to chase – but the report glossed over the negativity, and attempted to blame the difficulties on the complexities of adjusting totals for rain interruptions. 'The Playing Conditions operated satisfactorily although there was an obvious difficulty in the Sydney Semi-Final with the application of the Rule relating to the recalculation of the target score when the innings of the side batting second was interrupted. This was the first such occasion in over 75 matches played since the Rule was adopted in 1989, and serves to illustrate the difficulty in maintaining equity for both sides when a match is interrupted, particularly in its closing stages.'

The ICC appeared to take a blasé attitude to the inadequacy of the rain rule too. A congratulatory letter sent from Lt Col Stephenson to New Zealand Cricket directly after the tournament also made light of the episode. Stephenson referred to the 'slight hiccup with the rain regulation', but was quick to qualify that with 'which I know was approved by the Countries taking part'.

Speaking to Duckworth and Lewis about 1992, they were scathing of the rain rule. 'The injustice in the England v South Africa semi-final was largely created because it was two overs at the end which were lost, not at the beginning, which wouldn't have had such a big impact. Another match with such a scenario, but just as unfairly so, occurred on March 7 in Hamilton. India had only 32 overs to bat and scored 203/7. Zimbabwe were 104/1 in 19.1 when rain terminated the match. Who should be the winners? MPO was only able to work to complete numbers of overs and so, for 19 overs, the MPO target for the end of the 19th over was 159. How absurd!'

Their criticism continued: 'One of the many strengths of the DL method is that it takes account of the stage of the innings that the stoppage occurs – later on is more disadvantageous than early in the innings. Assuming India's shortened innings was due to a late start and not any interruptions, then, according to the DL tables, the par score after 19.1 overs (DL can handle fractions of overs just as easily) was 102. So instead of the absurd margin of defeat by 55 runs, Zimbabwe at 104/1 was two runs ahead of the DL par and would have been the winners! For their strong position at the abandonment, would anybody have complained? We doubt it.'

Although 1992 highlighted that MPO was not fit for purpose, the question of target revision had been debated for some time. The Cricket World Cup accelerated change, and the ACB was first to respond. The book *Duckworth Lewis: The Method and the Men Behind It* states that a competition run by the newspaper *The Australian* came up with the idea of tweaking MPO by discounting total runs by half a per cent for each over lost. It would be four years before Duckworth and Lewis's method would be published, and some time longer before its adoption.

The 1992 Cricket World Cup was not free from the shadow of corruption. Several players who played in the tournament would receive bans from cricket. None of those incidents, though, were ever directly linked to, any incidents during the 1992 tournament. Mohammed Azharuddin, Ajay Jadeja, Manoj Prabhakar, Salim Malik and Hansie Cronje received punishments for relationships with bookmakers. Others such as Chris Cairns, Aravinda de Silva, Arjuna Ranatunga, Wasim Akram, Alec Stewart, Dean Jones, Brian Lara and Mark Waugh were implicated in corruption scandals. One man was questioned about 1992, and that was Martin Crowe.

In November 2000, a report made by the Central Bureau of Investigation of India named Crowe as having accepted money from a bookmaker, MK Gupta, to provide information about the pitch and team news. It did state that Crowe had refused to 'fix any matches' when asked. Crowe responded by accepting that he had received money from an individual, but was being paid to write articles about the 1992 Cricket World Cup for publication in India. Gupta alleged that Crowe received US$20,000, but Crowe asserted that it was US$3,000 for ten articles.

The inquiry recognised mitigating factors in Crowe's conduct during the incident. 'These events all occurred at a time when Martin Crowe was under intense pressure. There had been significant issues surrounding his captaincy immediately before the World Cup, after an unsuccessful Test series against England. The inquiry was provided with articles which demonstrated that he and Simone Crowe [Crowe's then wife] were subject to intense speculation about their marriage and other intrusions into their personal life. He was under immense pressure, with the responsibilities of captain and batsman in a major international tournament. These circumstances must be reflected in any residual comment about his conduct.'

Crowe's ex-wife refused to testify at the inquiry, and was an alleged witness to Crowe meeting Gupta at his own home. Also, Crowe refuted the allegation that he was introduced to Gupta by Aravinda de Silva. Ironically, Gupta refused to cooperate with the New Zealand Cricket inquiry. Ultimately, the investigation found that Crowe was cleared of any wrongdoing and that his credibility and reputation were intact.

And so should Crowe's credibility and reputation be intact. His form in 1992 was phenomenal. Scoring the most runs, 456, and averaging 114, Crowe almost single-handedly took New Zealand to the final. Quite rightly, he was named player of the tournament and was awarded $5,000 and a Nissan 300 ZX Coupe car. For what it's worth, I do think New Zealand would have won the tournament if Crowe's hamstring hadn't been injured. Pakistan were playing excellent cricket, but something makes me think that Crowe would have pulled something out of the bag.

When speaking to Gavin Larsen about 1992, his voice oozed sincerity about Crowe. He convinced me that there was a New Zealand masterplan. 'We just had this amazing self-belief, had built within the unit, and one thing that Marty did right at the start of the tournament was to eliminate us thinking about the teams or the country names and the particular individuals within the team. We de-humanised them by ... we were playing the "yellow team" when we were playing Australia, we were playing the "green team" when we played Pakistan, we were playing the "red team" when we played Zimbabwe, and we were playing the "blue team" when we played England. And I found that incredibly effective actually, so we focused very much on our play, our game plan and when we knew things were going so well, we knew it was going to take a damn big effort from the opposition to knock us over.'

For Kepler and the South Africans, the rain rule didn't give them a fair chance of victory. It was unfair that England took the blame for the semi-final nonsense. Having been in isolation for over 20 years and then being thrust back on to the international scene, playing out against a paradigm shift in the political situation, the South Africans acquitted themselves superbly.

For England, the Cricket World Cup Final was a few weeks too late. Selecting an ageing side and picking up injuries on the way was always going to provide a test. Arguably, the final was one game that they wouldn't have played if the rain rule hadn't robbed us all of a finish to a fascinating contest. England's mix of batting strength and all-rounders gave a blueprint suggesting that limited-overs cricket success could be achieved by players who could bat and bowl. In the same way as New Zealand opened the bowling with a spinner, teams being able to bat right down the order was a way forward.

For the winners, Pakistan peaked at the right time. The batting skill of Inzamam-ul-Haq was undeniable. Wasim Akram's devastating wicket-taking ability was phenomenal. However, it was the experience of Imran Khan and Javed

Miandad that underpinned the turnaround in form. Like two virtuoso violinists, they played all the right notes. Imran's man-management skills were overt, while Miandad worked quietly at the crease, with words of encouragement, advice, suggestions and goodness knows what else.

Pakistan's victory was testament to the adage, 'It is not how you start the race or where you are during the race – it is how you cross the finish line that will matter.'

Scorecards
Appendix 1

Match 1 – February 22, 1992: New Zealand vs Australia (Eden Park, Auckland)
Toss: New Zealand   Umpires: Khizer Hayat & DR Shepherd
Crowd: 22,262   MOTM: MD Crowe
New Zealand won by 37 runs

New Zealand			Runs	Mins	Balls	4s	6s	SR
JG Wright		b McDermott	0	3	1	-	-	0.00
RT Latham	c Healy	b Moody	26	65	44	4	-	59.09
AH Jones	lbw	b Reid	4	16	14	1	-	28.57
MD Crowe*		not out	100	180	134	11	-	74.63
KR Rutherford		run out	57	88	71	6	-	80.28
CZ Harris		run out	14	14	15	2	-	93.33
IDS Smith†	c Healy	b McDermott	14	15	14	1	-	100.00
CL Cairns		not out	16	15	11	2	-	145.45
DN Patel								
GR Larsen								
W Watson								
Extras	(lb 6, w 7, nb 4)		17					
	50 overs (201 mins)		248 for 6					

Fall: 1-2 (Wright) 2-13 (Kirsten) 3-53 (Latham) 4-171 (Rutherford) 5-191 (Harris) 6-215 (Smith)

	O	M	R	W	Ave	SR	ER	Wide	NB
CJ McDermott	10	1	43	2	21.50	30.00	4.30	2	-
BA Reid	10	0	39	1	39.00	60.00	3.90	2	4
TM Moody	9	1	37	1	37.00	54.00	4.11	-	-
SR Waugh	10	0	60	0	-	-	6.00	2	-
PL Taylor	7	0	36	0	-	-	5.14	-	-
ME Waugh	4	0	27	0	-	-	6.75	1	-

Australia			Runs	Mins	Balls	4s	6s	SR
DC Boon		run out	100	176	131	11	-	76.34
GR Marsh	c Latham	b Larsen	19	60	56	2	-	33.93
DM Jones		run out	21	28	27	3	-	77.78
AR Border*	c Cairns	b Patel	3	13	11	-	-	27.27
TM Moody	c and	b Latham	7	10	11	-	-	63.64
ME Waugh	lbw	b Larsen	2	9	5	-	-	40.00
SR Waugh	c and	b Larsen	38	48	34	3	1	111.76
IA Healy†		not out	7	16	9	-	-	77.78
CJ McDermott		run out	1	4	1	-	-	100.00
PL Taylor	c Rutherford	b Watson	1	3	2	-	-	50.00
BA Reid	c Jones	b Harris	3	4	4	-	-	75.00
Extras	(lb 6, w 2, nb 1)		9					
	48.1 overs (190 mins)		211					

Fall: 1-62 (Marsh) 2-92 (Jones) 3-104 (Border) 4-120 (Moody) 5-125 (ME Waugh) 6-199 (SR Waugh) 7-200 (Boon) 8-205 (McDermott) 9-206 (Taylor) 10-211 (Reid)

	O	M	R	W	Ave	SR	ER	Wide	NB
CL Cairns	4	0	30	0	-	-	7.50	1	1
DN Patel	10	1	36	1	36.00	60.00	3.60	1	-
W Watson	9	1	39	1	39.00	54.00	4.33	-	-
GR Larsen	10	1	30	3	10.00	20.00	3.00	-	-
CZ Harris	7.1	0	35	1	35.00	43.00	4.88	-	-
RT Latham	8	0	35	1	35.00	48.00	4.37	-	-

Match 2 – February 22, 1992: England vs India (WACA Ground, Perth) – D/N

Toss: England
Crowd: 12,902
England won by 9 runs

Umpires: DP Buultjens & PJ McConnell
MOTM: IT Botham

England			Runs	Mins	Balls	4s	6s	SR
GA Gooch*	c Tendulkar	b Shastri	51	121	89	1	-	57.30
IT Botham	c More	b Kapil Dev	9	33	21	1	-	42.86
RA Smith	c Azharuddin	b Prabhakar	91	145	108	8	2	84.26
GA Hick	c More	b Banerjee	5	5	6	1	-	83.33
NH Fairbrother	c Srikkanth	b Srinath	24	47	34	1	-	70.59
AJ Stewart†		b Prabhakar	13	22	15	1	-	86.67
CC Lewis	c Banerjee	b Kapil Dev	10	10	6	1	-	166.67
DR Pringle	c Srikkanth	b Srinath	1	4	3			33.33
DA Reeve		not out	8	14	8	-	-	100.00
PAJ DeFreitas		run out	1	2	5	-	-	20.00
PCR Tufnell		not out	3	7	5	-	-	60.00
Extras	(b 1, lb 6, w 13)		20					
	50 overs (214 mins)		236 for 9					

Fall: 1-21 (Botham) 2-131 (Gooch) 3-137 (Hick) 4-197 (Fairbrother) 5-198 (Smith) 6-214 (Lewis) 7-222 (Pringle) 8-223 (Stewart) 9-224 (DeFreitas)

	O	M	R	W	Ave	SR	ER	Wide	NB
Kapil Dev	10	0	38	2	19.00	30.00	3.80	6	
M Prabhakar	10	3	34	2	17.00	30.00	3.40	-	-
J Srinath	9	1	47	2	23.50	27.00	5.22	5	-
ST Banerjee	7	0	45	1	45.00	42.00	6.43	-	-
SR Tendulkar	10	0	37	0	-	-	3.70	1	-
RJ Shastri	4	0	28	1	28.00	24.00	7.00	1	-

India			Runs	Mins	Balls	4s	6s	SR
RJ Shastri		run out	57	151	112	2	-	50.89
K Srikkanth	c Botham	b DeFreitas	39	63	50	7	-	78.00
M Azharuddin*	c Stewart	b Reeve	0	2	1	-	-	0.00
SR Tendulkar	c Stewart	b Botham	35	51	44	5	-	79.55
VG Kambli	c Hick	b Botham	3	6	11	-	-	27.27
PK Amre	run out	run out	22	44	31	-	-	70.97
Kapil Dev	c DeFreitas	b Reeve	17	24	18	2	-	94.44
ST Banerjee		not out	25	28	16	1	1	156.25
KS More†		run out	1	6	4	-	-	25.00
M Prabhakar		b Reeve	0	1	3	-	-	0.00
J Srinath		run out	11	10	8	-	-	137.50
Extras	(lb 9, w 7, nb 1)		17					
	48.1 overs (190 mins)		227					

Fall: 1-63 (Srikkanth) 2-63 (Azharuddin) 3-126 (Tendulkar) 4-140 (Kambli) 5-149 (Shastri) 6-187 (Kapil Dev) 7-194 (Amre) 8-200 (More) 9-201 (Prabhakar) 10-227 (Srinath)

	O	M	R	W	Ave	SR	ER	Wide	NB
DR Pringle	10	0	53	0	-	-	5.30	1	-
CC Lewis	9.2	0	36	0	-	-	3.86	5	1
PAJ DeFreitas	10	0	39	1	39.00	60.00	3.90	-	-
DA Reeve	6	0	38	3	12.67	12.00	6.33	1	-
IT Botham	10	0	27	2	13.50	30.00	2.70	-	-
PCR Tufnell	4	0	25	0	-	-	6.25	-	-

Match 3 – February 23, 1992: Sri Lanka vs Zimbabwe (Pukekura Park, New Plymouth)

Toss: Sri Lanka   Umpires: PD Reporter & SJ Woodward
Crowd: 3,100 (estimated)   MOTM: A Flower
Sri Lanka won by three wickets

Zimbabwe			Runs	Mins	Balls	4s	6s	SR
A Flower†		not out	115	215	152	8	1	75.66
WR James	c Tillakaratne	b Wickramasinghe	17	31	21	3	-	80.95
AJ Pycroft	c Ramanayake	b Gurusinha	5	31	22	-	-	22.73
DL Houghton*	c Tillakaratne	b Gurusinha	10	23	19	1	-	52.63
KJ Arnott	c Tillakaratne	b Wickramasinghe	52	66	56	4	1	92.86
AC Waller		not out	83	57	45	9	3	184.44
IP Butchart								
KG Duers								
EA Brandes								
MP Jarvis								
AJ Traicos								
Extras	(b 2, lb 6, w 13, nb 9)		30					
	50 overs (215 mins)		312 for 4					

Fall: 1-30 (James) 2-57 (Pycroft) 3-82 (Houghton) 4-167 (Arnott)

	O	M	R	W	Ave	SR	ER	Wide	NB
KIW Wijegunawardene	7	0	54	0	-	-	7.71	3	6
CPH Ramanayake	10	0	59	0	-	-	5.90	3	1
GP Wickramasinghe	10	1	50	2	25.00	30.00	5.00	1	2
AP Gurusinha	10	0	72	2	36.00	30.00	7.20	6	-
RS Kalpage	10	0	51	0	-	-	5.10	-	-
ST Jayasuriya	3	0	18	0	-	-	6.00	-	-

Sri Lanka			Runs	Mins	Balls	4s	6s	SR
RS Mahanama	c Arnott	b Brandes	59	100	89	4	-	66.29
MAR Samarasekera	c Duers	b Traicos	75	81	61	11	1	122.95
PA de Silva*	c Houghton	b Brandes	14	40	28	1	-	50.00
AP Gurusinha		run out	5	9	6	-	-	83.33
A Ranatunga		not out	88	117	61	9	1	144.26
ST Jayasuriya	c Flower	b Houghton	32	24	23	2	2	139.13
HP Tillakaratne†		b Jarvis	18	25	12	1	1	150.00
RS Kalpage	c Houghton	b Brandes	11	19	14	1	-	78.57
CPH Ramanayake		not out	1	2	1	-	-	100.00
KIW Wijegunawardene								
GP Wickramasinghe								
Extras	(lb 5, w 5)		10					
	49.2 overs (202 mins)		313 for 7					

Fall: 1-128 (Samarasekera) 2-144 (Mahanama) 3-155 (Gurusinha) 4-167 (de Silva) 5-212 (Jayasuriya) 6-273 (Tillakaratne) 7-308 (Kalpage)

	O	M	R	W	Ave	SR	ER	Wide	NB
MP Jarvis	9.2	0	51	1	51.00	56.00	5.46	1	-
KG Duers	10	0	72	0	-	-	7.20	-	-
EA Brandes	10	0	70	3	23.33	20.00	7.00	-	-
AJ Traicos	10	1	33	1	33.00	60.00	3.30	1	-
IP Butchart	8	0	63	0	-	-	7.87	3	-
DL Houghton	2	0	19	1	19.00	12.00	9.50	-	-

Match 4 – February 23, 1992: Pakistan vs West Indies (MCG, Melbourne)

Toss: West Indies

Crowd: 14,162

West Indies won by ten wickets

Umpires: SG Randell & ID Robinson

MOTM: BC Lara

Pakistan			Runs	Mins	Balls	4s	6s	SR
Ramiz Raja		not out	102	181	158	4	-	64.56
Aamer Sohail	c Logie	b Benjamin	23	53	44	3	-	52.27
Inzamam-ul-Haq	c Hooper	b Harper	27	46	39-		-	69.23
Javed Miandad*		not out	57	80	61	5	-	93.44
Salim Malik								
Ijaz Ahmed								
Wasim Akram								
Iqbal Sikander								
Wasim Haider								
Moin Khan†								
Aaqib Javed								
Extras	(b 1, lb 3, w 5, nb 2)		11					
50 overs (181 mins)			220 for 2					

Fall: 1-45 (Sohail) 2-97 (Inzamam)

	O	M	R	W	Ave	SR	ER	Wide	NB
MD Marshall	10	1	53	0	-	-	5.30	3	-
CEL Ambrose	10	0	40	0	-	-	4.00	1	2
WKM Benjamin	10	0	49	1	49.00	60.00	4.90	1	-
CL Hooper	10	0	41	0	-	-	4.10	-	-
RA Harper	10	0	33	1	33.00	60.00	3.30	-	-

West Indies			Runs	Mins	Balls	4s	6s	SR
DL Haynes		not out	93	192	144	7	-	64.58
BC Lara		retired hurt	88	150	101	11	-	87.13
RB Richardson*		not out	20	41	40	1	-	50.00
CL Hooper								
KLT Arthurton								
AL Logie								
RA Harper								
MD Marshall								
WKM Benjamin								
D Williams†								
CEL Ambrose								
Extras	(b 2, lb 8, w 7, nb 3)		20					
46.5 overs (192 mins)			221 for 0					

	O	M	R	W	Ave	SR	ER	Wide	NB
Wasim Akram	10	0	37	0	-	-	3.70	7	-
Aaqib Javed	8.5	0	42	0	-	-	4.75	-	2
Wasim Haider	8	0	42	0	-	-	5.25	-	1
Ijaz Ahmed	6	1	29	0	-	-	4.83	-	-
Iqbal Sikander	8	1	26	0	-	-	3.25	-	-
Aamer Sohail	6	0	35	0	-	-	5.83	-	-

APPENDICES

Match 5 – February 25: 1992: New Zealand vs Sri Lanka (Trust Bank Park, Hamilton)
Toss: New Zealand
Crowd: 8,268
New Zealand won by six wickets

Umpires: PD Reporter & DR Shepherd
MOTM: KR Rutherford

Sri Lanka			Runs	Mins	Balls	4s	6s	SR
RS Mahanama	c and	b Harris	80	175	131	6	-	61.07
MAR Samarasekera	c Wright	b Watson	9	25	20	1	-	45.00
AP Gurusinha	c Smith	b Harris	9	41	33	-	-	27.27
PA de Silva*		run out	31	61	45	2	-	68.89
A Ranatunga	c Rutherford	b Harris	20	40	26	2	-	76.92
ST Jayasuriya		run out	5	10	7	-	-	71.43
HP Tillakaratne†	c Crowe	b Watson	8	21	19	-	-	42.11
RS Kalpage	c Larsen	b Watson	11	20	17	-	-	64.71
CPH Ramanayake		run out	2	2	1	-	-	200.00
SD Anurasiri		not out	3	7	2	-	-	150.00
GP Wickramasinghe		not out	3	2	4	-	-	75.00
Extras	(b 1, lb 15, w 4, nb 5)		25					
	50 overs (208 mins)		206 for 9					

Fall: 1-18 (Samarasekera) 2-50 (Gurusinha) 3-120 (de Silva) 4-172 (Ranatunga) 5-172 (Mahanama) 6-181 (Jayasuriya) 7-195 (Tillakaratne) 8-199 (Ramanayake) 9-202 (Kalpage)

	O	M	R	W	Ave	SR	ER	Wide	NB
DK Morrison	8	0	36	0	-	-	4.50	1	2
W Watson	10	0	37	3	12.33	20.00	3.70	1	2
GR Larsen	10	1	29	0	-	-	2.90	1	-
CZ Harris	10	0	43	3	14.33	20.00	4.30	1	1
RT Latham	3	0	13	0	-	-	4.33	-	-
DN Patel	9	0	32	0	-	-	3.56	-	-

New Zealand			Runs	Mins	Balls	4s	6s	SR
JG Wright	c and	b Kalpage	57	89	76	9	-	75.00
RT Latham		b Kalpage	20	72	41	3	-	48.78
AH Jones	c Jayasuriya	b Gurusinha	49	106	77	4	-	63.64
MD Crowe*	c Ramanayake	b Wickramasinghe	5	25	23	-	-	21.74
KR Rutherford		not out	65	79	71	6	1	91.55
CZ Harris		not out	5	13	5	-	-	100.00
DN Patel								
IDS Smith†								
GR Larsen								
DK Morrison								
W Watson								
Extras	(lb 3, w 3, nb 3)		9					
	48.2 overs (195 mins)		210					

Fall: 1-77 (Latham) 2-90 (Wright) 3-105 (Crowe) 4-186 (Jones)

	O	M	R	W	Ave	SR	ER	Wide	NB
CPH Ramanayake	9.2	0	46	0	-	-	4.93	2	2
GP Wickramasinghe	8	1	40	1	40.00	48.00	5.00	1	-
SD Anurasiri	10	1	27	0	-	-	2.70	-	-
RS Kalpage	10	0	33	2	16.50	30.00	3.30	-	-
AP Gurusinha	4	0	19	1	19.00	24.00	4.75	-	-
A Ranatunga	4	0	22	0	-	-	5.50	-	-
ST Jayasuriya	2	0	14	0	-	-	7.00	-	-
PA de Silva	1	0	6	0	-	-	6.00	-	1

Match 6 – February 26, 1992: Australia vs South Africa (SCG, Sydney) – D/N

Toss: Australia
Crowd: 39,789
South Africa won by nine wickets

Umpires: BL Aldridge & SU Bucknor
MOTM: KC Wessels

Australia			Runs	Mins	Balls	4s	6s	SR
GR Marsh	c Richardson	b Kuiper	80	175	131	6	-	61.07
DC Boon		run out	9	25	20	1	-	45.00
DM Jones	c Richardson	b McMillan	9	41	33	-	-	27.27
AR Border*		b Kuiper	31	61	45	2	-	68.89
TM Moody	lbw	b Donald	20	40	26	2	-	76.92
SR Waugh	c Cronje	b McMillan	5	10	7	-	-	71.43
IA Healy†	c McMillan	b Donald	8	21	19	-	-	42.11
PL Taylor		b Donald	11	20	17	-	-	64.71
CJ McDermott		run out	2	2	1	-	-	200.00
MR Whitney		not out	3	7	2	-	-	150.00
BA Reid		not out	3	2	4	-	-	75.00
Extras	(lb 2, w 11, nb 4)		17					
	50 overs (215 mins)		170 for 9					

Fall: 1-42 (Boon) 2-76 (Marsh) 3-76 (Border) 4-97 (Jones) 5-108 (Moody) 6-143 (Healy) 7-146 (Waugh) 8-156 (Taylor) 9-161 (McDermott)

	O	M	R	W	Ave	SR	ER	Wide	NB
AA Donald	10	0	34	3	11.33	20.00	3.40	5	-
MW Pringle	10	0	52	0	-	-	5.20	1	2
RP Snell	9	1	15	0	-	-	1.67	-	-
BM McMillan	10	0	35	2	17.50	30.00	3.50	3	2
AP Kuiper	5	0	15	2	7.50	15.00	3.00	1	-
WJ Cronje	5	1	17	0	-	-	3.40	1	-

South Africa		Runs	Mins	Balls	4s	6s	SR
KC Wessels*	not out	81	173	148	9	-	54.73
AC Hudson	b Taylor	28	81	52	3	-	53.85
PN Kirsten	not out	49	91	88	1	-	55.68
WJ Cronje							
AP Kuiper							
JN Rhodes							
BM McMillan							
DJ Richardson†							
RP Snell							
MW Pringle							
AA Donald							
Extras	(lb 5, w 6, nb 2)	13					
	46.5 overs (173 mins)	171 for 1					

Fall: 1-74 (Hudson)

	O	M	R	W	Ave	SR	ER	Wide	NB
CJ McDermott	10	1	23	0	-	-	2.30	-	2
BA Reid	8.5	0	41	0	-	-	4.64	4	-
MR Whitney	6	0	26	0	-	-	4.33	-	-
SR Waugh	4	1	16	0	-	-	4.00	1	-
PL Taylor	10	1	32	1	32.00	60.00	3.20	1	-
AR Border	4	0	13	0	-	-	3.25	-	-
TM Moody	4	0	15	0	-	-	3.75	-	-

Match 7 -– February 27, 1992: Pakistan vs Zimbabwe (Bellerive Oval, Hobart)
Toss: Zimbabwe   Umpires: DP Buultjens & SG Randell
Crowd: 1,107   MOTM: Aamer Sohail
Pakistan won by 53 runs

Pakistan			Runs	Mins	Balls	4s	6s	SR
Ramiz Raja	c Flower	b Jarvis	9	25	16	1	-	56.25
Aamer Sohail	c Pycroft	b Butchart	114	178	136	12	-	83.82
Inzamam-ul-Haq	c Brandes	b Butchart	14	49	43	-	-	32.56
Javed Miandad	lbw	lbw b Butchart	89	125	94	5	-	94.68
Salim Malik		not out	14	24	12	-	-	116.67
Wasim Akram		not out	1	1	1	-	-	100.00
Imran Khan*								
Moin Khan†								
Iqbal Sikander								
Mushtaq Ahmed								
Aaqib Javed								
Extras	(lb 9, nb 4)		13					
50 overs (203 mins)			254 for 4					

Fall: 1-29 (Ramiz) 2-63 (Inzamam) 3-208 (Sohail) 4-253 (Miandad)

	O	M	R	W	Ave	SR	ER	Wide	NB
EA Brandes	10	1	49	0	-	-	4.90	-	4
MP Jarvis	10	1	52	1	52.00	60.00	5.20	-	-
AH Shah	10	1	24	0	-	-	2.40	-	-
IP Butchart	10	0	57	3	19.00	20.00	5.70	-	-
AJ Traicos	10	0	63	0	-	-	6.30	-	-

Zimbabwe			Runs	Mins	Balls	4s	6s	SR
KJ Arnott	c Wasim	b Iqbal	7	69	61	-	-	11.48
A Flower†	c Inzamam	b Wasim	6	34	21	-	-	28.57
AJ Pycroft		b Wasim	0	3	4	-	-	0.00
DL Houghton*	c Ramiz	b Aamer	44	92	82	3	-	53.66
AH Shah		b Aamer	33	55	58	2	-	56.90
AC Waller		b Wasim	44	53	36	3	1	122.22
IP Butchart	c Javed	b Aaqib	33	42	27	4	-	122.22
EA Brandes		not out	2	12	3	-	-	66.67
AJ Traicos		not out	8	7	7	-	-	114.29
MP Jarvis								
WR James								
Extras	(b 3, lb 15, w 6)		24					
50 overs (187 mins)			201 for 7					

Fall: 1-14 (Flower) 2-14 (Pycroft) 3-33 (Arnott) 4-103 (Shah) 5-108 (Houghton) 6-187 (Butchart) 7-190 (Waller)

	O	M	R	W	Ave	SR	ER	Wide	NB
Wasim Akram	10	2	21	3	7.00	20.00	2.10	3	-
Aaqib Javed	10	1	49	1	49.00	60.00	4.90	1	-
Iqbal Sikander	10	1	35	1	35.00	60.00	3.50	1	-
Mushtaq Ahmed	10	1	34	0	-	-	3.40	-	-
Aamer Sohail	6	1	26	2	13.00	18.00	4.33	-	-
Salim Malik	4	0	18	0	-	-	4.50	1	-

Match 8 – February 27, 1992: England vs West Indies (MCG, Melbourne) – D/N

Toss: England

Umpires: KE Liebenberg & SJ Woodward

Crowd: 18,521

MOTM: CC Lewis

England won by six wickets

West Indies

			Runs	Mins	Balls	4s	6s	SR
DL Haynes	c Fairbrother	b DeFreitas	38	85	68	5	-	55.88
BC Lara	c Stewart	b Lewis	0	6	2	-	-	0.00
RB Richardson*	c Botham	b Lewis	5	27	17	1	-	29.41
CL Hooper	c Reeve	b Botham	5	26	20	-	-	25.00
KLT Arthurton	c Fairbrother	b DeFreitas	54	130	101	2	2	53.47
AL Logie		run out	20	142	27	-	1	74.07
RA Harper	c Hick	b Reeve	3	20	14	-	-	21.43
MD Marshall		run out	3	13	8	-	-	37.50
D Williams†	c Pringle	b DeFreitas	6	19	19	-	-	31.58
CEL Ambrose	c DeFreitas	b Lewis	4	23	6	-	-	66.67
WKM Benjamin		not out	11	14	15	1	-	73.33
Extras	(lb 4, w 3, nb 1)		8					
	49.2 overs (207 mins)		157					

Fall: 1-0 (Lara) 2-22 (Richardson) 3-36 (Hooper) 4-55 (Haynes) 5-91 (Logie) 6-102 (Harper) 7-114 (Marshall) 8-131 (Williams) 9-145 (Arthurton) 10-157 (Ambrose)

	O	M	R	W	Ave	SR	ER	Wide	NB
DR Pringle	7	3	16	0	-	-	2.29	-	-
CC Lewis	8.2	1	30	3	10.00	16.67	3.60	-	1
PAJ DeFreitas	9	2	34	3	11.33	18.00	3.78	2	-
IT Botham	10	0	30	1	30.00	60.00	3.00	-	-
DA Reeve	10	1	23	1	23.00	60.00	2.30	1	-
PCR Tufnell	5	0	20	0	-	-	4.00	-	-

England

			Runs	Mins	Balls	4s	6s	SR
GA Gooch*	st Williams	b Hooper	65	130	101	7	-	64.36
IT Botham	c Williams	b Benjamin	8	56	28	-	-	28.57
RA Smith	c Logie	b Benjamin	8	29	28	1	-	28.57
GA Hick	c and	b Harper	54	73	55	3	1	98.18
NH Fairbrother		not out	13	33	28	1	-	46.43
AJ Stewart†		not out	0	3	1	-	-	0.00
DA Reeve								
CC Lewis								
DR Pringle								
PAJ DeFreitas								
PCR Tufnell								
Extras	(lb 7, w 4, nb 1)		12					
	39.5 overs (164 mins)		160 for 4					

Fall: 1-50 (Botham) 2-71 (Smith) 3-126 (Gooch) 4-156 (Hick)

	O	M	R	W	Ave	SR	ER	Wide	NB
CEL Ambrose	8	1	26	0	-	-	3.25	-	-
MD Marshall	8	0	37	0	-	-	4.62	2	-
WKM Benjamin	9.5	2	22	2	11.00	29.50	2.24	2	1
CL Hooper	10	1	38	1	38.00	60.00	3.80	-	-
RA Harper	4	0	30	1	30.00	24.00	7.50	-	-

Match 9 – February 28, 1992: India vs Sri Lanka (Harrup Park, Mackay)

Toss: Sri Lanka   Umpires: ID Robinson & DR Shepherd
Crowd: 4,172   MOTM: Not awarded
Match abandoned – no result

India		Runs	Mins	Balls	4s	6s	SR
K Srikkanth	not out	1	2	2	-	-	50.00
Kapil Dev	not out	0	2	0	-	-	0.00
M Azharuddin*							
SR Tendulkar							
VG Kambli							
PK Amre							
AD Jadeja							
KS More†							
M Prabhakar							
J Srinath							
SLV Raju							
Extras		0					
0.2 overs (2 mins)		1 for 0					

	O	M	R	W	Ave	SR	ER	Wide	NB
CPH Ramanayake	0.2	0	1	0	-	-	3.00	-	-

Sri Lanka

RS Mahanama
UC Hathurusinghe
AP Gurusinha
PA de Silva*
A Ranatunga
ST Jayasuriya
RS Kalpage
HP Tillakaratne†
CPH Ramanayake
KIW Wijegunawardene
GP Wickramasinghe

Match 10 – February 29, 1992: New Zealand vs South Africa (Eden Park, Auckland)

Toss: South Africa
Crowd: 27,450
New Zealand won by seven wickets

Umpires: Khizer Hayat & PD Reporter
MOTM: MJ Greatbatch

South Africa			Runs	Mins	Balls	4s	6s	SR
KC Wessels*	c Smith	b Watson	3	22	18	-	-	16.67
AC Hudson		b Patel	1	18	16	-	-	6.25
PN Kirsten	c Cairns	b Watson	90	156	129	10	-	69.77
WJ Cronje	c Smith	b Harris	7	30	22	-	-	31.82
DJ Richardson†	c Larsen	b Cairns	28	69	53	1	-	52.83
AP Kuiper		run out	2	2	2	-	-	100.00
JN Rhodes	c Crowe	b Cairns	6	17	13	-	-	46.15
BM McMillan		not out	33	44	40	1	-	82.50
RP Snell		not out	11	13	8	1	-	137.50
T Bosch								
AA Donald								
Extras	(lb 8, nb 1)		9					
50 overs (189 mins)			190 for 7					

Fall: 1-8 (Hudson) 2-10 (Wessels) 3-29 (Cronje) 4-108 (Richardson) 5-111 (Kuiper) 6-121 (Rhodes) 7-162 (Kirsten)

	O	M	R	W	Ave	SR	ER	Wide	NB
W Watson	10	2	30	2	15.00	30.00	3.00	-	1
DN Patel	10	1	28	1	28.00	60.00	2.80	-	-
GR Larsen	10	1	29	0	-	-	2.90	-	-
CZ Harris	10	2	33	1	33.00	60.00	3.30	-	-
RT Latham	2	0	19	0	-	-	9.50	-	-
CL Cairns	8	0	43	2	21.50	24.00	5.37	-	-

New Zealand			Runs	Mins	Balls	4s	6s	SR
MJ Greatbatch		b Kirsten	68	80	60	9	2	113.33
RT Latham	c Wessels	b Snell	60	117	69	7	-	86.96
AH Jones		not out	34	64	63	4	-	53.97
IDS Smith†	c Kirsten	b Donald	19	9	8	4	-	237.50
MD Crowe*		not out	3	17	9	-	-	33.33
KR Rutherford								
CZ Harris								
DN Patel								
CL Cairns								
GR Larsen								
W Watson								
Extras	(b 1, w 5, nb 1)		7					
34.3 overs (145 mins)			191 for 3					

Fall: 1-114 (Greatbatch) 2-155 (Latham) 3-179 (Smith)

	O	M	R	W	Ave	SR	ER	Wide	NB
AA Donald	10	0	38	1	38.00	60.00	3.80	1	1
BM McMillan	5	1	23	0	-	-	4.60	3	-
RP Snell	7	0	56	1	56.00	42.00	8.00	-	-
T Bosch	2.3	0	19	0	-	-	7.60	-	-
WJ Cronje	2	0	14	0	-	-	7.00	1	-
AP Kuiper	1	0	18	0	-	-	18.00	-	-
PN Kirsten	7	1	22	1	22.00	42.00	3.14	-	-

Match 11 – February 29, 1992: West Indies vs Zimbabwe (The Gabba, Brisbane)
Toss: Zimbabwe
Crowd: 2,221
West Indies won by 75 runs

Umpires: KE Liebenberg & SJ Woodward
MOTM: BC Lara

West Indies			Runs	Mins	Balls	4s	6s	SR
PV Simmons		b Brandes	21	60	45	3	-	46.67
BC Lara	c Houghton	b Shah	72	86	76	12	-	94.74
RB Richardson*	c Brandes	b Jarvis	56	102	67	2	2	83.58
CL Hooper	c Pycroft	b Traicos	63	72	67	5	1	94.03
KLT Arthurton		b Duers	26	28	18	2	2	144.44
AL Logie		run out	5	7	6	-	-	83.33
MD Marshall	c Houghton	b Brandes	2	11	10	-	-	20.00
D Williams†		not out	8	10	6	1	-	133.33
WKM Benjamin		b Brandes	1	5	4	-	-	25.00
AC Cummins								
BP Patterson								
Extras	(b 1, lb 6, w 2, nb 1)		10					
50 overs (194 mins)			264 for 8					

Fall: 1-78 (Simmons) 2-103 (Lara) 3-220 (Hooper) 4-221 (Richardson) 5-239 (Logie) 6-254 (Marshall) 7-255 (Arthurton) 8-264 (Benjamin)

	O	M	R	W	Ave	SR	ER	Wide	NB
EA Brandes	10	1	45	3	15.00	20.00	4.50	2	1
MP Jarvis	10	1	71	1	71.00	60.00	7.10	-	-
KG Duers	10	0	52	1	52.00	60.00	5.20	-	-
AH Shah	10	2	39	1	39.00	60.00	3.90	-	-
AJ Traicos	10	0	50	1	50.00	60.00	5.00	-	-

Zimbabwe			Runs	Mins	Balls	4s	6s	SR
KJ Arnott		retired hurt	16	55	36	1	-	44.44
A Flower†		b Patterson	6	23	20	-	-	30.00
AJ Pycroft	c Williams	b Benjamin	10	26	24	-	-	41.67
DL Houghton*	c Patterson	b Hooper	55	94	88	3	-	62.50
AC Waller	c Simmons	b Benjamin	0	13	9	-	-	0.00
ADR Campbell	c Richardson	b Hooper	1	27	18	-	-	5.56
AH Shah		not out	60	93	87	4	-	68.97
EA Brandes	c and	b Benjamin	6	16	9	-	-	66.67
AJ Traicos		run out	8	21	19	-	-	42.11
MP Jarvis		not out	5	6	4	1	-	125.00
KG Duers								
Extras	(lb 9, w 5, nb 8)		22					
50 overs (191 mins)			189 for 7					

Fall: 1-21 (Flower) 2-43 (Pycroft) 3-48 (Waller) 4-63 (Campbell) 5-132 (Houghton) 6-161 (Brandes) 7-181 (Traicos)

	O	M	R	W	Ave	SR	ER	Wide	NB
BP Patterson	10	0	25	1	25.00	60.00	2.50	1	-
MD Marshall	6	0	23	0	-	-	3.83	-	2
WKM Benjamin	10	2	27	3	9.00	20.00	2.70	3	3
AC Cummins	10	0	33	0	-	-	3.30	1	3
CL Hooper	10	0	47	2	23.50	30.00	4.70	-	-
KLT Arthurton	4	0	25	0	-	-	6.25	-	-

Match 12 – March 1, 1992: Australia vs India (The Gabba, Brisbane)

Toss: Australia Umpires: BL Aldridge & ID Robinson
Crowd: 11,734 MOTM: DM Jones
Australia won by one run (India required 236 runs from 47 overs)

Australia			Runs	Mins	Balls	4s	6s	SR
MA Taylor	c More	b Kapil Dev	13	18	22	-	-	59.09
GR Marsh		b Kapil Dev	8	41	29	1	-	27.59
DC Boon†	c Shastri	b Raju	43	76	61	4	-	70.49
DM Jones	c and	b Prabhakar	90	145	109	6	2	82.57
SR Waugh		b Srinath	29	48	48	1	-	60.42
TM Moody		b Prabhakar	25	28	23	3	-	108.70
AR Border*	c Jadeja	b Kapil Dev	10	17	10	-	-	100.00
CJ McDermott	c Jadeja	b Prabhakar	2	6	5	-	-	40.00
PL Taylor		run out	1	6	1	-	-	100.00
MG Hughes		not out	0	3	4	-	-	0.00
MR Whitney								
Extras	(lb 7, w 5, nb 4)		16					
	50 overs (198 mins)		237 for 9					

Fall: 1-18 (MA Taylor) 2-31 (Marsh) 3-102 (Boon) 4-156 (Waugh) 5-198 (Moody) 6-230 (Jones) 7-235 (Border) 8-236 (McDermott) 9-237 (PL Taylor)

	O	M	R	W	Ave	SR	ER	Wide	NB
Kapil Dev	10	2	41	3	13.67	20.00	4.10	1	3
M Prabhakar	10	0	41	3	13.67	20.00	4.10	2	1
J Srinath	8	0	48	1	48.00	48.00	6.00	1	-
SR Tendulkar	5	0	29	0	-	-	5.80	1	-
SLV Raju	10	0	37	1	37.00	60.00	3.70	-	-
AD Jadeja	7	0	34	0	-	-	4.86	-	-

India			Runs	Mins	Balls	4s	6s	SR
RJ Shastri	c Waugh	b Moody	25	75	67	1	-	37.31
K Srikkanth		b McDermott	0	13	10	-	-	0.00
M Azharuddin*		run out	93	147	103	10	-	90.29
SR Tendulkar	c Waugh	b Moody	11	19	19	1	-	57.89
Kapil Dev	lbw	b Waugh	21	26	21	3	-	100.00
SV Manjrekar		run out	47	50	42	3	1	111.90
AD Jadeja		b Hughes	1	5	4	-	-	25.00
KS More†		b Moody	14	13	8	2	-	175.00
J Srinath		not out	8	11	8	-	-	100.00
M Prabhakar		run out	1	1	1	-	-	100.00
SLV Raju		run out	0	1	0	-	-	-
Extras	(lb 8, w 5)		13					
	47 overs (185 mins)		234					

Fall: 1-6 (Srikkanth) 2-53 (Shastri) 3-86 (Tendulkar) 4-128 (Kapil Dev) 5-194 (Azharuddin) 6-199 (Jadeja) 7-216 (Manjrekar) 8-231 (More) 9-232 (Prabhakar) 10-234 (Raju)

	O	M	R	W	Ave	SR	ER	Wide	NB
CJ McDermott	9	1	35	1	35.00	54.00	3.89	1	-
MR Whitney	10	2	36	0	-	-	3.60	3	-
MG Hughes	9	1	49	1	49.00	54.00	5.44	-	-
TM Moody	9	0	56	3	18.67	18.00	6.22	-	-
SR Waugh	10	0	50	1	50.00	60.00	5.00	1	-

APPENDICES

Match 13 – March 1, 1992: England vs Pakistan (Adelaide Oval, Adelaide)

Toss: England

Crowd: 7,537

Match abandoned – no result

Umpires: SU Bucknor & PJ McConnell

MOTM: Not awarded

Pakistan			Runs	Mins	Balls	4s	6s	SR
Ramiz Raja	c Reeve	b DeFreitas	1	13	10	-	-	10.00
Aamer Sohail	c and	b Pringle	9	52	39	-	-	23.08
Inzamam-ul-Haq	c Stewart	b DeFreitas	0	1	1	-	-	0.00
Javed Miandad*		b Pringle	3	29	22	-	-	13.64
Salim Malik	c Reeve	b Botham	17	45	20	3	-	85.00
Ijaz Ahmed	c Stewart	b Small	0	16	15	-	-	0.00
Wasim Akram		b Botham	1	12	13	-	-	7.69
Moin Khan†	c Hick	b Small	2	25	14	-	-	14.29
Wasim Haider	c Stewart	b Reeve	13	46	46	1	-	28.26
Mushtaq Ahmed	c Reeve	b Pringle	17	54	42	1	-	40.48
Aaqib Javed		not out	1	24	21	-	-	4.76
Extras	(lb 1, w 8, nb 1)		10					
	40.2 overs (163 mins)		74					

Fall: 1-5 (Ramiz) 2-5 (Inzamam) 3-14 (Miandad) 4-20 (Sohail) 5-32 (Ijaz) 6-35 (Akram) 7-42 (Malik) 8-47 (Moin) 9-62 (Haider) 10-74 (Mushtaq)

	O	M	R	W	Ave	SR	ER	Wide	NB
DR Pringle	8.2	5	8	3	2.67	16.67	0.96	-	1
PAJ DeFreitas	7	1	22	2	11.00	21.00	3.14	7	-
GC Small	10	1	29	2	14.50	30.00	2.90	1	-
IT Botham	10	4	12	2	6.00	30.00	1.20	-	-
DA Reeve	5	3	2	1	2.00	30.00	0.40	-	-

England			Runs	Mins	Balls	4s	6s	SR
GA Gooch*	c Moin	b Wasim Akram	3	24	14	-	-	21.43
IT Botham	not out	not out	6	42	22	-	-	27.27
RA Smith	not out	not out	5	17	13	1	-	38.46
GA Hick								
NH Fairbrother								
AJ Stewart†								
CC Lewis								
DR Pringle								
DA Reeve								
PAJ DeFreitas								
GC Small								
Extras	(b 1, lb 3, w 5, nb 1)		10					
	8 overs (42 mins)		24 for 1					

Fall: 1-14 (Gooch)

	O	M	R	W	Ave	SR	ER	Wide	NB
Wasim Akram	3	0	7	1	7.00	18.00	2.33	3	1
Aaqib Javed	3	1	7	0	-	-	2.33	2	-
Wasim Haider	1	0	1	0	-	-	1.00	-	-
Ijaz Ahmed	1	0	5	0	-	-	5.00	-	-

Match 14 – March 2, 1992: South Africa vs Sri Lanka (Basin Reserve, Wellington)
Toss: Sri Lanka
Crowd: 3,802
Sri Lanka won by three wickets

Umpires: Khizer Hayat & Steve Woodward
MOTM: A Ranatunga

South Africa			Runs	Mins	Balls	4s	6s	SR
KC Wessels*	c and	b Ranatunga	40	130	94	-	-	42.55
AP Kuiper		b Anurasiri	18	53	44	3	-	40.91
PN Kirsten	c Hathurusinghe	b Kalpage	47	74	81	5	1	58.02
JN Rhodes	c Jayasuriya	b Wickramasinghe	28	27	21	2	-	133.33
MW Rushmere	c Jayasuriya	b Ranatunga	4	7	9	-	-	44.44
WJ Cronje	st Tillakaratne	b Anurasiri	3	10	6	-	-	50.00
BM McMillan		not out	18	35	22	-	-	81.82
RP Snell		b Anurasiri	9	10	5	2	-	180.00
DJ Richardson†		run out	0	1	0	-	*	
O Henry	c Kalpage	b Ramanayake	11	17	13	1	-	84.62
AA Donald		run out	3	9	6	-	-	50.00
Extras	(lb 9, w4, nb 1)		14					
	50 overs (192 mins)		198					

Fall: 1-27 (Kuiper) 2-114 (Kirsten) 3-114 (Wessels) 4-128 (Rushmere) 5-149 (Cronje) 6-153 (Rhodes) 7-165 (Snell) 8-165 (Richardson) 9-186 (Henry) 10-195 (Donald)

	O	M	R	W	Ave	SR	ER	Wide	NB
CPH Ramanayake	9	2	19	1	19.00	54.00	2.11	-	1
GP Wickramasinghe	7	0	32	1	32.00	42.00	4.57	1	-
SD Anurasiri	10	1	41	3	13.67	20.00	4.10	-	-
AP Gurusinha	8	0	30	0	-	-	3.75	-	-
RS Kalpage	10	0	38	1	38.00	60.00	3.80	2	-
A Ranatunga	6	0	26	2	13.00	18.00	4.33	1	-

Sri Lanka			Runs	Mins	Balls	4s	6s	SR
RS Mahanama	c Richardson	b McMillan	68	181	121	6	-	56.20
UC Hathurusinghe	c Wessels	b Donald	5	10	9	1	-	55.56
AP Gurusinha	lbw	b Donald	0	7	4	-	-	0.00
PA de Silva*		b Donald	7	27	16	1	-	43.75
HP Tillakaratne†	c Rushmere	b Henry	17	75	63	-	-	26.98
A Ranatunga		not out	64	96	73	6	-	87.67
ST Jayasuriya	st Richardson	b Kirsten	3	11	7	-	-	42.86
RS Kalpage		run out	5	21	11	-	-	45.45
CPH Ramanayake		not out	4	3	2	1	-	200.00
SD Anurasiri								
GP Wickramasinghe								
Extras	(b1, lb 7, w 13, nb 4)		25					
	49.5 overs (219 mins)		198 for 7					

Fall: 1-11 (Hathurusinghe) 2-12 (Gurusinha) 3-35 (de Silva) 4-87 (Tillakaratne) 5-154 (Mahanama) 6-168 (Jayasuriya) 7-189 (Kalpage)

	O	M	R	W	Ave	SR	ER	Wide	NB
BM McMillan	10	2	34	1	34.00	60.00	3.40	-	3
AA Donald	9.5	0	42	3	14.00	19.67	4.27	8	-
RP Snell	10	1	33	0	-	-	3.30	2	-
O Henry	10	0	31	1	31.00	60.00	3.10	2	1
AP Kuiper	5	0	25	0	-	-	5.00	1	-
PN Kirsten	5	0	25	1	-	30.00	5.00	-	-

320

Match 15 – March 3, 1992: New Zealand vs Zimbabwe (McLean Park, Napier)

Toss: Zimbabwe

Crowd: 6,581

Umpires: DP Buultjens & KP Liebenberg

MOTM: MD Crowe

New Zealand won by 48 runs (Zimbabwe required 154 runs in 18 overs)

New Zealand			Runs	Mins	Balls	4s	6s	SR
MJ Greatbatch		b Duers	15	27	16	2	-	93.75
RT Latham		b Brandes	2	10	6	-	-	33.33
AH Jones	c Waller	b Butchart	57	76	58	9	-	98.28
MD Crowe*		not out	74	64	44	8	2	168.18
CL Cairns		not out	1	4	2	-	-	50.00
KR Rutherford								
CZ Harris								
DN Patel								
IDS Smith†								
GR Larsen								
DK Morrison								
Extras	(b 7, lb 6)		13					
	20.5 overs (92 mins)		162 for 3					

Fall: 1-9 (Latham) 2-25 (Greatbatch) 3-154 (Jones)

	O	M	R	W	Ave	SR	ER	Wide	NB
EA Brandes	5	1	28	1	28.00	30.00	5.60	-	-
KG Duers	6	0	17	1	17.00	36.00	2.83	-	-
AH Shah	4	0	34	0	-	-	8.50	-	-
IP Butchart	4	0	53	1	53.00	24.00	13.25	-	-
MG Burmester	1.5	0	17	0	-	-	9.27	-	-

Zimbabwe			Runs	Mins	Balls	4s	6s	SR
A Flower†		b Larsen	30	45	27	5	-	111.11
AC Waller		b Morrison	11	14	11	1	1	100.00
DL Houghton*		b Larsen	10	19	14	2	-	71.43
IP Butchart	c Cairns	b Larsen	3	9	7	-	-	42.86
EA Brandes		b Harris	6	9	8	-	-	75.00
AJ Pycroft		not out	13	25	20	-	-	65.00
ADR Campbell	c Crowe	b Harris	8	6	9	1	-	88.89
AH Shah		b Harris	7	5	8	1	-	87.50
MG Burmester		not out	4	3	8	-	-	50.00
AJ Traicos								
KG Duers								
Extras	(lb 9, w 3, nb 1)		13					
	18 overs (68 mins)		105 for 7					

Fall: 1-22 (Waller) 2-40 (Houghton) 3-63 (Flower) 4-63 (Butchart) 5-75 (Brandes) 6-86 (Campbell) 7-97 (Shah)

	O	M	R	W	Ave	SR	ER	Wide	NB
DK Morrison	4	0	14	1	14.00	24.00	3.50	2	1
CL Cairns	2	0	27	0	-	-	13.50	-	-
GR Larsen	4	0	16	3	5.33	8.00	4.00	-	-
CZ Harris	4	0	15	3	5.00	8.00	3.75	1	-
RT Latham	3	0	18	0	-	-	6.00	-	-
MD Crowe	1	0	6	0	-	-	6.00	-	-

Match 16 – March 4, 1992: India vs Pakistan (SCG, Sydney) – D/N

Toss: India
Crowd: 10,330
India won by 43 runs

Umpires: PJ McConnell & DR Shepherd
MOTM: SR Tendulkar

India			Runs	Mins	Balls	4s	6s	SR
AD Jadeja	c Zahid	b Wasim Haider	46	118	81	2	-	56.79
K Srikkanth	c Moin	b Aaqib	5	41	40	-	-	12.50
M Azharuddin*	c Moin	b Mushtaq	32	61	51	4	-	62.75
VG Kambli	c Inzamam	b Mushtaq	24	60	42	-	-	57.14
SR Tendulkar		not out	54	91	62	3	-	87.10
SV Manjrekar		b Mushtaq	0	2	1	-	-	0.00
Kapil Dev	c Imran	b Aaqib	35	34	26	2	1	134.62
KS More†		run out	4	3	4	-	-	100.00
M Prabhakar		not out	2	2	1	-	-	200.00
J Srinath								
SLV Raju								
Extras	(lb 3, w 9, nb 2)		14					
	49 overs (210 mins)		216 for 7					

Fall: 1-25 (Srikkanth) 2-86 (Azharuddin) 3-101 (Jadeja) 4-147 (Kambli) 5-148 (Manjrekar) 6-208 (Kapil Dev) 7-213 (More)

	O	M	R	W	Ave	SR	ER	Wide	NB
Wasim Akram	10	0	45	0	-	-	4.50	5	2
Aaqib Javed	8	2	28	2	14.00	24.00	3.50	-	-
Imran Khan	8	0	25	0	-	-	3.12	1	-
Wasim Haider	10	1	36	1	36.00	60.00	3.60	1	-
Mushtaq Ahmed	10	0	59	3	19.67	20.00	5.90	1	-
Aamer Sohail	3	0	20	0	-	-	6.67	1	-

Pakistan			Runs	Mins	Balls	4s	6s	SR
Aamer Sohail	c Srikkanth	b Tendulkar	62	118	103	6	-	60.19
Inzamam-ul-Haq	lbw	b Kapil Dev	2	9	7	-	-	28.57
Zahid Fazal	c More	b Prabhakar	2	14	10	-	-	20.00
Javed Miandad		b Srinath	40	132	113	2	-	35.40
Salim Malik	c More	b Prabhakar	12	12	9	2	-	133.33
Imran Khan*		run out	0	12	5	-	-	0.00
Wasim Akram	st More	b Raju	4	9	8	-	-	50.00
Wasim Haider		b Srinath	13	41	25	-	-	52.00
Moin Khan†	c Manjrekar	b Kapil Dev	12	16	12	1	-	100.00
Mushtaq Ahmed		run out	3	5	4	-	-	75.00
Aaqib Javed		not out	1	15	12	-	-	8.33
Extras	(lb 6, w 15, nb 1)		22					
	48.1 overs (196 mins)		173					

Fall: 1-8 (Inzamam) 2-17 (Zahid) 3-105 (Sohail) 4-127 (Malik) 5-130 (Imran) 6-141 (Akram) 7-141 (Miandad) 8-161 (Moin) 9-166 (Mushtaq) 10-173 (Haider)

	O	M	R	W	Ave	SR	ER	Wide	NB
Kapil Dev	10	0	30	2	15.00	30.00	3.00	5	1
M Prabhakar	10	1	22	2	11.00	30.00	2.20	4	-
J Srinath	8.1	0	37	2	18.50	24.50	4.53	1	-
SR Tendulkar	10	0	37	1	37.00	60.00	3.70	5	-
SLV Raju	10	1	41	1	41.00	60.00	4.10	-	-

Match 17 – March 5, 1992: South Africa vs West Indies (Lancaster Park, Christchurch)

Toss: West Indies
Crowd: 12,116
South Africa won by 64 runs

Umpires: BL Aldridge & SG Randell
MOTM: MW Pringle

South Africa			Runs	Mins	Balls	4s	6s	SR
AC Hudson	c Lara	b Cummins	22	67	60	3	-	36.67
KC Wessels*	c Haynes	b Marshall	1	11	9	-	-	11.11
PN Kirsten	c Williams	b Marshall	56	124	91	2	-	61.54
MW Rushmere	st Williams	b Hooper	10	24	24	-	-	41.67
AP Kuiper		b Ambrose	23	31	29	-	1	79.31
JN Rhodes	c Williams	b Cummins	22	33	27	-	-	81.48
BM McMillan	c Lara	b Benjamin	20	44	29	2	-	68.97
DJ Richardson†		not out	20	41	26	1	-	76.92
RP Snell	c Haynes	b Ambrose	3	5	6	-	-	50.00
MW Pringle		not out	5	12	6	-	-	83.33
AA Donald								
Extras	(lb 8, w 3, nb 7)		18					
	50 overs (200 mins)		200 for 8					

Fall: 1-8 (Wessels) 2-51 (Hudson) 3-73 (Rushmere) 4-119 (Kuiper) 5-127 (Kirsten) 6-159 (Rhodes) 7-181 (McMillan) 8-187 (Snell)

	O	M	R	W	Ave	SR	ER	Wide	NB
CEL Ambrose	10	1	34	2	17.00	30.00	3.40	-	3
MD Marshall	10	1	26	2	13.00	30.00	2.60	-	-
WKM Benjamin	10	0	47	1	47.00	60.00	4.70	2	-
AC Cummins	10	0	40	2	20.00	30.00	4.00	-	4
CL Hooper	10	0	45	1	45.00	60.00	4.50	1	-

West Indies			Runs	Mins	Balls	4s	6s	SR
DL Haynes	c Richardson	b Kuiper	30	113	83	3	-	36.14
BC Lara	c Rhodes	b Pringle	9	14	13	2	-	69.23
RB Richardson*	lbw	b Pringle	1	7	3	-	-	33.33
CL Hooper	c Wessels	b Pringle	0	3	4	-	-	0.00
KLT Arthurton	c Wessels	b Pringle	0	6	4	-	-	0.00
AL Logie	c Pringle	b Kuiper	61	102	69	9	1	88.41
MD Marshall	c Rhodes	b Snell	6	14	10	1	-	60.00
D Williams†	c Richardson	b Snell	0	2	3	-	-	0.00
CEL Ambrose		run out	12	24	15	2	-	80.00
AC Cummins	c McMillan	b Donald	6	30	24	-	-	25.00
WKM Benjamin		not out	1	9	4	-	-	25.00
Extras	(lb 9, w 1)		10					
	38.4 overs (167 mins)		136					

Fall: 1-10 (Lara) 2-19 (Richardson) 3-19 (Hooper) 4-19 (Arthurton) 5-70 (Marshall) 6-70 (Williams) 7-116 (Haynes) 8-117 (Logie) 9-132 (Ambrose) 10-136 (Cummins)

	O	M	R	W	Ave	SR	ER	Wide	NB
AA Donald	6.4	2	13	1	13.00	40.00	1.95	1	-
MW Pringle	8	4	11	4	2.75	12.00	1.37	-	-
BM McMillan	8	2	36	0	-	-	4.50	-	-
RP Snell	7	2	16	2	8.00	21.00	2.29	-	-
AP Kuiper	9	0	51	2	25.50	27.00	5.67	-	-

Match 18 – March 5, 1992: Australia vs England (SCG, Sydney) – D/N

Toss: Australia　　　　　　　　　　　　　Umpires: SU Bucknor & Khizer Hayat
Crowd: 38,951　　　　　　　　　　　　　　MOTM: IT Botham
England won by eight wickets

Australia			Runs	Mins	Balls	4s	6s	SR
TM Moody		b Tufnell	51	131	91	3	-	56.04
MA Taylor	lbw	b Pringle	0	11	11	-	-	0.00
DC Boon		run out	18	29	27	2	-	66.67
DM Jones	c Lewis	b DeFreitas	22	78	50	2	-	44.00
SR Waugh		run out	27	65	43	2	-	62.79
AR Border*		b Botham	16	30	22	1	-	72.73
IA Healy†	c Fairbrother	b Botham	9	6	7	-	1	128.57
PL Taylor	lbw	b Botham	0	2	2	-	-	0.00
CJ McDermott	c DeFreitas	b Botham	0	1	2	-	-	0.00
MR Whitney		not out	8	33	27	1	-	29.63
BA Reid		b Reeve	1	21	22	-	-	4.55
Extras	(b 2, lb 8, w 5, nb 4)		19					
	49 overs (208 mins)		171					

Fall: 1-5 (MA Taylor) 2-35 (Boon) 3-106 (Jones) 4-114 (Moody) 5-145 (Border) 6-155 (Healy) 7-155 (PL Taylor) 8-155 (McDermott) 9-164 (Waugh) 10-171 (Reid)

	O	M	R	W	Ave	SR	ER	Wide	NB
DR Pringle	9	1	24	1	24.00	54.00	2.67	1	3
CC Lewis	10	2	28	0	-	-	2.80	2	-
PAJ DeFreitas	10	3	23	1	23.00	60.00	2.30	1	-
IT Botham	10	1	31	4	7.75	15.00	3.10	1	-
PCR Tufnell	9	0	52	1	52.00	54.00	5.78	-	1
DA Reeve	1	0	3	1	3.00	6.00	3.00	-	-

England			Runs	Mins	Balls	4s	6s	SR
GA Gooch*		b Waugh	58	157	115	7	-	50.43
IT Botham	c Healy	b Whitney	53	103	79	6	-	67.09
RA Smith		not out	30	66	60	5	-	50.00
GA Hick		not out	7	13	5	1	-	140.00
NH Fairbrother								
AJ Stewart†								
CC Lewis								
DR Pringle								
DA Reeve								
PAJ DeFreitas								
PCR Tufnell								
Extras	(lb 13, w 8, nb 4)		25					
	40.5 overs (171 mins)		173 for 2					

Fall: 1-107 (Botham) 2-153 (Gooch)

	O	M	R	W	Ave	SR	ER	Wide	NB
CJ McDermott	10	1	29	0	-	-	2.90	3	1
BA Reid	7.5	0	49	0	-	-	6.26	2	3
MR Whitney	10	2	28	1	28.00	60.00	2.80	1	-
SR Waugh	6	0	29	1	29.00	36.00	4.83	2	-
PL Taylor	3	0	7	0	-	-	2.33	-	-
TM Moody	4	0	18	0	-	-	4.50	-	-

Match 19 – March 7, 1992: India vs Zimbabwe (Trust Bank Park, Hamilton)
Toss: India   Umpires: SU Bucknor & Khizer Hayat
Crowd: 1,520   MOTM: SR Tendulkar
India won by 55 runs (Zimbabwe required 159 from 19.1 overs)

India			Runs	Mins	Balls	4s	6s	SR
K Srikkanth		b Burmester	32	50	32	5	-	100.00
Kapil Dev	lbw	b Brandes	10	19	14	-	1	71.43
M Azharuddin*	c Flower	b Burmester	12	14	15	2	-	80.00
SR Tendulkar	c Campbell	b Burmester	81	88	77	8	1	105.19
SV Manjrekar	c Duers	b Traicos	34	57	34	2	-	100.00
VG Kambli		b Traicos	1	2	2	-	-	50.00
AD Jadeja	c Shah	b Traicos	6	8	6	-	-	100.00
KS More†		not out	15	9	8	-	1	187.50
J Srinath		not out	6	6	4	1	-	150.00
M Prabhakar								
SLV Raju								
Extras	(lb 3, w 3)		6					
	32 overs (130 mins)		203 for 7					

Fall: 1-23 (Kapil Dev) 2-43 (Azharuddin) 3-69 (Srikkanth) 4-168 (Manjrekar) 5-170 (Kambli) 6-182 (Jadeja) 7-184 (Tendulkar)

	O	M	R	W	Ave	SR	ER	Wide	NB
EA Brandes	7	0	43	1	43.00	42.00	6.14	-	-
KG Duers	7	0	48	0	-	-	6.86	-	-
MG Burmester	6	0	36	3	12.00	12.00	6.00	3	-
AH Shah	6	1	38	0	-	-	6.33	-	-
AJ Traicos	6	0	35	3	11.67	12.00	5.83	-	-

Zimbabwe			Runs	Mins	Balls	4s	6s	SR
AH Shah		b Tendulkar	31	55	51	3	-	60.78
A Flower†		not out	43	66	56	3	-	76.79
AC Waller		not out	13	10	7	2	-	185.71
DL Houghton*								
AJ Pycroft								
IP Butchart								
ADR Campbell								
EA Brandes								
MG Burmester								
AJ Traicos								
KG Duers								
Extras	(b 1, lb 11, w 5)		17					
	19.1 overs (66 mins)		104 for 1					

Fall: 1-79 (Shah)

	O	M	R	W	Ave	SR	ER	Wide	NB
Kapil Dev	4	0	6	0	-	-	1.50	2	-
M Prabhakar	3	0	14	0	-	-	4.67	1	-
J Srinath	4	0	20	0	-	-	5.00	1	-
SR Tendulkar	6	0	35	1	35.00	36.00	5.83	1	-
SLV Raju	2.1	0	17	0	-	-	7.85	-	-

Match 20 – March 7, 1992: Australia vs Sri Lanka (Adelaide Oval, Adelaide)

Toss: Australia   Umpires: PD Reporter & ID Robinson
Crowd: 11,663   MOTM: TM Moody
Australia won by seven wickets

Sri Lanka			Runs	Mins	Balls	4s	6s	SR
RS Mahanama		run out	7	9	10	1	-	70.00
MAR Samarasekera	c Healy	b Taylor	34	87	63	3	-	53.97
AP Gurusinha	lbw	b Whitney	5	30	23	1	-	21.74
PA de Silva*	c Moody	b McDermott	62	133	83	2	-	74.70
A Ranatunga	c Jones	b Taylor	23	48	52	-	-	44.23
ST Jayasuriya	lbw	b Border	15	25	29	1	-	51.72
HP Tillakaratne†		run out	5	17	13	-	-	38.46
RS Kalpage		run out	14	25	15	1	-	93.33
CPH Ramanayake		run out	5	12	10	-	-	50.00
SD Anurasiri		not out	4	6	4	-	-	100.00
GP Wickramasinghe								
Extras	(b 3, lb 6, w 5, nb 1)		15					
	50 overs (200 mins)		189 for 9					

Fall: 1-8 (Mahanama) 2-28 (Gurusinha) 3-72 (Samarasekera) 4-123 (Ranatunga) 5-151 (Jayasuriya) 6-163 (de Silva) 7-166 (Tillakaratne) 8-182 (Ramanayake) 9-189 (Kalpage)

	O	M	R	W	Ave	SR	ER	Wide	NB
CJ McDermott	10	0	28	1	28.00	60.00	2.80	1	-
SR Waugh	7	0	34	0	-	-	4.86	4	1
MR Whitney	10	3	26	1	26.00	60.00	2.60	-	-
TM Moody	3	0	18	0	-	-	6.00	-	-
PL Taylor	10	0	34	2	17.00	30.00	3.40	-	-
AR Border	10	0	40	1	40.00	60.00	4.00	-	-

Australia			Runs	Mins	Balls	4s	6s	SR
TM Moody	c Mahanama	b Wickramasinghe	57	115	86	4	-	66.28
GR Marsh	c Anurasiri	b Kalpage	60	127	113	3	1	53.10
ME Waugh	c Mahanama	b Wickramasinghe	26	39	26	1	-	100.00
DC Boon		not out	27	44	37	-	2	72.97
DM Jones		not out	12	16	8	-	1	150.00
AR Border*								
SR Waugh								
IA Healy†								
PL Taylor								
CJ McDermott								
MR Whitney								
Extras	(lb 2, w 3, nb 3)		8					
	44 overs (172 mins)		190 for 3					

Fall: 1-120 (Moody) 2-130 (Marsh) 3-165 (ME Waugh)

	O	M	R	W	Ave	SR	ER	Wide	NB
GP Wickramasinghe	10	3	29	2	14.50	30.00	2.90	1	1
CPH Ramanayake	9	1	44	0	-	-	4.89	2	2
SD Anurasiri	10	0	43	0	-	-	4.30	-	-
AP Gurusinha	6	0	20	0	-	-	3.33	-	-
A Ranatunga	1	0	11	0	-	-	11.00	-	-
RS Kalpage	8	0	41	1	41.00	48.00	5.12	-	-

Match 21 – March 8, 1992: New Zealand vs West Indies (Eden Park, Auckland)

Toss: New Zealand
Crowd: 24,281
New Zealand won by five wickets

Umpires: PD Reporter & ID Robinson
MOTM: MD Crowe

West Indies			Runs	Mins	Balls	4s	6s	SR
DL Haynes	c and	b Harris	22	74	61	-	1	36.07
BC Lara	c Rutherford	b Larsen	52	104	82	-	-	63.41
RB Richardson*	c Smith	b Watson	29	68	54	1	-	53.70
CL Hooper	c Greatbatch	b Patel	2	10	9	-	-	22.22
KLT Arthurton		b Morrison	40	77	54	3	-	74.07
AL Logie		b Harris	3	4	4	-	-	75.00
MD Marshall		b Larsen	5	19	14	-	-	35.71
D Williams†		not out	32	26	24	5	-	133.33
WKM Benjamin		not out	2	1	1	-	-	200.00
CEL Ambrose								
AC Cummins								
Extras	(lb 8, w 7, nb 1)		16					
	50 overs (195 mins)		203 for 7					

Fall: 1-65 (Haynes) 2-95 (Lara) 3-100 (Hooper) 4-136 (Richardson) 5-142 (Logie) 6-156 (Marshall) 7-201 (Arthurton)

	O	M	R	W	Ave	SR	ER	Wide	NB
DK Morrison	9	1	33	1	33.00	54.00	3.67	2	1
DN Patel	10	2	19	1	19.00	60.00	1.90	1	-
W Watson	10	2	56	1	56.00	60.00	5.60	-	-
GR Larsen	10	0	41	2	20.50	30.00	4.10	-	-
CZ Harris	10	2	32	2	16.00	30.00	3.20	-	-
RT Latham	1	0	14	0	-	-	14.00	4	-

New Zealand			Runs	Mins	Balls	4s	6s	SR
MJ Greatbatch	c Haynes	b Benjamin	63	102	77	7	3	81.82
RT Latham	c Williams	b Cummins	14	51	27	1	-	51.85
AH Jones	c Williams	b Benjamin	10	42	35	-	-	28.57
MD Crowe*		not out	81	105	81	12	-	100.00
KR Rutherford	c Williams	b Ambrose	8	32	32	1	-	25.00
CZ Harris	c Williams	b Cummins	7	36	23	-	-	30.43
DN Patel		not out	10	27	18	-	-	55.56
IDS Smith†								
GR Larsen								
DK Morrison								
W Watson								
Extras	(lb 7, w 5, nb 1)		13					
	48.3 overs (200 mins)		206 for 5					

Fall: 1-67 (Latham) 2-97 (Jones) 3-100 (Greatbatch) 4-135 (Rutherford) 5-174 (Harris)

	O	M	R	W	Ave	SR	ER	Wide	NB
CEL Ambrose	10	1	41	1	41.00	60.00	4.10	3	-
MD Marshall	9	1	35	0	-	-	3.89	1	1
AC Cummins	10	0	53	2	26.50	30.00	5.30	1	-
CL Hooper	10	0	36	0	-	-	3.60	-	-
WKM Benjamin	9.3	3	34	2	17.00	28.50	3.58	-	-

Match 22 – March 8, 1992: Pakistan vs South Africa (The Gabba, Brisbane)

Toss: Pakistan   Umpires: BL Aldridge & SU Bucknor
Crowd: 8,108   MOTM: AC Hudson
South Africa won by 20 runs (Pakistan required 193 from 36 overs)

South Africa			Runs	Mins	Balls	4s	6s	SR
AC Hudson	c Ijaz	b Imran	54	97	81	8	-	66.67
KC Wessels*	c Moin	b Aaqib	7	32	26	-	-	26.92
MW Rushmere	c Aamer	b Mushtaq	35	86	70	2	-	50.00
AP Kuiper	c Moin	b Imran	5	13	12	-	-	41.67
JN Rhodes	lbw	b Iqbal	5	25	17	-	-	29.41
WJ Cronje		not out	47	78	53	4	-	88.68
BM McMillan		b Wasim	33	47	44	1	-	75.00
DJ Richardson†		b Wasim	5	9	10	-	-	50.00
RP Snell		not out	1	2	1	-	-	100.00
MW Pringle								
AA Donald								
Extras	(lb 8, w 9, nb 2)		19					
	50 overs (198 mins)		211 for 7					

Fall: 1-31 (Wessels) 2-98 (Hudson) 3-110 (Kuiper) 4-111 (Rushmere) 5-127 (Rhodes) 6-198 (McMillan) 7-207 (Richardson)

	O	M	R	W	Ave	SR	ER	Wide	NB
Wasim Akram	10	0	42	2	21.00	30.00	4.20	7	2
Aaqib Javed	7	1	36	1	36.00	42.00	5.14	2	-
Imran Khan	10	0	34	2	17.00	30.00	3.40	-	-
Iqbal Sikander	8	0	30	1	30.00	48.00	3.75	-	-
Ijaz Ahmed	7	0	26	0	-	-	3.71	-	-
Mushtaq Ahmed	8	1	35	1	35.00	48.00	4.37	-	-

Pakistan			Runs	Mins	Balls	4s	6s	SR
Aamer Sohail		b Snell	23	61	53	2	-	43.40
Zahid Fazal	c Richardson	b McMillan	11	63	46	1	-	23.91
Inzamam-ul-Haq		run out	48	70	45	5	-	106.67
Imran Khan*	c Richardson	b McMillan	34	70	53	5	-	64.15
Salim Malik	c Donald	b Kuiper	12	15	11	-	-	109.09
Wasim Akram	c Snell	b Kuiper	9	15	8	1	-	112.50
Ijaz Ahmed	c Rhodes	b Kuiper	6	4	3	1	-	200.00
Moin Khan†		not out	5	11	5	-	-	100.00
Mushtaq Ahmed		run out	4	5	4	-	-	100.00
Iqbal Sikander		not out	1	2	3	-	-	33.33
Aaqib Javed								
Extras	(lb 2, w 17, nb 1)		20					
	36 overs (162 mins)		173 for 8					

Fall: 1-50 (Sohail) 2-50 (Zahid) 3-135 (Inzamam) 4-136 (Imran) 5-156 (Malik) 6-157 (Akram) 7-163 (Ijaz) 8-171 (Mushtaq)

	O	M	R	W	Ave	SR	ER	Wide	NB
AA Donald	7	1	31	0	-	-	4.43	7	-
MW Pringle	7	0	31	0	-	-	4.43	3	1
RP Snell	8	2	26	1	26.00	48.00	3.25	1	-
BM McMillan	7	0	34	2	17.00	21.00	4.86	4	-
AP Kuiper	6	0	40	3	13.33	12.00	6.67	2	-
WJ Cronje	1	0	9	0	-	-	9.00	-	-

Match 23 – March 9, 1992: England vs Sri Lanka (Eastern Oval, Ballarat)

Toss: England

Crowd: 13,037

England won by 106 runs

Umpires: Khizer Hayat & PD Reporter

MOTM: CC Lewis

England			Runs	Mins	Balls	4s	6s	SR
GA Gooch*		b Labrooy	8	40	28	1	-	28.57
IT Botham		b Anurasiri	47	106	63	5	2	74.60
RA Smith		run out	19	46	39	2	-	48.72
GA Hick		b Ramanayake	41	73	62	3	-	66.13
NH Fairbrother	c Ramanayake	b Gurusinha	63	96	70	3	2	90.00
AJ Stewart†	c Jayasuriya	b Gurusinha	59	48	36	7	1	163.89
CC Lewis		not out	20	9	6	1	2	333.33
DR Pringle		not out	0	2	0	-	-	-
DA Reeve								
PAJ DeFreitas								
RK Illingworth								
Extras	(b 1, lb 9, w 9, nb 4)		23					
50 overs (213 mins)			280 for 6					

Fall: 1-44 (Gooch) 2-80 (Smith) 3-105 (Botham) 4-164 (Hick) 5-244 (Fairbrother) 6-268 (Stewart)

	O	M	R	W	Ave	SR	ER	Wide	NB
GP Wickramasinghe	9	0	54	0	-	-	6.00	3	-
CPH Ramanayake	10	1	42	1	42.00	60.00	4.20	3	4
GF Labrooy	10	1	68	1	68.00	60.00	6.80	2	-
SD Anurasiri	10	1	27	1	27.00	60.00	2.70	-	-
AP Gurusinha	10	0	67	2	33.50	30.00	6.70	1	-
ST Jayasuriya	1	0	12	0	-	-	12.00	-	-

Sri Lanka			Runs	Mins	Balls	4s	6s	SR
RS Mahanama	c Botham	b Lewis	9	31	19	1	-	47.37
MAR Samarasekera	c Illingworth	b Lewis	23	42	29	4	-	79.31
AP Gurusinha	c and	b Lewis	7	31	9	-	-	77.78
PA de Silva*	c Fairbrother	b Lewis	7	10	10	1	-	70.00
A Ranatunga	c Stewart	b Botham	36	67	51	6	-	70.59
HP Tillakaratne†		run out	4	40	30	-	-	13.33
ST Jayasuriya	c DeFreitas	b Illingworth	19	20	16	2	-	118.75
GF Labrooy	c Smith	b Illingworth	19	42	34	1	-	55.88
CPH Ramanayake	c and	b Reeve	12	35	38	-	-	31.58
SD Anurasiri	lbw	b Reeve	11	17	19	-	-	57.89
GP Wickramasinghe		not out	6	14	16	-	-	37.50
Extras	(lb 7, w 8, nb 6)		21					
44 overs (179 mins)			174					

Fall: 1-33 (Mahanama) 2-46 (Samarasekera) 3-56 (de Silva) 4-60 (Gurusinha) 5-91 (Tillakaratne) 6-119 (Ranatunga) 7-123 (Jayasuriya) 8-156 (Ramanayake) 9-158 (Labrooy) 10-174 (Anurasiri)

	O	M	R	W	Ave	SR	ER	Wide	NB
DR Pringle	7	1	27	0	-	-	3.86	1	3
CC Lewis	8	0	30	4	7.50	12.00	3.75	2	2
PAJ DeFreitas	5	1	31	0	-	-	6.20	3	1
IT Botham	10	0	33	1	33.00	60.00	3.30	1	-
RK Illingworth	10	0	32	2	16.00	30.00	3.20	-	-
DA Reeve	4	0	14	2	7.00	12.00	3.50	1	-

Match 24 – March 10, 1992: India vs West Indies (Basin Reserve, Wellington)

Toss: India
Crowd: 6,634
West Indies won by five wickets

Umpires: SG Randell & SJ Woodward
MOTM: CC Lewis

India

India			Runs	Mins	Balls	4s	6s	SR
AD Jadeja	c Benjamin	b Simmons	27	64	61	2	-	44.26
K Srikkanth	c Logie	b Hooper	40	101	70	2	-	57.14
M Azharuddin*	c Ambrose	b Cummins	61	89	84	4	-	72.62
SR Tendulkar	c Williams	b Ambrose	4	11	11	-	-	36.36
SV Manjrekar		run out	27	53	40	-	-	67.50
Kapil Dev	c Haynes	b Cummins	3	9	4	-	-	75.00
PK Amre	c Hooper	b Ambrose	4	14	8	-	-	50.00
KS More†	c Hooper	b Cummins	5	5	5	1	-	100.00
M Prabhakar	c Richardson	b Cummins	8	10	10	1	-	80.00
J Srinath		not out	5	7	5	-	-	100.00
SLV Raju		run out	1	2	1	-	-	100.00
Extras	(lb 6, w 5, nb 1)		12					
	49.4 overs (187 mins)		197					

Fall: 1-56 (Jadeja) 2-102 (Srikkanth) 3-115 (Tendulkar) 4-166 (Azharuddin) 5-171 (Kapil Dev) 6-172 (Manjrekar) 7-180 (More) 8-186 (Amre) 9-193 (Prabhakar) 10-197 (Raju)

	O	M	R	W	Ave	SR	ER	Wide	NB
CEL Ambrose	10	1	24	2	12.00	30.00	2.40	-	-
WKM Benjamin	9.4	0	35	0	-	-	3.62	4	-
AC Cummins	10	0	33	4	8.25	15.00	3.30	-	-
PV Simmons	9	0	48	1	48.00	54.00	5.33	1	1
CL Hooper	10	0	46	1	46.00	60.00	4.60	-	-
KLT Arthurton	1	0	5	0	-	-	5.00	-	-

West Indies

West Indies			Runs	Mins	Balls	4s	6s	SR
DL Haynes	c Manjrekar	b Kapil Dev	16	28	16	3	-	100.00
BC Lara	c Manjrekar	b Srinath	41	51	37	6	1	110.81
PV Simmons	c Tendulkar	b Prabhakar	22	27	20	2	1	110.00
RB Richardson*	c Srikkanth	b Srinath	3	19	8	-	-	37.50
KLT Arthurton		not out	58	101	99	3	-	58.59
AL Logie	c More	b Raju	7	15	10	1	-	70.00
CL Hooper		not out	34	70	57	3	-	59.65
D Williams†								
CEL Ambrose								
AC Cummins								
WKM Benjamin								
Extras	(lb 8, w 2, nb 4)		14					
	40.2 overs (158 mins)		195 for 5					

Fall: 1-57 (Haynes) 2-82 (Lara) 3-88 (Simmons) 4-98 (Richardson) 5-112 (Logie)

	O	M	R	W	Ave	SR	ER	Wide	NB
Kapil Dev	8	0	45	1	45.00	48.00	5.62	-	-
M Prabhakar	9	0	55	1	55.00	54.00	6.11	1	1
SLV Raju	10	2	32	1	32.00	60.00	3.20	1	-
J Srinath	9	2	23	2	11.50	27.00	2.56	-	3
SR Tendulkar	3	0	20	0	-	-	6.67	-	-
K Srikkanth	1	0	7	0	-	-	7.00	-	-
AD Jadeja	0.2	0	5	0	-	-	15.00	-	-

APPENDICES

Match 25 – March 10, 1992: South Africa vs Zimbabwe (Manuka Oval, Canberra)

Toss: South Africa
Crowd: 3,165
South Africa won by seven wickets

Umpires: SU Bucknor & DR Shepherd
MOTM: PN Kirsten

Zimbabwe			Runs	Mins	Balls	4s	6s	SR
WR James	lbw	b Pringle	5	12	12	-	-	41.67
A Flower†	c Richardson	b Cronje	19	71	44	-	-	43.18
AJ Pycroft	c Wessels	b McMillan	19	63	47	-	-	40.43
DL Houghton*	c Cronje	b Kirsten	15	75	53	-	-	28.30
AC Waller	c Cronje	b Kirsten	15	28	28	1	-	53.57
AH Shah	c Wessels	b Kirsten	3	10	4	-	-	75.00
EA Brandes	c Richardson	b McMillan	20	49	28	1	1	71.43
MG Burmester	c Kuiper	b Cronje	1	8	10	-	-	10.00
AJ Traicos		not out	16	49	40	1		40.00
MP Jarvis	c and	b McMillan	17	28	21	1	1	80.95
KG Duers		b Donald	5	9	10	-	-	50.00
Extras	(lb 11, w 13, nb 4)		28					
	48.3 overs (207 mins)		163					

Fall: 1-7 (James) 2-51 (Pycroft) 3-72 (Waller) 4-80 (Houghton) 5-80 (Shah) 6-115 (Flower) 7-117 (Burmester) 8-123 (Brandes) 9-151 (Jarvis) 10-163 (Duers)

	O	M	R	W	Ave	SR	ER	Wide	NB
AA Donald	9.3	1	25	1	25.00	57.00	2.63	1	1
MW Pringle	9	0	25	1	25.00	54.00	2.78	6	3
RP Snell	10	3	24	0	-	-	2.40	-	-
WJ Cronje	5	0	17	2	8.50	15.00	3.40	-	-
PN Kirsten	5	0	31	3	10.33	10.00	6.20	-	-
BM McMillan	10	1	30	3	10.00	20.00	3.00	6	-

South Africa			Runs	Mins	Balls	4s	6s	SR
KC Wessels*		b Shah	70	148	137	6	-	51.09
AC Hudson		b Jarvis	13	26	22	1	-	59.09
PN Kirsten		not out	62	138	103	3	-	60.19
AP Kuiper	c Burmester	b Brandes	7	9	9	-	-	77.78
JN Rhodes		not out	3	6	3	-	-	100.00
WJ Cronje								
BM McMillan								
MW Pringle								
RP Snell								
DJ Richardson†								
AA Donald								
Extras	(lb 4, w 2, nb 3)		9					
	45.1 overs (165 mins)		164 for 3					

Fall: 1-27 (Hudson) 2-139 (Wessels) 3-151 (Kuiper)

	O	M	R	W	Ave	SR	ER	Wide	NB
EA Brandes	9.1	0	40	1	40.00	55.00	4.36	1	1
MP Jarvis	9	2	23	1	23.00	54.00	2.56	-	2
MG Burmester	5	0	20	0	-	-	4.00	1	-
AH Shah	8	2	32	1	32.00	48.00	4.00	-	-
KG Duers	8	1	19	0	-	-	2.37	-	-
AJ Traicos	6	0	26	0	-	-	4.33	-	-

Match 26 – March 11, 1992: Australia vs Pakistan (WACA Ground, Perth) – D/N
Toss: Pakistan
Crowd: 21,214
Pakistan won by 48 runs

Umpires: KE Liebenberg & PD Reporter
MOTM: Aamer Sohail

Pakistan			Runs	Mins	Balls	4s	6s	SR
Aamer Sohail	c Healy	b Moody	76	150	106	8	-	71.70
Ramiz Raja	c Border	b Whitney	34	82	61	4	-	55.74
Salim Malik		b Moody	0	4	6	-	-	0.00
Javed Miandad	c Healy	b SR Waugh	46	90	75	3	-	61.33
Imran Khan*	c Moody	b SR Waugh	13	31	22	-	1	59.09
Inzamam-ul-Haq		run out	16	20	16	-	-	100.00
Ijaz Ahmed		run out	0	8	2	-	-	0.00
Wasim Akram	c ME Waugh	b SR Waugh	0	1	1	-	-	0.00
Moin Khan†	c Healy	b McDermott	5	13	8	-	-	62.50
Mushtaq Ahmed		not out	3	6	5	-	-	60.00
Aaqib Javed								
Extras	(lb 9, w 16, nb 2)		27					
	50 overs (210 mins)		220 for 9					

Fall: 1-78 (Ramiz) 2-80 (Malik) 3-157 (Sohail) 4-193 (Miandad) 5-194 (Imran) 6-205 (Ijaz) 7-205 (Akram) 8-214 (Inzamam) 9-220 (Moin)

	O	M	R	W	Ave	SR	ER	Wide	NB
CJ McDermott	10	0	33	1	33.00	60.00	3.30	3	-
BA Reid	9	0	37	0	-	-	4.11	4	2
SR Waugh	10	0	36	3	12.00	20.00	3.60	6	-
MR Whitney	10	1	50	1	50.00	60.00	5.00	2	-
TM Moody	10	0	42	2	21.00	30.00	4.20	1	-
ME Waugh	1	0	13	0	-	-	13.00	-	-

Australia			Runs	Mins	Balls	4s	6s	SR
TM Moody	c Salim	b Aaqib	4	22	18	-	-	22.22
GR Marsh	c Moin	b Imran	39	139	91	1	-	42.86
DC Boon	c Mushtaq	b Aaqib	5	22	15	1	-	33.33
DM Jones	c Aaqib	b Mushtaq	47	82	79	2	-	59.49
ME Waugh	c Ijaz	b Mushtaq	30	51	42	2	-	71.43
AR Border*	c Ijaz	b Mushtaq	1	4	4	-	-	25.00
SR Waugh	c Moin	b Imran	5	4	6	1	-	83.33
IA Healy†	c Ijaz	b Aaqib	8	19	15	-	-	53.33
CJ McDermott	lbw	b Wasim	0	5	2	-	-	0.00
MR Whitney		b Wasim	5	8	9	-	-	55.56
BA Reid		not out	0	4	0	-	-	-
Extras	(lb 7, w 14, nb 7)		28					
	45.2 overs (189 mins)		172					

Fall: 1-13 (Moody) 2-31 (Boon) 3-116 (Jones) 4-122 (Marsh) 5-123 (Border) 6-130 (SR Waugh) 7-156 (Healy) 8-162 (McDermott) 9-167 (ME Waugh) 10-172 (Whitney)

	O	M	R	W	Ave	SR	ER	Wide	NB
Wasim Akram	7.2	0	28	2	14.00	22.00	3.82	4	3
Aaqib Javed	8	1	21	3	7.00	16.00	2.62	6	1
Imran Khan	10	1	32	2	16.00	30.00	3.20	-	-
Ijaz Ahmed	10	0	43	0	-	-	4.30	4	3
Mushtaq Ahmed	10	0	41	3	13.67	20.00	4.10	-	-

Match 27 – March 12, 1992: New Zealand vs India (Carisbrook, Dunedin)
Toss: India
Umpires: PJ McConnell & ID Robinson
Crowd: 9,134
MOTM: MJ Greatbatch
New Zealand won by four wickets

India			Runs	Mins	Balls	4s	6s	SR
AD Jadeja		retired hurt	13	28	32	1	-	40.63
K Srikkanth	c Latham	b Patel	0	5	3	-	-	0.00
M Azharuddin*	c Greatbatch	b Patel	55	127	98	3	1	56.12
SR Tendulkar	c Smith	b Harris	84	122	107	6	-	78.50
SV Manjrekar	c and	b Harris	18	37	25	-	-	72.00
Kapil Dev	c Larsen	b Harris	33	27	16	5	-	206.25
ST Banerjee	c Greatbatch	b Watson	11	11	9	1	-	122.22
KS More†		not out	2	5	8	-	-	25.00
J Srinath		not out	4	3	3	-	-	133.33
M Prabhakar								
SLV Raju								
Extras	(b 1, lb 4, w 4, nb 1)		10					
	50 overs (183 mins)		230 for 6					

Fall: 1-4 (Srikkanth) 2-149 (Azharuddin) 3-166 (Tendulkar) 4-201 (Manjrekar) 5-222 (Kapil Dev) 6-223 (Banerjee)

	O	M	R	W	Ave	SR	ER	Wide	NB
CL Cairns	8	1	40	0	-	-	5.00	-	1
DN Patel	10	0	29	2	14.50	30.00	2.90	-	-
W Watson	10	1	34	1	34.00	60.00	3.40	-	-
GR Larsen	9	0	43	0	-	-	4.78	-	-
CZ Harris	9	0	55	3	18.33	18.00	6.11	2	-
RT Latham	4	0	24	0	-	-	6.00	2	-

New Zealand			Runs	Mins	Balls	4s	6s	SR
MJ Greatbatch	c Banerjee	b Raju	73	99	77	5	4	94.81
RT Latham		b Prabhakar	8	32	22	1	-	36.36
AH Jones		not out	67	160	107	8	-	62.62
MD Crowe*		run out	26	27	28	3	1	92.86
IDS Smith†	c (sub – Amre)	b Prabhakar	9	11	8	1	-	112.50
KR Rutherford	lbw	b Raju	21	25	22	3	1	95.45
CZ Harris		b Prabhakar	4	20	17	-	-	23.53
CL Cairns		not out	4	6	5	1	-	80.00
DN Patel								
GR Larsen								
W Watson								
Extras	(b 4, lb 3, w 4, nb 8)		19					
	47.1 overs (193 mins)		231 for 6					

Fall: 1-36 (Latham) 2-118 (Greatbatch) 3-162 (Crowe) 4-172 (Smith) 5-206 (Rutherford) 6-225 (Harris)

	O	M	R	W	Ave	SR	ER	Wide	NB
Kapil Dev	10	0	55	0	-	-	5.50	1	1
M Prabhakar	10	0	46	3	15.33	20.00	4.60	-	2
ST Banerjee	6	1	40	0	-	-	6.67	-	1
J Srinath	9	0	35	0	-	-	3.89	2	3
SLV Raju	10	0	38	2	19.00	30.00	3.80	1	-
SR Tendulkar	1	0	2	0	-	-	2.00	-	-
K Srikkanth	1.1	0	8	0	-	-	6.86	-	1

Match 28 – March 12, 1992: England vs South Africa (MCG, Melbourne) – D/N
Toss: England
Umpires: BL Aldridge & DP Buultjens
Crowd: 25,248
MOTM: AJ Stewart
England won by three wickets (England required 226 runs from 41 overs)

South Africa			Runs	Mins	Balls	4s	6s	SR
KC Wessels*	c Smith	b Hick	85	170	126	6	-	67.46
AC Hudson	c and	b Hick	79	132	115	7	-	68.70
PN Kirsten	c Smith	b DeFreitas	11	14	12	-	1	91.67
JN Rhodes		run out	18	25	23	-	-	78.26
AP Kuiper		not out	15	17	12	1	-	125.00
WJ Cronje		not out	13	14	15	-	-	86.67
BM McMillan								
DJ Richardson†								
RP Snell								
MW Pringle								
AA Donald								
Extras	(b 4, lb 4, w 4, nb 3)		15					
	50 overs (188 mins)		236 for 4					

Fall: 1-151 (Hudson) 2-170 (Kirsten) 3-201 (Wessels) 4-205 (Rhodes)

	O	M	R	W	Ave	SR	ER	Wide	NB
DR Pringle	9	2	34	0	-	-	3.78	2	3
PAJ DeFreitas	10	1	41	1	41.00	60.00	4.10	1	-
IT Botham	8	0	37	0	-	-	4.62	-	-
GC Small	2	0	14	0	-	-	7.00	1	-
RK Illingworth	10	0	43	0	-	-	4.30	-	-
DA Reeve	2.4	0	15	0	-	-	5.62	-	-
GA Hick	8.2	0	44	2	22.00	25.00	5.28	-	-

England			Runs	Mins	Balls	4s	6s	SR
AJ Stewart*†		run out	77	122	88	7	-	87.50
IT Botham		b McMillan	22	54	30	1	-	73.33
RA Smith	c Richardson	b McMillan	0	2	2	-	-	0.00
GA Hick	c Richardson	b Snell	1	4	4	-	-	25.00
NH Fairbrother		not out	75	133	83	6	-	90.36
DA Reeve	c McMillan	b Snell	10	29	15	-	-	66.67
CC Lewis		run out	33	29	22	4	-	150.00
DR Pringle	c Kuiper	b Snell	1	11	3	-	-	33.33
PAJ DeFreitas		not out	1	2	1	-	-	100.00
RK Illingworth								
GC Small								
Extras	(lb 3, w 1, nb 2)		6					
	40.5 overs (196 mins)		226 for 7					

Fall: 1-63 (Botham) 2-63 (Smith) 3-64 (Hick) 4-132 (Stewart) 5-166 (Reeve) 6-216 (Lewis) 7-225 (Pringle)

	O	M	R	W	Ave	SR	ER	Wide	NB
AA Donald	9	1	43	0	-	-	4.78	-	1
MW Pringle	8	0	44	0	-	-	5.50	1	1
RP Snell	7.5	0	42	3	14.00	15.67	5.36	-	-
BM McMillan	8	1	39	2	19.50	24.00	4.87	-	-
AP Kuiper	4	0	32	0	-	-	8.00	-	-
WJ Cronje	3	0	14	0	-	-	4.67	-	-
PN Kirsten	1	0	9	0	-	-	9.00	-	-

Match 29 – March 13, 1992: Sri Lanka vs West Indies (Berri Oval, Berri)
Toss: Sri Lanka
Crowd: 3,107
West Indies won by 91 runs

Umpires: DR Shepherd & SJ Woodward
MOTM: PV Simmons

West Indies			Runs	Mins	Balls	4s	6s	SR
DL Haynes	c Tillakaratne	b Ranatunga	38	78	47	3	1	80.85
BC Lara	c and	b Ramanayake	1	8	6	-	-	16.67
PV Simmons	c Wickramasinghe	b Hathurusinghe	110	153	125	8	2	88.00
RB Richardson*		run out	8	25	23	-	-	34.78
KLT Arthurton	c Tillakaratne	b Hathurusinghe	40	84	54	1	-	74.07
AL Logie		b Anurasiri	0	3	2	-	-	0.00
CL Hooper	c Gurusinha	b Hathurusinghe	12	12	12	1	-	100.00
D Williams†	c Tillakaratne	b Hathurusinghe	2	3	3	-	-	66.67
CEL Ambrose		not out	15	24	14	-	1	107.14
WKM Benjamin		not out	24	18	20	1	-	120.00
AC Cummins								
Extras	(lb 9, w 3, nb 6)		18					
	50 overs (208 mins)		268 for 8					

Fall: 1-6 (Lara) 2-72 (Haynes) 3-103 (Richardson) 4-194 (Simmons) 5-195 (Logie) 6-217 (Hooper) 7-223 (Williams) 8-228 (Arthurton)

	O	M	R	W	Ave	SR	ER	Wide	NB
GP Wickramasinghe	7	0	30	0	-	-	4.29	2	1
CPH Ramanayake	7	1	17	1	17.00	42.00	2.43	1	1
SD Anurasiri	10	0	46	1	46.00	60.00	4.60	-	-
AP Gurusinha	1	0	10	0	-	-	10.00	-	-
A Ranatunga	7	0	35	1	35.00	42.00	5.00	-	-
RS Kalpage	10	0	64	0	-	-	6.40	-	-
UC Hathurusinghe	8	0	57	4	14.25	12.00	7.12	-	4

Sri Lanka			Runs	Mins	Balls	4s	6s	SR
RS Mahanama	c Arthurton	b Cummins	11	87	50	-	-	22.00
MAR Samarasekera	lbw	b Hooper	40	48	41	4	1	97.56
UC Hathurusinghe		run out	16	35	25	-	-	64.00
PA de Silva*	c and	b Hooper	11	26	19	-	-	57.89
A Ranatunga	c Benjamin	b Arthurton	24	60	40	-	1	60.00
AP Gurusinha	c Richardson	b Ambrose	10	28	30	-	-	33.33
HP Tillakaratne†		b Ambrose	3	4	9	-	-	33.33
RS Kalpage		not out	13	51	40	-	-	32.50
CPH Ramanayake		b Arthurton	1	8	13	-	-	7.69
SD Anurasiri		b Benjamin	3	12	11	-	-	27.27
GP Wickramasinghe		not out	21	22	21	1	-	100.00
Extras	(lb 8, w 14, nb 2)		24					
	50 overs (190 mins)		177 for 9					

Fall: 1-56 (Samarasekera) 2-80 (Hathurusinghe) 3-86 (Mahanama) 4-99 (de Silva) 5-130 (Gurusinha) 6-135 (Tillakaratne) 7-137 (Ranatunga) 8-139 (Ramanayake) 9-149 (Anurasiri)

	O	M	R	W	Ave	SR	ER	Wide	NB
CEL Ambrose	10	2	24	2	12.00	30.00	2.40	6	-
WKM Benjamin	10	0	34	1	34.00	60.00	3.40	5	-
AC Cummins	9	0	49	1	49.00	54.00	5.44	3	1
CL Hooper	10	1	19	2	9.50	30.00	1.90	-	-
KLT Arthurton	10	0	40	2	20.00	30.00	4.00	-	1
PV Simmons	1	0	3	0	-	-	3.00	-	-

Match 30 – March 14, 1992: Australia vs Zimbabwe (Bellerive Oval, Hobart)
Toss: Zimbabwe   Umpires: BL Aldridge & SU Bucknor
Crowd: 7,411   MOTM: SR Waugh
Australia won by 128 runs

Australia			Runs	Mins	Balls	4s	6s	SR
TM Moody		run out	6	4	8	-	-	75.00
DC Boon		b Shah	48	92	84	4	-	57.14
DM Jones		b Burmester	54	123	71	4	-	76.06
AR Border*	st Flower	b Traicos	22	24	29	2	-	75.86
ME Waugh		not out	66	68	39	5	2	169.23
SR Waugh		b Brandes	55	48	43	4	-	127.91
IA Healy†	lbw	b Duers	0	3	2	-	-	0.00
PL Taylor		not out	1	3	1	-	-	100.00
CJ McDermott								
MR Whitney								
BA Reid								
Extras	(b 2, lb 8, w 2, nb 1)		13					
	46 overs (186 mins)		265 for 6					

Fall: 1-8 (Moody) 2-102 (Boon) 3-134 (Border) 4-144 (Jones) 5-257 (SR Waugh) 6-258 (Healy)

	O	M	R	W	Ave	SR	ER	Wide	NB
EA Brandes	9	0	59	1	59.00	54.00	6.56	-	1
KG Duers	9	1	48	1	48.00	54.00	5.33	1	-
MG Burmester	9	0	65	1	65.00	54.00	7.22	1	-
AH Shah	9	0	53	1	53.00	54.00	5.89	-	-
AJ Traicos	10	0	30	1	30.00	60.00	3.00	-	-

Zimbabwe			Runs	Mins	Balls	4s	6s	SR
AH Shah		run out	11	87	50	-	-	22.00
A Flower†	c Border	b SR Waugh	40	48	41	4	1	97.56
ADR Campbell	c ME Waugh	b Whitney	16	35	25	-	-	64.00
AJ Pycroft	c ME Waugh	b SR Waugh	11	26	19	-	-	57.89
DL Houghton*		b McDermott	24	60	40	-	1	60.00
AC Waller	c Taylor	b Moody	10	28	30	-	-	33.33
KJ Arnott		b Whitney	3	4	9	-	-	33.33
EA Brandes	c McDermott	b Taylor	13	51	40	-	-	32.50
MG Burmester	c Border	b Reid	1	8	13	-	-	7.69
AJ Traicos	c Border	b Taylor	3	12	11	-	-	27.27
KG Duers		not out	21	22	21	1	-	100.00
Extras	(lb 12, w 8, nb 2)		22					
	41.4 overs (174 mins)		137					

Fall: 1-47 (Shah) 2-51 (Flower) 3-51 (Pycroft) 4-57 (Campbell) 5-69 (Houghton) 6-88 (Waller) 7-97 (Arnott) 8-117 (Burmester) 9-132 (Traicos) 10-137 (Brandes)

	O	M	R	W	Ave	SR	ER	Wide	NB
CJ McDermott	8	0	26	1	26.00	48.00	3.25	3	1
BA Reid	9	2	17	1	17.00	54.00	1.89	-	1
SR Waugh	7	0	28	2	14.00	21.00	4.00	4	-
MR Whitney	10	3	15	2	7.50	30.00	1.50	-	-
TM Moody	4	0	25	1	25.00	24.00	6.25	1	-
PL Taylor	3.4	0	14	2	7.00	11.00	3.82	-	-

Match 31 – March 15, 1992: New Zealand vs England (Basin Reserve, Wellington)
Toss: New Zealand
Crowd: 13,612
New Zealand won by seven wickets

Umpires: SG Randell & ID Robinson
MOTM: AH Jones

England			Runs	Mins	Balls	4s	6s	SR
AJ Stewart*†	c Harris	b Patel	41	77	59	7	-	69.49
IT Botham		b Patel	8	21	25	1	-	32.00
GA Hick	c Greatbatch	b Harris	56	94	70	6	1	80.00
RA Smith	c Patel	b Jones	38	67	72	3	-	52.78
AJ Lamb	c Cairns	b Watson	12	39	29	-	-	41.38
CC Lewis	c and	b Watson	0	1	1	-	-	0.00
DA Reeve		not out	21	37	27	1	-	77.78
DR Pringle	c (sub - Latham)	b Jones	10	20	16	-	-	62.50
PAJ DeFreitas	c Cairns	b Harris	0	3	1	-	-	0.00
RK Illingworth		not out	2	3	2	-	-	100.00
GC Small								
Extras	(b 1, lb 7, w 4)		12					
	50 overs (185 mins)		200 for 8					

Fall: 1-25 (Botham) 2-95 (Stewart) 3-135 (Hick) 4-162 (Smith) 5-162 (Lewis) 6-169 (Lamb) 7-189 (Pringle) 8-195 (DeFreitas)

	O	M	R	W	Ave	SR	ER	Wide	NB
DN Patel	10	1	26	2	13.00	30.00	2.60	-	-
CZ Harris	8	0	39	2	19.50	24.00	4.87	1	-
W Watson	10	0	40	2	20.00	30.00	4.00	1	-
CL Cairns	3	0	21	0	-	-	7.00	1	-
GR Larsen	10	3	24	0	-	-	2.40	1	-
AH Jones	9	0	42	2	21.00	27.00	4.67	-	-

New Zealand			Runs	Mins	Balls	4s	6s	SR
MJ Greatbatch	c DeFreitas	b Botham	35	51	37	4	1	94.59
JG Wright		b DeFreitas	1	5	5	-	-	20.00
AH Jones		run out	78	123	113	13	-	69.03
MD Crowe*		not out	73	105	81	4	-	90.12
KR Rutherford		not out	3	27	12	-	-	25.00
CZ Harris								
IDS Smith†								
CL Cairns								
DN Patel								
GR Larsen								
W Watson								
Extras	(lb 9, w 1, nb 1)		11					
	40.5 overs (157 mins)		201 for 3					

Fall: 1-5 (Wright) 2-62 (Greatbatch) 3-171 (Jones)

	O	M	R	W	Ave	SR	ER	Wide	NB
DR Pringle	6.2	1	34	0	-	-	5.37	1	1
PAJ DeFreitas	8.3	1	45	1	45.00	51.00	5.29	-	-
IT Botham	4	0	19	1	19.00	24.00	4.75	-	-
RK Illingworth	9	1	46	0	-	-	5.11	-	-
GA Hick	6	0	26	0	-	-	4.33	-	-
DA Reeve	3	0	9	0	-	-	3.00	-	-
GC Small	4	0	13	0	-	-	3.25	-	-

Match 32 – March 15, 1992: India vs South Africa (Adelaide Oval, Adelaide)

Toss: South Africa
Crowd: 6,272
South Africa won by six wickets

Umpires: DP Buultjens & Khizer Hayat
MOTM: PN Kirsten

India			Runs	Mins	Balls	4s	6s	SR
K Srikkanth	c Kirsten	b Donald	0	5	5	-	-	0.00
SV Manjrekar		b Kuiper	28	72	53	-	-	52.83
M Azharuddin*	c Kuiper	b Pringle	79	125	77	6	-	102.60
SR Tendulkar	c Wessels	b Kuiper	14	14	14	1	-	100.00
Kapil Dev		b Donald	42	33	29	3	1	144.83
VG Kambli		run out	1	4	3	-	-	33.33
PK Amre		not out	1	3	1	-	-	100.00
J Srinath		not out	0	1	0	-	-	-
M Prabhakar								
KS More†								
SLV Raju								
Extras	(lb 7, w 6, nb 2)		15					
	30 overs (133 mins)		180 for 6					

Fall: 1-1 (Srikkanth) 2-79 (Manjrekar) 3-103 (Tendulkar) 4-174 (Kapil Dev) 5-177 (Kambli) 6-179 (Azharuddin)

	O	M	R	W	Ave	SR	ER	Wide	NB
AA Donald	6	0	34	2	17.00	18.00	5.67	3	-
MW Pringle	6	0	37	1	37.00	36.00	6.17	2	2
RP Snell	6	1	46	0	-	-	7.67	-	-
BM McMillan	6	0	28	0	-	-	4.67	-	-
AP Kuiper	6	0	28	2	14.00	18.00	4.67	1	-

South Africa			Runs	Mins	Balls	4s	6s	SR
AC Hudson		b Srinath	53	85	73	4	-	72.60
PN Kirsten		b Kapil Dev	84	104	86	7	-	97.67
AP Kuiper		run out	7	13	6	-	-	116.67
JN Rhodes	c Raju	b Prabhakar	7	8	3	-	1	233.33
KC Wessels*		not out	9	13	6	1	-	150.00
WJ Cronje		not out	8	9	6	1	-	133.33
BM McMillan								
DJ Richardson†								
RP Snell								
AA Donald								
MW Pringle								
Extras	(lb 10, nb 3)		13					
	29.1 overs (118 mins)		181 for 4					

Fall: 1-128 (Hudson) 2-149 (Kuiper) 3-157 (Kirsten) 4-163 (Rhodes)

	O	M	R	W	Ave	SR	ER	Wide	NB
Kapil Dev	6	0	36	1	36.00	36.00	6.00	-	-
M Prabhakar	5.1	1	33	1	33.00	31.00	6.39	-	-
SR Tendulkar	6	0	20	0	-	-	3.33	-	-
J Srinath	6	0	39	1	39.00	36.00	6.50	-	3
SLV Raju	6	0	43	0	-	-	7.17	-	-

Match 33 – March 15, 1992: Pakistan vs Sri Lanka (WACA Ground, Perth)
Toss: Sri Lanka
Umpires: KE Liebenberg & PJ McConnell
Crowd: 3,071
MOTM: Javed Miandad
Pakistan won by four wickets

Sri Lanka			Runs	Mins	Balls	4s	6s	SR
RS Mahanama		b Wasim	12	35	36	1	-	33.33
MAR Samarasekera	st Moin	b Mushtaq	38	106	59	1	-	64.41
UC Hathurusinghe		b Mushtaq	5	32	29	-	-	17.24
PA de Silva*	c Aamer	b Ijaz	43	64	56	2	-	76.79
AP Gurusinha	c Salim	b Imran	37	77	54	2	-	68.52
A Ranatunga	c (sub – Zahid)	b Aamer	7	18	19	-	-	36.84
HP Tillakaratne†		not out	25	44	34	3	-	73.53
RS Kalpage		not out	13	16	14	-	-	92.86
CPH Ramanayake								
GP Wickramasinghe								
KIW Wijegunawardene								
Extras	(lb 15, w 11, nb 6)		32					
50 overs (201 mins)			212 for 6					

Fall: 1-29 (Mahanama) 2-48 (Hathurusinghe) 3-99 (Samarasekera) 4-132 (de Silva) 5-158 (Ranatunga) 6-187 (Gurusinha)

	O	M	R	W	Ave	SR	ER	Wide	NB
Wasim Akram	10	0	37	1	37.00	60.00	3.70	2	4
Aaqib Javed	10	0	39	0	-	-	3.90	3	2
Imran Khan	8	1	36	1	36.00	48.00	4.50	-	-
Mushtaq Ahmed	10	0	43	2	21.50	30.00	4.30	2	-
Ijaz Ahmed	8	0	28	1	28.00	48.00	3.50	3	-
Aamer Sohail	4	0	14	1	14.00	24.00	3.50	1	-

Pakistan			Runs	Mins	Balls	4s	6s	SR
Aamer Sohail	c Mahanama	b Ramanayake	1	11	10	-	-	10.00
Ramiz Raja	c Gurusinha	b Wickramasinghe	32	92	56	3	-	57.14
Imran Khan*	c de Silva	b Hathurusinghe	22	98	69	2	-	31.88
Javed Miandad	c Wickramasinghe	b Gurusinha	57	99	84	3	-	67.86
Salim Malik	c Kalpage	b Ramanayake	51	98	66	2	-	77.27
Inzamam-ul-Haq		run out	11	15	11	-	-	100.00
Ijaz Ahmed		not out	8	11	6	1	-	133.33
Wasim Akram		not out	5	7	5	1	-	100.00
Moin Khan†								
Mushtaq Ahmed								
Aaqib Javed								
Extras	(lb 12, w 9, nb 8)		29					
49.1 overs (219 mins)			216 for 6					

Fall: 1-7 (Sohail) 2-68 (Ramiz) 3-84 (Imran) 4-185 (Miandad) 5-201 (Malik) 6-205 (Inzamam)

	O	M	R	W	Ave	SR	ER	Wide	NB
KIW Wijegunawardene	10	1	34	0	-	-	3.40	-	7
CPH Ramanayake	10	1	37	2	18.50	30.00	3.70	4	-
GP Wickramasinghe	9.1	0	41	1	41.00	55.00	4.47	1	-
AP Gurusinha	9	0	38	1	38.00	54.00	4.22	1	-
UC Hathurusinghe	9	0	40	1	40.00	54.00	4.44	2	1
RS Kalpage	2	0	14	0	-	-	7.00	1	-

Match 34 – March 18, 1992: New Zealand vs Pakistan (Lancaster Park, Christchurch)

Toss: Pakistan   Umpires: SU Bicknor & SG Randell
Crowd: 9,974   MOTM: Mushtaq Ahmed
Pakistan won by seven wickets

New Zealand			Runs	Mins	Balls	4s	6s	SR
MJ Greatbatch	c Javed	b Mushtaq	42	106	67	5	1	62.69
RT Latham	c Inzamam	b Aaqib	6	18	9	1	-	66.67
AH Jones	lbw	b Wasim	2	5	3	-	-	66.67
MD Crowe*	c Aamer	b Wasim	3	23	20	-	-	15.00
KR Rutherford		run out	8	41	35	-	-	22.86
CZ Harris	st Moin	b Mushtaq	1	6	6	-	-	16.67
DN Patel	c Mushtaq	b Aamer	7	27	13	-	-	53.85
IDS Smith†		b Imran	1	5	4	-	-	25.00
GR Larsen		b Wasim	37	86	80	3	-	46.25
DK Morrison	c Inzamam	b Wasim	12	55	45	1	-	26.67
W Watson		not out	5	17	13	-	-	38.46
Extras	(b 3, lb 23, w 12, nb 4)		42					
	48.2 overs (199 mins)		166					

Fall: 1-23 (Latham) 2-26 (Jones) 3-39 (Crowe) 4-85 (Rutherford) 5-88 (Harris) 6-93 (Greatbatch) 7-96 (Smith) 8-106 (Patel) 9-150 (Morrison) 10-166 (Larsen)

	O	M	R	W	Ave	SR	ER	Wide	NB
Wasim Akram	9.2	0	32	4	8.00	14.00	3.43	9	2
Aaqib Javed	10	1	34	1	34.00	60.00	3.40	1	2
Mushtaq Ahmed	10	0	18	2	9.00	30.00	1.80	2	-
Imran Khan	8	0	22	1	22.00	48.00	2.75	-	-
Aamer Sohail	10	1	29	1	29.00	60.00	2.90	-	-
Ijaz Ahmed	1	0	5	0	-	-	5.00	-	-

Pakistan			Runs	Mins	Balls	4s	6s	SR
Aamer Sohail	c Patel	b Morrison	0	1	1	-	-	0.00
Ramiz Raja		not out	119	173	155	16	-	76.77
Inzamam-ul-Haq		b Morrison	5	12	8	1	-	62.50
Javed Miandad	lbw	b Morrison	30	123	85	1	-	35.29
Salim Malik		not out	9	34	23	1	-	39.13
Imran Khan*								
Ijaz Ahmed								
Wasim Akram								
Moin Khan†								
Mushtaq Ahmed								
Aaqib Javed								
Extras	(lb 1, w 1, nb 2)		4					
	44.4 overs (173 mins)		167 for 3					

Fall: 1-0 (Sohail) 2-9 (Inzamam) 3-124 (Miandad)

	O	M	R	W	Ave	SR	ER	Wide	NB
DK Morrison	10	0	42	3	14.00	20.00	4.20	-	2
DN Patel	10	2	25	0	-	-	2.50	-	-
W Watson	10	3	26	0	-	-	2.60	-	-
CZ Harris	4	0	18	0	-	-	4.50	-	-
GR Larsen	3	0	16	0	-	-	5.33	-	-
AH Jones	3	0	10	0	-	-	3.33	-	-
RT Latham	2	0	13	0	-	-	6.50	-	-
KR Rutherford	1.4	0	11	0	-	-	6.60	1	-
MJ Greatbatch	1	0	5	0	-	-	5.00	-	-

APPENDICES

Match 35 – March 18, 1992: England vs Zimbabwe (Lavington Sports Oval, Albury)
Toss: England
Crowd: 5,645
Zimbabwe won by nine runs

Umpires: BL Aldridge & Khizer Hayat
MOTM: EA Brandes

Zimbabwe

Zimbabwe			Runs	Mins	Balls	4s	6s	SR
WR James	c and	b Illingworth	13	55	46	1	-	28.26
A Flower†		b DeFreitas	7	17	16	1	-	43.75
AJ Pycroft	c Gooch	b Botham	3	24	13	-	-	23.08
KJ Arnott	lbw	b Botham	11	43	33	-	-	33.33
DL Houghton*	c Fairbrother	b Small	29	90	74	2	-	39.19
AC Waller		b Tufnell	8	15	16	1	-	50.00
AH Shah	c Lamb	b Tufnell	3	21	16	-	-	18.75
IP Butchart	c Fairbrother	b Botham	24	42	36	2	-	66.67
EA Brandes	st Stewart	b Illingworth	14	25	24	1	-	58.33
AJ Traicos		not out	0	12	6	-	-	0.00
MP Jarvis	lbw	b Illingworth	6	9	6	-	-	100.00
Extras	(lb 8, w 8)		16					
	46.1 overs (182 mins)		134					

Fall: 1-12 (Flower) 2-19 (Pycroft) 3-30 (James) 4-52 (Arnott) 5-65 (Waller) 6-77 (Shah) 7-96 (Houghton) 8-127 (Butchart) 9-127 (Brandes) 10-134 (Jarvis)

	O	M	R	W	Ave	SR	ER	Wide	NB
PAJ DeFreitas	8	1	14	1	14.00	48.00	1.75	2	-
GC Small	9	1	20	1	20.00	54.00	2.22	1	-
IT Botham	10	3	23	3	7.67	20.00	2.30	4	-
RK Illingworth	9.1	0	33	3	11.00	18.33	3.60	-	-
PCR Tufnell	10	2	36	2	18.00	30.00	3.60	1	-

England

England			Runs	Mins	Balls	4s	6s	SR
GA Gooch*	lbw	b Brandes	0	1	1	-	-	0.00
IT Botham	c Flower	b Shah	18	45	34	4	-	52.94
AJ Lamb	c James	b Brandes	17	29	26	2	-	65.38
RA Smith		b Brandes	2	15	13	-	-	15.38
GA Hick		b Brandes	0	12	6	-	-	0.00
NH Fairbrother	c Flower	b Butchart	20	132	77	-	-	25.97
AJ Stewart†	c Waller	b Shah	29	94	96	3	-	30.21
PAJ DeFreitas	c Flower	b Butchart	4	14	17	-	-	23.53
RK Illingworth		run out	11	28	20	-	-	55.00
GC Small	c Pycroft	b Jarvis	5	20	18	-	-	27.78
PCR Tufnell		not out	0	3	0	-	-	-
Extras	(b 4, lb 3, w 11, nb 1)		19					
	49.1 overs (201 mins)		125					

Fall: 1-0 (Gooch) 2-32 (Lamb) 3-42 (Botham) 4-42 (Smith) 5-43 (Hick) 6-95 (Stewart) 7-101 (DeFreitas) 8-108 (Fairbrother) 9-124 (Illingworth) 10-125 (Small)

	O	M	R	W	Ave	SR	ER	Wide	NB
EA Brandes	10	4	21	4	5.25	15.00	2.10	-	-
MP Jarvis	9.1	0	32	1	32.00	55.00	3.49	2	-
AH Shah	10	3	17	2	8.50	30.00	1.70	3	-
AJ Traicos	10	4	16	0	-	-	1.60	-	-
IP Butchart	10	1	32	2	16.00	30.00	3.20	6	1

Match 36 – March 18, 1992: Australia vs West Indies (MCG, Melbourne) – D/N

Toss: Australia   Umpires: PD Reporter & DR Shepherd

Crowd: 47,572   MOTM: DC Boon

Australia won by 57 runs

Australia			Runs	Mins	Balls	4s	6s	SR
TM Moody	c Benjamin	b Simmons	42	95	70	3	-	60.00
DC Boon	c Williams	b Cummins	100	173	147	8	-	68.03
DM Jones	c Williams	b Cummins	6	19	14	-	-	42.86
AR Border*	lbw	b Simmons	8	12	10	1	-	80.00
ME Waugh	st Williams	b Hooper	21	38	31	-	-	67.74
SR Waugh		b Cummins	6	18	14	-	-	42.86
IA Healy†		not out	11	22	11	-	-	100.00
PL Taylor		not out	10	9	6	1	-	166.67
CJ McDermott								
MR Whitney								
BA Reid								
Extras	(lb 3, w 3, nb 6)		12					
50 overs (196 mins)			216 for 6					

Fall: 1-107 (Moody) 2-128 (Jones) 3-141 (Border) 4-185 (ME Waugh) 5-189 (Boon) 6-200 (SR Waugh)

	O	M	R	W	Ave	SR	ER	Wide	NB
CEL Ambrose	10	0	46	0	-	-	4.60	2	6
WKM Benjamin	10	1	49	0	-	-	4.90	-	-
AC Cummins	10	1	38	3	12.67	20.00	3.80	-	-
CL Hooper	10	0	40	1	40.00	60.00	4.00	1	-
PV Simmons	10	1	40	2	20.00	30.00	4.00	-	-

West Indies			Runs	Mins	Balls	4s	6s	SR
DL Haynes	c Jones	b McDermott	14	27	24	2	-	58.33
BC Lara		run out	70	180	97	3	-	72.16
PV Simmons	lbw	b McDermott	0	1	1	-	-	0.00
RB Richardson*	c Healy	b Whitney	10	50	44	-	-	22.73
KLT Arthurton	c McDermott	b Whitney	15	16	15	1	-	100.00
AL Logie	c Healy	b Whitney	5	14	15	-	-	33.33
CL Hooper	c ME Waugh	b Whitney	4	16	11	-	-	36.36
D Williams†	c Border	b Reid	4	17	15	-	-	26.67
WKM Benjamin	lbw	b SR Waugh	15	34	21	2	-	71.43
CEL Ambrose		run out	2	12	7	-	-	28.57
AC Cummins		not out	5	8	10	-	-	50.00
Extras	(b 3, lb 5, w 3, nb 4)		15					
42.4 overs (182 mins)			159					

Fall: 1-27 (Haynes) 2-27 (Simmons) 3-59 (Richardson) 4-83 (Arthurton) 5-99 (Logie) 6-117 (Hooper) 7-128 (Williams) 8-137 (Lara) 9-150 (Ambrose) 10-159 (Benjamin)

	O	M	R	W	Ave	SR	ER	Wide	NB
CJ McDermott	6	1	29	2	14.50	18.00	4.83	-	3
BA Reid	10	1	26	1	26.00	60.00	2.60	2	1
MR Whitney	10	1	34	4	8.50	15.00	3.40	-	-
SR Waugh	6.4	0	24	1	24.00	40.00	3.60	-	-
PL Taylor	4	0	24	0	-	-	6.00	-	-
TM Moody	6	1	14	0	-	-	2.33	1	-

1st Semi-Final – March 21, 1992: New Zealand vs Pakistan (Eden Park, Auckland)

Toss: New Zealand
Crowd: 32,439
Pakistan won by four wickets

Umpires: SU Bucknor & DR Shepherd
MOTM: Inzamam-ul-Haq

New Zealand

New Zealand			Runs	Mins	Balls	4s	6s	SR
MJ Greatbatch		b Aaqib	17	41	22	-	2	77.27
JG Wright	c Ramiz	b Mushtaq	13	57	44	1	-	29.55
AH Jones	lbw	b Mushtaq	21	60	53	2	-	39.62
MD Crowe*		run out	91	132	83	7	3	109.64
KR Rutherford	c Moin	b Wasim	50	68	68	5	1	73.53
CZ Harris	st Moin	b Iqbal	13	15	12	1	-	108.33
IDS Smith†		not out	18	21	10	3	-	180.00
DN Patel	lbw	b Wasim	8	10	6	1	-	133.33
GR Larsen		not out	8	7	6	1	-	133.33
DK Morrison								
W Watson								
Extras	(b 4, lb 7, w 8, nb 4)		23					
	50 overs (209 mins)		262 for 7					

Fall: 1-35 (Greatbatch) 2-39 (Wright) 3-87 (Jones) 4-194 (Rutherford) 5-214 (Harris) 6-221 (Crowe) 7-244 (Patel)

	O	M	R	W	Ave	SR	ER	Wide	NB
Wasim Akram	10	0	40	2	20.00	30.00	4.00	2	4
Aaqib Javed	10	2	45	1	45.00	60.00	4.50	2	-
Mushtaq Ahmed	10	0	40	2	20.00	30.00	4.00	-	-
Imran Khan	10	0	59	0	-	-	5.90	3	-
Iqbal Sikander	9	0	56	1	56.00	54.00	6.22	1	-
Aamer Sohail	1	0	11	0	-	-	11.00	-	-

Pakistan

Pakistan			Runs	Mins	Balls	4s	6s	SR
Aamer Sohail	c Jones	b Patel	14	26	20	1	-	70.00
Ramiz Raja	c Morrison	b Watson	44	81	55	6	-	80.00
Imran Khan*	c Larsen	b Harris	44	98	93	1	2	47.31
Javed Miandad		not out	57	125	69	4	-	82.60
Salim Malik	c (sub - Latham)	b Larsen	1	4	2	0	-	50.00
Inzamam-ul-Haq		run out	60	48	37	7	1	162.16
Wasim Akram		b Watson	9	12	8	1	-	112.50
Moin Khan†		not out	20	15	11	2	1	181.81
Iqbal Sikander								
Mushtaq Ahmed								
Aaqib Javed								
Extras	(b 4, lb 10, w 1)		15					
	49 overs (207 mins)		264 for 6					

Fall: 1-30 (Sohail) 2-84 (Ramiz) 3-134 (Imran) 4-140 (Malik) 5-227 (Inzamam) 6-238 (Akram)

	O	M	R	W	Ave	SR	ER	Wide	NB
DN Patel	10	1	50	1	50.00	60.00	5.00	-	-
DK Morrison	9	0	55	0	-	-	6.11	1	-
W Watson	10	2	39	2	19.50	30.00	3.90	-	-
GR Larsen	10	1	34	1	34.00	60.00	3.40	-	-
CZ Harris	10	0	72	1	72.00	60.00	7.20	-	-

2nd Semi-Final – March 22, 1992: England vs South Africa (SCG, Sydney) – D/N

Toss: South Africa   Umpires: BL Aldridge & SG Randell
Crowd: 35,088   MOTM: GA Hick
England won by 19 runs (South Africa required 252 off 43 overs)

England			Runs	Mins	Balls	4s	6s	SR
GA Gooch*	c Richardson	b Donald	2	15	8	-	-	25.00
IT Botham		b Pringle	21	38	27	3	-	77.78
AJ Stewart†	c Richardson	b McMillan	33	87	58	4	-	56.90
GA Hick	c Rhodes	b Snell	83	133	90	9	-	92.22
NH Fairbrother		b Pringle	28	64	50	1	-	56.00
AJ Lamb	c Richardson	b Donald	19	27	22	1	-	86.36
CC Lewis		not out	18	37	17	2	-	105.88
DA Reeve		not out	25	13	14	4	-	178.57
PAJ DeFreitas								
RK Illingworth								
GC Small								
Extras	(b 1, lb 7, w 9, nb 6)		23					
45 overs (210 mins)			252 for 6					

Fall: 1-20 (Gooch) 2-39 (Botham) 3-110 (Stewart) 4-183 (Fairbrother) 5-187 (Hick) 6-221 (Lamb)

	O	M	R	W	Ave	SR	ER	Wide	NB
AA Donald	10	0	69	2	34.50	30.00	6.90	5	2
MW Pringle	9	2	36	2	18.00	27.00	4.00	2	4
RP Snell	8	0	52	1	52.00	48.00	6.50	2	-
BM McMillan	9	0	47	1	47.00	54.00	5.22	-	-
AP Kuiper	5	0	26	0	-	-	5.20	-	-
WJ Cronje	4	0	14	0	-	-	3.50	-	-

South Africa			Runs	Mins	Balls	4s	6s	SR
KC Wessels*	c Lewis	b Botham	17	17	23	1	-	73.91
AC Hudson	lbw	b Illingworth	46	78	53	6	-	86.79
PN Kirsten		b DeFreitas	11	30	26		-	42.31
AP Kuiper		b Illingworth	36	62	44	5	-	81.82
WJ Cronje	c Hick	b Small	24	72	46	1	-	52.17
JN Rhodes	c Lewis	b Small	43	61	39	3	-	110.26
BM McMillan		not out	21	41	21	-	-	100.00
DJ Richardson†		not out	13	19	10	1	-	130.00
RP Snell								
MW Pringle								
AA Donald								
Extras	(lb 17, w 4)		21					
43 overs (193 mins)			232 for 6					

Fall: 1-26 (Wessels) 2-61 (Kirsten) 3-90 (Hudson) 4-131 (Kuiper) 5-176 (Cronje) 6-206 (Rhodes)

	O	M	R	W	Ave	SR	ER	Wide	NB
IT Botham	10	0	52	1	52.00	60.00	5.20	3	-
CC Lewis	5	0	38	0	-	-	7.60	-	-
PAJ DeFreitas	8	1	28	1	28.00	48.00	3.50	1	-
RK Illingworth	10	1	46	2	23.00	30.00	4.60	-	-
GC Small	10	1	51	2	25.50	30.00	5.10	-	-

Final – March 25, 1992: England vs Pakistan (MCG, Melbourne) – D/N

Toss: Pakistan   Umpires: BL Aldridge & SU Bucknor

Crowd: 87,182   MOTM: Wasim Akram

Pakistan won by 22 runs

Pakistan			Runs	Mins	Balls	4s	6s	SR
Aamer Sohail	c Stewart	b Pringle	4	20	19	-	-	21.05
Ramiz Raja	lbw	b Pringle	8	36	26	1	-	30.77
Imran Khan*	c Illingworth	b Botham	72	159	110	5	1	65.45
Javed Miandad	c Botham	b Illingworth	58	125	98	4	-	59.18
Inzamam-ul-Haq		b Pringle	42	46	35	4	-	120.00
Wasim Akram		run out	33	21	19	4	-	173.68
Salim Malik		not out	0	2	1	-	-	0.00
Moin Khan†								
Ijaz Ahmed								
Aaqib Javed								
Mushtaq Ahmed								
Extras	(lb 19, w 6, nb 7)		32					
	50 overs (212 mins)		249 for 6					

Fall: 1-20 (Sohail) 2-24 (Ramiz) 3-163 (Miandad) 4-197 (Imran) 5-249 (Inzamam) 6-249 (Akram)

	O	M	R	W	Ave	SR	ER	Wide	NB
DR Pringle	10	2	22	3	7.33	20.00	2.20	3	5
CC Lewis	10	2	52	0	-	-	5.20	1	2
IT Botham	7	0	42	1	42.00	42.00	6.00	1	-
PAJ DeFreitas	10	1	42	0	-	-	4.20	-	-
RK Illingworth	10	0	50	1	50.00	60.00	5.00	-	-
DA Reeve	3	0	22	0	-	-	7.33	1	-

England			Runs	Mins	Balls	4s	6s	SR
GA Gooch*	c Aaqib	b Mushtaq	29	93	66	1	-	43.94
IT Botham	c Moin	b Wasim	0	12	6	-	-	0.00
AJ Stewart†	c Moin	b Aaqib	7	22	16	1	-	43.75
GA Hick	lbw	b Mushtaq	17	49	36	1	-	47.22
NH Fairbrother	c Moin	b Aaqib	62	97	70	3	-	88.57
AJ Lamb		b Wasim	31	54	41	2	-	75.61
CC Lewis		b Wasim	0	1	1	-	-	0.00
DA Reeve	c Ramiz	b Mushtaq	15	38	32	-	-	46.88
DR Pringle		not out	18	29	16	1	-	112.50
PAJ DeFreitas		run out	10	13	8	-	-	125.00
RK Illingworth	c Ramiz	b Imran	14	9	11	2	-	127.27
Extras	(lb 5, w 13, nb 6)		24					
	49.2 overs (213 mins)		227					

Fall: 1-6 (Botham) 2-21 (Stewart) 3-59 (Hick) 4-69 (Gooch) 5-141 (Lamb) 6-141 (Lewis) 7-180 (Fairbrother) 8-183 (Reeve) 9-208 (DeFreitas) 10-227 (Illingworth)

	O	M	R	W	Ave	SR	ER	Wide	NB
Wasim Akram	10	0	49	3	16.33	20.00	4.90	6	4
Aaqib Javed	10	2	27	2	13.50	30.00	2.70	3	1
Mushtaq Ahmed	10	1	41	3	13.67	20.00	4.10	1	-
Ijaz Ahmed	3	0	13	0	-	-	4.33	2	-
Imran Khan	6.2	0	43	1	43.00	38.00	6.79	-	1
Aamer Sohail	10	0	49	0	-	-	4.90	1	-

Appendix 2

TEAM

Highest totals

Team	Score	Overs	RR	I	Opposition	Ground	Match Date
Sri Lanka	313/7	49.2	6.34	2	v Zimbabwe	New Plymouth	February 23, 1992
Zimbabwe	312/4	50	6.24	1	v Sri Lanka	New Plymouth	February 23, 1992
England	280/6	50	5.60	1	v Sri Lanka	Ballarat	March 9, 1992
West Indies	268/8	50	5.36	1	v Sri Lanka	Berri	March 13, 1992
Australia	265/6	46	5.76	1	v Zimbabwe	Hobart	March 14, 1992
Pakistan	264/6	49	5.38	2	v New Zealand	Auckland	March 21, 1992
West Indies	264/8	50	5.28	1	v Zimbabwe	Brisbane	February 29, 1992
New Zealand	262/7	50	5.24	1	v Pakistan	Auckland	March 21, 1992
Pakistan	254/4	50	5.08	1	v Zimbabwe	Hobart	February 27, 1992
England	252/6	45	5.60	1	v South Africa	Sydney	March 22, 1992

By runs

Winner	Margin	Target	Opposition	Ground	Match Date
Australia	128 runs	266	v Zimbabwe	Hobart	March 14, 1992
England	106 runs	281	v Sri Lanka	Ballarat	March 9, 1992
West Indies	91 runs	269	v Sri Lanka	Berri	March 13, 1992
West Indies	75 runs	265	v Zimbabwe	Brisbane	February 29, 1992
South Africa	64 runs	201	v West Indies	Christchurch	March 5, 1992
Australia	57 runs	217	v West Indies	Melbourne	March 18, 1992
India	55 runs	159	v Zimbabwe	Hamilton	March 7, 1992
Pakistan	53 runs	255	v Zimbabwe	Hobart	February 27, 1992
New Zealand	48 runs	154	v Zimbabwe	Napier	March 3, 1992
Pakistan	48 runs	221	v Australia	Perth	March 11, 1992

By wickets

Winner	Margin	Balls Rem	Target	Overs	Opposition	Ground	Match Date
West Indies	10 wickets	19	221	46.5	v Pakistan	Melbourne	February 23, 1992
South Africa	9 wickets	13	171	46.5	v Australia	Sydney	February 26, 1992
England	8 wickets	55	172	40.5	v Australia	Sydney	March 5, 1992
New Zealand	7 wickets	93	191	34.3	v South Africa	Auckland	February 29, 1992
Australia	7 wickets	36	190	44.0	v Sri Lanka	Adelaide	March 7, 1992
South Africa	7 wickets	29	164	45.1	v Zimbabwe	Canberra	March 10, 1992
New Zealand	7 wickets	55	201	40.5	v England	Wellington	March 15, 1992
Pakistan	7 wickets	32	167	44.4	v New Zealand	Christchurch	March 18, 1992

CATCHES

Most catches

Player	M	I	Ct
KC Wessels (SA)	9	9	7
NH Fairbrother (ENG)	9	9	6
CL Cairns (NZ)	5	5	5
AR Border (AUS)	8	8	5
GR Larsen (NZ)	9	9	5
DA Reeve (ENG)	9	9	5
PAJ DeFreitas (ENG)	10	10	5
GA Hick (ENG)	10	10	5

Wicketkeeper Dismissals

Player	M	I	Dis	Ct	St
DJ Richardson (SA)	9	9	15	14	1
D Williams (WI)	8	8	14	11	3
Moin Khan (PAK)	10	10	14	11	3
IA Healy (AUS)	7	7	9	9	0
AJ Stewart (ENG)	10	10	9	8	1
KS More (INDIA)	8	7	7	6	1
A Flower (ZIM)	8	8	7	6	1
HP Tillakaratne (SL)	8	8	7	6	1
IDS Smith (NZ)	9	9	5	5	0

BATTING

Most runs

Player		M	I	NO	Runs	HS	Ave	BF	SR	100	50	0	4s	6s
MD Crowe	NZ	9	9	5	456	100*	114.00	502	90.83	1	4	0	45	6
Javed Miandad	PAK	9	9	2	437	89	62.42	698	62.60	0	5	0	27	0
PN Kirsten	SA	8	8	2	410	90	68.33	616	66.55	0	4	0	28	2
DC Boon	AUS	8	8	1	368	100	52.57	534	68.91	2	0	0	34	2
Ramiz Raja	PAK	8	8	2	349	119*	58.16	539	64.74	2	0	0	35	0
BC Lara	WI	8	8	1	333	88*	47.57	408	81.61	0	4	1	34+	1+
M Azharuddin	INDIA	8	7	0	332	93	47.42	425	78.11	0	4	1	29	1
Aamer Sohail	PAK	10	10	0	326	114	32.60	515	63.30	1	2	1	32	0
AH Jones	NZ	9	9	2	322	78	46.00	523	61.56	0	3	0	41	0
MJ Greatbatch	NZ	7	7	0	313	73	44.71	356	87.92	0	3	0	32	13
KC Wessels	SA	9	9	2	313	85	44.71	583	53.68	0	3	0	23	0
AC Hudson	SA	8	8	0	296	79	37.00	467	63.38	0	3	0	32	0
NH Fairbrother	ENG	9	7	2	285	75*	57.00	412	69.17	0	3	0	15	2
SR Tendulkar	INDIA	8	7	1	283	84	47.16	334	84.73	0	3	0	24	1
DM Jones	AUS	8	8	1	276	90	39.42	407	67.81	0	2	0	18	3
GA Hick	ENG	10	9	1	264	83	33.00	334	79.04	0	3	1	24	2
A Ranatunga	SL	8	7	2	262	88*	52.40	322	81.36	0	2	0	23	2
AJ Stewart	ENG	10	8	1	259	77	37.00	365	70.95	0	2	0	30	1
DL Haynes	WI	7	7	1	251	93*	41.83	443	56.65	0	1	0	23	2
RS Mahanama	SL	8	7	0	246	80	35.14	456	53.94	0	3	0	19	0
A Flower	ZIM	8	8	2	246	115*	41.00	386	63.73	1	0	0	18	1
KLT Arthurton	WI	8	7	1	233	58*	38.83	351	66.38	0	2	1	12	4
Inzamam-ul-Haq	PAK	10	10	0	225	60	22.50	240	93.75	0	1	1	17	1
MAR Samarasekera	SL	6	6	0	219	75	36.50	273	80.21	0	1	0	24	2
GA Gooch	ENG	8	8	0	216	65	27.00	419	51.55	0	3	1	17	0

Highest averages

Player		M	I	NO	Runs	HS	Ave	BF	SR	100	50	0	4s	6s
MD Crowe	NZ	9	9	5	456	100*	114.00	502	90.83	1	4	0	45	6
PN Kirsten	SA	8	8	2	410	90	68.33	616	66.55	0	4	0	28	2
BM McMillan	SA	9	5	3	125	33*	62.50	154	81.16	0	0	0	4	0
Javed Miandad	PAK	9	9	2	437	89	62.42	698	62.60	0	5	0	27	0
Ramiz Raja	PAK	8	8	2	349	119*	58.16	539	64.74	2	0	0	35	0
NH Fairbrother	ENG	9	7	2	285	75*	57.00	412	69.17	0	3	0	15	2
DC Boon	AUS	8	8	1	368	100	52.57	534	68.91	2	0	0	34	2
A Ranatunga	SL	8	7	2	262	88*	52.40	322	81.36	0	2	0	23	2
BC Lara	WI	8	8	1	333	88*	47.57	408	81.61	0	4	1	34+	1+
M Azharuddin	INDIA	8	7	0	332	93	47.42	425	78.11	0	4	1	29	1

Highest strike rates

Player		M	I	NO	Runs	HS	Ave	BF	SR	100	50	0	4s	6s
CC Lewis	ENG	9	6	2	81	33	20.25	52	155.76	0	0	2	8	2
ST Banerjee	INDIA	2	2	1	36	25*	36.00	25	144.00	0	0	0	2	1
IDS Smith	NZ	9	5	1	61	19	15.25	44	138.63	0	0	0	9	0
Kapil Dev	INDIA	8	8	1	161	42	23.00	128	125.78	0	0	0	15	3
J Srinath	INDIA	8	6	5	34	11	34.00	28	121.42	0	0	0	1	0
RP Snell	SA	9	4	2	24	11*	12.00	20	120.00	0	0	0	3	0
CL Cairns	NZ	5	3	3	21	16*	-	18	116.66	0	0	0	3	0
KS More	INDIA	8	6	2	41	15*	10.25	37	110.81	0	0	0	3	1
Wasim Akram	PAK	10	8	2	62	33	10.33	61	101.63	0	0	1	7	0
ME Waugh	AUS	5	5	1	145	66*	36.25	144	100.69	0	1	0	8	2

High scores

Player	Runs	Balls	4s	6s	SR	Team/Opposition/Ground /Match Date
Ramiz Raja	119*	155	16	0	76.77	Pakistan v New Zealand, Christchurch, March 18, 1992
A Flower	115*	152	8	1	75.65	Zimbabwe v Sri Lanka, New Plymouth, February 23, 1992
Aamer Sohail	114	136	12	0	83.82	Pakistan v Zimbabwe, Hobart, February 27, 1992
PV Simmons	110	125	8	2	88.00	West Indies v Sri Lanka, Berri, March 13, 1992
Ramiz Raja	102*	158	4	0	64.55	Pakistan v West Indies, Melbourne , February 23, 1992
MD Crowe	100*	134	11	0	74.62	New Zealand v Australia, Auckland, February 22, 1992
DC Boon	100	133	11	0	75.18	Australia v New Zealand, Auckland, February 22, 1992
DC Boon	100	147	8	0	68.02	Australia v West Indies, Melbourne, March 18, 1992

BOWLING

Most wickets

Player		M	I	O	Md	R	W	BBI	Ave	Econ	SR	4	5
Wasim Akram	PAK	10	10	89.4	3	338	18	4-32	18.77	3.76	29.80	1	0
IT Botham	ENG	10	10	89	7	306	16	4-31	19.12	3.43	33.30	1	0
Mushtaq Ahmed	PAK	9	8	78	3	311	16	3-41	19.43	3.98	29.20	0	0
CZ Harris	NZ	9	9	72.1	4	342	16	3-15	21.37	4.73	27.00	0	0
EA Brandes	ZIM	8	8	70.1	7	355	14	4-21	25.35	5.05	30.00	1	0
AA Donald	SA	9	9	78	5	329	13	3-34	25.30	4.21	36.00	0	0
M Prabhakar	INDIA	8	7	57.1	5	245	12	3-41	20.41	4.28	28.50	0	0
AC Cummins	WI	6	6	59	1	246	12	4-33	20.50	4.16	29.50	1	0
W Watson	NZ	8	8	79	11	301	12	3-37	25.08	3.81	39.50	0	0
BM McMillan	SA	9	9	73	7	306	11	3-30	27.81	4.19	39.80	0	0
PAJ DeFreitas	ENG	10	10	85.3	12	319	11	3-34	29.00	3.73	46.60	0	0
Aaqib Javed	PAK	10	10	84.5	11	328	11	3-21	29.81	3.86	46.20	0	0
WKM Benjamin	WI	8	8	79	8	297	10	3-27	29.70	3.75	47.40	0	0
MR Whitney	AUS	7	7	66	12	215	9	4-34	23.88	3.25	44.00	1	0
AP Kuiper	SA	9	8	41	0	235	9	3-40	26.11	5.73	27.30	0	0
Kapil Dev	INDIA	8	7	58	2	251	9	3-41	27.88	4.32	38.60	0	0
GR Larsen	NZ	9	9	76	7	262	9	3-16	29.11	3.44	50.60	0	0
DA Reeve	ENG	9	8	34.4	4	126	8	3-38	15.75	3.63	26.00	0	0
MW Pringle	SA	7	7	57	6	236	8	4-11	29.50	4.14	42.70	1	0
DN Patel	NZ	9	8	79	8	245	8	2-26	30.62	3.10	59.20	0	0
CJ McDermott	AUS	8	8	73	5	246	8	2-29	30.75	3.36	54.70	0	0
J Srinath	INDIA	8	7	53.1	3	249	8	2-23	31.12	4.68	39.80	0	0
RK Illingworth	ENG	6	6	58.1	2	250	8	3-33	31.25	4.29	43.60	0	0
SR Waugh	AUS	8	8	60.4	1	277	8	3-36	34.62	4.56	45.50	0	0
RP Snell	SA	9	9	72.5	10	310	8	3-42	38.75	4.25	54.60	0	0
CL Hooper	WI	8	8	80	2	312	8	2-19	39.00	3.90	60.00	0	0

Best averages

Player		M	I	O	Md	R	W	BBI	Ave	Econ	SR	4	5
DA Reeve	ENG	9		34.4	4	126	8	3-38	15.75	3.63	26.00	0	0
PN Kirsten	SA	8		18	1	87	5	3-31	17.40	4.83	21.60	0	0
Wasim Akram	PAK	10		89.4	3	338	18	4-32	18.77	3.76	29.80	1	0
DL Houghton	ZIM	8		2	0	19	1	1-19	19.00	9.50	12.00	0	0
IT Botham	ENG	10		89	7	306	16	4-31	19.12	3.43	33.30	1	0
UC Hathurusinghe	SL	4		17	0	97	5	4-57	19.40	5.70	20.40	1	0
Mushtaq Ahmed	PAK	9		78	3	311	16	3-41	19.43	3.98	29.20	0	0
M Prabhakar	INDIA	8		57.1	5	245	12	3-41	20.41	4.28	28.50	0	0
AC Cummins	WI	6		59	1	246	12	4-33	20.50	4.16	29.50	1	0
CZ Harris	NZ	9		72.1	4	342	16	3-15	21.37	4.73	27.00	0	0

Best economy rates

Player		M	I	O	Md	R	W	BBI	Ave	Econ	SR	4	5
BP Patterson	WI	1		10	0	25	1	1-25	25.00	2.50	60.00	0	0
O Henry	SA	1		10	0	31	1	1-31	31.00	3.10	60.00	0	0
DN Patel	NZ	9		79	8	245	8	2-26	30.62	3.10	59.20	0	0
MR Whitney	AUS	7		66	12	215	9	4-34	23.88	3.25	44.00	1	0
DR Pringle	ENG	8		66.4	15	218	7	3-8	31.14	3.27	57.10	0	0
CJ McDermott	AUS	8		73	5	246	8	2-29	30.75	3.36	54.70	0	0
IT Botham	ENG	10		89	7	306	16	4-31	19.12	3.43	33.30	1	0
GR Larsen	NZ	9		76	7	262	9	3-16	29.11	3.44	50.60	0	0
CEL Ambrose	WI	7		68	6	235	7	2-24	33.57	3.45	58.20	0	0
GC Small	ENG	5		35	3	127	5	2-29	25.40	3.62	42.00	0	0

Best strike rates

Player	M	I	O	Md	R	W	BBI	Ave	Econ	SR	4	5
DL Houghton	ZIM	8	2	0	19	1	1-19	19.00	9.50	12.00	0	0
UC Hathurusinghe	SL	4	17	0	97	5	4-57	19.40	5.70	20.40	1	0
PN Kirsten	SA	8	18	1	87	5	3-31	17.40	4.83	21.60	0	0
RJ Shastri	INDIA	2	4	0	28	1	1-28	28.00	7.00	24.00	0	0
DA Reeve	ENG	9	34.4	4	126	8	3-38	15.75	3.63	26.00	0	0
CZ Harris	NZ	9	72.1	4	342	16	3-15	21.37	4.73	27.00	0	0
AP Kuiper	SA	9	41	0	235	9	3-40	26.11	5.73	27.30	0	0
M Prabhakar	INDIA	8	57.1	5	245	12	3-41	20.41	4.28	28.50	0	0
Mushtaq Ahmed	PAK	9	78	3	311	16	3-41	19.43	3.98	29.20	0	0
AC Cummins	WI	6	59	1	246	12	4-33	20.50	4.16	29.50	1	0

Best bowling figures in an innings

Player	O	M	R	W	Econ	Team/Opposition/Ground/Match Date
MW Pringle	8	4	11	4	1.37	South Africa v West Indies, Christchurch, March 5, 1992
EA Brandes	10	4	21	4	2.10	Zimbabwe v England, Albury, March 18, 1992
CC Lewis	8	0	30	4	3.75	England v Sri Lanka, Ballarat, March 9, 1992
IT Botham	10	1	31	4	3.10	England v Australia, Sydney, March 5, 1992
Wasim Akram	9.2	0	32	4	3.42	Pakistan v New Zealand, Christchurch, March 18, 1992
AC Cummins	10	0	33	4	3.30	West Indies v India, Wellington, March 10, 1992
MR Whitney	10	1	34	4	3.40	Australia v West Indies, Melbourne, March 18, 1992
UC Hathurusinghe	8	0	57	4	7.12	Sri Lanka v West Indies, Berri, March 13, 1992

PARTNERSHIPS
Highest partnerships by wicket

Wkt	R	Partners	Team/Opposition/Ground/Match Date
1st	175*	DL Haynes, BC Lara	West Indies v Pakistan, Melbourne, February 23, 1992
2nd	127	M Azharuddin, SR Tendulkar	India v New Zealand, Dunedin, March 12, 1992
3rd	145	Aamer Sohail, Javed Miandad	Pakistan v Zimbabwe, Hobart, February 27, 1992
4th	118	MD Crowe, KR Rutherford	New Zealand v Australia, Auckland, February 22, 1992
5th	145*	A Flower, AC Waller	Zimbabwe v Sri Lanka, New Plymouth, February 23, 1992
6th	83*	KLT Arthurton, CL Hooper	West Indies v India, Wellington, March 10, 1992
7th	46	DL Haynes, AL Logie	West Indies v South Africa, Christchurch, March 5, 1992
8th	33	GF Labrooy, CPH Ramanayake	Sri Lanka v England, Ballarat, March 9, 1992
9th	44	GR Larsen, DK Morrison	New Zealand v Pakistan, Christchurch, March 18, 1992
10th	28*	RS Kalpage, GP Wickramasinghe	Sri Lanka v West Indies, Berri, March 13, 1992

Highest partnerships by runs

Partners	Runs	Wkt	Team/Opposition/Ground/Match Date
DL Haynes & BC Lara	175*	1st	West Indies v Pakistan, Melbourne, February 23, 1992
KC Wessels & AC Hudson	151	1st	South Africa v England, Melbourne, March 12, 1992
A Flower & AC Waller	145*	5th	Zimbabwe v Sri Lanka, New Plymouth, February 23, 1992
Aamer Sohail & Javed Miandad	145	3rd	Pakistan v Zimbabwe, Hobart, February 27, 1992
Imran Khan & Javed Miandad	139	3rd	Pakistan v England, Melbourne, March 25, 1992
AH Jones & MD Crowe	129	3rd	New Zealand v Zimbabwe, Napier, March 3, 1992
RS Mahanama & MAR Samarasekera	128	1st	Sri Lanka v Zimbabwe, New Plymouth, February 23, 1992
AC Hudson & PN Kirsten	128	1st	South Africa v India, Adelaide, March 15, 1992
M Azharuddin & SR Tendulkar	127	2nd	India v New Zealand, Dunedin, March 12, 1992
Ramiz Raja & Javed Miandad	123*	3rd	Pakistan v West Indies, Melbourne, February 23, 1992
TM Moody & GR Marsh	120	1st	Australia v Sri Lanka, Adelaide, March 7, 1992
MD Crowe & KR Rutherford	118	4th	New Zealand v Australia, Auckland, February 22, 1992
RB Richardson & CL Hooper	117	3rd	West Indies v Zimbabwe, Brisbane, February 29, 1992
Ramiz Raja & Javed Miandad	115	3rd	Pakistan v New Zealand, Christchurch, March 18, 1992
MJ Greatbatch & RT Latham	114	1st	New Zealand v South Africa, Auckland, February 29, 1992
ME Waugh & SR Waugh	113	5th	Australia v Zimbabwe, Hobart, March 14, 1992
KC Wessels & PN Kirsten	112	2nd	South Africa v Zimbabwe, Canberra, March 10, 1992
GA Gooch & RA Smith	110	2nd	England v India, Perth, February 22, 1992
AH Jones & MD Crowe	108	3rd	New Zealand v England, Wellington, March 15, 1992
GA Gooch & IT Botham	107	1st	England v Australia, Sydney, March 5, 1992
TM Moody & DC Boon	107	1st	Australia v West Indies, Melbourne, March 18, 1992
MD Crowe & KR Rutherford	107	4th	New Zealand v Pakistan, Auckland, March 21, 1992
Javed Miandad & Salim Malik	101	4th	Pakistan v Sri Lanka, Perth, March 15, 1992

Appendix 3

BATTING

Australia batting averages

Player	M	I	NO	R	HS	Ave	BF	SR	100	50	0	4s	6s
DC Boon	8	8	1	368	100	52.57	534	68.91	2	0	0	34	2
DM Jones	8	8	1	276	90	39.42	407	67.81	0	2	0	18	3
ME Waugh	5	5	1	145	66*	36.25	144	100.69	0	1	0	8	2
GR Marsh	5	5	0	151	60	30.20	360	41.94	0	1	0	8	1
SR Waugh	8	7	0	187	55	26.71	239	78.24	0	1	0	12	1
TM Moody	8	8	0	202	57	25.25	337	59.94	0	2	0	13	0
MR Whitney	7	3	2	22	9*	22.00	51	43.13	0	0	0	2	0
IA Healy	7	6	2	51	16	12.75	68	75.00	0	0	1	2	1
AR Border	8	7	0	60	22	8.57	85	70.58	0	0	1	4	0
MA Taylor	2	2	0	13	13	6.50	31	41.93	0	0	1	0	0
BA Reid	6	4	2	9	5*	4.50	35	25.71	0	0	0	0	0
PL Taylor	7	6	2	17	10*	4.25	21	80.95	0	0	1	1	0
CJ McDermott	8	5	0	9	6	1.80	22	40.90	0	0	2	0	0
MG Hughes	1	1	1	0	0*	-	4	0	0	0	0	0	0

England batting averages

Player	M	I	NO	R	HS	Ave	BF	SR	100	50	0	4s	6s
NH Fairbrother	9	7	2	285	75*	57.00	412	69.17	0	3	0	15	2
DA Reeve	9	5	3	79	25*	39.50	96	82.29	0	0	0	5	0
AJ Stewart	10	8	1	259	77	37.00	365	70.95	0	2	0	30	1
GA Hick	10	9	1	264	83	33.00	334	79.04	0	3	1	24	2
RA Smith	8	8	2	193	91	32.16	333	57.95	0	1	1	20	2
GA Gooch	8	8	0	216	65	27.00	419	51.55	0	3	1	17	0
IT Botham	10	10	1	192	53	21.33	329	58.35	0	1	1	21	2
CC Lewis	9	6	2	81	33	20.25	52	155.76	0	0	2	8	2
AJ Lamb	4	4	0	79	31	19.75	118	66.94	0	0	0	5	0
RK Illingworth	6	3	1	27	14	13.50	32	84.37	0	0	0	2	0
DR Pringle	8	5	2	30	18*	10.00	38	78.94	0	0	0	1	0
GC Small	5	1	0	5	5	5.00	18	27.77	0	0	0	0	0
PAJ DeFreitas	10	5	1	16	10	4.00	32	50.00	0	0	1	0	0
PCR Tufnell	4	2	2	3	3*	-	5	60.00	0	0	0	0	0

India batting averages

Player	M	I	NO	R	HS	Ave	BF	SR	100	50	0	4s	6s
M Azharuddin	8	7	0	332	93	47.42	425	78.11	0	4	1	29	1
SR Tendulkar	8	7	1	283	84	47.16	334	84.73	0	3	0	24	1
RJ Shastri	2	2	0	82	57	41.00	179	45.81	0	1	0	3	0
ST Banerjee	2	2	1	36	25*	36.00	25	144.00	0	0	0	2	1
J Srinath	8	6	5	34	11	34.00	28	121.42	0	0	0	1	0
SV Manjrekar	6	6	0	154	47	25.66	195	78.97	0	0	1	5	1
AD Jadeja	6	5	1	93	46	23.25	180	51.66	0	0	0	5	0
Kapil Dev	8	8	1	161	42	23.00	128	125.78	0	0	0	15	3
K Srikkanth	8	8	1	117	40	16.71	211	55.45	0	0	3	14	0
PK Amre	4	3	1	27	22	13.50	40	67.50	0	0	0	0	0
KS More	8	6	2	41	15*	10.25	37	110.81	0	0	0	3	1
VG Kambli	5	4	0	29	24	7.25	57	50.87	0	0	0	0	0
M Prabhakar	8	4	1	11	8	3.66	14	78.57	0	0	1	1	0
SLV Raju	7	2	0	1	1	0.50	1	100.00	0	0	1	0	0

New Zealand batting averages

Player	M	I	NO	R	HS	Ave	BF	SR	100	50	0	4s	6s
MD Crowe	9	9	5	456	100*	114.00	502	90.83	1	4	0	45	6
AH Jones	9	9	2	322	78	46.00	523	61.56	0	3	0	41	0
GR Larsen	9	2	1	45	37	45.00	86	52.32	0	0	0	4	0
MJ Greatbatch	7	7	0	313	73	44.71	356	87.92	0	3	0	32	13
KR Rutherford	9	7	2	212	65*	42.40	311	68.16	0	3	0	21	3
RT Latham	7	7	0	136	60	19.42	218	62.38	0	1	0	17	0
JG Wright	4	4	0	71	57	17.75	126	56.34	0	1	1	10	0
IDS Smith	9	5	1	61	19	15.25	44	138.63	0	0	0	9	0
DN Patel	9	3	1	25	10*	12.50	37	67.56	0	0	0	1	0
DK Morrison	5	1	0	12	12	12.00	45	26.66	0	0	0	1	0
CZ Harris	9	6	1	44	14	8.80	78	56.41	0	0	0	3	0
CL Cairns	5	3	3	21	16*	-	18	116.66	0	0	0	3	0
W Watson	8	1	1	5	5*	-	13	38.46	0	0	0	0	0

Pakistan batting averages

Player	M	I	NO	R	HS	Ave	BF	SR	100	50	0	4s	6s
Javed Miandad	9	9	2	437	89	62.42	698	62.60	0	5	0	27	0
Ramiz Raja	8	8	2	349	119*	58.16	539	64.74	2	0	0	35	0
Aamer Sohail	10	10	0	326	114	32.60	515	63.30	1	2	1	32	0
Imran Khan	8	6	0	185	72	30.83	351	52.70	0	1	1	13	4
Inzamam-ul-Haq	10	10	0	225	60	22.50	240	93.75	0	1	1	17	1
Salim Malik	10	9	3	116	51	19.33	150	77.33	0	1	1	8	0
Moin Khan	10	5	2	44	20*	14.66	50	88.00	0	0	0	3	1
Wasim Haider	3	2	0	26	13	13.00	70	37.14	0	0	0	1	0
Wasim Akram	10	8	2	62	33	10.33	61	101.63	0	0	1	7	0
Mushtaq Ahmed	9	4	1	27	17	9.00	56	48.21	0	0	0	1	0
Zahid Fazal	2	2	0	13	11	6.50	50	26.00	0	0	0	1	0
Ijaz Ahmed	7	4	1	14	8*	4.66	26	53.84	0	0	2	2	0
Aaqib Javed	10	2	2	2	1*	-	33	6.06	0	0	0	0	0
Iqbal Sikander	4	1	1	1	1*	-	3	33.33	0	0	0	0	0

South Africa batting averages

Player	M	I	NO	R	HS	Ave	BF	SR	100	50	0	4s	6s
PN Kirsten	8	8	2	410	90	68.33	616	66.55	0	4	0	28	2
BM McMillan	9	5	3	125	33*	62.50	154	81.16	0	0	0	4	0
KC Wessels	9	9	2	313	85	44.71	583	53.68	0	3	0	23	0
AC Hudson	8	8	0	296	79	37.00	467	63.38	0	3	0	32	0
WJ Cronje	8	6	3	102	47*	34.00	148	68.91	0	0	0	6	0
DJ Richardson	9	5	2	66	28	22.00	99	66.66	0	0	1	3	0
JN Rhodes	9	8	1	132	43	18.85	146	90.41	0	0	0	5	1
MW Rushmere	3	3	0	49	35	16.33	103	47.57	0	0	0	2	0
AP Kuiper	9	8	1	113	36	16.14	158	71.51	0	0	0	9	1
RP Snell	9	4	2	24	11*	12.00	20	120.00	0	0	0	3	0
O Henry	1	1	0	11	11	11.00	13	84.61	0	0	0	1	0
AA Donald	9	1	0	3	3	3.00	6	50.00	0	0	0	0	0
MW Pringle	7	1	1	5	5*	-	6	83.33	0	0	0	0	0
T Bosch	1	-	-	-	-	-	-	-	-	-	-	-	-

Sri Lanka batting averages

Player	M	I	NO	R	HS	Ave	BF	SR	100	50	0	4s	6s
A Ranatunga	8	7	2	262	88*	52.40	322	81.36	0	2	0	23	2
MAR Samarasekera	6	6	0	219	75	36.50	273	80.21	0	1	0	24	2
RS Mahanama	8	7	0	246	80	35.14	456	53.94	0	3	0	19	0
PA de Silva	8	7	0	175	62	25.00	257	68.09	0	1	0	9	0
GF Labrooy	1	1	0	19	19	19.00	34	55.88	0	0	0	1	0
RS Kalpage	7	6	2	67	14	16.75	111	60.36	0	0	0	2	0
ST Jayasuriya	6	5	0	74	32	14.80	82	90.24	0	0	0	5	2
HP Tillakaratne	8	7	1	80	25*	13.33	180	44.44	0	0	0	4	1
SD Anurasiri	5	4	2	21	11	10.50	36	58.33	0	0	0	0	0
AP Gurusinha	8	7	0	73	37	10.42	159	45.91	0	0	1	3	0
UC Hathurusinghe	4	3	0	26	16	8.66	63	41.26	0	0	0	1	0
CPH Ramanayake	8	6	2	25	12	6.25	65	38.46	0	0	0	1	0
GP Wickramasinghe	8	3	3	30	21*	-	41	73.17	0	0	0	1	0
KIW Wijegunawardene	3	-	-	-	-	-	-	-	-	-	-	-	-

West Indies batting averages

Player	M	I	NO	R	HS	Ave	BF	SR	100	50	0	4s	6s
BC Lara	8	8	1	333	88*	47.57	408	81.61	0	4	1	34	1
DL Haynes	7	7	1	251	93*	41.83	443	56.65	0	1	0	23	2
KLT Arthurton	8	7	1	233	58*	38.83	351	66.38	0	2	1	12	4
PV Simmons	4	4	0	153	110	38.25	191	80.10	1	0	1	13	3
WKM Benjamin	8	6	4	54	24*	27.00	59	91.52	0	0	0	4	0
CL Hooper	8	7	1	120	63	20.00	180	66.66	0	1	1	9	1
RB Richardson	8	8	1	132	56	18.85	265	49.81	0	1	0	5	2
AL Logie	8	7	0	101	61	14.42	133	75.93	0	1	1	10	2
D Williams	8	6	2	52	32*	13.00	70	74.28	0	0	1	6	0
CEL Ambrose	7	4	1	33	15*	11.00	42	78.57	0	0	0	2	1
AC Cummins	6	2	1	11	6	11.00	34	32.35	0	0	0	0	0
MD Marshall	5	4	0	16	6	4.00	42	38.09	0	0	0	1	0
RA Harper	2	1	0	3	3	3.00	14	21.42	0	0	0	0	0
BP Patterson	1	-	-	-	-	-	-	-	-	-	-	-	-

Zimbabwe batting averages

Player	M	I	NO	R	HS	Ave	BF	SR	100	50	0	4s	6s
A Flower	8	8	2	246	115*	41.00	386	63.73	1	0	0	18	1
AC Waller	8	8	2	192	83*	32.00	191	100.52	0	1	1	19	5
AH Shah	7	7	1	160	60*	26.66	270	59.25	0	1	0	12	0
DL Houghton	8	7	0	165	55	23.57	340	48.52	0	1	0	11	0
KJ Arnott	5	5	1	94	52	23.50	201	46.76	0	1	0	5	1
IP Butchart	5	3	0	60	33	20.00	70	85.71	0	0	0	6	0
AJ Traicos	8	5	3	35	16*	17.50	81	43.20	0	0	0	1	0
EA Brandes	8	6	1	71	23	14.20	101	70.29	0	0	0	5	1
MP Jarvis	5	3	1	28	17	14.00	31	90.32	0	0	0	2	1
WR James	4	3	0	35	17	11.66	79	44.30	0	0	0	4	0
MG Burmester	4	3	1	17	12	8.50	37	45.94	0	0	0	0	0
AJ Pycroft	8	7	1	50	19	8.33	131	38.16	0	0	2	0	0
KG Duers	6	2	1	7	5	7.00	20	35.00	0	0	0	0	0
ADR Campbell	4	3	0	13	8	4.33	48	27.08	0	0	0	2	0

BOWLING

Australia bowling averages

Player	M	I	O	M	R	W	BBI	Ave	Econ	SR	4	5	Ct	St
MR Whitney	7	7	66	12	215	9	4-34	23.88	3.25	44.00	1	0	0	0
PL Taylor	7	6	37.4	1	147	5	2-14	29.40	3.90	45.20	0	0	1	0
CJ McDermott	8	8	73	5	246	8	2-29	30.75	3.36	54.70	0	0	2	0
TM Moody	8	8	49	2	225	7	3-56	32.14	4.59	42.00	0	0	2	0
SR Waugh	8	8	60.4	1	277	8	3-36	34.62	4.56	45.50	0	0	2	0
MG Hughes	1	1	9	1	49	1	1-49	49.00	5.44	54.00	0	0	0	0
AR Border	8	2	14	0	53	1	1-40	53.00	3.78	84.00	0	0	5	0
BA Reid	6	6	54.4	3	209	3	1-17	69.66	3.82	109.30	0	0	0	0
ME Waugh	5	2	5	0	40	0	0-13	-	8.00	-	0	0	4	0

England bowling averages

Player	M	I	O	M	R	W	BBI	Ave	Econ	SR	4	5	Ct	St
DA Reeve	9	8	34.4	4	126	8	3-38	15.75	3.63	26.00	0	0	5	0
IT Botham	10	10	89	7	306	16	4-31	19.12	3.43	33.30	1	0	4	0
GC Small	5	5	35	3	127	5	2-29	25.40	3.62	42.00	0	0	0	0
PAJ DeFreitas	10	10	85.3	12	319	11	3-34	29.00	3.73	46.60	0	0	5	0
CC Lewis	9	6	50.4	5	214	7	4-30	30.57	4.22	43.40	1	0	4	0
DR Pringle	8	8	66.4	15	218	7	3-8	31.14	3.27	57.10	0	0	2	0
RK Illingworth	6	6	58.1	2	250	8	3-33	31.25	4.29	43.60	0	0	3	0
GA Hick	10	2	14.2	0	70	2	2-44	35.00	4.88	43.00	0	0	5	0
PCR Tufnell	4	4	28	2	133	3	2-36	44.33	4.75	56.00	0	0	0	0

India bowling averages

Player	M	I	O	M	R	W	BBI	Ave	Econ	SR	4	5	Ct	St
M Prabhakar	8	7	57.1	5	245	12	3-41	20.41	4.28	28.50	0	0	1	0
Kapil Dev	8	7	58	2	251	9	3-41	27.88	4.32	38.60	0	0	0	0
RJ Shastri	2	1	4	0	28	1	1-28	28.00	7.00	24.00	0	0	1	0
J Srinath	8	7	53.1	3	249	8	2-23	31.12	4.68	39.80	0	0	0	0
SLV Raju	7	6	48.1	3	208	5	2-38	41.60	4.31	57.80	0	0	1	0
ST Banerjee	2	2	13	1	85	1	1-45	85.00	6.53	78.00	0	0	2	0
SR Tendulkar	8	7	41	0	180	2	1-35	90.00	4.39	123.00	0	0	2	0
AD Jadeja	6	2	7.2	0	39	0	0-5	-	5.31	-	0	0	2	0
K Srikkanth	8	2	2.1	0	15	0	0-7	-	6.92	-	0	0	4	0

New Zealand bowling averages

Player	M	I	O	M	R	W	BBI	Ave	Econ	SR	4	5	Ct	St
CZ Harris	9	9	72.1	4	342	16	3-15	21.37	4.73	27.00	0	0	4	0
W Watson	8	8	79	11	301	12	3-37	25.08	3.81	39.50	0	0	1	0
AH Jones	9	2	12	0	52	2	2-42	26.00	4.33	36.00	0	0	2	0
GR Larsen	9	9	76	7	262	9	3-16	29.11	3.44	50.60	0	0	5	0
DN Patel	9	8	79	8	245	8	2-26	30.62	3.10	59.20	0	0	2	0
DK Morrison	5	5	40	1	180	5	3-42	36.00	4.50	48.00	0	0	1	0
CL Cairns	5	5	25	1	161	2	2-43	80.50	6.44	75.00	0	0	5	0
RT Latham	7	7	23	0	136	1	1-35	136.00	5.91	138.00	0	0	3	0
MJ Greatbatch	7	1	1	0	5	0	0-5	-	5.00	-	0	0	4	0
MD Crowe	9	1	1	0	6	0	0-6	-	6.00	-	0	0	3	0
KR Rutherford	9	1	1.4	0	11	0	0-11	-	6.60	-	0	0	3	0

Pakistan bowling averages

Player	M	I	O	M	R	W	BBI	Ave	Econ	SR	4	5	Ct	St
Wasim Akram	10	10	89.4	3	338	18	4-32	18.77	3.76	29.80	1	0	1	0
Mushtaq Ahmed	9	8	78	3	311	16	3-41	19.43	3.98	29.20	0	0	2	0
Aaqib Javed	10	10	84.5	11	328	11	3-21	29.81	3.86	46.20	0	0	2	0
Imran Khan	8	7	60.2	2	251	7	2-32	35.85	4.16	51.70	0	0	1	0
Aamer Sohail	10	7	40	2	184	4	2-26	46.00	4.60	60.00	0	0	3	0
Iqbal Sikander	4	4	35	2	147	3	1-30	49.00	4.20	70.00	0	0	0	0
Wasim Haider	3	3	19	1	79	1	1-36	79.00	4.15	114.00	0	0	0	0
Ijaz Ahmed	7	7	36	1	149	1	1-28	149.00	4.13	216.00	0	0	4	0
Salim Malik	10	1	4	0	18	0	0-18	-	4.50	-	0	0	3	0

South Africa bowling averages

Player	M	I	O	M	R	W	BBI	Ave	Econ	SR	4	5	Ct	St
PN Kirsten	8	4	18	1	87	5	3-31	17.40	4.83	21.60	0	0	2	0
AA Donald	9	9	78	5	329	13	3-34	25.30	4.21	36.00	0	0	1	0
AP Kuiper	9	8	41	0	235	9	3-40	26.11	5.73	27.30	0	0	3	0
BM McMillan	9	9	73	7	306	11	3-30	27.81	4.19	39.80	0	0	4	0
MW Pringle	7	7	57	6	236	8	4-11	29.50	4.14	42.70	1	0	1	0
O Henry	1	1	10	0	31	1	1-31	31.00	3.10	60.00	0	0	0	0
RP Snell	9	9	72.5	10	310	8	3-42	38.75	4.25	54.60	0	0	1	0
WJ Cronje	8	6	20	1	85	2	2-17	42.50	4.25	60.00	0	0	3	0
T Bosch	1	1	2.3	0	19	0	0-19	-	7.60	-	0	0	0	0

Sri Lanka bowling averages

Player	M	I	O	M	R	W	BBI	Ave	Econ	SR	4	5	Ct	St
UC Hathurusinghe	4	2	17	0	97	5	4-57	19.40	5.70	20.40	1	0	1	0
A Ranatunga	8	4	18	0	94	3	2-26	31.33	5.22	36.00	0	0	1	0
SD Anurasiri	5	5	50	3	184	5	3-41	36.80	3.68	60.00	0	0	1	0
GP Wickramasinghe	8	7	60.1	5	276	7	2-29	39.42	4.58	51.50	0	0	2	0
AP Gurusinha	8	7	48	0	256	6	2-67	42.66	5.33	48.00	0	0	2	0
CPH Ramanayake	8	8	64.4	6	265	5	2-37	53.00	4.09	77.60	0	0	4	0
RS Kalpage	7	6	50	0	241	4	2-33	60.25	4.82	75.00	0	0	3	0
GF Labrooy	1	1	10	1	68	1	1-68	68.00	6.80	60.00	0	0	0	0
KIW Wijegunawardene	3	2	17	1	88	0	0-34	-	5.17	-	0	0	0	0
PA de Silva	8	1	1	0	6	0	0-6	-	6.00	-	0	0	1	0
ST Jayasuriya	6	3	6	0	44	0	0-12	-	7.33	-	0	0	4	0

West Indies bowling averages

Player	M	I	O	M	R	W	BBI	Ave	Econ	SR	4	5	Ct	St
AC Cummins	6	6	59	1	246	12	4-33	20.50	4.16	29.50	1	0	0	0
BP Patterson	1	1	10	0	25	1	1-25	25.00	2.50	60.00	0	0	1	0
WKM Benjamin	8	8	79	8	297	10	3-27	29.70	3.75	47.40	0	0	4	0
PV Simmons	4	3	20	1	91	3	2-40	30.33	4.55	40.00	0	0	1	0
RA Harper	2	2	14	0	63	2	1-30	31.50	4.50	42.00	0	0	1	0
CEL Ambrose	7	7	68	6	235	7	2-24	33.57	3.45	58.20	0	0	1	0
KLT Arthurton	8	3	15	0	70	2	2-40	35.00	4.66	45.00	0	0	1	0
CL Hooper	8	8	80	2	312	8	2-19	39.00	3.90	60.00	0	0	4	0
MD Marshall	5	5	43	3	174	2	2-26	87.00	4.04	129.00	0	0	0	0

Zimbabwe bowling averages

Player	M	I	O	M	R	W	BBI	Ave	Econ	SR	4	5	Ct	St
DL Houghton	8	1	2	0	19	1	1-19	19.00	9.50	12.00	0	0	4	0
EA Brandes	8	8	70.1	7	355	14	4-21	25.35	5.05	30.00	1	0	2	0
IP Butchart	5	4	32	1	205	6	3-57	34.16	6.40	32.00	0	0	0	0
MG Burmester	4	4	21.5	0	138	4	3-36	34.50	6.32	32.70	0	0	1	0
AJ Traicos	8	7	62	5	253	6	3-35	42.16	4.08	62.00	0	0	0	0
MP Jarvis	5	5	47.3	4	229	5	1-23	45.80	4.82	57.00	0	0	0	0
AH Shah	7	7	57	9	237	5	2-17	47.40	4.15	68.40	0	0	1	0
KG Duers	6	6	50	2	256	3	1-17	85.33	5.12	100.00	0	0	2	0

Bibliography

Books

Alfred, L., *The Art of Losing: Why the Proteas Choke at the Cricket World Cup* (Cape Town: Penguin Random House South Africa, 2012).

Ambrose, C., *Sir Curtly Ambrose: Time to Talk* (London: Aurum Press Ltd, 2015).

Baldwin, M., *The History of the Cricket World Cup* (London: Sanctuary Publishing, 2003).

Boon, D., *Under the Southern Cross* (Sydney: HarperCollins Publishers, 1996).

Border, A., *Beyond Ten Thousand* (Nedlands: Swan Publishing, 1993).

Botham, I., *Botham: My Autobiography* (London: CollinsWillow, 1994).

Browning, M. & Grapsas, J., *A Complete History of World Cup Cricket* (London: New Holland Publishers, 2014).

Bryden, C., *Return of the Prodigal* (Johannesburg: Sunday Times with Jonathan Ball Publishers, 1992).

Crace, J., *Wasim and Waqar: Imran's Inheritors* (London: Boxtree, 1993).

Crowe, M., *Out on a Limb: My Own Story* (Auckland: Reed Publishing, 1995).

De Silva, A., *Aravinda – My Autobiography* (Edinburgh: Mainstream Publishing, 1999).

Donald, A., *White Lightning* (Glasgow: CollinsWillow, 1999).

Duckworth, F., & Lewis, T., *Duckworth Lewis: The Method and the Men Behind It* (Cheltenham: SportsBooks, 2011).

Gooch, G. & Keating, F., *Gooch: My Autobiography* (London: CollinsWillow, 1996).

Greatbatch, M. & Harding, J., *Boundary Hunter* (Auckland: Hodder Moa Beckett Publishers, 1996).

Griffiths, E*., Glory Days: Forty Years of One-day Cricket 1963– 2003* (London: Viking, 2003).

Griffiths, E., *Kepler: The Biography* (London: Pelham Books, 1994).

Haigh, G., *The Cricket War 30th Anniversary Edition* (Melbourne: Melbourne University Press, 2007).

Harris, C. & Leggat, D., *Harry: The Chris Harris Story* (Auckland: Celebrity Books, 1999).

Healy, I., *Hands and Heals* (Sydney: HarperCollins Publishers, 2000).

Knight, J., *Mark Waugh: The Biography* (Sydney: HarperCollins Publishers, 2002).

Lara, B. & Scovell, B., *Beating the Field: My Own Story* (London: Corgi, 1996).

Lewis, C., *Crazy: My Road to Redemption* (Stroud: The History Press, 2017).

Lister, S., *Fire in Babylon: How the West Indies Cricket Team Brought a People to Its Feet* (London: Random House, 2015).

McDonald, I. (ed.), *Benson & Hedges World Cup 1992* (Scoresby: Magenta Press, 1992).

Majumdar, B., *Eleven Gods and a Billion Indians: The On and Off the Field Story of Cricket in India and Beyond* (New Delhi: Simon & Schuster India, 2018).

Miller, P. & Tickner, D., *28 Days' Data – England's Troubled Relationship with One-day Cricket* (Worthing: Pitch Publishing, 2016).

Murray, P.A., *The World Championship of Cricket* (Sydney: Stirling Publishers, 1985).

Nicholls, J.L., *Cricket Corruption: The Guilty Named and Shamed* (London: UK Book Publishing, 2016).

Oborne, P., *Wounded Tiger: A History of Cricket in Pakistan* (London: Simon & Schuster, 2014).

Procter, M. & Murphy, P., *South Africa: The Years of Isolation and Return to International Cricket* (Harpenden: Queen Anne Press, 1994).

Ray, A., *One-Day Cricket: The Indian Challenge* (New Delhi: HarperCollins Publishers India, 1994).

Romanos, J., *Martin Crowe: Tortured Genius* (Auckland: Hodder Moa Beckett Publishers, 1995).

Samiuddin, O., *The Unquiet Ones: A History of Pakistan Cricket* (Uttar Pradesh: HarperCollins Publishers India, 2014).

Smith, P. (ed.), *World Cup Cricket 1992: The Complete Record* (Poole: The Five Mile Press, 1992).

Stewart, A., *Playing for Keeps* (London: BBC Books, 2004).

Tennant, I., *Imran Khan* (London: Gollancz/Witherby, 1995).

Waugh, S., *Out of My Comfort Zone* (Camberwell: Viking, 2005).

Wilde, S., *Ian Botham: The Power and the Glory* (London: Simon & Schuster, 2012).

Woods, D., *World Cricket: Reflections on the 1992 World Cup* (Bristol: Broadcast Books, 1992).

Newspapers, Journals and Periodicals

ABC Cricket Book – India Tour of Australia 1991/92

Australian Cricket 1991/92 Guide

Benson & Hedges World Series Guide 1991/92

Border Mail

Canberra Times

Cricketer – February / March / April 1992

Cricketer International – March / April / May 1992

Cricket World Cup '92 – Richard Hecht in association with Fotopacific

Daily Mercury

Daily Telegraph

How's That! On tour with South Africa in India, the World Cup and the West Indies

Murray Pioneer

National Nine Tour Guide 1991/92

New Zealand Herald

New Zealand Cricket News – World Cup Special

Official Players' Handbook

Otago Daily Times

SA Cricket News – World Cup Commemorative Issue – March 1992

Sydney Morning Herald

Wisden Cricket Monthly – February / March / April 1992

Yearbooks

Benaud, R. (ed.), *Cricket Yearbook 1992* (Melbourne: Hamlyn Australia, 1992).

Derriman, M. (ed.), *The ABC Australian Cricket Almanac* (Sydney: ABC Books, 1992).

Engel, M. (ed.), *Wisden Cricketers' Almanack* (London: John Wisden & Co Ltd, 1993).

Lemmon, D. (ed.), *Benson and Hedges Cricket Year* (11th ed.) (London: Headline Book Publishing, 1992).

McConnell, L. (ed.), *Radio New Zealand Sport Cricket Annual 1992* (21st ed.) (Auckland: Moa Beckett Publishers, 1992).

Miller, A. (ed.), *Allen's Australian Cricket Annual 1991/92* (5th ed.) (Busselton: Globe Press, 1992).

Payne, F. & Smith, I. (ed.), *The 1992 Shell Cricket Almanack of New Zealand* (Auckland: Moa Beckett Publishers, 1992).

Robertson, A., *Cricket Alight! World Series Cricket* (Singapore: Golden Press, 1979).

Internet

CricketArchive
CricketWeb.net
ESPNcricinfo
Howstat.com
Howzstat Cricket Database
Wikipedia
YouTube

Index